The Virgin Mary as Alchemical and Lullian Reference in Donne

The Apple-Zimmerman Series in Early Modern Culture
Susquehanna University Press
Editors: Phyllis Rackin, University of Pennsylvania
Carole Levin, University of Nebraska

This interdisciplinary series will include books that examine a wide range of aesthetic works and moments in their original cultural milieu. This would include, for example, the works of Shakespeare and his contemporaries as the products of the burgeoning theatrical industry, designed for the entertainment of heterogeneous audiences who lived in a rapidly changing world where politics, religion, national identity, and gender roles were all subjects of contestation and redefinition. We solicit manuscripts from fields including, but not limited to, literature, history, philosophy, religion, and political science, in order to enable a truly multifaceted understanding of the early modern period.

Titles in This Series

Marguerite A. Tassi, *The Scandal of Images: Iconoclasm, Eroticism, and Painting in Early Modern English Drama*

Ann A. Hurley, *John Donne's Poetry and Early Modern Visual Culture*

Roberta Albrecht, *The Virgin Mary as Alchemical and Lullian Reference in Donne*

The Virgin Mary as Alchemical and Lullian Reference in Donne

Roberta Albrecht

Selinsgrove: Susquehanna University Press

© 2005 by Rosemont Publishing & Printing Corp.

All rights reserved. Authorization to photocopy items for interal or personal use, or the internal or personal use of specific clients, is granted by the copyright owner, provided that a base fee of $10.00, plus eight cents per page, per copy is paid directly to the Copyright Clearance Center, 222 Rosewood Drive, Danvers, Massachusetts 01923. [1-57591-094-2/05 $10.00 + 8¢ pp, pc.]

Associated University Presses
2010 Eastpark Boulevard
Cranbury, NJ 08512

The paper used in this publication meets the requirements of the American National Standard for Permanence for Printed Library Materials Z39.48-1984.

Library of Congress Cataloging-in-Publication Data

Albrecht, Roberta, 1945–
  The Virgin Mary as alchemical and Lullian reference in Donne / Roberta Albrecht.
    p. cm. — (The Apple-Zimmerman series in early modern culture)
  Includes bibliographical references (p.   ) and index.
  ISBN 1-57591-094-2 (alk. paper)
  1. Donne, John, 1572–1631—Criticism and interpretation. 2. Christian poetry, English—Early modern, 1500–1700—History and criticism. 3. Christianity and literature—England—History—17th century. 4. Sermons, English—17th century—History and criticism. 5. Mary, Blessed Virgin, Saint—in literature. 6. Llull, Ramon, 1232?–1316—Influence. 7. Donne, John, 1572–1631—Religion. 8. English poetry—Spanish influences. 9. Alchemy in literature. I. Title. II. Series.

PR2248.A66 2005
821'.3—dc22

2005003404

PRINTED IN THE UNITED STATES OF AMERICA

To Jude

Contents

List of Illustrations	9
Preface	11
Introduction: Theological Alchemy	19
1. Emblems of Making	57
2. Donne's Doctrine of Mary	78
3. Mnemotechnics in the Sermons and Poems	94
4. *Ars Sacra Poetica*	134
Conclusion: *Schekhina*	158
Notes	181
Glossary	227
Selected Bibliography	233
Index	251

Illustrations

1. Jean Pol and Herman de Limbourg, *The Court of Heaven* from *Belles Heures de Jean, Duc de Berry*.   28
2. *Sanctum Sanctorum* from Giovanni Agostino Pantheo, *Theoria Transmvtationis Metallicae cum Voarchadúmia*.   34
3. The Ouroboros. Figure 3 from H. J. Sheppard, "The Ouroboros and the Unity of Matter in Alchemy: A Study in Origins."   36
4. Crozier Head in the form of the Ouroboros (figures in the volute missing).   37
5. Crozier Head with Virgin and Child on recto (the Crucifixion on verso).   38
6. Cabalistic Table from Giovanni Agostino Pantheo, *Theoria Transmvtationis Metallicae cum Voarchadúmia*.   43
7. "Jonah and the Whale" from Sebastian Münster, *Cosmographia Universalis*.   52
8. The Virgin suckling the Child, Michael Maier, *Symbola aureae mensae*.   58
9. "Phoenix with Two Hearts," from Henry Hawkins, *Parthenos*.   62
10. The Virgin as *Sedes Sapientiae* Trampling the Dragon.   68
11. "The Androgyne Crushing the Dragon."   69
12. *Madonna and Child with Saints* (and Egg). Piero della Francesca.   70
13. *The Elements in the Egg* from *Turba philosophorum*.   71
14. Ivory Tabernacle with Virgin and Child.   73
15. Figure of the Androgyne holding the Philosopher's Egg.   74
16. Pelican vessel.   75
17. Mystical figure from Ramon Lull's *Ars brevis*.   87

18. Combinatory figure from Ramon Lull's *Ars brevis*. 101
19. *Princess Elizabeth, Later Queen of Bohemia* by Robert Peake the Elder. 111
20. "The Holy Virgin with the Child, as Patron Saint of Sailors." 137
21. Detail of female figure from Robert Fludd, *Utriusque Cosmi Historia*. 173

Preface

THIS STUDY BRINGS TOGETHER THREE SEPARATE SUBJECTS: THE Hermetic-cabalist alliance formed in the fifteenth century and how it influenced Donne, the *ars combinatoria* of Ramon Lull and how it influenced both Donne and his readers, and the religious controversies of the Elizabethan, Jacobean, and Caroline eras and how these affected the way Donne wrote. All three subjects are venues in which a single phenomenon, the presence of Mary in his texts, can be investigated. The evidence argues that we have underestimated the power of her image in his thought.

The main concern here is Mary as alchemical code and how ideas associated with this code helped Donne confront the problem of residual Catholicism. The main force behind this study is Stanton J. Linden's *Darke Hierogliphicks* (1996), which investigates the nonsatirical use of alchemical discourse by Donne and others. Supplementing it is the work of two others: Gareth Roberts's *The Mirror of Alchemy* (1994) and Lyndy Abraham's *A Dictionary of Alchemical Imagery* (1999). Also important are studies by new historicists of how Protestant print culture changed the way Renaissance readers read.

Kevin Sharpe and Steven N. Zwicker's *Reading, Society and Politics in Early Modern England* (2003), for example, argues that Protestant humanism encouraged individual readers to construct their own exegeses of texts no longer considered the property of an elite clergy. Readers belonged to specific interpretive communities, and these determined the ideological context for what meanings they made of the text. My investigation indicates Donne's special concern for his community of "adept" readers, that is, those readers who had acquired a taste for alchemical discourse, and especially those influenced by pseudo-Lullian mnemotechnics.

Though many Renaissance readers appropriated Lull's theory of *ars combinatoria* from secondary sources, we know that Donne himself studied the original. His personal copy of *Duodecim Principia Philosophiae* (1516) bears his pencil markings in the margins, a sign of his careful attention. His knowledge of cabalistic investigative practices, which had also influenced Lull, was supplemented by other pseudo-Lullian sources such as *De auditu kabbalistico,* familiar to all Renaissance Lullists.

The cabalists investigated divinity by combining abstract things such as numbers, names, and shapes. Alchemists sought to discover the same secrets by studying corporeal images, which, they thought, expressed various aspects of divinity. Because Renaissance readers had acquired a large vocabulary of alchemical and cabalistic signs, they naturally combined these according to the pseudo-Lullian methodologies they had learned. Donne was able to capitalize upon this situation, addressing readers who he knew would understand certain sensitive issues in specific ways. Whether he introduced corporeal images, hieroglyphs, algebra, or signs of the zodiac, he could assume a reader predisposed to make meaning by combining "this" with "that." He provided the "heterogeneous ideas" and expected his readers to yoke them together, not necessarily by violence.

Ironically, the new Protestant print culture had provided both readers and writers with a way to cling to the past. Although Protestants had tried to erase papist images by substituting similar things, their efforts were frustrated by Lullist mnemotechnics that insisted upon dredging up Roman icons. The diagrams I have compiled only begin to indicate how Renaissance readers came into possession of the text, constructing—from images and numbers and signs—dissenting values. They also begin to indicate how the individual writer or reader was able to protect his or her conscience. Finally, these diagrams suggest ways that pre-Reformation *culture* was protected and kept alive. When images of Mary, for example, were introduced into a poem or a sermon, readers, both Protestant and other, were compelled to make choices, deciding for themselves the exegesis of this Marian text.

Religious authorities had hoped that irenic policies would ease the transition from the Roman Church to the English Church, and Donne's own tolerance marks him as a child of his time. The "cross-confessionalism" that Anthony Milton says characterized the arts of Donne's time[1] suggests different ideologies coexisting in one Church. However, certain religious factions took advantage of this situation to seize political power. Ironically, the newly formed "Arminian" and "Puritan" camps, which existed by virtue of this tolerance, ended up starting a holy war.

Moderate Calvinists had been part of the Church of England for a long time. Gradually, a minority of radical Calvinists gained power. Early in 1603, for example, Sir Oliver Cromwell visited England's future king in Scotland and, shortly thereafter, entertained him as James I at home. Both rendezvous were efforts to prepare for Puritan success. Later at the Synod of Dort (1618–19), the king gave way to the hyper-Calvinists, who defined themselves according to certain tenets, including the doctrine of "total depravity."

This doctrine comes from Calvin's description of the contagion of sin as "rotten branches . . . from a rotten root."[2] "Even infants themselves," Calvin wrote, "have the seed enclosed within them. Indeed, their whole nature is a seed of sin."[3] Since "none of the soul remains pure," even man's will "can have no power for righteousness."[4] Hence, total depravity stripped all mankind, including newborns, of any vestige of good, including good intentions and good works, leaving man's nature without one spark of divinity. Except God do *all* the work, man, even with *all* his good works, is damned.

Opposing these radical Calvinists were the Arminians, who believed in man's essential goodness. Like Luther, they thought that "God is present in all creatures," even as the Holy Trinity.[5] Donne, as Herbert and later Crashaw, was attracted to this Arminian doctrine. Nicholas Tyacke remarks the "Arminian preaching . . . of John Donne at Paul's Cross," where he disparaged radical Calvinists as those who "despise others as men whom nothing can save."[6] For Donne, alchemical discourse became a way to express his belief in man's essential goodness. Alchemists believed that all base matter contains manifestations of the divine. Therefore, by works, or the *opus*, it is possible to break down, putrefy, separate, reunite, and finally resurrect that same material as perfect gold. It is no accident that Abraham's "Index of alchemical and literary authors" includes Luther's name but not Calvin's.

Each time Donne used alchemical discourse, he knew that a certain community of adept readers would understand. The female element was crucial to the opus. Always she joined the male in the alembic, celebrating the alchemical wedding and afterward rising through the retort as the glorified Stone. Christian cabalists embraced the same theory in a different form. Through the Hebrew *Zohar*, they learned that *Schekhina*, the female part of the Deity, created the world. To some humanists, this logic, which followed the natural order, made sense. Various theorists called this female various things. Pico della Mirandola called her *Hochmah*, or Wisdom. Lull, in spite of the fact that he hoped to convert Muslims and Jews by his art, sometimes called her Mary, sometimes Mercy. Naturally, he gave her an intercessory function. Aware of these Hermetic, cabalistic, and Lullian traditions, Donne sometimes called her Mary, sometimes something else.

My study of these references begins with the earlier work of Louis L. Martz, particularly his investigations of the meditative traditions influencing Renaissance poems. His article, published long ago, continues to challenge us today:

> One should also recall that a renewal of devotion to the Virgin, especially encouraged by the Jesuits, was one of the strongest spiritual movements of the Counter-Reformation. Imitation of Christ and Imitation of the Virgin were together fostered by meditation on the Rosary, which, like other forms of methodical meditation, was assuming its modern form in the century preceding the birth of Donne.[7]

This line of inquiry has been interrupted by Barbara Lewalski's *Protestant Poetics* (1979), which inspired a wave of criticism intended to track down Protestant doctrines in Renaissance poems. Now, however, scholars are beginning to return to the study of Counter-Reformation influences, as Martz had suggested so long ago.

Alison Shell's *Catholicism, Controversy, and the English Literary Imagination, 1558–1660* (1999) explores anti-Catholic movements during the Tudor and Stuart eras. Having established Martz's work as an important base, she proceeds to study the marginalization of Catholics by English Protestants, and particularly how this phenomenon affected Counter-Reformation Catholic poets. R. V. Young's *Doctrine and Devotion in Seventeenth-Century Poetry: Studies in Donne, Herbert, Crashaw, and Vaughan* (2000) also studies how Counter-Reformation sensibilities and ideas influenced the culture of early modern England. Arthur F. Marotti's *Catholicism and Anti-Catholicism in Modern English Texts* (1999) examines, among other things, the way the new Protestant print culture began to blur pre-Reformation images, creating a shift from the icon to the word. Theresa DiPasquale's award-winning *Literature and Sacrament: The Sacred and the Secular in John Donne* (1999) pursues the influence of Roman Catholic meditational materials. Catholic handbooks and the cycle of the liturgical year, she says, have been neglected by scholars bent upon studying primarily Protestant manuals and treatises. A recent collection of essays, entitled *John Donne and the Protestant Reformation* (2003), surveys Donne's commitment to the Church of England, including his drive toward the unity of all Protestants. My own study investigates Donne's Lullian mnemotechnics, which helped him include "all" in his vision of the "catholique" church. In fact, it shows how this post-Reformation poet restored things once lost, including man's divine nature, including the female nature in God.

I had hoped to accomplish my task during Professor Martz's lifetime. Instead, he leaves me with these words:

I think you are right in arguing that Donne's Catholic background shines through most of his writings. I had not thought of the presence of Mary in his sermons, but I would be interested to see what evidence you have for her presence.[8]

Linking the Mary of alchemy with the Mary of Counter-Reformation theology has helped me understand what Donne meant by numerous sermon references to her. I am naturally glad, but I am also sorry that Professor Martz can never respond.

The Virgin Mary as Alchemical and Lullian Reference in Donne

Introduction: Theological Alchemy

THAT DONNE'S CATHOLIC BACKGROUND "SHINES" THROUGH HIS poems was long ago observed by Louis L. Martz.[1] That current scholarship continues to study this phenomenon is evidenced by numerous books and articles on how the Anglo-Catholic controversy has influenced English literature. Some treat the broader social and historical context, some specific poems.[2] Concerning *La Corona,* for example, Theresa DiPasquale builds upon Patrick F. O'Connell's observation that Mary is the "model for all believers," particularizing her as Donne's own role model in the creative process.[3] George Klawitter examines shifts in Donne's Marian theology from "A Litanie" to his later sermons, concluding that "ideas learned early are not easily discarded."[4] And Raymond-Jean Frontain discovers in the *Second Anniversary* Donne's "attempt to replace Dante's Virgin Mary" with a Protestant version of the same.[5] Altogether, these argue her continuing presence in his mind.

Linked with this body of criticism are studies of alchemical ideas influencing Renaissance literature. These include the work of Edgar Hill Duncan and Joseph Mazzeo in the 1940s and 1950s and now the work of such scholars as Stanton J. Linden and Lyndy Abraham, both of whom have renewed interest in this subject. Some studies seek to determine ways in which alchemical theories and their respective codes influenced texts written by Christian writers, especially those most susceptible to the Christian cabalists. Whatever their respective theses, scholars working in this field respect the importance of memory in creating and responding to texts.[6]

Though not everyone acknowledges him, Marsilio Ficino (1433–99) is partly responsible for devising a system of memory that joined Christian and Hermetic thought. Ficino based his concept of memory upon the *Corpus Hermeticum,* a text that was rediscovered in the fifteenth century and subsequently translated into Latin by him.[7] The result was a melding of images, both Christian and alchemical, including codes from the Jewish cabala. Christian cabalists, like

Ficino and Pico della Mirandola (1463–94), devised systems of memory that employed these codes as a way to express their own peculiar doctrines and theories.

They took, for example, the attributes of wisdom and glory (the Hebrew word for God) from the cabala and attached them to Mary. Hence, she became *Sapientia* (wisdom) or *Schekhina* (glory), the female principle emanating from God.[8] Another example of such melding occurred when Christian alchemists associated the Mother of Christ with the Maker of the Philosopher's Stone. St. Bernard (1090?–1153) was an early exponent of this way of explaining doctrine. His Hermetic Cult of Mary employed the language of alchemy in order to express the role of the priest during the spiritual Opus, whereby Christ the Stone was made and whereby every Christian is likewise made anew.[9] So Ficino's work supplements the doctrines of the older and revered Bernard, forging a powerful weapon, as it were, in stone.

Eventually, during that period we now call early modern England, Donne used Hermetic discourse as a way to invite various reading communities to discover their own, sometimes dissenting, views. When he did this, he proved—to what was quickly becoming a reading nation—that the writer, like his readers, would always be free to engage in the "strenuous acts" of making meaning.[10] An important by-product of this cultural phenomenon was that he and his readers cooperated to protect and perpetuate England's medieval iconography.

Donne employs many images and codes from sources both Catholic and Protestant, pagan and Christian, forbidden and tolerated. I have been particularly impressed by the way he sometimes uses an alchemical code, not just as an occasional reference, but as the organizing principle of a poem. Clearly he meant to address, along with the general audience, a specific reading community, eliciting responses from them that were based upon knowledge both esoteric and exoteric.

Current interest in the subject of alchemy is evidenced by the number of dictionaries and related works recently published.[11] This body of scholarship demonstrates that many modern readers are also studying how to become adept. Obviously, without *some* knowledge of alchemical codes we cannot comprehend how some of Donne's readers understood his poems. In spite of the considerable effort required, I agree with Rosemond Tuve that at least a "reading knowledge" of another's language is useful:

[S]ymbols are a language which enables poems to be permanently valid, and . . . if we will learn the language, which is in some cases an archaic and difficult one, we shall not mistake the poet's tone of voice but accurately take his meanings even across intervening centuries.[12]

This study builds upon the work of others by probing the meanings, both the "hows" and the "whys," of specific codes, especially as they apply to Mary. Assisting me in this endeavor are certain new historicists who investigate how culture is made.

These study a related subject, that is, the problem of residual Catholicism during the Elizabethan, Jacobean, and Caroline eras.[13] Since historians, unlike scientists, cannot prove causality by experiment, they must work with less precise categories, discovering an array of causes for a given effect or effects. Nicholas Tyacke, David Cressy, Julian Davies, Anthony Milton, Peter Lake, Kevin Sharpe, and numerous others have helped us understand the complexities arising from policies of practical tolerance in early modern England.

Tyacke, for example, studies the phenomenon of a rising Arminianism during the Caroline era.[14] Though the term *Arminianism* has sometimes been abused,[15] it is generally considered to be compatible with the idea that man, as a creature, is *not wholly* corrupt. Because man retains some vestiges of goodness, it is possible, by means of the refining powers of the sacraments, to rescue him from sin. This doctrine derived, in part, from the antideterminism of Epicurus as expounded in Lucretius's *De Rerum Natura*. So the doctrine that each particle in nature endures incorruptible had a long history before the Arminians appropriated it. Tyacke concludes that obdurate English Calvinists, with their predestinarianism, compelled an Arminian reaction.[16] The Hermetic theory postulating that base elements contain pure, that pure substance will be drawn out when the base is purged, is, in some respects, analogous. Happily, Donne could use alchemical theory to express his own version of Arminian doctrine but in such a way that radical Puritans, predisposed to blindness, could not see.

David Cressy, who studies the Protestant attempt to erase Catholic images and rituals, helps us make sense of the strange and exotic codes Donne used. *Bonfires and Bells* investigates how paranoia and anti-Catholicism cooperated with national memory in such a way that Reformation efforts were sometimes frustrated.[17] The result was a rich vocabulary of ceremony wherein Roman Catholicism could survive, albeit in disguised form. The Church of England, of course, needed to establish its authority by successfully confronting the issue of residual Catholicism. Its line of attack was two-pronged: either erase popish forms by outlawing them or provide Protestant substitutes. The latter, they hoped, would persuade people to reinvest their faith in something similar, not the same. Cressy explains why this strategy sometimes succeeded but often failed. My study builds upon Cressy's work, arguing that Donne substituted a form of Mary that functioned within the Protestant framework, inviting Christians other than Roman Catholics to worship her in "altared" form.[18]

Intellectuals, both Catholic and other, trying to survive in this more limited world that England had become, inoculated their language with "other" languages and images from a larger world. Fortunately, Protestantism allowed each believer to determine his or her own meaning.[19] As a result, early modern England became "a culture of self-fashioning."[20] Donne, always adeptly self-fashioning, inoculated his texts with images from Catholic, Hermetic, cabalistic, and Gnostic sources. His poems are filled with things not necessarily allowed, certainly not encouraged. Nevertheless, he invites the adept reader "to unfold the personal meaning of Scripture, to apply the sacred texts [even their *alchemical* texts] to the self."[21]

When the Reformed Church erased Catholic images, Cressy observes, it could not find successful replacements. The result was psychic instability or "dis-ease" among those dependent upon visual discourse. His more recent work, *Birth, Marriage, and Death* (1997), studies this phenomenon in terms of the language and rituals connected with religious ceremonies.[22] I shall rely upon his insights when I study *La Corona*. As I see it, Donne was able to exploit a Protestant mistake. Already schooled in various language systems, he understood that esoteric codes, woven into poetry and sermons, would be recognized by a certain community of readers. They understood that "humanism educated and enabled readers to perform their own readings, and to construct their own, often dissenting, values and politics."[23] Instead of the apple of discord, he dropped seeds of gold in his verse, allowing his readers to harvest what meaning they would.

Cressy shows how a similar phenomenon occurred during the revision of the English calendar. The old calendar dedicated numerous holy days to the memory of certain saints. English reformers of the sixteenth century, repelled by the Catholic doctrine of the intercession of saints, removed most of the saints' days, which had proliferated during the early part of that century. Nevertheless, they understood the impact of this old calendar upon daily life, including the routines of business and law.[24] The Inns of Court, for example, continued to function as usual, retaining many of the saints' days as legal holidays, thereby preventing erasure, thereby perpetuating memory. Donne was able to exploit this cultural phenomenon. That few have noticed this indicates a need for investigation.

In a sense my work answers Kevin Sharpe's challenge to traditionalists within his own field. His observation that historians of republican discourse "have largely ignored the visual, the symbolic, and the emblematic"[25] is important to all of us working in this period. Studying the relations between political and aesthetic change is a way for historians to challenge the artificial boundaries separating literature from politics. But it is also a way to challenge literary critics concerning what has too long been perceived as Donne's "Protestant poetics."

Both the Tudors and the Stuarts, and particularly the radical Puritans, overlooked images of Mary that continued to sustain Catholic memory and that, therefore, undermined Protestant ceremonies.[26] Sharpe has demonstrated how the persistence of monarchical imagery undermined Commonwealth efforts. Similarly, I believe that national memory rebelled against numerous attempts to eradicate iconography of the Virgin. This study of exotic codes—both Hermetic and cabalistic, both Roman Catholic and pagan—in seventeenth-century verse shows how Donne managed to avoid, or accommodate, political and religious issues. Alchemical discourse, as he developed it, became a kind of *concordia discors,* addressing the need to include what others were attempting to expel.

Stanton J. Linden has noted that England continued to be enamored of alchemy even during a time when Francis Bacon and the new philosophy were questioning its value.[27] I would add that alchemical discourse undermined Protestant efforts to enforce the Reformation; for the failure of Tudor and Stuart England to establish a purely Protestant poetics can be partly attributed to the persistence of Catholic imagery already attached to this language—to this alchemical discourse—that refused to go away.[28] Although the practice of alchemy had been banned in the fifteenth century,[29] and although alchemy had become the butt of satire by the beginning of the seventeenth, Linden has shown that Donne was "aware of its literary potential."[30] In fact, he says, Donne's "nonsatirical uses [of alchemy] outweigh those that are satirical in nature."[31] Why?

Donne used poetry to heal the rifts made by religious and political upheaval. Satire seeks to improve society. Satirists heal society by holding up a mirror reflecting people's faults. They know that some of their readers are blind; however, they also expect that others, seeing themselves in the mirror, will reform. During the English Renaissance, satirists held up the mirror to fools who had fallen prey to charlatanism and superstition and to knaves who had victimized the credulous. This is a form of healing. Donne, however, sought a different kind.

He used the language of alchemy to heal a society torn by religious strife. He dredged up images from the past, images held dear by some of his readers but images to which others were blind. For these latter the images were dormant. As sleeping dogs, they posed no threat. The rest recognized certain codes and, moreover, reinvented the text according to *their own understanding* of them. For many, Hermetic discourse was a soothing balm because it mended the rift between present and past. Donne appreciated not only its literary potential but also the freedom it gave him to express potentially dangerous truths with impunity.[32]

I agree with John Shawcross that the reader's text, that is, what the reader understands, should be distinguished from the author's text, or "the text the author has provided for the reader to read, with all its potentialities."[33] Donne, for example, provides his readers with easily recognizable genres, tropes, and forms. These conventions are the "constants" in his text.[34] But he also implements the "variables," for example, alchemical codes, which he expects his readers to reinvent in their own way.[35] The resultant text belongs to each reader alone.

This study will examine some of these variables. It will demonstrate how Donne provided his readers with a sense of order and stability during difficult times. In this respect it proves Albert H. Tricomi's thesis that texts "simultaneously make and reproduce culture."[36] Donne, in fact, illustrates this phenomenon as he creates language that looks backward and forward. We shall examine "how" he does this, at the same time trying to understand "why."

In order to address the question "why," certain elements of the past *outside* the field of literature must be retrieved. In order to understand his world, we must, like archaeologists, sift through the layers of silt separating it from ours, sometimes selecting evidence uncongenial or unfamiliar. Much we cannot know, but some of the signs, reconstituted, begin to recover a past, not necessarily *the* past, but "a historicized past" that makes sense.[37]

Iconography of the Virgin Mary

The Church of England, as we know, inherited many of its traditions from Rome. These included religious feasts and holy days dedicated to the perpetual memory of saints. Some of these were retained, transformed into Protestant feast days or similar liturgical rites. David

Cressy, discussing the consequences of the parliament of Edward VI in 1552, lists twenty-seven holy days, plus fifty-two Sundays—seventy-nine days altogether—annually devoted to prayer and worship.[38] Two feasts devoted to the Virgin Mary were among those retained: the Purification of the Virgin, celebrated February 2, and Lady Day (or the Feast of the Annunciation), celebrated March 25. Also, naturally, Mary continued to be the subject of the important doctrine of the virgin birth, whereby she was distinguished as the only human parent of Christ. Exactly how this virgin birth translated into Mary's position in the Godhead was an issue to be debated throughout church history, touching Roman Catholics and Protestants alike.

Certainly Protestants could not entirely avoid the traditions of medieval iconography, which had argued through pictures her place with God. Because she was considered eternal, medieval artists cared little whether their portraits envisioned her as adult or as swaddling child in the mind of God; for Mary, like the Word himself, was "in the beginning." Of course, not all pictures conveyed the same meaning. Lurking beneath, always, were contrary doctrines concerning the position of Mary in, with, or beside the Godhead. Medieval artists (or rather their patrons) espoused one of two views: either the Virgin, at some point, became God, or she remained essentially human. The way one answered this question determined his or her position as Immaculist or Maculist.

Both Bernard of Clairvaux and Thomas Aquinas (1226?–74) believed that Mary had been sanctified in the womb of her mother Anne. Like John the Baptist, also sanctified in the womb, she needed a Redeemer.[39] Accordingly, they did not consider her exempt from the need of Christ's redeeming power. She was, however, thought to be qualified as conduit or intercessory force between God and mankind.[40] Bernard proclaimed her *not the Source,* which is God himself, but the *aqueduct* through which the Source flows. Adam's Eve, he said, had plunged her children down into woe. As aqueduct, or intercessor, this Second Eve reestablished them in heaven. This is compatible with Bernard's own vision wherein Mary suckled him at her breast.[41] It is also compatible with Bernard's spiritual alchemy. Donne, as we shall see, later developed this Hermetic concept of Mary as conduit of grace and spiritual power.

Bernard reinforced his belief in the Virgin as intercessor by establishing certain precepts for his Cistercian order. Among them was the alchemical motto: "Laborare est Orare."[42] The Cistercians, deeply devoted to Mary, considered their function similar to that of Christ's bride, often referring to themselves in feminine and maternal terms. Bernard's imagery, for example, often depicts or implies the breastfeeding priest who sometimes wishes for relief from maternal duties:

> Take note however that she [Christ's bride] yearns for one thing and receives another. In spite of her longing for the repose of contemplation she is burdened with the task of preaching; and despite her desire to bask in the bridegroom's presence she is entrusted with cares of begetting and rearing children.[43]

When later separated from his brothers at Clairvaux, Bernard wrote, "My children are snatched from my breast before it is time. Those whom I have 'begotten' in the Gospel . . . I am not allowed to rear."[44] Though these examples demonstrate Bernard's profound devotion to Mary, they also help clarify and refine his basic belief that Mary was *not* God.[45] His was an essentially Maculist position, one that opposed the then developing doctrine of the Immaculate Conception.

One early exponent of the doctrine was Petrus Comestor, who in 1150 claimed that the Virgin Mary received from her parents their flesh but not their sin of concupiscence. Peter Abelard (1079–1142) had even earlier championed this doctrine by supporting a feast day (December 8) devoted to the Nativity of the Virgin. When he did this, Abelard, who believed that Aristotle's logic could be applied to the truths of faith, defied the mysticism of his contemporary, Bernard. The latter's famous letter to the Canons of Lyons naturally condemned this practice, championed by his rival. It also established his opposition to a doctrine that rendered Mary inextricably bound up in the Trinity.

Among those who later opposed Bernard was Duns Scotus (1266–1308). As Augustine before him, Scotus ascribed actual sin to every child of Adam, *excluding* the Virgin Mother. By cunning argument, the *Doctor subtilis* assured her preservation from original sin, making her God. This evolving doctrine was semiofficially recognized in 1476, when Pope Sixtus IV, a Franciscan, ordered a special office to the Nativity of the Virgin.[46] One result was an accumulation of iconography depicting Mary as part of the Trinity.

Also contributing to this concept of Mary as God was the occultist vision of Ramon Lull (1235–1316). How Lull came to appropriate the "Kabbalistic Sefirot" into his Christian version of *dignitates Dei* is still being discussed.[47] One source suggests that, by the Renaissance, certain memory devices were already based upon a combination of the Hebrew cabala and the art of Ramon Lull.[48] At any rate, Lull's influence was profound. According to Frances Yates, "Lullism is no unimportant side-issue in the history of Western civilization. Its influence over five centuries was incalculably great."[49] "In fact," she observes, "it is perhaps hardly an exaggeration to say that Lullism is one of the major forces in the Renaissance."[50] Lull himself could not have anticipated these results, which began with his alliance with the Franciscans. Nevertheless, when his theories were embraced by them, a coalition of sorts was formed.[51] When Sixtus IV promoted the new doctrine of the Immaculate Conception, it found welcome support in the theories of Ramon Lull. Unwittingly, a force had been set in motion, and this pseudo-Lullist/Immaculist alliance would prevail even through the seventeenth century. In opposition to Dominican concepts of memory (based upon Thomistic sense-oriented images), Lull's system of memory was based upon names (signifying abstract things that cannot be pictured in corporeal form).[52] Among these names are those of the Virgin Mary and the Holy Spirit.[53] Hence Lull's "completely abstract and imageless" system joined with the very sense-oriented images it sought to resist.[54] In its origins Lull's system of memory was scientific. His method, much like the cabalist practice, was to use letters and geometrical figures as the basis of inquiry, a fairly complicated manner of proceeding. His was a system whereby numbers, names, and letters from the Hebrew alphabet matched the attributes of God manifest on nine different levels. Ironically, these abstract principles were appropriated by the Franciscans and other later pseudo-Lullists, who yoked them with the "corporeal similitudes" of classical memory. Lull himself would have considered this manner of proceeding incongruous. Nevertheless it did occur. Moreover, Donne acquired knowledge from numerous Franciscan cabalists, evidencing his attraction to these mingled codes.[55] What this phenomenon means in terms of his doctrine of Mary is yet to be investigated.

As corporeal similitude, the Virgin Mary had no part in Lull's own *Liber ad memoriam confirmandam,* where repetition was the main rule. However, as *one of the attributes of God,* her importance was great indeed. Some Renaissance readers, confronted by such images as this below, understood, even in the pseudo-Lullian sense, the abstract principle of Mary as attribute of God.

Luther's breach with Rome involved the breaking of many idols as well as the discarding of many beliefs. The Virgin Mary was an obvious first target. If the just were to live by faith alone, they certainly did not need Mary. Reformation iconoclasm began to erase her. Eventually images would be smashed in churches and chapels. Statues of the Virgin would be decapitated. What could not be erased, however, was the sense of her essential role in mankind's salvation. Whether the position was Maculist or Immaculist, her role, whether as Creator

Figure 1: Pol, Jean, and Herman de Limbourg. *The Court of Heaven* from *Belles Heures de Jean, Duc de Berry.* French (ca. 1406–9). The Metropolitan Museum of Art, the Cloisters Collection, Purchase, 1954. (54.1.1,f.218).

or intercessory force, persisted in human memory. Though the Reformation destroyed much, it could not touch the more profound center of Roman Catholicism, which was the image of Mary in the hearts of believers.

Why she refused to budge remains a mystery. Perhaps, it has been suggested, man could find nothing to replace her. At any rate emblems and pictures incorporated by the Church during the Middle Ages haunted men's minds even throughout the English Renaissance, a highly visual age. Perhaps, after all, this persistence of memory proves the power of images to inform and persuade.

In spite of hairsplitting particulars over the doctrine of the Immaculate Conception, medieval iconography, bolstered by pseudo-Lullism, often portrayed Mary "as the Trinity or as one of the three persons in the Trinity."[56] Illustrations of Genesis, for example, frequently show her with the Father, illustrations from the Apocalypse with the Son, and illustrations from Isaiah with the Holy Spirit. Furthermore, scenes of the Coronation of Mary usually include the Trinity.[57] Though later Protestant poets did not embrace the ideas informing this iconography, they were aware of the images and of their power to convey spiritual truths.

But some Renaissance poets were also aware that the power invested in images was complemented by the greater power invested in combinations of the same. These poets discovered "very congenial" comrades in cabalistic theory and in the Neoplatonism of Ramon Lull, who had already appropriated the cabala into his art of combinations.[58] The mission of Lull's *Ars memorativa*, according to Yates, was to create a system compatible with all three major Western religions (Jewish, Christian, and Muslim). "He believed that if he could persuade Jews and Muslims to do the Art with him, they would become converted to Christianity."[59] To accomplish this goal he tried to adduce proof from cabalistic texts for the Trinity, arguing it was common to all three religions.[60] Also he focused on the names of God (common to all), attributes such as "the good," "the wise," "the eternal," and so on. Naturally, Lull's placement of Mary in his schema is important to my work, which also suggests the reason why Donne found himself intrigued by the power of names to communicate essential truths.

Lull's *Ars memorativa* was modified numerous times over the years and later appropriated, at least in part, by the English language reformers of the early seventeenth century. Their goals were essentially the same, that is, the conversion of the Jews to Christianity.[61] Both Lull and the English linguists sought to compile a *perfect* language, a language based upon memory images. This language was to be that which all could read so that all might be saved. It would realize "the utopian ideal of the return to Adamic purity and innocence" and implement "kabbalistic aids towards this end."[62] Naturally, this language would be some form of Hebrew. It would be a language that employed Arabic numerals, alchemical symbols, Egyptian hieroglyphics, algebra, magic, and cabalistic analyses. Francis Bacon and Elias Ashmole were among those English language reformers working toward this end.[63] For Bacon the model would be the Chinese cryptograms.[64] For Donne, who in his own way participated in this movement, the model would be the cabala. The cabalists, he wrote, "are the Anatomists of words, and have a Theologicall Alchimy to draw soveraigne tinctures and spirits from plain and grosse literall matter."[65] Noteworthy is the fact that Calvin and others had rejected the "famous proof of the Trinity from Christian kabbalah," first cited in the twelfth century and repeated throughout the Middle Ages.[66] Hence Donne's affirmation of Christian cabalist doctrine is his way of planting himself firmly against what David Cressy calls a "minority of godly precisians [who] sought to safeguard the advances of the Reformation."[67] Also noteworthy is Donne's belief that names express the essential nature of things. Like Ramon Lull, he believed that "names are to instruct us, and express natures and essences."[68] With this in mind, we shall study Donne's names, and especially the name of Mary.

Donne devised his own version of Lull's system. To what extent he determined to convert the Jews is a question reserved for the conclusion of this study. We do know that Cromwellian policy was inspired by a vision of Israel converted and that the London authorities sought to establish both a synagogue and a Jewish cemetery.[69] Since the goals of Ramon Lull and of republican England were, in some respects, the same, Donne was naturally encouraged to consider the place of the Jews in his vision of a unified church. Although he did not live to experience the impact of Cromwellian policies, he was nevertheless aware of the philo-Semitic movement that was gathering strength in England during the early part of the seventeenth century. How these issues translate into poetry is yet to be studied. At this point I merely note that during the 1650s Thomas Tany, one of the philo-Semitic millenarians, "denied that God is the Father, and proclaimed that Christ is Mary and Mary is Christ."[70] This strange doctrine did not come from nowhere.

Donne had inherited many images of Mary from his Roman Catholic ancestors and employed some in his poetry and sermons. Hence, throughout his life, he proved her value. Always fascinated with the poet's and priest's role as *maker*, his own identity was bound

INTRODUCTION: THEOLOGICAL ALCHEMY

up with the *idea* of Mary. As archaeologists, we shall dig down into the culture of the period, discovering his various versions of Mary, trying to determine what this phenomenon means in terms of the literature and in terms of English culture. If, for example, the image of the Virgin is simply a commonplace, merely one of numerous conventions associated with Protestant feast days or with the elaborate system of metaphors contrived either as celebrations of Elizabeth, the Virgin Queen, or as elegies lamenting the death of a young lady, then this study would have nowhere to go. If, on the other hand, he employed images of Mary in unconventional ways, even as part of his poetics of salvation, then that matter should be studied.

David Cressy begins to answer the question when he discusses the mystery surrounding childbearing ceremonies. During the sixteenth and seventeenth centuries, he writes, "Very few men gained intimate entry to the birthroom or knew what happened behind the screen."[71] Nevertheless, the miracle and mystery of childbirth was full of spiritual meaning and therefore compelled attention, so much so that some men, determined to participate in the ritual, actually disguised themselves as women in order to get on the other side of the veil.[72] Cressy concludes that

> the childbearing woman underwent a series of transformations affecting her physical, hormonal, emotional, social, domestic, and cultural condition. From conception to quickening, through all the anxieties of carrying and gestation, to the climax of labour, parturition, and recovery and the rewards of suckling and motherhood, each woman participated in a series of commonly shared experiences.[73]

I suspect that Donne tried to gain access to the birth room, even playing the role of spiritual midwife, in order to universalize these "commonly shared experiences" to include men, but also to erase distinctions between the exalted and the humble, between one religious faction and another.[74] His kind of alchemy was meant to heal the factions and frictions dividing English culture. St. Bernard, after all, had set the precedent as mothering priest suckling his children, even in the spiritual alchemical sense. When Donne entered the birth room, it became for him the *sanctum sanctorum* (the adept's laboratory) where the opus (the spiritual work) is performed, where the Philosopher's Stone (the Child) is born. All of this fits in neatly with the developing Arminian doctrine that salvation is based upon works (not just faith), a position the radical Calvinist minority abhorred.

The reader's task, as suggested above, is complicated by the fact that Donne was attracted to Hermetic discourse and occultist linguistics as a means to express theological truths, including those "truths" still lingering from England's Catholic past. In a sense he helped secure the (not always smooth) transformation from a Catholic to a Protestant culture without provoking undue offense. Like the early reformers, he had learned that abolishing rites by declaration meant little to those who meant to retain them. Donne meant to retain some of these rites. So, along with moderate Puritans and mainstream Anglicans, he participated in the "re-Catholicization" of England, reinstituting the element of magic, which for many seemed to have departed.[75] His manner of proceeding was subtle and compatible with his metaphysical bent of mind, a way of thinking that harked back to Heraclitus and Hippocrates.[76] Implementing esoteric codes allowed him to explore with impunity important issues such as the nature of God and the nature of spiritual birth. Codes of alchemy provided a way to retrieve the magic, a way to sustain and protect religious values and beliefs already established in the public consciousness even during changing times. Like it or not, we must study these codes, even when they at first seem not to apply.

Alchemical Symbols of Creation and Eternity

Alchemy developed alongside Christianity in the Western world. Though a predecessor to this pseudoscience, Heraclitus (ca. 535–475 BC) may have been the first Western thinker to begin to perceive what would evolve into the alchemistic principle of fire. He thought fire to be the underlying substance of the universe; all other elements were merely transformations of it. The Hermetic alchemists appropriated this idea, attaching it to various symbols, the phoenix, for example, which the Egyptians understood as a symbol of the regenerative Nile, rising and falling along with the sun's progress through the sky.

Hermetic alchemy was inspired by the need to know. As a field of inquiry, it falls somewhere between intellectual and spiritual knowledge, between fact and faith. Sometimes alchemists sought practical ends, but more usually theoretical ones. As mentioned above, alchemy, at least as a practical art, was banned in England in the fifteenth century, but that did not prevent Elizabethans from cultivating it as a hobby or even as a serious discipline. Later, John Dee (1527–1608), a favorite of Elizabeth, was still able to obtain a license.[77] For seven years Dee worked with Edward Talbot, now known as Edward Kelly (1555–97), hoping to discover divine knowledge.[78] In order to conduct their experiments, Dee and Kelly were able to draw upon traditions of medieval magic and its attendant visual logic, including Lullian geometry. It is no coincidence that Donne knew about Lull from Dee. Sir Robert Cotton, Donne's friend, had added works from Dee's library to his own.[79] Because Dee was a Lullist and because he was among "the most influential figures in the thought of Elizabethan England," he assured Ramon Lull's place in the Renaissance mind.[80] Donne was no exception. Though Lull himself seems to have taken on alchemy only as a hobby, Dee, and consequently the Renaissance, saw it otherwise. The scene below, for example, a woodcut for Giovanni Pantheo's *The Theory of the Transmutation of Metals* (1550), illustrates a setting very familiar to Renaissance readers. The triangle encompassing the Philosopher's head (*Sapientia*) may derive from Lull, whose allegory, *Arbor scientiae*, describes Triangle as "nearer to the soul of man and to God" than any other shape.[81] Pantheo's depiction of the *sanctum sanctorum* is standard. In fact, it is one of several such woodcuts of alchemical furnaces and other apparatuses in his treatise.[82] Included here are the necessary fire (discussed above) but also the necessary shapes. The triangle encompassed by fire is, as noted above, a sign of Lull's Trinity but also a sign of the mysterious Philosopher's Stone, foundation of all Hermetic art, whether practical or theoretical. The Philosopher's Stone to be resurrected from these refining fires is indicated by the eternal circle. This scene depicts the practical Hermetic arts: but, whether practical or theoretical, alchemy's esoteric techniques aimed at the discovery of truth. The goal was to find (or at least understand) that animating material that constituted life's core. If the adept could accomplish this, he could command (or understand) all the mechanisms that control life.

Western alchemy evolved from the pre-Socratic Greeks, but it became a special field of pseudoscientific inquiry under Hermes Trismegistus, or Mercurius (fourth century AD), reputed author of a body of syncretistic works on philosophy and religion. The so-called Hermetic writings, combining elements of Neoplatonic, Judaic, Gnostic, and cabalistic Theosophy, were presumably contrived to check the ascendancy of Christianity.[83] Alchemy, in other words, intended to refute Christianity by providing other answers to mankind's more profound questions: Who is God? What is man's relationship with Him/Her/It? What is the nature of the Universe? Of Death? Of the Creative Act?

The followers of Hermes Trismegistus, whose name was translated by the Greeks from the Egyptian *Thoth*, devised a series of symbols or emblems as alchemical equivalents to Heraclitus's fire and other

Figure 2: *Sanctum Sanctorum* from Giovanni Agostino Pantheo, *Theoria Transmutationis Metallicae cum Voarchadúmia*. Milan, 1550. Science, Industry, and Business Library, the New York Public Library, Astor, Lenox, and Tilden Foundations.

forces in the universe. Among these was the phoenix, mentioned above, burning itself to ashes, whence came numbers of other birds, silver and gold. Another was the sun itself. Visual "logic" was important in alchemistic doctrines. To those working in the occult sciences, as well as in the Hermetic, images took several forms, including tables, letters or names, and emblems. Those, like John Dee, who hoped to acquire the "magic" contained therein, were compelled to inspect the image by gazing upon it.[84] Understanding this much is something but not all. For other threads of doctrine from other very different sources were also woven into the warp and woof of these same images and understood in similar ways.

As H. J. Sheppard has shown, Gnosticism formed a familiar alliance with alchemy so that the one could sometimes be understood by the other.[85] In order to begin to disentangle the various threads from which such images as the above were woven, we must understand what those threads were. Nor need we fear getting all tangled up in them. Because of their polysemic nature, they bear scrutiny, as under a microscope. If Renaissance readers found pleasure in the exercise (and we know that the emblem books were ubiquitous), then so might we, as long as we keep in mind the various traditions feeding into them. Gnosticism, which is based upon a system of thought seemingly opposed to Christianity, is one such tradition.

Gnosticism, which sought to discover true knowledge through revelation and ecstatic experience, and alchemy, which sought to probe divine secrets by studying the natural world, employed some of the same expressions and symbols for the same or similar ends. One emblem common to both was the Ouroboros, the "Serpent that Eats His Own Tail," a representation of transmutation and a symbol of eternity. Its origins are ancient. The Babylonians and Chaldeans thought that it encompassed the heavens. The Phoenicians called it their "sun-serpent," which reproduced itself annually. It can be no accident that Donne twice seized upon this emblem as an organizing principle for his poems. In Stoic doctrine the Ouroboros symbolized cosmic creation and destruction by fire.[86] Donne seems to have been introduced to the emblem by his great-granduncle, Thomas More, although it had found its way into Christian iconography long before. One example is the Ouroboros composing the ivory crozier head below, the figure in the volute missing. Beside this crozier is another, the volute containing a figure of the Virgin and Child. Here the branch of Jesse assumes the same shape and gesture as the Ouroboros. Those gazing upon it were invited to see something like the

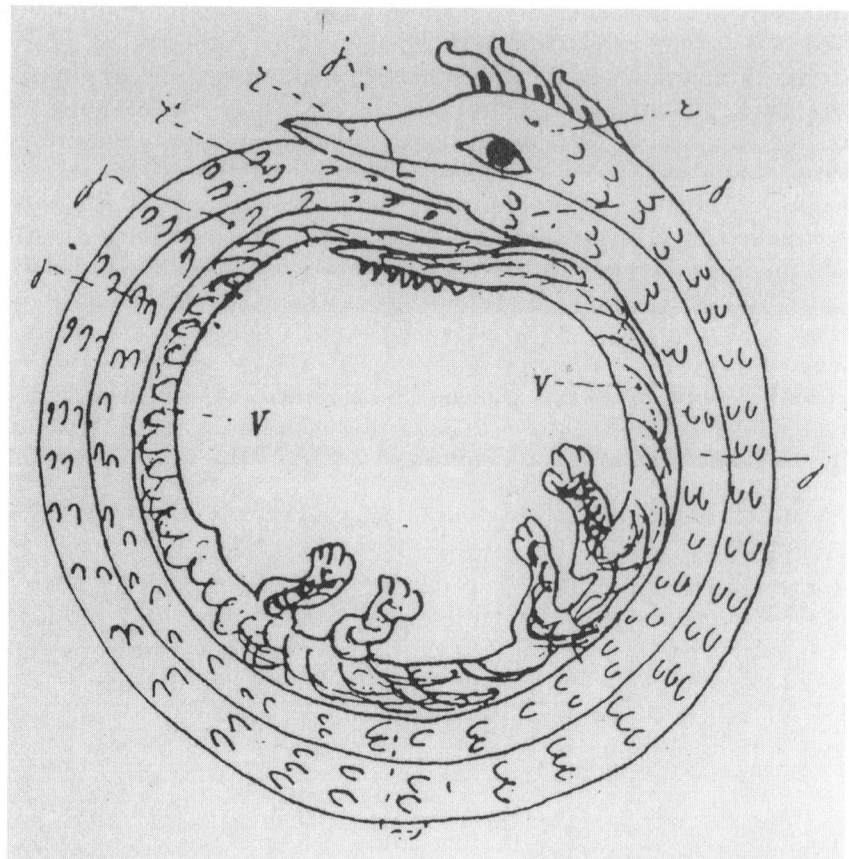

Figure 3: The Ouroboros. Figure 3 from H. J. Sheppard, "The Ouroboros and the Unity of Matter in Alchemy: A Study in Origins," *Ambix* 10 (June 1962): 83–96.

other. It is important to remember that this same Ouroboros was common among the Gnostic sects. As serpent-worshippers, Sheppard reminds us, these people considered the World Soul to be symbolic of Christ or Sophia (Wisdom).[87] Hence, they developed the myth of *Pistis Sophia*, another kind of Eve, who fell from the sphere of light, her Spouse. Donne, in his sermons and poems, plays with this Gnostic concept of Wisdom, also portraying a divinity without "sexual difference," also demanding that women "lose their femaleness in order to be subsumed into the larger 'male' group, whose actual sex was no longer significant."[88] Because Mary, at least in her role as Wisdom, had already become a symbol of cosmic importance, Donne

Figure 4: Crozier Head in the form of the Ouroboros (figures in the volute missing). French (twelfth to thirteenth century). The Metropolitan Museum of Art, Gift of J. Pierpont Morgan, 1917. (17.190.232).

is able to attach her to the alchemical concept of "wisdom," making interesting pictures for his readers to inspect.

Paracelsus (ca. 1493–1541), influenced by Lullian medical theories,[89] is one example of this phenomenon. He developed the idea that mercury, sulfur, and salt were ultimate constituents of matter.

Figure 5: Crozier Head with Virgin and Child on recto (the Crucifixion on verso). French (fourteenth century). The Metropolitan Museum of Art, Gift of J. Pierpont Morgan, 1917. (17.190.278).

Since salt was considered a purifying agent, it was "associated with Sapientia (wisdom)," especially when it was depicted as the "crowned virgin."[90] Paracelsus thought of these elements as the *tria prima*, likening them to the Trinity (hence Lull's Trinity). Naturally, the Virgin's identity was established here. The Philosopher's Stone, which emerged from *tria prima*, he called "Adam, who carried his own invisible Eve hidden in his body . . . united by the Supreme God."[91]

Other alchemists developed a four-element theory based upon Earth, Air, Fire, and Water. Some tenaciously held to Heraclitus's concept of fire, developing various theories of the "fire seed" that feeds the earth. No matter the specific brand or flavor, the primary business of alchemy, from the Middle Ages through the Renaissance, was to probe a greater reality than organized religion allowed.

Alchemists argued their case just as medieval theologians had done: by bringing visual codes into the front line of battle. During the late fifteenth century certain Christian humanists began to study these alchemical codes. The result was a kind of tennis match, or rather a volley, between two camps (one of them a coalition of Hermetic, cabalistic, and Gnostic teachings). Christian emblems, for example, bounced into the pagan court and were returned as something other. What these Christians received was something not the same, but not so new that it could not be incorporated back into their thought.[92] The mnemotechnics differed slightly. Hermetics used images to express their theories, and cabalists used arithmetical devices to express their doctrines. Those who studied both sets of codes (and that would include more or less every Renaissance gentleman) were faced with an interesting situation. Codes of the adept's magic and codes of God's miracles began to mingle in the imagination. The result was a strange duet, producing, at least for the poet, unusual song.[93]

Memory

Memory is the thing that knits these Hermetic images and these cabalistic and Gnostic ideas to Renaissance texts. Augustine's theory of memory had already provided a theoretical basis for Christian writing and preaching. Augustine, using the pseudo-Ciceronian *Ad Herennium* as model, thought of memory as a vast treasure-house with "roomy chambers" containing countless images stored there by the senses:

> When I am in this storehouse, I demand that what I wish should be brought forth, and some things immediately appear; others require to be longer sought after, and are dragged, as it were, out of some hidden receptacle. . . . All of which takes place when I repeat a thing from memory.[94]

The kinds of images Augustine cites range from the purely visual (light and colors) to the auditory to the less easily defined gustatory ("all flavors by that of the mouth") and tactile ("what is hard or soft, hot or cold").[95]

> All these does that great receptacle of memory, with its many and indescribable departments, receive, to be recalled and brought forth when required; each, entering by its own door, is laid up in it. And yet the things themselves do not enter it, but only the images of the things perceived are there ready at hand for thought to recall.[96]

Donne adapted Augustine's more static classical theories (as opposed to Lull's very mobile system to be discussed below) to his own writing, sometimes scattering esoteric emblems throughout his texts. Once, in a sermon, he even discussed the function of memory, reminding his congregation that throughout the ages, the Church had had to resort to pictures in order to compensate for illiteracy. This view of memory is yet another legacy from his great-granduncle, Thomas More, who had firmly believed in images as the language of salvation.[97] But pictures alone, Donne cautions, are ineffectual unless kept alive and transported by memory:

> They had wont to call Pictures in the Church, the lay-mans book, because in them, he that could not read at all, might read much. The ignorantest man that is, even he that cannot read a Picture, even a blinde man, hath a better book in himself; In his own memory. . . .[98]

Several scholars, besides John Chamberlin, have written about the phenomenon of memory in Donne.[99] But more needs to be done.

First of all, we must acknowledge that alchemical images do not move through the filter of the mind as other signaling systems, that is, horizontally, from this to that. Although artists may employ mnemonic devices, giving their viewers one familiar category to match with another, alchemical theorists work from another base. When Sir Joshua Reynolds, for example, depicts a British naval officer in the posture of the familiar *Apollo Belvedere*,[100] he expects his viewer to match the man with the god, almost as equals. But when the illustrator of an alchemical treatise depicts a worm or a rock, he expects his reader to derive the same comparison, albeit by way of a very different kind of "match." Because the very nature of alchemy is transformation, that is, the reconstitution of base things (below) into divine (above), alchemical images move through the filter of the mind vertically (from mineral or vegetable to spirit).[101] Early alchemists sought to discover the secret of each mineral in order to gain some control over the material world and to compel reunion with the divine. This is also the theoretical basis of Donne's system of memory.

It is not, however, entirely disengaged from that classical system of memory distinguished by the author of the *Ad Herennium* (a book every Renaissance gentleman read). This kind of memory investigates images against memorized backgrounds, trying to achieve some kind of synthesis. Backgrounds are like the wax tablets upon which images are written.[102] Donne's genius is to situate his "forrain wisdom," or Hermetic and cabalistic signs, against familiar Christian settings. Naturally, some of his readers were disturbed.

He did have his predecessors, however. Certain Christian humanists had already laid the foundation for this kind of "obscure writing," linking doctrines of the cabala and Hermetic theories with Christianity and, thereby, articulating *with impunity* dissenting views. Marsilio Ficino, for example, had translated the *Corpus Hermeticum* into Latin, developing a system of memory based upon it. Pico della Mirandola, his pupil, had likewise assimilated Hermetic and cabalistic teachings into his own, more diverse, system of thought. Pico studied carefully portions of the cabala that a Jewish convert had translated into Latin for him.[103] Donne's frequent citations of Pico indicate both his interest and his respect. Taking a page from Pico's book, Donne began with the same "fragments" of knowledge and proceeded to develop his own system. In this respect, he joined the league of Christian Hermetists, established a century before.

These included Johann Reuchlin (1455–1522), a famous Hebraist, who had hoped to restore magic to philosophy.[104] John Chamberlin argues that both Pico and Reuchlin profoundly influenced Donne.[105] Donne often cites both in the *Essays* and the *Sermons*, and he seems to have been familiar with Reuchlin's *De Arte Cabbalistica* (1517).[106] Though the increasing disunity between Protestants and Catholics, especially toward the end of the sixteenth century, brought disappointment to everyone involved in the Christian cabalist movement, the wheels of memory had been set in motion and could not be stopped immediately.[107] Why? In order to establish the authority of the Church of England, the language and images of Catholicism had to be erased. That did not happen. Subversive texts insured that the "magic" of Roman Catholic rituals would prevail, that the Protestant Reformation in England would always be limited, that the power of the individual to follow the dictates of his or her own conscience would ultimately survive. Visual codes from "occult memory systems" (sometimes letters "represented by images," sometimes emblems imposed as mnemonic devices) assisted this process.[108] Donne uses this situation to his advantage. When he introduces a strange code into a poem, situating it against some familiar background, he invites his readers to make their own meaning, or "magic," out of it.[109]

Yates explains that Christian humanists were committed to the discovery and use of "spiritual magic."[110] Heinrich Agrippa himself, she reminds us, had achieved the "synthesis of magic and religion, through cabala, which Pico had adumbrated and which Reuchlin carried further."[111] Of course this magic was "white magic guided by good and angelic forces which ensured protection from evil powers."[112] The Virgin Mary was one such talisman, for she was invoked to drive away demon specters.[113] And this magic was often expressed by emblems imbued with power. Memory was the key. As they remembered these codes, Christian humanists linked images immediately before them with others previously seen (whether as altarpieces or as illustrations in alchemical treatises or as names designating God's attributes). This is how they learned to read and to understand.

Lyndy Abraham explains occult linguistics as a system whereby images sometimes substituted for letters, letters sometimes for images.[114]

> [I]f, for instance, an object resembled the shape of a particular letter, it would be used to represent that letter (e.g., an open pair of scissors for the letter "X"). Alternatively, images of birds, trees, or animals would be used to represent the letter which was the initial letter of their name. . . . When the images are placed together, the word that is to be recalled is formed.[115]

Citing Yates, she characterizes this visual alphabet "of infantile simplicity, like teaching a child to remember 'C' through the picture of a Cat."[116] This kind of reading, Abraham says, is similar to that of the Druid alphabet, where images from nature are translated by the initial letters of their names. Hence "N" translates "nightingale."[117] The following copy of a page from Pantheo's treatise indicates similar mnemotechnics in his cabalistic system, which assigned numbers to letters from the Greek, Latin, and Hebrew alphabets.[118] On another page Pantheo provides a list of names, which, he says, all mean the same thing. When either letters or names engage the memory, then important associations can be made. Abraham uses Marvell's "Upon Appleton House," which contains codes that cannot be understood apart from certain occult "secrets," to illustrate a similar phenomenon. Hence, she says, the poem is a good example of the Renaissance penchant for complicated wordplay. Also it serves as "a memory map for those who want to regain the Paradisal state."[119] We have already noted the Renaissance attempt to create an international language based upon either Chinese cryptograms (Francis Bacon's model) or cabalistic combinations of names (Jan Amos Comenius's model). As stated before, both aimed at emulation of the "perfect" language of Adam and Eve. So "to regain the Paradisal state" seems to have been written into Renaissance psychology as well as philosophy, and memory was the key.

In this regard, the influence of Ramon Lull during the Renaissance remains great. Pico himself acknowledged the profound influence of Lull's *ars combinatoria* upon his own system of revolving alpha-

PRIMA.
Schema literarum ad Voarchadú-miam pertinentium.

Quarti cara-
cteres litera-
rum Voar-
chadumica-
rum.

אבגדהוזחט

- Aleph . A . e . i . —
- . o . u .
- Beth . B .
- Gimel . G .
- Daleth . D .
- He . H .
- Vau . V .
- Zain . Z .
- Cheth . Ch .
- Tcrh . T .

יכךלממנןס

- Iod . I .
- Caph . C . & ch .
- Lamed . L .
- Mem . M .
- Nun . N .
- Samech . S .

Figure 6: Cabalistic Table from Giovanni Agostino Pantheo, *Theoria Transmvtationis Metallicae cum rchadúmia*. Milan, 1550. Science, Industry, and Business Library, the New York Public Library, or, Lenox, and Tilden Foundations.

bets and letter combinations.[120] In order to make sense of how Mary, as icon or code, functions in the *memoria* of Donne, we must follow Lull's track, which is one of memory in motion. Lull's system of memory differed from the scholastics in that it was based upon the attributes of God (which he settled as nine): *Bonitas, Magnitudo, Eternitas, Potestas, Sapientia, Voluntas, Virtus, Veritas, Gloria.* Some of these attributes, at least in Lull's system, belonged to Mary, the Mother of Christ.

Lull's *Ars Magna* (1305–8) developed alongside Augustine's classical rhetoric but was no part of it, except that it seems to have attracted the attention of the Franciscans. Perhaps this was because the Franciscans, unlike the Dominicans, had no memory system of their own. At any rate, during the next century, it was a Franciscan pope (Sixtus IV) who ordered a special office to the Nativity of the Virgin. One immediate result of his directive would be the creation of numerous images associating Mary with the Trinity. Another eventual result would be official acceptance of the doctrine of the Immaculate Conception. So the Franciscan appropriation of Lull's *Ars Magna* seems to have established Mary as an even more powerful force.[121] Since the friars were highly mobile, dissemination of this "new" Mary—a dynamic, or *moving,* force in memory—spread quickly.

The "most significant aspect of Lullism," according to Yates, is that "Lull introduces movement into memory."[122]

> The figures of his Art, on which its concepts are set out in the letter notation, are not static but revolving. One of the figures consists of concentric circles, marked with the letter notations standing for the concepts, and when these wheels revolve, combinations of the concepts are obtained. In another revolving figure, triangles within a circle pick up related concepts. These are simple devices, but revolutionary in their attempt to represent movement in the psyche.[123]

It is very important to note Lull's accomplishment here. When he brought *motion* into the process of making meaning, he radically revised the way memory had always been perceived.

Those who know the work of John Dee, for example, immediately see the difference. Dee's system of knowing, as mentioned above, was highly influenced by Lull. However, his method whereby *memoria* functions is closer to his classical models. Dee had argued that magical images or the characters containing them "operate as figures to be 'inspected', rather than as a text to be 'read'."[124] Those who hoped to be empowered by them, gazed upon them, one at a time. Dee's way of defining the function of memory differs little, at least as a process, from the meditative practices of Ignatius of Loyola (1491–

1556). Lull's method, however, is much more progressive in that it reached into the future, touching seventeenth-century readers who already enjoyed reading polysemic texts. Whereas Dee supposes that magic comes from matching this static thing with that static thing,[125] Lull perceives memory in motion, many things from diverse cultures and systems, joining together to say something like but not the same. In order to illustrate Lull's concept of memory, another analogy must be found.

I have argued elsewhere that memory in Donne's *Holy Sonnets* functions according to theories of modern cinema. Particularly the theory of montage seems to apply.[126] Since most of us have at least a rudimentary grasp of the principles of modern cinema, the analogy may serve well. Who is to say, after all, that mnemotechnics, which began with the Greeks and continued through the Renaissance, cannot evolve into twentieth-century art forms?

Montage

Montage illustrates Lull's *Ars memorativa* and, as by-product, the medieval theory of *memoria*. Augustine believed that codes approximating each other were transferred by memory from place past to place present. Lull, as we have just observed, introduced the concept of motion to memory. Donne seemed to understand both principles, constructing language and selecting images in such a way that his congregations/readers could join images past with images present in order to apprehend, in the Lullian sense, a larger spiritual reality.

Montage as cinematic principle is the same, for it is a process whereby images in films are read both vertically and horizontally, not just side by side. It is usually defined as a series of adjacent shots that relate to each other in such a way that memory of the first image causes the mind, when it encounters the next, to think of "something like something else." In the grammar of film, the image translates to word. Words alone, however, are insufficient to move the text. The function of montage in film is to move the text by means of the dialectic between two adjacent images. When this occurs, more than mere matching of "word" with letter results. Memory acts as linking verb between images, resulting in a statement, something larger than the sum of the parts.

Montage reads like Chinese hieroglyphics, another good analogy (and more complicated than static systems because it suggests memory in motion). A picture of a dog and another of a mouth means "to bark." A picture of a fountain and another of an eye means "to weep."

The yoking is done by the mind, but it cannot perform this function without memory. This process of reading moves beyond "this equals that." The mind is forced to move images backward, to that place where they were first encountered, simultaneously adding whatever new meaning the present moment invites, which is movement forward. The process is cerebral, the memory is central, and the transfer dual. As the narrative (mise-en-scène) moves forward in a linear way, montage moves back and forth, down and up, remembering the past in order to create a new present.

ARS MEMORATIVA

This is a good illustration of Ramon Lull's theory of *memoria*, for it is far from static. Yates contrasts the static schemata of Augustine's memory buildings, in which images are stored in rooms, to the continuously moving symbols of Lull's combinatory tables and diagrams. These latter, she says, had a profound influence upon Lullists during the English Renaissance:

> Think of the great mediaeval encyclopaedic schemes, with all knowledge arranged in static parts, made yet more static in the classical art by the memory buildings [Augustine's conceptual metaphor] stocked with the images. And then think of Lullism, with its algebraic notations, breaking up the static schemata into new combinations on its revolving wheels. The first art is the more artistic, but the second is the more scientific.[127]

Ramon Lull's carefully constructed system of *ars combinatoria* (whereby memory's revolving wheels create intriguing conjunctions and, sometimes, disjunctions) became, in its pseudo-Lullian form, a pervasive influence throughout the English Renaissance. Numerous references to it, especially as it was assimilated by various systems of memory, can be found in Thorndike's multivolume study of magic. Nevertheless, seventeenth-century poets did have numerous other treatises upon which to draw for theories of memory.

MERGING SYSTEMS

These included the *Ad Herennium*, where the author instructs those who have learned mnemonics to place images against definite backgrounds and to have these backgrounds in a series, so that we may never by confusion in their order be prevented from following the images—proceeding from any background we wish, whatsoever its place in the series, and whether we go forwards or backwards—nor from delivering orally what has been committed to the backgrounds.[128]

According to one principle of montage, filmmakers construct similar images against different backgrounds, creating a dramatic situation that compels viewers' minds to move backward and forward in order to understand. This "modern" idea is actually Lull's, though the earlier Augustine had urged those who create texts to enrich them by "complication." Complication, John Chamberlin explains, is a process that "involves the memory, for the mind draws out these implications and associations by ruminating upon the words of the text, recalling similar but different instances of them elsewhere in Scripture, and distinguishing multiple significations."[129]

Augustine's metaphor, rumination, seems a strange way to explain *memoria,* or how the memory works:

> propterea inde per recordationem potuere depromi, forte ergo sicut de ventre cibus ruminando, sic ista de memoria recordando proferuntur.[130]
>
> [Perchance, therefore, even as meat is by chewing of the cud brought up again out of the belly, so by recalling are these [images] brought up again out of the memory.][131]

Actually the depiction of memory as a cow chewing its cud is common to medieval theories, and it represents both parts of the process whereby things are remembered and interpreted. The image itself is the cud, which must be chewed by the intellect before understanding can take place.[132] Thus Augustine follows the prescribed method, implementing a metaphor firmly rooted in the natural world in order to teach higher principles. According to Mary Carruthers, "Metaphors which are digestive activities are so powerful and tenacious that 'digestion' should be considered another basic functional model for the complementary activities of reading and composition, collection and recollection."[133] Augustine uses the image of the cow chewing its cud to describe memory as the "stomach of the soul," arguing that its purpose is divine, making the transfer of knowledge primarily vertical.

Donne, like George Herbert, appropriated the metaphor of digestion, embedding it in his poetry in order to extend the usual meaning to its alchemical counterpart. When he did this, he complicated the text beyond the usual, placing even greater demands upon his readers. Donne employed alchemical (and cabalistic) codes in order to express Mary. Very often these codes are so similar to the more familiar Christian icons that the reader's memory is compelled to move back and forth in two directions and his or her mind is compelled to make fine distinctions. These distinctions include systems of languages already learned but also religious and political predispositions.[134] The diagram below gives some idea of how the process of making meaning works:

IMAGE REVOLVING OUTSIDE TEXT
^
^
IMAGE OF MARY IN TEXT

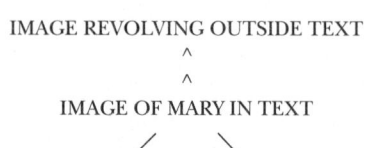

Reader meditates by means of: Author creates by means of:
Memory of Christian icons   Images (Christian/alchemic)
Memory of Hermetic and   Names/numbers from cabala
cabalistic emblems   Arranged backgrounds

Simply matching images of Mary against similar or different backgrounds is not sufficient grounds for interpretation. As John Shawcross reminds us, the reader's task is to recognize the constants that the author has supplied, meanwhile perceiving the available variables. These variables include "what has been put into the work under scrutiny by the author."[135] Among these variables are all the possible attitudes, associations, and experiences the reader can supply.[136] I will add that both the constants and the variables are attached to memory and that the author intends for his readers to implement memory as part of these associations and experiences. Memory supplies the verb that will translate the combination of visual code and associative experience into statement. That verb is, naturally, linking, but even this is deceptively simple. Those of us who remember our elementary grammar, remember that linking verbs take two forms: 1) the state of being verbs (is, are, was, were, be, being, been) and 2) the more elusive others (appears, seems, grows, becomes). Whereas the first invites declaration, "This *is* that," the latter can only ask questions, albeit rhetorical ones, "To what extent is this the same as that?" The first may be defined as the language of simile. The second represents the language of metonymy or synecdoche.

The occult emblem from nature (whether mineral, vegetable, or animal) evokes the spiritual force behind it. So when Renaissance readers encountered such an image, a "crucified" snake, for example, they were forced to think in several directions including Moses's lifting up of the serpent in the wilderness (itself the Old Testament antetype of Christ) and the synoptic image symbolizing the unity of sulfur and mercury (or whatever equivalents were in their memory banks). These they had to interpret within the context or background provided. Not an easy task.

The habit of reading such complicated texts in such complicated ways continued throughout the English Renaissance. According to Lina Bolzoni, the art of simultaneously revealing and concealing was considered to be "the product of virtuoso skill and play."[137] Milton's attraction to occult and Hermetic images, along with certain cabalistic theories, some of which he implemented as occasional references in his poems, is well documented.[138] According to David Katz, Milton's Garden of Eden was a "utopian image . . . important for both Jews and Christians in the seventeenth century: the state of language before Adam's Fall was the distant goal."[139] Donne used cabalistic combinations and occult references in order to complicate his texts, thus proving his virtuosity. However, he also implemented these codes in order to transfer ideas vertically, aspiring toward some lost Eden, his response to Reformation iconoclasm. The images themselves are fairly easy to cite. What is more difficult to discern is the mental gymnastics behind this kind of magic, which transforms the baser things of nature into the divine.

Thorndike cites examples of occult emblems coming from three different kingdoms. The mineral is represented by several ancient coins, gems, and seals. The vegetable by leaves of tansy with white flowers from "the Tridentine Alps." The animal is represented by the *monoceros*, a horselike creature having a horn in its forehead, a head like a deer, and a mane like a young mule.[140] Each of these Hermetic images should be viewed as an intercessory link from the low to the high. As "white magic" it contains spiritual power. An emblem of copper, for example, is a link to Venus. An emblem of silver to the moon. The glue behind this linking, the secret itself, has different names according to various treatises. Sometimes the glue that binds is mercury and sometimes *pneuma*. One dictionary of alchemical terms defines pneuma as the "spirit or Breath of God (in Greek and Coptic magical texts)."[141]

According to H. J. Sheppard the Gnostics considered warmth and moisture an important provision for the "impelling action" of pneuma, analogous to the provisions of growth already observed in the animal and vegetable world.[142] Both the Gnostics and the alchemists perceived pneuma as something that links things. The Gnostics, moreover, distinguished pneuma, at least in the divine state, as asexual or androgynous. The Stoics, like the Gnostics and, often, the alchemists, saw pneuma as divine, a force emitted from the Divine that, "like a gradually ascending scale of perfections," connected mankind with Divine Wisdom.[143] For Donne, this pneuma linking souls to God is sometimes Mary and sometimes her equivalent in "word" or "shape."

Since pictures played a key role in Hermetic theory, we should look for significance beyond the obvious, especially when we study Donne. Yet little has been done to confront the numerous images of Mary in his poems and sermons. One recent study, for example, notes the picture of Adam and Eve in Donne's chambers, citing it among the "images and emblems" that served as Donne's models for "religious instruction and imitation."[144] Yet Adam and Eve were also Hermetic codes woven into Donne's theological alchemy. The picture in his private chambers is indeed significant, not as supposed, but as it provides clues to his system of magic. Understanding the image helps us understand how, if not why, he was able to incorporate a "multivalent vision of reality and of knowledge" into his poetry and sermons.[145] Such emblems, one scholar says, were not mere word games but rather "a method of revealing reality":

> The polysemic nature of an emblem constituted a more authentic representation of reality than could a representation that claimed to express a single objective truth. An emblem thus was more real than, say, a microscopic observation, unless of course the microscope observation could be interpreted as an emblem.[146]

What we are about to do is study Mary as emblem or image in order to discover her as mnemonic device containing—not just one but several—powerful secrets. As emblem she calls up "things like other things," revealing or discovering many dimensions of reality, traveling sideways and vertically in spiraling motion, emanating even from the mind of God, which is the Origin of all Reality.

Both Donne and Herbert celebrated the acquisition of "forrain wisdome," which allowed them a measure of freedom in creating things like others but not the same. We know this because they spoke about it. Herbert, for example, weaves secular knowledge into his theology, declaring that it can be converted to Christian use:

> All forrain wisdome doth amount to this,
> To take all that is given; whether wealth,
> Or love, or language; nothing comes amisse:
> A good digestion turneth all to health:
>
> (ll. 355–58)[147]

Herbert's reference to "digestion," the same code employed by Augustine, is an allusion to the alembic as "stomach." Alchemists thought of transmutation as a sort of digestion. The solvents used during the early stages in the process were likened to saliva, which helps transform crude materials into wholesome food. Sometimes these acids were given fantastic names, like "stomach of the ostrich," thought to be capable of digesting even the most recalcitrant materials. Sometimes these acids were pictured as animals "swallowing the sun or the moon."[148] Illustrations of this phenomenon in alchemical texts include Joseph "fed" to the well and Jonah to the whale.[149] The illustration below, from Sebastian Münster's *Cosmographia Universalis* (1614), a copy of which Donne gave to a friend,[150] is a good example of how the biblical story of Jonah joins with the alchemical concept of mastication in the Renaissance mind. Unlike most modern readers, the community of readers confronted by Münster's atlas understood this image in *both* its biblical and alchemical sense. Jonah, who had been told by God to go to Nineveh and cry against the wickedness of its people, disobeyed, fleeing instead to Tarshish.[151] God cured Jonah by placing him in the belly-alembic of a great fish. Its digestive juices worked upon the prophet, healing him in various stages until finally he was cast upon the shore transmuted. In the end, this reconstituted Jonah went to Nineveh as ordered, urging its people to cease striving against God. Hence, the subject of Jonah's story is unity in the cosmos, which is the theme of Münster's atlas.

Donne uses such imagery, imagery associated with swallowing and digestion, in this same alchemical sense. Michael Schoenfeldt has observed a similar phenomenon in Francis Bacon's political writing, citing Paracelsian theories of medicine as Bacon's source for the concept of health in the body politic.[152] Cultural xenophobia, he notes, considered outsiders, "such as Jews, Catholics and witches," as a disease to be either expelled or cured by internalization.[153] Donne invariably chose the latter method, employing alchemical discourse, to express a vision of restored health and harmony in the body politic.

When he employs the image of the alchemical stomach, for example, he means it as a metaphor for medieval *memoria* but also as a metaphor for *theological alchemy* (Johann Reuchlin's term and, as we have seen, a term Donne appropriated as his own in the *Essays*).[154] When Milton uses the language of alchemy to describe angel digestion in *Paradise Lost*, he intends it as an *isolated* metaphor.[155] Donne, however, employs alchemical discourse not just occasionally but so that it becomes central to his epistemology. Donne's verse letter to Edward Herbert (1610) is a good example:

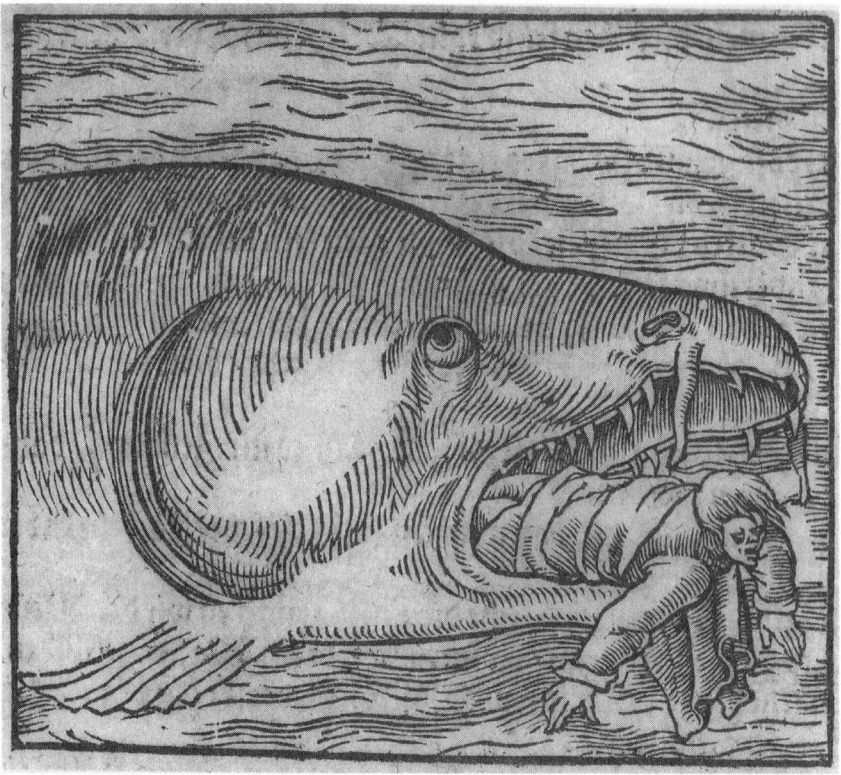

Figure 7: "Jonah and the Whale" from Sebastian Münster, *Cosmographia Universalis* (Basel, 1614). Rare Books Division, the New York Public Library, Astor, Lenox, and Tilden Foundations.

> . . . for Man into himselfe can draw
> All, All his faith can swallow, 'or reason chaw.[156]

His reference is to the mind, the seat of intellectual activity, but he encodes it as the stomach/alembic, that place that breaks down and dissolves otherwise contrary elements, gluing them together again as something not only whole but also wholesome.

> All that is fill'd, and all that which doth fill,
>   All the round world, to man is but a pill,
> In all it workes not, but it is in all
>   Poysonous, or purgative, or cordiall,
> For, knowledge kindles Calentures in some,
>   And is to others ice *Opium*.
>
>   (ll. 39–44)

The alchemists believed that human saliva contained healing powers sufficient to kill vipers and scorpions.[157] So Donne depicts here the ruminating philosopher capable of swallowing all knowledge with impunity. It is no accident that Ralph Waldo Emerson, a great admirer of Donne, appropriated this same code as an expression of his poetics of transcendental alchemy.[158]

Nor is it an accident that Donne's reference to wholesome digestion is contained in this particular letter, a response to Lord Herbert's *De Veritate*. Nicholas Tyacke reminds us that the views expressed by Herbert were compatible with Arminian teachings and particularly with the doctrine of free will.[159] Kevin Sharpe and Steven Zwicker remind us that reading itself "was understood as digestatory in every real sense."[160] So Donne's allusion to swallowing and chewing "all" is significant in that it encourages nourishment, rather than amputation, as a means to health. Although ardent Calvinists would cut away Jews and Catholics and anyone else threatening their "ideal" state, Lord Herbert and Donne, both "big feeders" in books, would seek a more gentle way. In 1610, when this letter was written, these Calvinists were merely a stubborn minority, but eventually they would become a force so dangerous that Donne himself, as Dean of St. Paul's, would feel compelled to condemn them publicly.[161] Lord Herbert, sensing the danger beforehand, decided to confront radical Calvinists publicly in *De Veritate*, but that is not to say that Donne lacked the same prescience. He only needed to discover more subtle ways to express dissent.

Heather Meakin has distinguished Donne's discourse as either dilatory or closed, his subject determining which is employed.[162] I would amend this dichotomy to define, by comparison, the "open" discourse of Arminianism, the spirit of which Donne embraced, against the "closed" discourse of radical Calvinism.[163] Hermetic codes and occult language systems, which he already knew and which his contemporaries were now attempting to compile as an international or "catholic" language, contributed to his peculiar brand of open discourse. For him it became a means to express more tolerant views. Whereas radical Puritans would eventually, during the Caroline period, insist upon holy war, upon escalating by whatever means the conflicts between Roman Catholicism and the Church of England, the prevailing attitude among conservatives was one of tolerance.[164]

Tolerance, it was believed, would accommodate various points of view, allowing numerous religious factions to coexist in peace. The only ones later excluded from this tolerance were recusants, who some Laudians thought to be a threat to true religion.[165] Ironically, the tolerant policies of James I were responsible for an eventual shift in power from the throne to a theocracy. Though he acceded to the throne as the friend of a powerful Puritan minority, he quickly distanced himself from them, especially in the matter of the divisive "puritan blueprint." Because James was determined to practice tolerance, he refused support for the Puritan plan to purge both church and state. Thus radical Puritan hopes were dashed at the Hampton Court Conference of 1604,[166] only to reassert themselves later. Eventually, Calvinism (with its doctrines of total depravity, unconditional election, limited atonement, and irresistible grace) would wage war against Arminianism (with its doctrines of free will and good works—including the sacraments and ceremony) and win.

Donne was aligned with the Arminian side, at least in spirit. During the early decades of the century, he had experienced various Calvinist attacks against the very images he held dear. One way to attack an image is to ignore it, and to Donne, the Virgin had been ignored. True, she was the subject of two Anglican feast days, but except as she was part of the important Protestant doctrine of Christ's virgin birth, she was not in the picture. Donne's poetics restored her, making Mary once again a vital force. Because he understood the threat Puritan radicals would eventually pose, he determined to carve out a larger space in which to think and be. This meant developing language that would counteract Puritan derogation and neglect, including what Anthony Milton calls their "anti-papal overreaction" to "Rome's idolatry" and the concomitant profanity they committed when they dishonored the Blessed Virgin.[167] Donne's dilemma could be likened to that of the son of a blind man, determined to confine him to an imageless world. He learned to restore with impunity images that his father could not, indeed *would not,* see.

One of Donne's sermons provides us with a good example of the way he used alchemical codes to express Arminian views. Since his subject was spiritual change or transformation, the alchemical opus was an apt way to illustrate the doctrine that man is *not,* after all, totally depraved, that there is within the individual something to be rescued or drawn out. Whether or not this happens depends upon works and will. For the "great work," or alchemical transmutation, is prefaced upon the same. Donne's sermon is a good example of how "forrain wisdome," including esoteric terms, helped him express Christian doctrine.

He distinguishes several distinct steps in the opus, each of which has its analogue in the spiritual order. The context is David's desire to become "whiter than snow" (Psalms 51:7 [King James version]):

> Therefore David who was metal tried seven times in the fire, and desired to be such gold as might be laid up in God's treasury, might consider, that in transmutation of metals, it is not enough to come to a calcination, or a

liquefaction of the metal, (that must be done) nor to an ablution, to sever dross from pure, nor to a transmutation, to make it a better metal, but there must be a fixion, a settling thereof, so that it shall not evaporate into nothing, nor return to his former nature. Therefore he saw that he needed not only a liquefaction, a melting into tears, not only an ablution and a transmutation, those he had by this purging and this washing, this station in the church of God, and this present sanctification there, but he needed *fixionem,* an establishment . . . that under the seal of his blessed Spirit, he might ever dwell in that calm, in that assurance, in that acquiescence, that as he is in a good state this minute, he shall be in no worse, whensoever God shall be pleased to translate him.[168]

Unlike the Calvinists, whose security rested in the doctrine of the perseverance of the saints, Donne was always worried that his faith might prove fugitive, hence his emphasis upon the need to be established by *fixionem,* the final stage.[169] Others called this final stage *projectionem.* At any rate, this sermon illustrates how codes of magic, including color symbolism, combine with the language of Scripture in order to provoke new thoughts concerning the divine opus whereby the Philosopher's Stone is born.

Donne's alchemical references allow the sermon text, as Shawcross has observed, "to be uncovered by the reader," who calls up "further allusions, rendering the text a different text."[170] Donne can assume the reader's general knowledge of the "constants" he provides. But the "variables," which the reader supplies, are what render the text elastic. Donne knows that alchemical signs are among these variables, and he expects his congregation to read into his sermon their own peculiar versions of the opus, including the implied color imagery.

Alchemical theorists generally aspired toward the birth of the red Philosopher's Stone, red because it symbolized resurrection.[171] So the adept among Donne's congregation naturally envisioned his analogy to the stages of the opus as a progression of colors from black to white to red. There was little consensus among alchemists, however, concerning the names and number of steps leading to this. George Ripley offers twelve:

> As for your better understanding, first I will set downe ye names of ye twelve gates, then will I apply this one key to every lock, & so shall appeare ye plaine truth discovered;
>
> The twelve Gates
>
> | 1 Calcination | 5 Putrifaction | 9 Fermentation |
> | 2 Dissolution | 6 Congelation | 10 Exaltation |
> | 3 Seperation [*sic*] | 7 Cibation | 11 Multiplication |
> | 4 Conjunction | 8 Sublimation | 12 Projection[172] |

Ripley explains that the "Wheele of Philosophy" will cleanse elements "from crudity to fixation . . . from black to white, from white to red, which truly hee calleth ye wheele."[173] Donne's sermon indicates that he has digested Ripley's theory (or something like it), converting it into his own doctrine of redemption. This is not as interesting, however, as the questions it inspires, especially the question of the virgin/Virgin's cooperation in the process. In this respect, Donne is more subtle.

1
Emblems of Making

As EMBLEM, THE VIRGIN SUCKLING HER CHILD WAS AN IMPORTANT alchemical code. Its origins seem to antedate Christianity and may be traced back to the figure of Roman Charity, breastfeeding her people.¹ Naturally Donne, who recognized the power of this seminal image or *device,* was quick to appropriate it.² Medieval alchemists had already discovered in the image a vivid comparison between the birth of the Philosopher's Stone and the Nativity, especially in the associative alchemical virgin's milk. As elixir, virgin's milk transforms the White Queen into the, perhaps androgynous, Mighty Red King.³ Writing for an audience fundamentally memorial, Donne was able to superimpose the variable, that is, the alchemical virgin suckling (above), over the constant, more conventional images from medieval iconography, complicating the text for many. When confronted with this kind of polysemic imagery, his readers are challenged to apply knowledge to context in order to understand how the Hermetic level of discourse coheres or conflicts with traditional Christian doctrine.

This does not mean that all readers recognize the Hermetic codes embedded in Donne's poems. Still, the alchemical signs are there for those readers who will or can construct them as statements. Like Herbert, Donne rarely employs the linking verb *is* in his *memoria.* Rather, he invites his readers to interpret alchemical codes by means of the more elusive *appears, seems,* and *becomes.* Hence, Donne asks only the rhetorical question: "Is this as it appears?"

Indeed, for the most part, Donne avoided overt statements concerning Mary. In fact, his preaching generally demonstrated that he was keenly aware of "the necessity of being not only harmless as the dove but also politically wise as the serpent if he was to achieve success in the profession he had adopted."⁴ Sometimes, however, he did venture statements from the pulpit concerning the Virgin's role in the process of salvation.

Donne's first appearance at St. Paul's Cross, the outdoor facility next to the Cathedral, put him in the spotlight where he could be

AVREAE MENSAE. LIB. XI.   509

LAPIS, VT INFANS, LACTE NVTRIENDVS est virginali.

Elchior Cibinensis Vngarus, si populi tribum spectemus in genere, alias Transsyluanus habetur, vir Religiosus & Sacerdotali ordini initiatus, vt verus artifex arcana huius scientiæ abditissimæ sub forma sacra, nempe Missæ, comprehendit & adumbrauit. Vidit enim hic vir doctus, quod Lapidi philosophico attribueretur quasi Natiuitas, vita, sublimatio seu igne passio, atque hinc mors in nigro & tenebroso colore; denique resurrectio & vita in rubeo & perfectissimo co-
Sss 3   lore,

Figure 8: The Virgin suckling the Child, "The Stone, like a child, must be nourished with virgin milk." Michael Maier, Symbola aureae mensae (Frankfurt, 1617). The British Library (90:25,509).

viewed by many distinguished people, including aldermen and councilmen of the city of London. The occasion was the anniversary of James's accession to the throne. Knowing the king might require a copy of his sermon text, he prepared it carefully, taking as part of his assignment the usual attacks upon Puritans and the church in Rome. Here he publicly declared the position expected of any loyal Anglican:

> I know the Fathers are frequent in comparing and paralleling *Eve,* the Mother of Man, and *Mary* the Mother of God. But, God forbid any should say, That the Virgin Mary concurred to our good, so, as *Eve* did to our ruine. . . . it cannot be said, in that sense, or that manner, that by one women innocence entred, and life: The Virgin *Mary* had not the same interest in our salvation, as *Eve* had in our destruction; nothing that she did entred into that treasure, that ransom that redeemed us.[5]

According to one member of Donne's congregation, the sermon was "exceedingly well liked generally."[6] Donne's modern editors, however, are not so sure, declaring this particular sermon to have been "planned rather too deliberately for the occasion . . . at least, less moving than many another."[7] The fact that Donne spoke as he did, especially early in his priestly career, should not surprise us. Only the most credulous, however, will believe his declaration, that "nothing that she did entred into that treasure . . . that redeemed us," entire. If we are to understand Donne's whole mind, we must pursue other texts, retaining this early sermon as reference.

Some six years later he preached a Christmas sermon at St. Paul's Cathedral. On this occasion he defined the fullness of Christ in terms of plenitude, listing first among his New Testament attributes the faith of Stephen and the works of Dorcas. Having placed faith and works before his congregation, Donne proceeds to press for still greater fullness, insisting next upon "The Virgin Mary [who] is full of Grace; and Grace is a fulnesse above both; above faith and works too, for that is the meanes to preserve both. . . ."[8] Perhaps this statement seems not very remarkable when placed within its context as a sermon preached on Christmas Day, when thoughts of Mary and of plenitude are natural. The force of Donne's statement, however, cannot be overlooked and, in fact, demands attention.

One reason is that during the previous century English recusants had come to regard Christmas as a time when they could assert their Catholicism by celebrating the Virgin. Subsequent legislation rendered these same Catholics vulnerable.[9] Of this Donne was keenly aware. Nevertheless, his comment on Mary's role in the process of salvation, putting her plenitude above Luther's faith, must have been startling.

Already we begin to see evidence that Donne employs alchemical codes when speaking of the Virgin. *Grace,* technically, is a term from Christian theology. Since Barbara Lewalski's *Protestant Poetics* (1979) much ink has been spilled on the subject of grace—whether it is the product of free will, how it cooperates with mankind's efforts, whether it is prevenient or subsequent—but little attention has been paid to its Hermetic counterpart. The alchemists appropriated grace, when it bounced across the net and into their court. When it volleyed back into Donne's court, it had been transformed into something like something else, not the same. He accepted the gift and used it. Other emblems, likewise transformed, he received. Plenitude, which he associates (in his sermon above) with Mary, had also taken on alchemical significance as one of the attributes of the phoenix.

Phoenix

Composed of both sexes, the phoenix was born every five or six hundred years out of its own burning nest. Out of this nest, numerous small birds emerged, the implication being that death has re-created more than just the original, multiplying birth far beyond the two-in-one originally born.

The phoenix is featured by various Renaissance emblematists, usually depicted during the act of self-sacrifice and self-renovation. It thereby anticipates several Christian doctrines, including Christ's Resurrection and the resurrection of mankind. Perhaps the emblem most familiar to modern students is that from Geffrey Whitney's *A Choice of Emblems* (1586), so often reproduced in textbooks. But Whitney is one among many. During the nineteenth century one scholar discovered an interesting clue to Mary's identity as phoenix. It came in the form of an emblem attached to a poem. Donne appropriated this presumably familiar image as his own. Significantly, it depicted Mary and Christ as that Heavenly Phoenix upon which all mankind depends.

Henry Green's survey of emblems in Shakespeare includes "a singular application of the Phoenix emblem which existed before and during Shakespeare's time, but of which I find no pictorial representation until 1633."[10] The image referred to is from Henry Hawkins's poem, *The Virgin.* The poem attached to the emblem, now almost forgotten, is not so very important, except as it explains the visual element. Digging down even to that relatively recent layer of literary history may get us closer to what Renaissance poets meant, and to how their readers understood.

The emblem depicts the phoenix with two hearts united, Hawkins explaining this phenomenon as "the hearts of the Virgin-Mother and her Son."[11] As is usual in sixteenth- and seventeenth-century emblem practice, picture and word explain each other. In fact, Huston Diehl reminds us, seventeenth-century epistemology "makes no distinction between pictures and words."[12] With that in mind I supply the opening lines, the rest to be discussed later:

> Behold, how Death aymes with his mortal dart,
> And wounds a Phoenix with a twin-like hart.
> These are the harts of Jesus and his Mother
> So linkt in one, that one without the other
> Is not entire.
>
> (ll. 1–5)[13]

It can be no accident that Crashaw employed the same device of two hearts joined in "Sancta Maria Dolorum." The more subtle Donne, at least in his Christmas sermon, merely suggests this, observing that "The Virgin Mary is full of Grace . . . above faith and works too."

The alchemists had seized upon the phoenix as symbol of the fire necessary to all important phases of transmutation (transformation from one substance or state into another) and sublimation (the transformation from solid to gaseous state or from gaseous to solid without becoming liquid).[14] Donne, of course, knew that the phoenix represented union between Christ and Mary, but he also understood it to represent alchemical transmutation. Knowing both traditions, he was able to make them cohere so that the phoenix becomes God residing in the warmth of Mary's womb. Naturally, the God he makes is composed of male and female parts, including the Womb of God who made all things in the beginning. At least that is the hypothesis.

Like any hypothesis, the question must be answered by proof. We begin to test it by studying the ways Donne depicts the concepts of heat and augmentation. Most Renaissance readers knew the alchemical doctrine of *multiplication*. They also knew that multiplication cannot occur without heat. Donne capitalized upon this knowledge of Hermetic principles, employing esoteric language he knew would be understood as variables, at least by his more adept readers. Huston Diehl observes that Renaissance readers, generally, derived aesthetic pleasure from figuring out relationships that seemed not to exist. These readers, he says, "valued riddles and particularly enjoyed the

Hawkins' Parthenos, 1633.

"Behold, how Death aymes with his mortal dart,
And wounds a Phœnix with a twin-like hart.
These are the harts of Jesus and his Mother
So linkt in one, that one without the other
Is not entire. They (sure) each others smart
Must needs sustaine, though two, yet as one hart.
One Virgin-Mother, Phenix of her kind,
And we her Sonne without a father find.
The Sonne's and Mothers paines in one are mixt,
His side, a Launce, her soule a Sword transfixt.
Two harts in one, one Phenix loue contriues : *
One wound in two, and two in one reuiues."

Figure 9: "Phoenix with Two Hearts," representing "the Virgin-Mother and her Son." From Henry Hawkins, *Parthenos* (1633). In Henry Green, *Shakespeare and the Emblem Writers* (London: Trübner, 1870), 384. General Research Division, the New York Public Library, Astor, Lenox, and Tilden Foundations.

pleasure of interpreting the obscure, the enigmatic, and the esoteric."[15] Donne naturally exploited this situation.

Some of his depictions of Mary are a puzzle that can only be solved by reading her womb as the alembic, the mint, the egg—the place where multiplication or plenitude occurs. Since the alembic per se was also considered an image of the adept's soul, which must be pure lest the opus fail, Donne was compelled to write himself into the puzzle, along with Mary. Such is the case in *La Corona*. Eluned Crawshaw helps us understand this phenomenon in Donne when he observes that, in spiritual alchemy, "metals might represent the alchemist and the degree of purity they reached would consequently indicate the adept's own level of spiritual attainment."[16] This says much about Donne's perception of himself as a poet and also about his theological alchemy as he developed it in his sermons.

One word of caution concerning the phoenix: it was also a standard Renaissance trope, so it could be employed in a dual sense, representing two constants. Usually it simply meant something "startling," "unique," or "brilliant." Queen Elizabeth herself was often referred to as *phoenix*. Sometimes, however, those who attached that image to her meant it to be understood alchemically. John Owen's epigram on "The Offspring of the Virgin Queen" argues her "fecundity," in spite of her childlessness:

> England, and Scotland's, blessed unity:
> The issue was of your virginity.
> She is more glorious, who unites two states,
> Then she, who like the Vulgar generate.

John Watkins interprets this depiction of Elizabeth's reign as one that has "achieved the miracle of virginal procreation," making of her both a phoenix and the Virgin.[17] By "virginal procreation" Watkins means that Elizabeth's death in 1603 spawned greater religious tolerance, the "death of the virgin" resulting in spiritual renewal.

Usually, however, the phoenix as reference meant "something extraordinary." Both Donne and Crashaw employed these conventions (what Shawcross would call "constants"), so we must learn to distinguish *which* constant, or else mar the sense. The phoenix as Renaissance trope is not particularly interesting, but when the variables, that is, the theological and the alchemical meanings, begin to mix, an intriguing network of ideas develops. In the sermons, for example, Donne describes the Riddle in Heaven as a dual-natured Phoenix. As Protector-god hovering over England, it is both the aggressive "male" eagle and the mild "female" hen, or rather dove.[18] Taken together, the eagle and the dove define phoenix.

Donne probed deeply what the cabalists called *Schekhina* ("glory"), what the Gnostics considered to be "the first feminine principle which emanates from the Supreme Being or God,"[19] and what I will call the female nature in God. The alchemical phoenix, composed of both sexes, helped him express what Christianity and Hermetism already believed, that death and dissolution must precede Creation, but also that more universal, Hermetic belief that death, dissolution, and resurrection can only be accomplished by the union of male and female.

One version of the phoenix myth includes the presence of a worm among the ashes of the dying bird. From this worm a new phoenix is born. Donne's sermon preached for the churching of the Countess of Bridgewater provides variables of this story. Distinguishing male corruption (or ashes) from *female* nourishment (or the worm), Donne allows his audience to understand this female worm as that which feeds the alchemical chick: "I shall say to corruption, Thou art my father, and to the worme, Thou art my Mother."[20] Some among his congregation joined the constant, "ashes to ashes," with the variable, the worm of the phoenix chick, in order to make new meaning. This way of depicting the miracle of resurrection seems to be Donne's invention, his own way of translating alchemical theory into Christian doctrine.

Another of Donne's sermons, delivered before Princess Elizabeth, daughter of King James, and Frederick, the Elector Palatine, also implies the female element in salvation, this time by providing variables of Mary herself.[21] His subject is grace, and he defines it as the *middle nature* in the blood, which gives birth to the individual soul.[22] Each member of his congregation must make sense of this variable, this "middle nature," implementing his or her own experience and knowledge, in order to determine whether Donne's version of grace has anything to do with Mary, "full of Grace." Princess Elizabeth, as we shall see, had good reason to think so. "This grace," Donne says, "which . . . grows out of that which is in you already . . . grows into more and more grace."[23] A few observations now may help to establish the context for what will be discussed later.

Not all of Donne's contemporaries would have understood *grace*, even as a theological term, in the same way. Calvinist readers would have thought of it as irresistible grace, integral with the doctrine of total depravity, which says that man's will is so corrupt he cannot even choose salvation. Hence this grace is limited to the elect, and God, presumably masculine, must put it there. Works, including the sacraments and ceremony, but also man's *unreliable* will, have nothing to do with the matter. Arminians, on the other hand, would understand that grace, "which . . . grows out of that which is in you already," as innate goodness. Good works, including the sacraments and ceremony, but also man's ability to *choose* God, grow into grace, which grows into more grace. When Donne writes the variable of alchemical grace into his text, he allows *both* kinds of readers, Arminians and Calvinists, to make their own texts with impunity. We might say that this is Donne's own way of implementing Arminian tolerance. Those readers who understood the alchemical codes also understood good works as a variable. The rest were blind to this matter.

As noted above, alchemical grace is the initial stage in the *opus*. The secrets of alchemy were thought to be imparted only to those upon whom grace had been bestowed. Adepts accordingly prepared themselves before entering the *sanctum sanctorum*. All knew, Edward Kelly wrote, that the Philosopher's Stone could only be obtained by grace.[24] Hence, Donne in the *Holy Sonnets* asks, "But who shall give thee that grace to beginne?" This *grace*, even as he employs it here, is another sign that his language is dual.[25]

Hatching Hens and the Mothering Body

Readers carefully following this argument have begun to perceive a common theme in this network of images. Joined to the image of grace (likened to the *middle nature* in blood) are womb (along with the phenomenon of multiple births), mint (where coins are "born," as children, stamped on both sides with the images of both parents), nest (in which the bisexual phoenix dies in flames), and grave ("alive" with activity between father corruption and mother worm). All of these are alchemical terms that help Donne express the mysteries of spiritual regeneration. He also employs some variables—phoenix, hen, and egg—each of which indicates particular attributes of the Virgin. In *The First Anniversarie*, for example, Donne uses hen imagery to probe correspondences between Elizabeth Drury's body and a world bereft of her. Albert H. Tricomi calls such cross-referencing "a metonymic transposition."[26] The genre Donne implements is encomium, a form familiar to his readers. But within this form he situates variables that invite self-fashioning readers to transpose as their own. One such variable is the hen, whose chicks are bereft of protection now that Elizabeth Drury is gone. Because "Shee is dead," the world is vulnerable:

> The clouds conceiue not raine, or doe not powre
> In the due birth-time, downe the balmy showre.
> Th'Ayre doth not motherly sit on the earth,

> To hatch her seasons, and giue all things birth.
> Spring-times were common cradles, but are toombes;
> And false-conceptions fill the generall wombs.
>
> (ll. 380–86)[27]

The informed reader perceives Donne's alchemical thought, understanding that earth, air, fire (implied by "hatch"), and water are all involved in the creative process ("Spring-times"). Like a hen watching over her chickens, protecting them with her wings, Elizabeth Drury used to sustain the world. As metonymy, the image of hen suggests the protective warmth of the Virgin's womb. Also the image of tomb/womb suggests that a world without a virgin is stillborn.

So far the context seems to be Christian, sometimes mixed with Hermetism. Donne, however, was able to attach to these images other doctrines from the Hebrew cabala. His memory, like that of others, was already oriented toward cabalistic teachings, which cannot be dissociated from Ramon Lull's mnemotechnics already discussed. As Yates has observed, "the stimulus behind Renaissance occult memory was the Renaissance Hermetic tradition."[28] When certain Christian humanists sought to synthesize Jewish and Christian ideas, they naturally included both occult and Hermetic theories. Pico della Mirandola, founder of the Hermetic-cabalist tradition, is one example.[29] Pico looked to the Hebrew doctrine of the *sephiroth* in order to explain Creation.

According to the philosophy of the cabala, the *sephiroth* is the means whereby the Infinite emanates into the finite. Heinrich Cornelius von Nettesheim Agrippa (1486–1535) defined the *sephiroth* as simply emanated "wisdom."[30] Acknowledging a three-personed God (Father, Son, and Holy Spirit), the *sephiroth* also declared a Limitless God presiding over all. This God is not limited in person or sex. THE ONE is gradually revealed to the earnest seeker through intermediaries. Naturally, Mary could be woven into this faith and assigned a role of greater importance.

Archangelus, for example, believed that the cabala proved Mary's intercessory powers, making her an important link in emanation. She was the one responsible for the "dual nature of Jesus."[31] The cabala, he said, also indicates her intercessory role, as "the beneficent virgin, queen of heaven."[32] In 1510 Agrippa glorified the entire female sex when he cited the Virgin's close relationship with the Tetragrammaton, or the four-letter word for God that cannot be expressed.[33] Using the alphabetical technique, or *gematria* (which is the cabalistic habit of assigning numbers to letters of the alphabet), Agrippa proved "a closer correspondence between the name 'Eve' and the

Tetragrammaton than exists between the name 'Adam' and that supreme four-letter name of God."[34] This discovery allowed Christian humanists to attach new meaning to already established codes from medieval iconography.

According to church doctrine, Mary and Christ, when they repaired paradise, became Second Eve and Second Adam. Naturally medieval iconographers often depicted her holding an apple.[35] Also, as noted above, Ramon Lull attached to the Virgin that attribute of God called *Sapientia*, a name, he argued, even Muslims and Jews could accept. The origins of this emblem of the dragon subdued by Mary/Sapientia and Christ can be traced back to earliest history, even to the late third or early second millennium BC.[36] In trampling the dragon, Christ and Second Eve combine to crush Satan. When this Christian image combines with its alchemical counterpart, the result is something new, not the same. We discover a fluidity of categories, which we must study in order to understand new meaning. The alchemical dragon, symbolizing primal chaos, stations itself at the doorway to secrets. Anyone who wishes to penetrate those secrets must kill it. The androgyne, depicted below, conquers the dragon in order that the Work may be born. The artist who fashioned the medieval statuette was merely expressing the generally accepted notion of Mary as Second Eve, of Mary as source of Wisdom. The Hermetic emblem illustrates what happens when Christian symbols are served across the net into another court. They return as things transformed.

If Donne ever read Agrippa's statement, cited above, he was able to link it with the idea of Mary as Second Eve, the doctrine of the *sephiroth*, and the name of God.[37] After all, it is but a short step from Eve to Second Eve, from Adam to Second Adam. Mary, by implication, is central to Creation, is closer to THE ONE than Second Adam/Christ. Also attached to this literary device, at least for some of Donne's readers, may have been the concept of Mary as "Second Eve." Because the Virgin repaired the work of first Eve, She was considered her antithesis. At any rate, it is no accident that the Hermetic egg attached itself to Christian iconography. Piero della Francesca's painting, *Madonna and Child with Saints* (1472–74) illustrates this phenomenon in Christian art. The Egg poised above Mary answers the Star of David at her feet, making her a link between the Old and New Testaments and the Egg a link between Christian and Hebrew mystical thought.

The concept of World Egg may reach as far back as the fifth millennium BC, so neither alchemists nor Christians invented it.[38] Nevertheless, alchemists used it to explain the opus, or birthing of the

Figure 10: The Virgin as *Sedes Sapientiae* Trampling the Dragon. Statuette of Enthroned Virgin and Child. She holds an apple, symbol of Second Eve, and the Child holds an orb. N. Spanish (thirteenth century). The Metropolitan Museum of Art, the Cloisters Collection, 1972. (1972.143)

Figure 11: "The Androgyne Crushing the Dragon." Illustration for *Tractus alchemici* (sixteenth century). Leiden University Library, ms. Voss. Chym. F. 29, fol. 96r.

Figure 12: *Madonna and Child with Saints* [and Egg]. Piero della Francesca (ca. 1410/20–1492). Pinacoteca di Brera. Milan. Su concessione del Ministero per i Beni e le Attività Culturali.

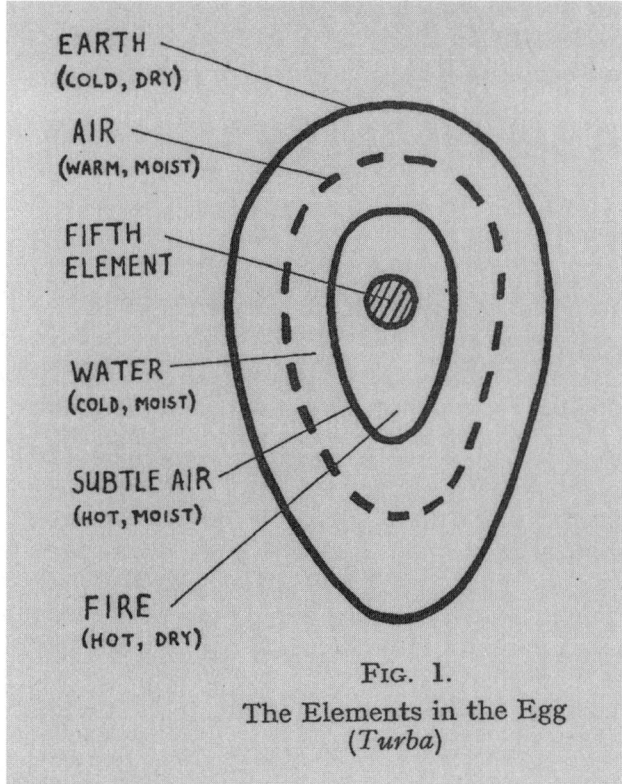

Figure 13: *The Elements in the Egg* from *Turba philosophorum* (twelfth century?). Figure 1 from H. J. Sheppard, "Egg Symbolism in Alchemy," *Ambix* 6 (1958).

alchemical Child. Edward Kelly, for example, used it to represent the vessel of the *opus alchymicum* over which God presides.[39] The Philosopher's Egg was understood according to various stages in the process. The yolk, for example, is Fire (at least in the four-element theory).[40] In other theories a mysterious fifth element, sometimes called *quintessence*, is included. The figure above illustrates the elements that compose this Egg: The twelfth-century *Turba philosophorum* was an important text often quoted in alchemical treatises.[41] According to the *Turba*, the middle of the yolk contains a mysterious fifth element, out of which a chick is born.[42] Because it is near perfection, this fifth element dominates the other four. Sometimes it is called quintessence, sometimes nothing, for, like the Tetragrammaton, it is inexpressible and therefore has no name.

By the late Middle Ages the alchemical egg had become polysemic, bearing specifically Christian meanings alongside the profane.[43] We have already begun to see Donne, in *The First Anniversarie,* depicting the virgin's womb as the alembic. This subject will be discussed in more detail in the chapter that follows. Sometimes, in the sermons for example, Donne uses metonymy as a literary device to depict the World Egg, out of which God's children are hatched by the Holy Spirit.[44] When he does this, he blurs the edges of gender. Defining the Holy Ghost as Creator, Donne transforms the usual convention of Spirit that "moved upon the face of the waters" into that of hatching hen:

> And yet, *Quia manet semen dei,* because the seed of *God* hath remained in thee, *Incubat Spiritus,* the Holy Ghost hath sat upon that seed, and hatched a new Creature in thee, a modest, but yet infallible assurance of the Mercy of thy God.[45]

Associations with Mary are implied, if by no other means than evocation of familiar images of the Holy Ghost descending upon Mary prior to her conception of Christ. Also implied is reversal of the center of power from the conventional male to the female, a variation of the constant; for the woman who bestows the gift of life, her womb providing a Savior, simultaneously becomes a center of power.

Two allusions in Donne's sermon, cited above, specifically the references to "seed" and "hatched," invite his readers, by "picture-thinking," to join these devices with other things. All would derive from what Sheppard has called "the universal symbol of creation," the World Egg.[46] Among these might be the Philosopher's Egg, which Sheppard says is symbolic of the redemption of man's soul.[47] At any rate, Donne's literary device in the sermon is metonymy, which invites each member of his congregation to construct his or her own text. The brooding hen mingles in the reader's mind with the dove hovering above Mary, an image already embedded in Christian memory. This process is the means whereby Donne, the author, manages to make and to reproduce culture. His readers' texts will vary according to the ways their memories interact with his text. Some will remember other instances whereby Mary is associated with hatching, with eggs, with power. The statuette below illustrates this phenomenon. Here Mary actually holds an egg, though sometimes the egg is near or beside her. The informed viewer will naturally make connections between this egg-bearer and Christian doctrine but also, perhaps, with Hermetic theory, which appropriates the image. Modern viewers may not "see" the egg, inserting instead an orb. But that is because their memories do not contain the *alchemical* egg, a commonplace during the century that produced the statue. The image

1: EMBLEMS OF MAKING 73

Figure 14: Ivory Tabernacle with Virgin and Child. Both the Virgin and Child hold egg-shaped orbs. French (early fourteenth century). The Metropolitan Museum of Art, Robert Lehman Collection, 1975. (1975.1.1553).

above and the image below, at least for medieval viewers, mingled in intriguing ways. Superimposed, the Virgin and Christ became the Androgyne, holding the Philosopher's Egg and beginning its progress through the alembic as male and female elements. This image also has its analogue in ancient history.[48] As indicated above, some Renaissance readers, when they looked upon emblems depicting the hearts of Christ and Mary joined, understood these as images of the Heavenly Phoenix.[49] This strange joining, they understood, somehow miraculously made Creation, in the same way that the alchemical Androgyne, already joined, makes the Stone. Certainly both images were present in Donne's imagination when he wrote of the Virgin in *La Corona:*

> Ere by the spheares time was created, thou
> Wast in his minde, who is thy Sonne, and Brother,
> Whom thou conceiv'st, conceiv'd; yea thou art now
> Thy Makers maker, and thy Fathers mother.
>
> (ll. 23–26)

Figure 15: Figure of the Androgyne holding the Philosopher's Egg. Illustration for *La Toyson d'or, par Salomon Trismosin, précepteur de Paracelse*. Bibliothèque nationale de France.

Pelican Power

Before leaving the aviary of alchemical and religious thought, we must recognize the pelican, which Donne also uses to depict either Mary or Christ. Various emblem books of the period contain references to the pelican mother who pierces her breast in order to nourish her children with her blood. Geffrey Whitney's *A Choice of Emblems* (1586) is one example. The comment beside the image reads, "The Pellican, for to revive her younge, / Doth peirce her brest, and geve them of her blood."[50] Intrigued by this image, Shakespeare used it in *Hamlet* and, with a witty reversal, in *King Lear*.[51] But the pelican also had its alchemical meaning as a particular kind of still or retort resembling the bird with its beak to its breast. In this sense it becomes a symbol not just of nourishment but also of power. Edward Kelly mentions the pelican as a vessel used to "elevate the calces of metals."[52] Gareth Roberts notes that in alchemical theory the "good wife and mother" is sometimes depicted as "a wife who kills herself to bring life to her child."[53]

There is evidence that the pelican and the phoenix were sometimes conflated in alchemical thought. This phenomenon may be more than occasional and certainly more than accidental. For when the "mother" pelican is conflated with the androgynous phoenix, she

Figure 16: Pelican vessel. Illustration for Giovanni Baptista della Porta, *De distillationibus libri* IX (Strassburg, 1609). The British Library (BL. 1037.1.15 [*1*], p. 41).

loses her otherwise exclusively female identity. Edward Kelly, for example, in *Two Excellent Treatises on the Philosopher's Stone* (1676), explains an illustration for what he calls "alchemical opposition": "A very red Sun is pouring blood into an urinal . . . the Moon lying on her back in blackish water. . . . On the hill stands a Phoenix, biting its breast, out of which drops blood, the same being drunk by its young."[54] Kelly says that this section of his treatise, "The Conjunction of Sun and Moon," was written "upon the testimony of Marsilius Ficinus."[55]

Since Ficino's influence was pervasive among the metaphysical poets, we may reasonably conclude that Donne learned the value of this alchemical pelican/phoenix partly from him. By introducing the image into his text, he invited adept readers to see God—whether Mary or Christ—reinvested with creative power. His famous sermon, *Death's Duel,* is a good example of this, for it offers a startling vision of the pelican, a vision that compels his congregation to make meaning out of variables. Those who recognize the alchemical equivalent are invited to gaze upon the Virgin as well.

Tricomi thinks that "the sexual mothering body" is an example of female power.[56] He argues that the pelican device, as Webster uses it in *The Duchess of Malfi,* provides a way to explore the phenomenon of power within power, which he says is a way "to treat the multivocalism that is part of the ceaseless play of culture."[57] As pelican, he observes, Webster's otherwise totally subdued duchess engineers a reversal of power by warning her enemies: "A many hungry guests have fed upon me; / Thine will be a poor reversion" (4.2.210).[58] Thus she makes herself, her body, the center from which all must eat or die of starvation.[59] As Tricomi says, "Whatever there is in life that's worth having proceeds from her. She is the pelican mother who, Christ-like, with her life's blood nurses those who cannot live without her. . . . Her caregiving body . . . suckles everyone, even her enemies."[60] Just before she is strangled, the duchess again asserts her power: "Go tell my brothers, when I am laid out, / They then may feed in quiet" (4.2.245–46). Hence she assumes her rightful place as that one who nourishes both the family and, by implication, the state, making or rather *restoring* herself as the center of power. It can be no accident that Donne's *The First Anniversarie,* which emphasizes the power of Elizabeth Drury to feed and sustain the world, has been cited as a possible source for Webster's play.[61]

The alchemical pelican still or vessel also symbolized the red elixir of that stage of the opus called multiplication.[62] Cibation, when the infant Stone is fed with mercurial blood, is a preface to multiplication, when the power of the elixir is augmented "more than a thousandfold through the reiterated dissolution and coagulation of the matter in the mercurial water."[63] Donne's decision to include this variable in his last sermon, *Death's Duel*, was a natural consequence of the alchemical discourse he had cultivated throughout his career.

Once, for example, when he preached before Lucy, Countess of Bedford, he constructed a strange vision of "those breasts which God puts out to us . . . which flow from him to us."[64] One variable of God's milk was virgin's milk. Since Renaissance ladies, as well as men, were keen students of the Hermetic arts, we can assume that this alchemical allusion was understood by some. By the time of *Death's Duel*, however, Donne had transformed the image to the pelican's bloody breast: "[Let us] *hang* upon *him* that *hangs* upon the *Crosse*, ther *bath* in his *teares*, there *suck* at his *wounds*. . . ."[65] Here Christ, as mother breastfeeding her children from self-inflicted wounds, reinvests woman with power.

So now some of the "tarot" cards are out on the table, ready for further investigation. I do apologize to those readers who, thinking they would encounter in this chapter a more traditional view of Mary, have instead been assaulted by a barrage of strange references. That cannot be helped. These represent some of the enduring images of sixteenth- and seventeenth-century *memoria*. They provide some of the raw materials from which Renaissance readers made meaning. In the following chapters, I will study the possible meanings of images of Mary as we find them in specific works by Donne. This cannot be done except by investigating the sources, sometimes difficult to distinguish because so intertwined. Lullism, for example, once prominent in Renaissance culture, became so confused with Hermetism that now it is difficult to find. At any rate, Donne's readers, when they encountered certain images, remembered things like something else not quite forgot (at least not yet). These "forrain" things they linked as statements, or at least as questions. In fact, Donne still provides us—those of us reading him in the twenty-first century—with constants and variables, sometimes strange, situated against backgrounds, sometimes foreign.[66] Having done this much, he rests, leaving us to discover, if we can, the *Schekhina* magic that "shines through" his poems.[67]

2
Donne's Doctrine of Mary

DONNE'S DOCTRINE OF MARY, AND THE ALCHEMICAL CODES THAT express it, emerge from his Catholic background.

FAMILY

Through the maternal line his Catholic legacy included John Heywood, the poet and epigrammatist, who had long served the Tudors, and, even more important, Heywood's wife Elizabeth, niece of Sir Thomas More, lord chancellor during the reign of Henry VIII. As a child Donne would have been taught to regard this famous Catholic martyr, his great-granduncle, with some degree of awe. More's contributions to English politics and culture were well known, especially the *Utopia*, published in Latin in 1516 and translated into English in 1551.

It is no accident that the religion of More's Utopians was marked by tolerance and what Frances Yates calls "Hermetic influence."[1] The wise Utopians understood that individuals must exercise freedom of choice, particularly in religious issues. The God(s) they worshipped varied greatly. Some chose the sun, some the moon. It mattered not, for the wisest knew that God, the Highest, could never be explained. According to More's story, some Utopians, recently converted to Christianity, became too zealous, condemning other religions and causing strife. These the Utopians disciplined and, if they resisted, banished.

The example of More's Utopians stands in sharp contrast to the kind of "practical tolerance" later Elizabethans exercised toward Catholics. Anthony Milton's study of this issue helps us understand how Protestants and Catholics sustained an "uneasy—perhaps contradictory—coexistence."[2] Donne's poetry, emerging during this culture in transition, naturally reflects "time present" (maintaining via media in order to avoid unnecessary political and religious strife) but also "time past," specifically "England's own Roman Catholic past," which Milton calls "a form of Roman Catholicism . . . not alien or *exotic* [emphasis mine] but familiar, even reassuring."[3] I would refine this description to include the *exotic*. Because the exotic was also familiar, it too was "reassuring." By the exotic I mean Hermetism, especially the emblems of alchemical discourse familiar to Protestants and Catholics alike.

More's father kept such an emblem in his home. All who lived with it, all who grew up with it, all who visited—contemplated this symbol. It was the Ouroboros, a figure of the serpent of eternity, which his father kept "on a *fyne paynted clothe*" in his house.[4] C. S. Lewis describes it as a serpent that "lies sleeping with his tail in his mouth."[5] So the child More had this (Figure 3) for his teething ring, and he bequeathed this exotic *and* familiar thing to Donne.

Yates, we know, has observed the resemblance between More's Utopian converts and "Christian Hermetists."[6] Her survey of the humanist tradition also implies Pico as source, especially as he studied the matter of natural magic, that is, "natural sympathies, natural Orphic incantations, magic signs and images naturally interpreted."[7] In 1510 More had published a Latin biography of Pico della Mirandola, so we know that Christian cabalism was on his mind. That Donne also admired Pico is evidenced by the numerous times he quotes him in the *Essays, Biathanatos,* and the *Sermons.*[8] Surely Donne was among those late sixteenth-century writers who Yates says turned to "religious hermetism as a palliative" during times of religious strife.[9] But if Donne found a palliative in alchemical discourse, he also found his dilemma to be, in some respects, more complicated than that of his great-granduncle.

It has been said that when we are asked a question, we discover who we are.[10] When Henry VIII asked Thomas More to subscribe to the Act of Supremacy, making him head of the newly conceived Church of England, More knew who he was. He would not betray his faith, denying Christ's vicar in Rome. But then that posed another question: How would he treat with a king demanding a lie? More's keen legal mind seized upon silence as his most powerful weapon. Silence, he hoped, would allow him to remain faithful to his church, and that same silence, he hoped, would save him from Henry's ax. That it did not is history, and part of that history is Donne's. We can only guess the impact of More's example upon him. Surely, as John Carey argues, he was anxious.[11] Indeed he had need to be, for even as a boy, he knew that the position of Catholics in England was precarious. Or was it?

David Hickman has argued that the Reformation in England was marked, in the beginning, by a fairly easy transition. He observes that "the continued repetition of traditional roles through a period of dramatic religious change, eased rather than hindered the transition to Protestant modes of thought."[12] David Cressy, referring to early modern English history, seems to take the same position when he observes that "[i]ndividualism and communitarianism were entwined in tension throughout this time, as they had been for as far back as the evidence allows us to go."[13] Both historians show us how Protestants, hoping to make the religious transition easier, tried to erase some Catholic traditions, retaining others in altered form. Ironically, Cressy argues, popery was kept alive, even by these "altered" forms. That is, certain community rituals—like birthings, baptisms, marriages, and funerals—retained, at least in popular memory, some of the trappings of a Catholic past.

Changes in the ritual of baptism may serve as one example. During Roman Catholic baptisms, Cressy says, "the priest put hallowed salt into the mouth of the infant" and applied "holy oil or unction . . . to the child's breast."[14] But Protestants rejected these "papist" substances, salt and oil, as well as the sign of the cross.[15] Other practices were also rejected. During baptismal ceremonies, for example, Protestants banished "such popish elaborations as the figure of a 'dove let down.'"[16] Nothing, however, could prevent individuals from *interpreting* water, the only symbol allowed, as purifying salt and consecrating oil. These, along with the sign of the cross, could be kept alive in memory.

The language of alchemy allowed Donne to reinvest such Protestant rituals as the above with some of their original Catholic elements. Even when he became an Anglican priest (and there is every reason to believe that he was sincere in his faith), theological alchemy allowed him to perpetuate some of the great traditions of English culture, including its Catholic past, which necessarily included the Virgin. It also allowed him to appeal to a wider audience. Again, one example may serve to illustrate how this worked.

Cited above is Donne's sermon analogy between spiritual regeneration and alchemical transmutation. In this sermon, he likened the stage that Christians call "baptism" to "ablution . . . this purging and this washing."[17] The term, "ablution," is esoteric because specific to Hermetism, but it is also compatible with the Christian (both Protestant and Catholic) idea of baptism as "the means to . . . transformation."[18] By using this specifically Hermetic term, Donne invites his congregation to rediscover the Virgin as variable. When and if this happens, they will also rediscover "salt," the emblem for the alchemical virgin. According to one recent dictionary of alchemical terms, "The crowned virgin symbolizes purity, and is associated with

Sapientia (wisdom) and salt."[19] Alchemically, the virgin is also Mercury, symbolized by the hieroglyphic monad in the shape of a cross. So Donne's seemingly innocuous reference to "ablution" allows him to retrieve such Catholic traditions as salt and, perhaps for some, the sign of the cross in baptism.[20] Of course, Donne's text is innocent, for those who do not see these elements will not be harmed.

As suggested, Donne did this in order to perpetuate his culture and in order to retrieve certain fading symbols during England's long Reformation (from the mid-sixteenth to the mid-seventeenth century). Symbols and images were naturally threatened by the Protestant emphasis on the "word." Speaking on this issue, Arthur F. Marotti cites the new Protestant print culture as the reason for the "diminishment of the importance of visual communication."[21] One consequence of this culture in transition, a transition from image to word, was that the "magic" contained in images, their power to arrest and captivate the imagination, was also disappearing from religion.

This is particularly true where Hermetic emblems, which had attached themselves to Catholic images, were concerned. Protestants rejected all forms of superstition, including amulets and charms, chants and potions. Many such relics of magic concerned the Virgin Mary. When Protestants rejected the charms, they rejected the Virgin's power.

As mentioned above, Pico and other humanists had devised a Christian cabala based on magic. Johann Reuchlin joined with Pico, hoping to restore magic to philosophy. Yates cites Agrippa, *De occulta philosophia* (1510), as yet another "synthesis of magic and religion, through cabala, which Pico had adumbrated and which Reuchlin carried further."[22] Though Reformation tactics eventually put an end to the Christian humanist movement, the popular imagination still depended on magic. That imagination was kept alive, partly, by pictures.

Anthony Milton observes that "Protestant England was in fact littered with Roman Catholic ideas, books, images and people."[23] Even Protestant churches, he says, "were still dominated [until the 1640s] by the images and physical structures of the Catholic past."[24] Still, he admits, they "generally held Rome to be guilty of idolatry in her doctrine and practice of the invocation of the angels and saints, and especially of the Virgin Mary."[25] So a kind of "iconophobia" did remain: fear that images of the Virgin could undermine Protestant power. To retain her image, except in modified Protestant form, was to retain her magic.

As already mentioned, some English linguists sought to devise a language of symbols that would reinvest language with what David

Katz calls "the mystical qualities of the Adamic vernacular and the purity of language in the Garden of Eden."[26] What was most important to these linguistic theorists, he says, "was this magical element."[27] Naturally, they studied the work of Giordano Bruno and Ramon Lull, which sought to "found universal memory systems on magic images."[28] Donne studied this matter too.

In this respect, therefore, his writing simply, or not so simply, reflects the time. Forging his own kind of cultural transition, he found a way to keep images of the Virgin in his poems and sermons, thereby keeping the magic in religion. More particularly, he found a way to keep the female principle—understood in different ways by Gnostics, Hermetists, cabalists, and Catholics—in the Godhead. Because Donne recognized a more diverse audience than the narrowly limited Protestant aesthetic allowed, he used strategies similar to those of Lull, Pico, and More in order to accommodate crypto-Catholic aesthetics without offending Protestants.[29]

Thomas More was a firm believer in the powers invested in images and emblems. "Many," More said, "shall with God's grace, though they never read word of scripture, come as well to heaven."[30] Even as a Protestant, Donne could see that the alteration of a powerful Mary—attached to the vital center of every Christian's birth and death—into a pale form of that Mary—as subject of two Anglican feast days—was a cultural loss.[31] Although she was still, technically, honored and still the subject of pulpit oratory, her essential place in the rituals of birth and death was gone.[32] Eventually, during the course of Donne's life, this Protestant diminishment would sometimes grow into blatant irreverence.[33]

Between youth and maturity he had witnessed many such changes. References to Mary quietly disappeared in preambles to wills, so that more and more people were "bequeathing the soul to God and Christ alone."[34] Eventually, these testaments would openly renounce the Virgin's mediation, forsaking "all other means brought in by man and his invention,"[35] including the five Ave Marias usually said at mass.[36] Step by step, a powerful few were stripping religion of saints' days and candles and bells.[37] Candles, of course, were associated with the Virgin, especially since Candlemas (February 2) celebrated her purification with candlelit processions. Candlemas remained an important Anglican feast day. But by the end of Donne's career, some were taking offense at the candles![38] Generally, however, moderation prevailed for the sake of the masses, who were the "heartland of England." Because these clung to the old ways and its patterns of outward form,[39] they were accommodated. Donne would capitalize upon this situation, giving England back some of her magic.

Persecution

Not so easy was the situation of his immediate family. Because some were zealous Catholics, they suffered in a way Donne would not.

The Ellesmere manuscripts, owned by Donne's onetime employer Thomas Egerton, document anti-Catholic legislation enacted between 1581 and 1606.[40] The list of proceedings against recusants included various offenses: practice and seducing (treason), knowing and not discovering a Jesuit or priest (forfeiture), receiving and maintaining Jesuits or priests within the realm (felony), or pretending to have any authority to persuade others toward obedience to the pope (treason).[41] Though the young Donne's personal credo is somewhat obscure, the fact that these laws threatened certain members of his family cannot be denied.

In 1581, when Donne was only nine, his uncle Jasper Heywood arrived from the Continent. Heywood was a poet and translator of Seneca's plays, eight of his poems having been included in "The Paradise of Dainty Devices," the most popular and most often reprinted of Elizabethan miscellanies. But his mission to England was not to convert people to poetry. Rather he had left his post as professor of moral theology in the Jesuit College at Dillingen, Bavaria, in order to supervise the re-Catholicization of England. If Anthony Milton's distinction between what Protestant Englishmen considered to be "good papists" and "bad papists" stands, then Jasper Heywood was definitely a bad papist.[42] As it turned out, he was forced to supervise Jesuit efforts from jail.[43]

When this happened, John Donne and his brother Henry were about to begin their formal education. Knowing they would have to take the Oath of Conformity in order to receive degrees, they lied about their ages when they matriculated at Hart Hall, Oxford, in 1584.[44] At that time, he may have heard of the notorious Lullist, Giordano Bruno, who had lectured on philosophy at Oxford from April to June, 1583. Bruno did not stay long. Neither the authorities nor the students could endure his anti-Aristotelian views, which were essentially the views of Ramon Lull.[45] (In 1600 Bruno was pronounced a heretic and burned in Rome.) At any rate, Bruno's departure for Paris in 1585 more or less coincided with Jasper Heywood's deportation in January of the same year.

Heywood was captured and imprisoned in the Tower in 1583. According to Peter Lake and Michael Questier, the post-1570 Tower, as other London prisons, was filthy and brutal but offered "relative freedom" to its inmates.[46] In 1584 Donne, now twelve years old, paid a Christmas visit to his uncle there. On the surface such a visit seems normal. If the Tower, or more particularly Jasper Heywood's quarters in it, was among those prisons that had became Catholic centers of worship, then Donne's uncle may have given him religious instruction, along with a kind welcome, as a Christmas gift.[47] Dennis Flynn, however, thinks that Donne's mother used this occasion to convey secretly into her brother's presence William Weston, his replacement as Jesuit superior in England.[48] That Jasper Heywood was eventually released (to suffer deportation rather than death) could not have entirely erased from Donne's mind the tension of this hour.

The next few years of his life remain informed conjecture. We shall probably never be able to reconstruct them in any satisfactory way. Nevertheless, they mark the beginning of Donne's interest in the Lullian theories, which influenced him throughout his career as poet and as Anglican priest. They also indicate that his youthful interest in Hermetism was further encouraged by the friendships he formed.

The evidence indicates that Donne may have traveled in Spain and Italy between 1585 and 1587 with William Stanley, the Earl of Derby's second son, "who had accompanied his father [to Paris in January 1585]."[49] This father was Henry Stanley, fourth Earl of Derby and longtime friend of Jasper Heywood. The Earl of Derby was sent to Paris to award the Order of the Garter to Henry III.[50] Jasper Heywood and his sister, Donne's mother, seemingly conspired to get him out of harm's way by arranging this trip to the Continent as a member of the ambassador's retinue.[51]

Henry Stanley's entourage arrived in Calais on 14 February 1585 and proceeded to Paris, where they were housed in the Louvre, awaiting the ceremony of 28 February.[52] Henry III presumably took the Oath of the Garter near the church of the Augustinian friars, where afterward Vespers were sung in lieu of a Mass.[53] At this time, Heywood and a few other deported priests arrived in Paris, so Donne may have had opportunity to visit his uncle again. He may also have procured his personal copy of Lull's *Duodecim Principia Philosophiae* (Paris, 1516).[54] At any rate, when Stanley departed for England some few weeks later, Donne remained on the Continent, perhaps traveling with young William Stanley in Italy and Spain, perhaps with Lull's work in his pocket.

If indeed Donne traveled in Spain, we can be sure that he heard of the famous legend of Ramon Lull (1232–1316?) and, possibly, of certain aspects of Lull's "spiritual logic." We know that Philip II (who reigned 1556–98) was a great admirer of Lull.[55] Certainly, the king's ardent Lullism would have been felt among his people. Also we know that, somewhere along the line, Donne marked his copy of Lull's *Principia*, thereby indicating the care with which he read it.[56]

Ramon Lull

According to Geoffrey Keynes, "the great majority of . . . [the books Donne had in his library] were published before the appearance of *Pseudo-Martyr* in 1610," and he seems to have gathered many of these in preparation for that work.[57] Whether *Duodecim Principia Philosophiae* was part of his research for *Pseudo-Martyr,* we cannot tell. All we know is that Lull, either directly or via Bruno, Pico, and Dee, influenced Donne's own art of memory.

Manuel Duran has distinguished Lull's system as one that requires observers to become involved:

> If the stream of sensations that reaches us incessantly, day and night, has to be tamed and put to good use, then we, as observers, cannot remain passive and uninvolved. Phenomena have to be sorted out, analyzed, related to each other—and to the observer.[58]

Lull's art demanded that aspects of the world, including the inner world of the mind, must be understood in terms of the myriad aspects of God. Hence the contemplative life must cohere with the active. Those who wish to comprehend God, who is a Book to be read, must actively work upon that Text, making what meaning they can or will.

Significantly, Lull explored other cultures (including Sufi poetry) and other religions (including the Islamic *hadras* or Divine Attributes) in order to read and understand this Divine Book.[59] Like Jasper Heywood, he too was a missionary, except that his ambition was to convert Jews and Muslims to the universal Christian Church. According to one scholar, Lull wanted "to heal the world's cultural wounds . . . to make the world a place marked by religious and cultural unity."[60] Like Donne's great-granduncle, Lull was also a famous martyr (or so legend would have it).[61] Also, at least by the fifteenth century, Lull's ability to transmute base metals into gold had become famous. Actually alchemy was merely his hobby, but that did not prevent his fame as an alchemist from growing. During the English Renaissance numerous pseudo-Lullian alchemical texts were published and purchased by enthusiastic readers.[62]

Lull, Pico, and Donne

As far as Donne's later "theological alchemy" is concerned, one link with Lull was Pico della Mirandola, who also studied the mystical version of cabala, Lull's original source. Yates says that "in his Conclusions and Apology, Pico states that one type of cabala is an *ars combinandi,* done with revolving alphabets, and he further states that this art is like 'that which is called amongst us the *ars Raymundi,*' that is the Art of Ramon, or Raymond Lull."[63] At this point, it may be important to note that the Virgin Mary and also the Holy Ghost, as two *separate* entities, were invoked by Lull before doing the art. Donne cited Pico in the *Essays, Biathanatos,* and the sermons. John Chamberlin mentions Pico's *Heptaplus* as one explicit reference in Donne's *Essays.*[64] This is an important clue, since it helps establish connections among Donne's "*Of the Name of God,*" Pico's treatise on Creation, and Lull's *ars combinatoria,* a combination of the names of God, which is a way of understanding all of Creation. "All Lull's arts," writes Yates, "are based on Names or attributes of God, on concepts such as *Bonitas, Magnitudo, Eternitas, Potestas, Sapientia, Voluntas, Virtus, Veritas, Gloria.* Lull calls such concepts the 'Dignities of God.'"[65] Among these, it should be noted, are two attributes, wisdom and glory, specifically associated with Mary. Donne's *Essays* take from Pico, and by implication Lull, the idea of "the Mysteries of these names."[66] Donne proceeds to distinguish the "Essence" of God as "the Name of *four* letters; for the Name, *I am,* is derived from the same root."[67] His commentary is compatible with the ideas of Lull, Pico's source for *Heptaplus,* at least as Frances Yates explains it.

Lull did not indulge in corporeal images. However, he did consider Mary one of God's attributes, invoking her mystical Name as one of the Divine Names of God upon which he urged his followers to meditate.[68] One basic rule in his art was repetition, and Lull's own synoptic diagram for the *Ars brevis* indicates that all nine of God's names or attributes were repeated as combinations. The letter in the center stands for the "ALL" of the Tetragrammaton (YHWH or JHYH), the vocalized YaHWeH often substituted for the word regarded as ineffable and treated as a mysterious symbol of the name of God. As noted in the introduction, in 1510 Agrippa emphasized the Virgin's close relationship with the Tetragrammaton, arguing her name, as second Eve, closer to it than Adam.

The letter in the center of Lull's diagram suggests the female principle in God, and so does the figure in the middle. It (the shape of the letter "K") symbolizes the ninth and final attribute in Lull's schema, "glory." Glory was the equivalent of *Schekhina* in the cabala, which the Gnostics defined as Sophia, or Wisdom, emanating from God, and the Jews as *hokhmah,* or "the emanation of God's glory . . . *and* spouse of the Lord."[69]

Motion is what makes these combinations of attributes work in Lull's system. It is his great contribution to Renaissance *memoria.*

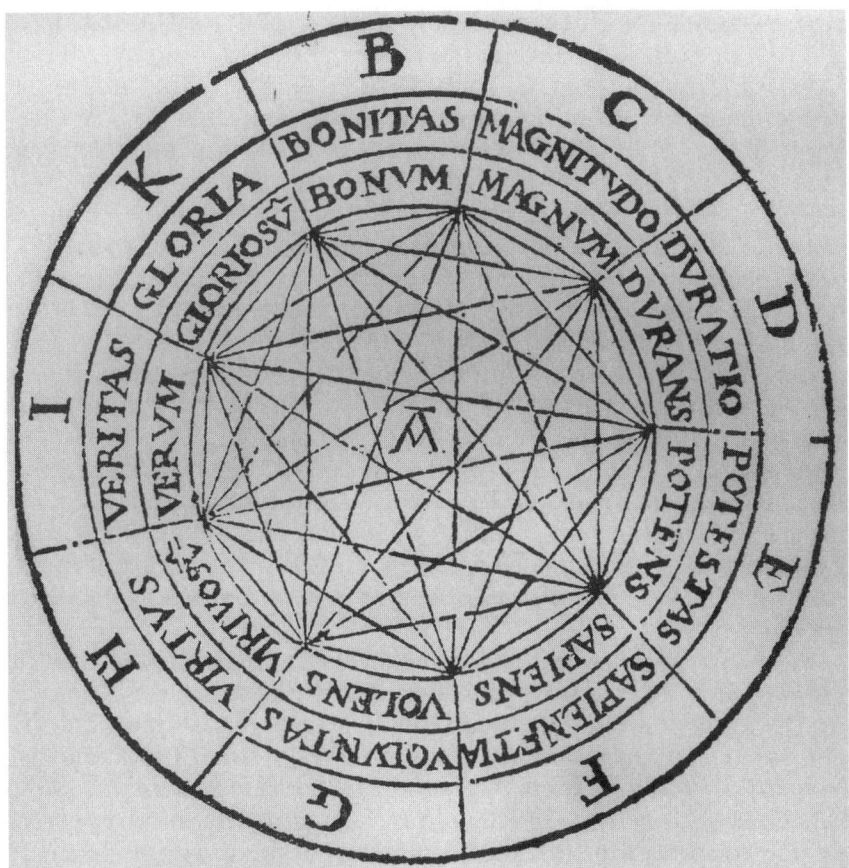

Figure 17: Mystical figure from Ramon Lull's *Ars brevis* (*Opera*, Strassburg, 1617). Reproduced as figure 5 in Frances Yates, *The Art of Memory* (University of Chicago Press, 1966).

Nicholas Tyacke illustrates just how pervasive combinations, as a way of thought, had become during the English Renaissance. In 1635, he says, the Oxford University syllabus was issued "in diagrammatic form. The resulting sheet, dedicated to Laud, shows the day and hour of each lecture, by means of a series of concentric circles with a sun in the middle; the moon, representing Monday."[70] Tyacke observes that the motif of this diagram is Copernican. I would add, however, that its origins are rooted in the mnemotechnics of Ramon Lull.

Yates thinks that Lull's *Ars memorativa* was strongly influenced by the cabalistic practice of meditating "on combinations of the sacred

Hebrew alphabet, which, according to mystical theory, contains . . . all the Names of God."[71] Names were therefore important to Lull's *ars ascendendi* because they designated God's attributes, becoming the rungs on a ladder, helping mankind transcend to *THE ONE*. According to Yates, "The figures of his Art . . . are not static but revolving. One of the figures consists of concentric circles . . . and when these wheels revolve, combinations of concepts are obtained."[72] Even as later pseudo-Lullists conceived this system, combinations continued to be an important element in *memoria*. Donne, especially, learned to use combinations to reinvest God with powers that had been lost when Mary disappeared from religion.

Current scholarship continues to wrestle with the matter of Lull's profound influence upon Pico, and Pico's even more profound influence upon Western civilization.[73] So understanding Pico is a way of understanding Lull. I would add that understanding the Lullist, John Dee, may also prove useful. Dee freely mixed magic with science, so he may not be the best example of Ramon Lull's "spiritual logic." Nevertheless, Donne did have access to Dee's papers, and he may have been among the sources of Donne's secondhand knowledge of *ars combinatoria*.

Kevin Sharpe's investigation of the library of Sir Robert Cotton (1586–1631) leads to the conclusion that Donne had access to works by Dee.[74] By Elizabethan standards, Cotton's library was vast. His collection contained antiquarian studies and some more esoteric treatises, including papers by Dee, whose "priceless pieces" came to him "only indirectly" by exchange.[75] Thereafter, numerous persons contacted Cotton in order to gain access to the works of Dee.[76] In fact, Cotton's library contained more than Dee's papers, as one inspection proved. In 1692 Richard Lapthorne reported that he found at Cotton's Westminster house "Dr. Dee's instruments of coniuration in cakes of bee's wax, almost petrified, with the images, lines, and figures on it."[77] Cotton's kinswoman, Lucy Harrington, sponsored numerous writers, including Donne. Presumably, he had access to this famous library belonging to one whom he long considered his friend.[78]

Other sources of Donne's knowledge of Lull have also been suggested. Evelyn Simpson's survey of Donne's Spanish authors, for example, includes Raymond of Sebond, author of *Liber Naturae sive Creaturarum*, to which Donne alludes in the *Essays*.[79] According to Mark Johnston, Raymond of Sebond "was a well-known Lullist of the fifteenth century and if Donne was familiar with his work, then he certainly knew of Llull's ideas [i.e., other than those expressed in *Principia*, which we know Donne owned]."[80]

In ways such as these Donne became familiar with Ramon Lull's "spiritual logic" and its concomitant analytical methodology. Lull, as Bruno later, was attracted to cabalistic speculation as an antidote to what he considered to be waning scholasticism.[81] Sensing that logic, at least Aristotelian logic, had failed to lead mankind to truth, he turned to mathematics and science. Later, Copernicus (1473–1543), Kepler (1571–1630), and Galileo (1564–1642) would do the same. So Renaissance thinkers were already predisposed toward Lull, who had defined the world as a divine book written in a language of spiritual logic.

Lull's logic begins with Unity as the divine Principle ordering a seemingly chaotic world. It then works backward, trying to discover the principles of this Order in everything. Donne seems to have employed this kind of logic in *The Anniversaries,* in his sonnet on the Church ("Show me deare Christ"), and in his sonnet sequence, *La Corona.* All of these were written years later, in the case of *The Anniversaries,* twenty-seven years after his travels in Spain.

More Persecution

By 1591, six years after Jasper Heywood's deportation from England, John and Henry Donne had left Oxford without degrees and were now students in London at Lincoln's Inn, one of the four legal societies comprising the Inns of Court. By 1594 the fourth Earl of Derby was dead and William, his second son, was also admitted to Lincoln's Inn.[82] So young Stanley and Donne could continue to share common interests, including alchemy and related topics.[83] Before Stanley's matriculation, however, something had occurred to feed Donne's fears.

In May 1593 a young priest was discovered in Henry Donne's chambers. Both were arrested, taken to the Clink, then removed to plague-ridden Newgate prison, where Henry Donne shortly died. The priest was executed in February 1594, drawn and quartered. At this point young John Donne may have seriously reviewed the life of his famous ancestor, considering what kind of silence was best.

Pseudo-Martyr, published in 1611, is Donne's declaration that he will not die in the manner of Thomas More and his brother. In fact, he confronts the Roman Catholic Church with its responsibility for these victims:

> as I am a Christian, I have been ever kept awake in a meditation of martyrdom, by being derived from such a stock and race as, I believe, no family which is not of far larger extent . . . hath endured and suffered

more in their persons and fortunes for obeying the teachers of the Roman doctrine than it hath done.[84]

Donne argues in *Pseudo-Martyr* that the Catholic Church has played false with its people, luring them not to "glorious" martyrdom but to senseless death. Among Rome's victims, he says, are members of his family. With this tract, Donne *seems* to have severed all ties with his Catholic past.

Donne in the Pulpit

All of us who have been deprived, Susanne Langer says, will seek to survive by adapting to the situation. The tree bereft of sunshine and the fish whose tail has been bitten will live, or not live, depending upon its ability to adjust. The tree grows very thin while it reaches beyond the barriers toward the light of the sky above. The fish simply, or not so simply, learns to swim a different way. This is the "grammar" of accommodation.[85] Donne's grammar was the same, for he learned a manner of discourse that reinvested God with attributes lost when the Virgin Mary was eliminated from religion. He took his former Catholicism, in altered form, to the Anglican pulpit.

John Donne was ordained deacon and priest at St. Paul's Cathedral, 23 January 1615. As his career developed, he had to adjust to various attitudes toward what used to be his church. Sometimes Anglican priests were expected to denounce Catholicism from the pulpit. One such time was 5 November, when England celebrated her survival of the Gunpowder Plot of 1605. Donne complies with the demands of the occasion, attacking papists, declaring "detestation of their Doctrines," remarking their "ingratefull intemperance" and the fact that "they, did make Treason an article of Religion."[86] Surely he knew, even as he spoke, that English memory had already attached to the Gunpowder Plot the myth that Protestant England, like little David, had slain the Catholic Goliath. The irony of this situation could not have been entirely lost on him.

A peculiarly English version of the "David myth" developed after Elizabeth I, the Virgin Queen, had overcome the Spanish "dragon." One immediate response, David Cressy says, typifies England's general reaction to the defeat of the Armada: "Though the Dragon be driven into his den, yet is his sting and poison still in force."[87] Elizabeth's triumph resulted in "the cult of Elizabeth," celebrated on 17 November, the day of her accession.[88] Protestants encouraged this new wave of sentiment as a way of supplanting the cult of the Virgin, replacing it with their own version. The later failure of the Gunpowder Plot, again in November, provided another opportunity to rewrite the same story. Consequently, the celebrations of 1588 and 1605 were conflated in the public mind. Both events became signs of "providential protection."[89] Because memory was being kept alive in this manner, it "fed into the renewed wave of anti-Spanish hysteria that was sweeping through late-Jacobean and early-Caroline England."[90]

But then, ironically, the Virgin Mary was also entangled in these events. People could not forget her as *the* Virgin Queen, who with Christ, had slain the Dragon (Figure 10). Protestants, who had hoped to marginalize her, unwittingly restored her to power (at least in the minds of some). Lady Day (25 March) coincided with the accession of James I (24 March), so it was decided to celebrate them at the same time.[91] Hence Protestants, who had conspired to remove Mary from the center of power, inadvertently encouraged what they did not intend, perpetuating images of the Virgin subduing the Dragon. Cooperating with this phenomenon were midsummer rites of bonfires meant to drive away dragons, along with other, perhaps Druidic, rituals featuring dragons.[92] All—midsummer rites with bonfires and dragons, celebrations of the triumphs of Elizabeth I and James I over "dragons"—were conflated in memory with medieval icons depicting the Virgin and Christ. Donne must have been aware of this, even as he preached his Gunpowder Plot sermon of 1622, when he and other Protestants helped keep her memory alive.

Donne was not responsible for this phenomenon. English culture and accidents of history had already accomplished this feat. He did not need, therefore, to mention "the dragon" per se in his text, the context having been established already. He did, however, understand that his congregation would make connections between the "Murdring peece . . . meant to discharge"[93] and the sulphur of the alchemical dragon that "never flies away from the fire."[94] The Catholic attempt to "shake and discompose Gods building,"[95] is answered in memory by that dual-natured Mercurius, that Mother and Son, whose divine protection is certain.

Other sermons by Donne show him actually taking control of the situation, implementing codes that might cause his congregation to reflect in certain ways. We shall have occasion to study some of these.

Sometimes, as when James I was negotiating a Spanish marriage for Prince Charles (1623–24), Donne was caught up in the power struggles that ensued. When called upon to support James's policies, he acted with discretion, his conduct, described by Milton as "the careful *via media*," exemplary.[96] The matter is too complicated to review here, but one aspect may illustrate Donne's dilemma.[97] Both the Earl of Arundel and the Marquis of Buckingham endorsed this match between Protestant England and Catholic Spain. Thomas Howard, Earl of Arundel, was Sir Robert Cotton's friend, so Donne was already politically aligned with him. George Villiers, Marquis of Buckingham, had used his influence with James I to get Donne his position as dean of St. Paul's.[98] So at first Donne's friendships with these three—Arundel, Cotton, and Buckingham—provoked no problem, since all supported the Spanish match. For Donne's part, his position from the pulpit was what mattered, and his sermons naturally reflected this new, more complicated, attitude toward papists. Later, however, strife between Arundel and Buckingham may have given Donne some discomfort. When Parliament advised the king to terminate marriage negotiations with Spain, Buckingham urged a French alliance instead, but Arundel rejected this. The subsequent struggle between these two, both Donne's friends, persisted into the reign of Charles I, when Arundel's "grand reception" for the new king at Cotton's Westminster home was simply ignored.[99] Such vicissitudes in England's attitude toward Rome (and in Donne's friends toward each other) demanded tact and complicated his position. As far as this study is concerned, I note only that English culture was sometimes predisposed to tolerate, if not accommodate, Catholic sensibilities, or aesthetics, though not Catholic doctrine itself. Especially late in his career, Donne could soften his attacks on Rome.

He also had to adjust to various struggles within the Church of England itself. A series of conflicts began when James I refused to endorse the "puritan blueprint" at the Hampton Court Conference of 1604. Nicholas Tyacke has described this plan as a "wholesale attack on the existing administration as being corrupt."[100] As a result of this rejection, two groups, already opposed, surfaced as ardent enemies: the increasingly stubborn Calvinists, disillusioned by the king's failure to comply with their demands to purify the Church[101] and, responding to them, the equally stubborn Arminians determined to withstand Puritan assaults by their "defence of man as a creature not wholly corrupt."[102] Donne aligned himself with the rising Arminian, anti-Calvinist faction within the English Church. This was a natural position for him to take because Arminian doctrine emphasized the vital role of works in salvation. It was therefore more compatible with Donne's theological alchemy. His remarks at St. Paul's Cross, Tyacke notes, illustrate his Arminian stand. Here he speaks against those who "in an over-valuation of their own purity despise others as men whom nothing can save [and] will abridge and contract the large mercies of God in Christ . . . But with the Lord there is *copiosa redemptio,* plentifull redemption, and an overflowing cup of mercy."[103] Donne's preaching, Tyacke says, "almost certainly had the approval of higher authority, for we know that Laud, as Bishop of London, required to see copies of Paul's Cross sermons before they were preached."[104] Eventually, William Laud's reforms allowed Arminianism to flourish, and, as a by-product, invited friendlier relations with Rome. Arminian elements within the Church of England were happy to restore images of Christ's mother that had quietly, over the years, disappeared.[105] The Virgin had come back, even, Anthony Milton observes, as *The Female Glory*.[106]

Laud's reforms were a powerful influence through the first part of the reign of Charles I (1625–49).[107] These included celibacy (encouraged but not required) and the erection of images, including the Blessed Virgin.[108] Fortunately, Donne missed the regicide that abruptly ended this story. Nevertheless, throughout his career he could not escape doing battle with papists and Puritan radicals alike. In the end, he thought of himself as the pelican priest piercing his own breast in order to sustain his people through difficult times.[109]

That is one aspect of Donne's psychology. Another aspect is attached to his family. His occasional diatribes against Catholicism, though required by given situations, are nevertheless poised against the examples of his uncle Jasper, his brother, and More himself. To shake off a church is one thing, to disengage from family another. According to Anthony Milton, "English Protestants were anxious to be reassured that their ancestors who died before the Reformation had been saved, despite having held Roman Catholic beliefs."[110] Protestant clergy addressed this psychological need, assuring these people that their ancestors had, in the pre-Reformation Latin Church, all the means to salvation. Donne himself had a ready answer in the teachings of More.

More's enduring influence on Donne, sometimes observed, needs further discussion.[111] Both More and his contemporary, Stephen Gardiner, had argued that images were more powerful than words.[112] Gardiner aptly states this point: "If the cross be a truth, and if it be true that Christ suffered, why may we not have a writing thereof such as all can read, that is to say an image?"[113] More's example prompted Donne to restore Mary's fading image, reinvesting her with the power she once had. In order to accomplish this, he learned to implement Lullian geometry, an abstract system of thinking, along with Hermetic codes, a system of corporeal emblems, in discourse. It was the magic imbued in the emblems that Donne wanted to restore.

3
Mnemotechnics in the Sermons and Poems

DONNE'S ATTITUDE TOWARD MARY IS DIFFICULT TO TRACE IN THE sermons because it is not consistent. The discrepancy between his early sermon at St. Paul's Cross and his later Christmas sermon at St. Paul's Cathedral begins to illustrate this problem. Reviewing those texts now may prove useful.

At St. Paul's Cross he had publicly announced a Maculist position, limiting the role of Mary in accomplishing mankind's salvation:

> God forbid any should say, That the Virgin *Mary* concurred to our good, so, as *Eve* did to our ruine . . . [for] The Virgin *Mary* had not the same interest in our salvation, as *Eve* had in our destruction."[1]

Six years later at St. Paul's Cathedral he would modify, if not reverse, this position to that approaching the Immaculist, defining the fullness of Christ in terms of the plenitude of Mary's womb, insisting that "The Virgin *Mary* is full of Grace; and Grace is . . . above [Luther's] faith and [Roman] works."[2] Once having heard Donne speak this much, the prudent reader will look for suppressed references to Mary every time he discusses the respective roles of faith and works.

Every student of rhetoric knows that emphasis falls upon the first and last items in a list, what is "in between" enjoying less notice. That Donne places Mary in the middle is significant. This middle component in the process of salvation, that which he must, albeit reluctantly, express—this is what deserves notice. Donne's reversal of position, a typical Donnean strategy, that John Carey has identified as a "switch-round," can best be understood by attending carefully to what he says elsewhere "in the middle," including the "between" times of his silences.[3] Donne's silences have been distinguished as areas of which he speaks once or twice, but never again, except in between.[4] When the sermon literature offers such bold statements as the above, then ceases to speak again, Donne is employing silence as a weapon against a potentially hostile religious community.

Donne's sermons express the quintessential God behind Creation.

"Fixe upon God any where," he says, "and you shall find him a Circle; He is with you now, when you fix upon him; He was with you before, for he brought you to this fixation."[5] In these words, many among Donne's congregation would see the Ouroboros, the serpent of eternity ending where it began, "in a reversion to the primary state."[6] The alchemists had already considered *materia prima* as the original stuff of Creation from which all things come. Chief among their symbols for *materia prima* was the pure virgin. She represented the menstrue, which contained the seeds of all things. From *materia prima*, or the pure virgin, was born the Philosopher's Stone. We should not ignore references to these in Donne's sermons and verse. Nor should we conclude that they merely serve as occasional metaphors. For Donne was an alchemical theorist in the sense that H. J. Sheppard defines, that is, for him alchemy was "a mental condition."[7]

Christian alchemists, Sheppard explains, developed a complement to the practical side of alchemy, which they eschewed.[8] Their disposition was to study instead various stages of the opus as they applied to the spiritual process. "Why the adept should feel the urge to seek his redemption in this way is, perhaps, better sought in terms of the depth psychology of the late C. G. Jung."[9]

The two sermons cited above illustrate this phenomenon as it applies to Mary's dynamics in the spiritual opus. Alchemical and occult references, especially as they apply to her, show Donne trying to determine her role in salvation. In spite of Reformation phallocentricity, he cannot, as alchemical theorist, relinquish the female component. So we see him trying to put flesh back on the eviscerated Protestant metaphor, which is really word stripped of the image informing it. In alchemical terms, the Mary he had known in his youth had been calcinated to some radically reduced form, even to powder. In order to reconstitute her, he devises his own version of theological alchemy. Hence he invades the Church of England internally, by a Counter-Reformation within. This requires tact and care.[10] Although both the poetry and the sermons provide fragmented versions of the female principle in God, none or few could be considered offensive to Protestant minds. Nevertheless, numerous bits and pieces of calcinated Mary compel the supposition that he intended, eventually, some reconstituted form.

Trinity

The Mary Donne makes is not easily recognizable because he manages to universalize her, incorporating her attributes into the Trinity.

His models for this were naturally the Immaculists who allowed the Virgin to be inextricably bound with the Godhead, always including her in the iconography of the Trinity. But Donne had other models to follow when he envisioned Mary. The divine attributes of Ramon Lull (who followed his own path alongside the Catholic Church) were among them. Lull wove Mary into a general Trinitarian structure, reflecting the Godhead but also the trinity in man.[11]

In fact Lull described Mary in Trinitarian terms, distinguishing her as "Mother of Mercy" or the "mediatrix between God and man."[12] As such her attributes were compassion, mercy, and justice. He thereby gave her power to intercede between God and the just.[13] Because she was Jesus's mother, she was imbued with power and compassion. Her mercy was compounded because it could not be bestowed apart from justice (usually considered God's prerogative). Because these two must coexist, Lull insisted that "both justice and mercy [be attributed] to Mary."[14] Mary gives grace to the sinner because she has been given grace by God.[15] So, in the Lullian system, she has been designated by God as intermediary. Her attributes—compassion, mercy, and justice—are also among the nine Lullian attributes of God. Therefore, she is woven into the Trinity as "assisting efficient cause," but not in the way Aristotle meant it. According to Lull's spiritual logic, She is Adonai, "the Lord with thee." *The Art of Contemplation* distinguishes Her as "Virtue, Truth and Glory—that is the Son of God . . . pre-eminent in Virtue, Truth and Glory over all other creatures."[16]

Alchemical theorists had developed similar views of creation, citing, beyond the essential "Trinity," a fourth or even a fifth mysterious element, immortal and incorruptible. Paracelsus demonstrated Lull's influence by his theory of *tria prima*.[17] If all matter was composed of sulfur, salt, and mercury, there must be a spiritual analogue for each (hence Lull's Trinity). According to Paracelsus, mercury (which was both active and volatile) possessed the power to join otherwise recalcitrant materials. However, he was careful to distinguish between common mercury and the "most abstruse, compounded Mercury," implying a fourth element crucial to successful completion of the opus.[18] This latter he defined as "perfect Mercury extracted by Nature and Art: that is, the artificially prepared and true hermaphrodite Adam, and the microcosm."[19] The Stone reborn of this Mercury, Paracelsus says, has "acquired the force of things above and things below."[20]

Upon the product of this marriage, that is, the alchemical Child, are stamped the colors of the phoenix, which Paracelsus describes as "the whiteness and the redness combined in it."[21] Hence Paracelsus

3: MNEMOTECHNICS IN THE SERMONS AND POEMS

effects a Trinity: the father (red), the mother (white), and the stone (both red and white), which cannot be reborn except by the power of perfect Mercury. The nature of this kind of mercury, which joined red sulfur with white salt, is hermaphroditic.

Donne follows the cues of his Catholic ancestry as well as Paracelsus when he depicts Mary with the Trinity (Figure 1). The alchemical concept of Mercury, specifically that kind of Mercury distinguished as *Argent-vive*, proved useful in expressing this essentially Immaculist view.[22] After all, "perfect Mercury," as Paracelsus defines it, and the Child thereby produced can hardly be considered "natural." In this sense, Paracelsus's description of transmutation aptly expresses the doctrine of the Immaculate Conception, as well as the "artificial" Virgin Birth. Donne explores the same issues, but in order to do this he studies the Virgin in fragments, one alchemical attribute at a time.

Sometimes she (as perfect Mercury) is only suggested by the image of Christ suckling his children. Sometimes perfect Mercury is the Holy Ghost, brooding over God's spiritual nest or interceding on behalf of these hatchlings. Sometimes Mary is transformed to otherwise Father, a Female engendering her progeny of Christians, or sometimes as Father, she takes the form of Wisdom, presiding over and making original thought. Among Donne's analogues was *Sapientia*, which the alchemists always associated with the Virgin, symbol of *prima materia*. Sapientia was among Lull's nine attributes of God, but some scholars believe that Edmund Spenser's *Sapience* (in *An Hymne of Heavenly Beauty*) resembles "the Virgin of the Catholic religion."[23] At any rate, when Donne attaches otherwise female attributes to Christ, to the Father, to the Holy Spirit, and when he attaches attributes of the Trinity to Mary, he is suggesting, albeit subtly, an essentially Immaculist view. His evolving theological alchemy allows this to happen.

When he preached before King James's Catholic queen, for example, he explained the nature of God in terms of husband and wife, codes understood as contrary elements joined in the alchemical marriage bed. Christ, he said, is the husband and Wisdom the wife. Hence God "is expressed in both sexes, man and woman" (Figure 11).[24] When he preached before Lucy, Countess of Bedford, he offered up a vision of God's female nature, implementing another emblem from alchemy, remarking "those breasts which God puts out to us . . . which flow from him to us."[25] Among Donne's alchemical sources is Aphrodite, goddess born of the sea, from which all things originate. One familiar emblem included an epigram by which Aphrodite urges, "Let my breasts pour forth to thee twin streams of blood and milk."[26] A concomitant emblem is that of the virgin suckling the Stone (Figure 8). When he preached his last sermon, he particularized Christ's breasts as those of the mother pelican, urging his congregation to "*suck* at his *wounds*,"[27] (Figure 16). And when he preached his first published sermon, he used the story of Jael, slayer of Sisera, to discuss spiritual propagation by a Mother-God, the "hatching hen," yet another emblem to be understood in its alchemical sense (Figures 13 and 15).[28]

These are but several examples of Donne's using alchemical discourse to explain theological issues. Since these codes were already familiar to his audience, they allowed him some degree of latitude in expressing covertly his idea of God. His vision of the hatching hen, for example, is analogous to the creation of the Philosopher's Stone and would have conveyed the message that somehow God is the "fiery hen" heating the incubator.[29] Hence his angle of vision shifts with his codes from text to text, giving his audience various partial views of the female principle residing in the Trinity—in the Father, the Son, and the Holy Ghost.

Medieval icons, cabalistic mnemonic devices, and alchemical emblems mingled in his mind, allowing him to invent new ways to express and understand God. The context for these medieval icons, as well as those from the Christian cabala, was the doctrine of the Immaculate Conception. This doctrine, by preserving Mary from original sin, assured her place with God. Though Donne chose his own way, this basic belief in Mary's role in salvation was not altogether lost upon him. His mind's eye was capable of seeing her with the Father, with the Son, with the Holy Spirit. In her coronation he could see her included with the Trinity (Figure 1).[30] But he could also see the crowned Virgin as alchemical purity, as that salt that cleanses and regenerates metals, and as that name that defied any corporeal form.

"The Annuntiation and Passion"

"The Annuntiation and Passion" illustrates Donne's theological alchemy, which begins with his title. The idea of annunciation, of course, is the prophecy of the Virgin Birth, "*Ecce, virgo concipiet et pariet filium.*" Christian alchemists appropriated this event, making it correspond with the newly joined fetus in the alembic, about to become the Philosopher's Stone. Passion refers at once to Christ's crucifixion and to the black stage (the *nigredo*), when elements are reduced by fire to a more malleable powder. These are only first signs, and given the title alone, no one would probably notice the alchemical sense.

However, Donne immediately introduces an emblem or code that cannot be ignored. When such an image introduces any metaphysical poem ("The Flea," for example), understanding readers know to look for various manifestations of it throughout the poem. Such is the case here.

"The Annuntiation and Passion" studies Donne's vision of the Trinity and specifically Mary's relationship with it. The occasion of the poem was a combination of two Anglican feast days, the Feast of the Annunciation (also called Lady Day) and the Feast of the Passion. In 1608 they happened to fall on the same day.[31] Donne takes advantage of the occasion to write a poem about both. His poem takes the shape of a story narrated by the human soul, recording what she sees. What she sees is a "circle embleme," the Ouroboros (Figure 3). Thus from the beginning Donne provides his reader with the context, in fact the organizing principle, of his poem.

The Ouroboros generally symbolized the unity of matter and "in particular the Work which had neither beginning nor end."[32] Adept readers will begin to look for signs of this cosmic unity, where the "first and last concurre" (l. 5). Indeed time does collapse as events from the "beginning" are juxtaposed with events from the "end." Mary awaits the birth of God's Son at the same time he is being crucified:

> She [the Soul] sees at once the virgin mother stay
> Reclus'd at home, Publique at Golgotha.
> Sad and rejoyc'd shee's seen at once, and seen
> At almost fiftie, and at scarce fifteene.
> At once a Sonne is promis'd her, and gone,
> Gabriell gives Christ to her, He her to John;
> Not fully'a mother, Shee's in Orbitie,
> At once receiver and the legacie;
>
> (ll. 11–18)

Throughout her narration of Mary's life, the soul is given free rein to move backward and forward, joining, like the alchemical Ouroboros, the beginning with the end. In alchemy, of course, the emblem represents the cyclic nature of events, from inception to growth to final reversion. The idea of the Ouroboros is All, that contained within its circle is All, and if not All, then nothing.[33]

The figure of the Ouroboros becomes more interesting when we observe the three circles of which it is composed. These three concentric rings are color-coded, the outer red, the middle yellow, and the inner green.[34] Sometimes these colors are interpreted as symbols for gold, silver, and mercury. A Trinitarian structure, in other words, is written into the symbol. No one has noticed, as far as I know, the correlation between these "familiar" emblems and Ramon Lull's famous combinatory figure.

F. Sherwood Taylor, writing in 1949, observes the differences between Lull's abstract symbolism (i.e., his "numbers of tables" and "letters of the alphabet" and "combinations of . . . letters") and the corporeal images most alchemists used (i.e., "the picturesque array of green lions and tail-eating dragons").[35] Though the observation is generally correct and the comparison useful, I suspect that somewhere along the line these two systems sometimes joined. (Probably one was served across the net and returned as both.) Sheppard's study of the Ouroboros suggests that this is indeed the case.

Though the Ouroboros is generally considered a corporeal figure, it can nevertheless take on the characteristics of Lull's combinatory table. The three concentric circles represent the essential Unity of Matter.[36] It can be no accident that Lull's stylized version of the same Ouroboros, that which he designed for his *Ars brevis*, represents the same. His three concentric circles reflect the Trinity on different levels, including the trinity in man. Augustine believed that man understands according to three powers: the intellect, the will, and the memory. Lull's synoptic diagram illustrates the method whereby all may investigate the attributes of God. The outer circle (inscribed with letters signifying God's names) is stationary; but the other two move, revolving within it (as circles within the Ouroboros presumably do). As noted above, Lull's nine attributes of God were designated goodness, greatness, eternity, power, wisdom, will, virtue, truth, and glory. To each is assigned a letter (B, C, D, etc.). We also remember that Lull attributed to the Virgin certain names: virtue, truth, and glory (in *The Art of Contemplation*) and compassion, mercy, and justice (in the *Libre de Sancta Maria*).

We have no reason to believe that the Ouroboros, symbolizing the stages in the alchemical work, is stationary, though the outer "red" ring, representing the final stage, may be. However, the inner rings (whether yellow and green or black and orange) indicate the dynamics of the opus, that which Christian alchemists considered a progress from "Passion, [to] Death and [to the] Resurrection of Christ."[37] We cannot know that Donne, when he chose the Ouroboros as organizing principle for "The Annuntiation and Passion," had Lull's *Ars brevis* in mind, but certain references in the poem indicate his concern with the stages in religious experience leading to a state of perfection as well as inner illumination.

As Donne constructs the "circle embleme," both Christ and Mary (both the Annunciation and the Passion) are contained within it.

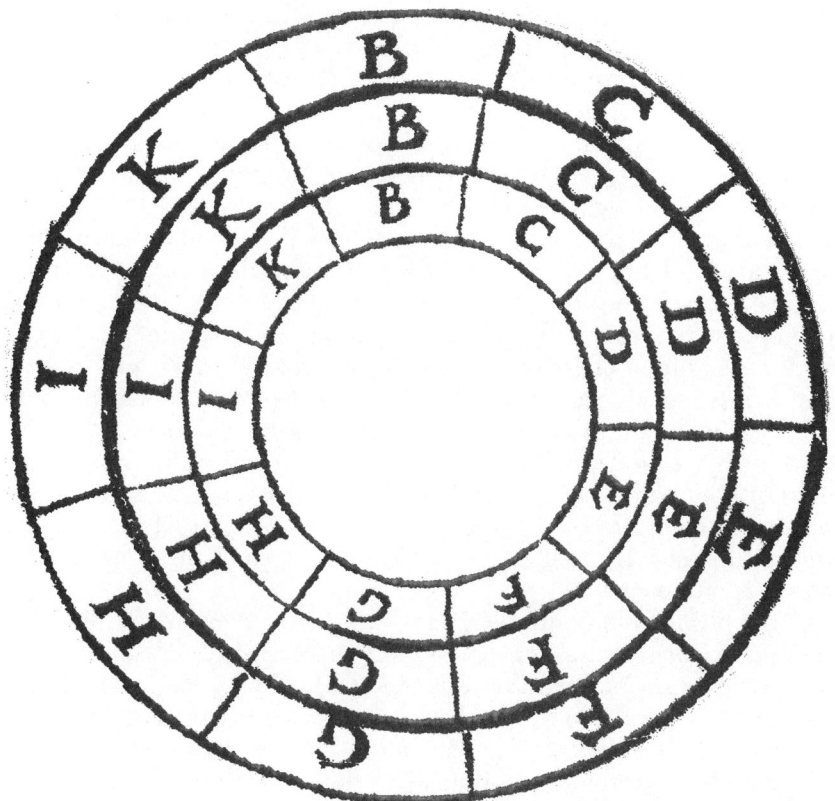

Figure 18: Combinatory figure from Ramon Lull's *Ars brevis* (*Opera*, Strassburg, 1617). Reproduced as figure 6 in Frances Yates, *The Art of Memory* (University of Chicago Press, 1966).

Naturally, chiasmus is also written into this "circle," functioning something like the principle of montage in film. Because Christ and Mary are eternal, the story must read back and forth simultaneously. Gabriel, for example, gives and at the same time *takes back* his gift. Christ is given to Mary, but *at the same time* she is given to John at Golgotha. At age fifteen she has him; at age fifty not. Mary observes Christ, "Her Maker put to making" (l. 9). On Golgotha he has planted himself, has felled himself (l. 8). She is "Not fully'a mother" but "in Orbitie" (l. 17). Here Donne's references are to the round alembic, which is her Womb, and to the planet Mercury, which moves in the same oval orbit. The color of the Egg/Womb is cinnabar.[38] So is Mercurius both white and red.[39] When Donne makes the colors and shapes collapse, he blends together several streams of thought.

John Dee had argued that true astronomers agree that Mercury moves in "an oval orbit."[40] Those among Donne's readers who understood Mary's "Orbitie" as that of Mercury, saw her as alchemical androgyne. As such, she is "the magical arcanum, the transformative substance without which the opus cannot be performed."[41] She is "the mother of all metals, the substance from which all other metals are created."[42] She feeds the infant Stone with mercurial blood (Figure 8). Her roundness therefore exceeds the usual limitations of femaleness. Though she loses her child, she becomes celestial Mother. As Queen of Heaven, she is "the legacie" (l. 18), not just the receiver. As legacy, She joins with Christ, joins with the Trinity. She becomes, in alchemical terms, the opus itself, which is what the Ouroboros symbolizes (Figure 5). All this magic Donne puts in his poem by making the shapes (which in themselves represent "finished products") collapse, by making Gabriel's "Ave" meet Christ's "Consummatum est." He makes the Ouroboros perfect when he makes the outer circle red.

At this point I am compelled to review certain features of Ramon Lull's *Ars memorativa,* which profoundly influenced Renaissance culture (at least in its pseudo-Lullian forms) and by extension John Donne. Pico della Mirandola had confused the cabalist *ars combinandi* with Lull's *ars combinatoria,* but this false attribution did not matter because Renaissance Lullists understood the pseudo-Lullian *De auditu kabbalistico* "as a genuine work by Lull and it confirmed them in their belief that Lullism was a kind of cabalism."[43] According to Yates, Pico's mistake provided Christian cabalists with a windfall, what they considered to be their own special Christian *cabala.*[44]

Donne seems to have been among those attracted to the idea. His *ars sacra,* especially as it is illustrated in "The Annuntiation and Passion," seems to implement Lull's *ars combinatoria* in a way that resembles montage. Of course we already know that Chinese cryptograms inspired such Renaissance thinkers as Francis Bacon and Elias Ashmole to consider new forms of language. So it is not strange that Donne also came up with this ancient system of thinking. Nevertheless, the way he implemented it in his poems represents a rather profound moment in the culture of early modern England.

His images, like Lull's names and symbols, revolve. Sometimes they cohere; sometimes they clash; but always they provoke his readers to make some sort of intelligent response. "The Annuntiation and Passion" is constructed in such a way that they are compelled to create out of two adjacent images a third image or idea. Anticipating Sergei

Eisenstein,[45] he joins his contemporaries, as coparticipants in the new Protestant print culture, in experimental discourse.

"The Annuntiation and Passion" superimposes two images. Like Lull's combinatory figure, the events of the Annunciation and the Passion revolve in concentric circles, meeting (as they did in 1608), jarring the memories of Donne's readers and compelling them to compose sentences using linking verbs like *is* and *seems* in order that they might articulate "something like something else but not the same." In this sense, they too make the opus. Here are some of the available materials, to be explained below:

```
              THREE CONCENTRIC CIRCLES OF THE:
            /                                    \
      OUROBOROS                        LULL'S COMBINATORY FIGURE
            /                                    \
   RED, YELLOW, GREEN/BLACK              INTELLECT, WILL, MEMORY
            /                                    \
IN ALCHEMY: SULFUR, SALT, MERCURY   IN AUGUSTINE: THREE POWERS OF THE SOUL
                              ^
1st CIRCLE (RED): CHRIST/MARY—(stationary)—ETERNITY—ANNUNCIATION AND PASSION
2nd CIRCLE (YELLOW): THE CHURCH—(revolving)—MIRROR OF GOD'S BIRTH AND DEATH
3rd CIRCLE (BLACK): HUMANKIND—(revolving)—CHRISTENINGS AND FUNERALS
                              ^
                          GOD'S OPUS
                         DONNE'S OPUS
                         READER'S OPUS
```

This is a great deal (though by no means all) for Donne's understanding readers to consider. The poem proceeds to describe the function of the Church, which is to bring these two (the Angel's "Ave" and Christ's "Consummatum est") together. Donne likens God's Spirit to the "fiery Pillar" (l. 31) in the Old Testament and his Church to the cloud (l. 32), both of which lead "home." Because these feasts (Lady Day and the Passion) have fallen on the same day, he is able to continue the process of synthesis with which his poem began. (This is the dialectical process that creates a third meaning out of the original two meanings of adjacent images or ideas.) He uses this same chiasmus when discussing the Church.

Death joins conception. Creation joins Creator. Entrance becomes exit. Christ's "imitating Spouse" joins these contraries on earth when she institutes these two feasts:

> This Church, by letting these daies joyne, hath shown
> Death and conception in mankinde is one.
> Or 'twas in him the same humility,
> That he would be a man, and leave to be:

> Or as creation he hath made, as God,
> With the last judgement, but one period,
> His imitating Spouse would joyne in one
> Manhoods extremes: He shall come, he is gone:
>
> (ll. 33–40)

The pillar of fire led Israel through the wilderness at night; the pillar of cloud led her by day. So God's Spirit will lead his children during their long "night" on earth, and the Church, a human institution, will direct his children by day. They are to stay close to the Church because she represents God. ("So God by his Church, neerest to him, wee know, / And stand firme, if wee by her motion goe," ll. 29–30.) If God's children will look into the mirror, which is the Church he has provided, they will see what direction he wants them to go.

Perhaps this is a good time to consider the Hermetic concept of the "mirror image" (or the alchemical *Emerald Table*), alluded to several times in the poem, for example, "but the next starre thereto, / Which showes" (ll. 26–27). The *Emerald Table* defines the Hermetic worldview that everything ruling above has its correspondent in things below. Hence the microcosm reflects the macrocosm. According to Stanton Linden, Latin versions of the *Emerald Table* "were frequently included in collections with the *Mirror* [Roger Bacon's *Mirror of Alchemy*, 1614]."[46] It is, he says, "without question, the most sacred of alchemical texts deriving from the ancient world, and its survival in numerous manuscripts and early printed books is evidence of keen interest well into the Renaissance."[47] According to some stories, the Emerald Table was "found resting in the hands of the entombed Hermes Trismegistus."[48] According to others, it fell from the forehead of Lucifer when he was cast down from heaven. At any rate, the conceptual metaphor throughout is that of the darkened glass affording only glimpses of a higher Truth. In this sense the *Emerald Table* represents the middle ground between fact and faith.

Donne's allusions in "The Annuntiation and Passion" indicate that, in terms of Christian tradition, the Church is this mirror, is this middle ground. She is in the inner circle reflecting the eternal outer circle. Through churchings and christenings, she supervises human births ("he shall come," l. 39). Through funerals she supervises mankind's deaths ("he shall go," l. 39). Hence she represents the essential Unity of Matter ("His imitating spouse would join in one / Manhood's extremes," ll. 39–40). As such, the Church reflects Christ's coming and Mary's conception, Christ's death and Resurrection. In an alchemical sense, the glue that binds the body and soul is mercurial blood or milk, which must be fed to the maturing Stone.

Donne's allusion is to both: both the "imitating Spouse" that joins and the blood or milk of Mercury that binds:[49]

> Or as though one blood drop, which thence did fall,
> Accepted, would have serv'd, he yet shed all;
> So though the least of his paines, deeds, or words,
> Would busie'a life, she all this day affords;
> This treasure then, in grosse, my Soule uplay,
> And in my life retaile it every day.
>
> (ll. 41–46)

That one drop of Christ's precious blood could suffice to pay for all is consistent with the other codes embedded in this passage. One drop becomes as one day (which the Church affords to celebrate this one moment). Moreover, this one day becomes a treasure, stored up in bulk ("in grosse . . . uplay"). In pseudo-Lullian terms, that one drop is *menstrues* of the third, essential sort. George Ripley quotes Ramon Lull as he defines it: "The third essentiall of Sunne and Moone . . . And Mercurie of mettalls essentiall, / Is the principle of our stone materiall."[50] So one drop of Christ's blood translates to one drop of essential Mercury, which is, according to Ripley's definition, a marriage of the Sun and Moon. Donne thereby defines Mary's conception, already equated with Christ's death, as that same precious drop.

We must understand that God's "imitating Spouse" (l. 39) is not Mary. However, the Church is also a maker; for she this very day "would joyne in one / Manhoods extremes." Mary and Christ, the original Makers, have taught the Church to make. This is how Donne makes his own circle, which is his poem, just.

Pictures

That Donne persisted in meditating upon the Holy Virgin is evidenced by a portrait of her, kept in his private dining room while he was dean of St. Paul's. We do not know whether this painting was of the Virgin only or of a group. Neither do we know the artist, whether Titian or some other. All we know is that Donne valued this portrait enough to keep it near him. Partly for this reason, Edmund Gosse believed that Donne still "hankered after some tenets of the Roman faith," observing:

> Donne would not have kept for ever before his eyes in privacy, and have passed on to Lord Doncaster (then Earl of Carlisle), as a peculiar treasure, a painting of the Virgin Mary, unless they had both preserved a

tender interest in her cult, and were equally out of sympathy with the iconoclastic puritanism of the age in England.[51]

Not only is Donne's portrait indicative of his private musings, it also hints that Mary functioned in some way as his Muse. Evidently he was still telling his beads, but not in the usual way, not in the way he had been taught as a child.

Metaphoric Codes: Metonymy and Synecdoche

While Donne was gazing upon Mary in his private chambers, he was also drawing various pictures of her for his congregation. Even before taking Anglican vows he had scattered many images of her throughout the divine poems and early verse. Sometimes, like Emerson's Sphinx or Melville's Yilla, the images are elusive, conveying multiple meanings fragment by fragment. Donne's images of Mary are usually just that. The only way to attach these fragments to their originals is to learn to discern them as types, their various guises assuming two commonly recognized forms—metonymy and synecdoche. Though both of these categories are slippery in the application, sometimes defying their limitations, they can nonetheless prove useful distinctions.

Sometimes Donne's visions of Mary are expressed in the language of metonymy, naming as substitute for the Virgin an object or attribute closely associated with her: the crown becomes Mary, Queen of Heaven; the book becomes Mary, student of prophecy, holding God's book in her hand or reading it from a lectern, poised for Gabriel's announcement. The language of metonymy enables Donne innocently to present his Protestant audience with otherwise controversial ideas about the Virgin. Since such metaphors are imbued with multiple meanings, they do not offend. Metonymy allows his Protestant audience to close their eyes partly, avoiding what they would not want to see, indeed are *not required* to see, in order to comprehend some doctrine.

Yet another example of Donne's squinting at the Virgin through the language of metonymy is his description of Elizabeth Drury's earthbound soul. When loosed, this earthly virgin becomes the string connecting all mankind with heaven, where she resides to intercede for them. No need to see the rosary beads, for Donne is not telling them aloud.

Sometimes Donne employs synecdoche, naming a part to signify the whole. For example, he makes specific references to physical attributes of the female nature *in* God, the breasts of the nursing Christ or the womb of the Maker-God. Though this language does not necessarily require Donne's Protestant audience to look, even glance, at the Virgin Mary, it does compel them to acknowledge the female nature of God. Many among his congregation would have recognized the alchemical code embedded in the image of the Virgin suckling her child.[52] This emblem was sometimes employed to compare the birth of the Stone with the Nativity. In other words, those who knew the code were indeed compelled to look at the Virgin, determining for themselves the meaning of Donne's vision.

One example is a sermon of 1627, preached in commemoration of Lady Danvers, George Herbert's mother. Here Donne both particularizes and expands the image of nursing mother so that it becomes his own nurse giving him Christian milk and his own mother, nursing him in her womb with Christian blood:

> How many, how great *Nations* perish, without ever hearing the name of Christ; But God wrapt mee up in his Covenant, and deriv'd mee from *Christian Parents;* I suck'd *Christian* bloud, in my Mothers wombe, and *Christian* milke at my Nurses breast.[53]

Donne's congregation would have understood the human mother, giving suck, as God's vehicle to impart grace (the grace of the Covenant). Some would have also recognized the familiar alchemical code. Among these some may have suspected Donne's perception of himself as spiritual mother, feeding his congregation the Word of God. However, lurking behind the image is yet another matter not easily understood, except by some. That is Donne's alchemical thinking concerning the doctrine of grace.

Although *grace* had already been appropriated into the language of the alchemists, Donne later developed it as operative principle in his own peculiar theological alchemy.[54] Both of these subjects (grace and Donne's perception of himself as *maker*) will be discussed below.

The Book

When Donne employs metonymy, his allusions to Mary are usually blurred so that they look "awry and squint."[55] That is because the metaphor is only loosely associated with her, simultaneously allowing other meanings. Nevertheless, his roving eye reserves at least a corner in which the Virgin can safely reside. One illustration of Donne's squinting is the book metaphor he often attaches to Mary. It is perhaps natural that Donne used the book as metonymic reference when alluding to the Virgin. One issue naturally attached to it is her intercessory role in salvation.

We know that the *Emerald Table* was important to alchemical theory. Moreover, as metaphor, it expressed the mirror or glass through which all must look or which all must read in order to find Truth. We know that Ramon Lull, Donne's mentor, thought of Mary as intercessor between God and Man,[56] thereby becoming a Book, which all who wish to be saved must read. Donne's ambivalence is understandable, especially when we consider his position before he took Anglican vows. Toward the end of Elizabeth's reign, when she was pressed to name a successor, she demurred. Her unwillingness fueled the hopes of some that a Catholic might yet sit upon the throne, a thing not beyond reason.[57] Even Lord Essex, under whom Donne once served, became a magnet for such schemes.[58] Though Donne kept his silence, we can be fairly certain he was interested.

When he depicts the Virgin as or with her book, he reattaches her to England's pre-Reformation past. Mary, throughout medieval church history, had been perceived as the intercessor between mankind and God. Similarly, as Wisdom, or the *Emerald Table*, she represents the thing that joins the seekers below, confined to the microcosm, with the Truth above. This is what Lull calls the "Mercurie of mettalls essentiall," whereby the "Elements joyne."[59] As that One who joins things, Mary represents the middle ground.

The book, as metonymic reference, restores her capacity to join things. Whatever the background, whether alchemical or theological, the emblem expresses this joining. In alchemical theory the crowned Virgin is *Sapientia* or Wisdom. As *Sapientia,* the Virgin dissolves, cleanses, and regenerates metals. When Donne employs the book metaphor, therefore, he invites adept readers to consider both Virgins: the Virgin of Scripture, often portrayed with her book in hand, but also the Virgin of alchemy, representing Wisdom. An example of the first can be found in Figure 10, where the Virgin, as *Sedes Sapientiae,* along with the Christ child, tramples the Dragon. "The Dragon is not killed, but by his Brother and his Sister; not by one of them alone, but by both together."[60]

Donne's secular poem, "Valediction of the booke," possibly written in July 1611, is an example of his devoting an entire exercise to exploring the possibilities of the book image.[61] Among the emerging meanings is the idea of "maker," that is, the maker of books not only makes "children" but also emulates God. In Donne's poem the woman first appears as poetess, greater than the Cumaean Sibyl, Pindar, Lucan, and even Homer. Her lover is the speaker, also her counselor, who will interpret her book. Their love letters, he says, will become manuscripts to be studied by others. Therein future lovers shall read precepts whereby to rule their lives. The lovers' Record is the Eternal Book, and their learning is safe because it is closed to the uninitiated. Subjects in this book include science, the music of the spheres (which normal persons cannot hear), and the poetry of angels. Mystical philosophers, the followers of Hermes Trismegistus (astrologers and alchemists), Neoplatonist abstractionists of love, cabalistic typologists—all will find secret knowledge in this Record. (Lawyers and statesmen, if they can read at all, will probably find nothing of interest here.) Nevertheless, the book that these lovers have become shames all other texts. The last nine lines of Donne's poem is a catalogue of other poems he has written or will write. He alludes to his "Lecture upon the Shadow" when he writes "Sun, or starres, are fitliest view'd / At their brightest" (ll. 60–61) and where, therefore, the "darke eclipses" (l. 64) are to be feared. "A Valediction forbidding mourning" is meant by "absence tryes how long this love will bee" (l. 58). "The Extasie" is referred to when the lover claims to "studie thee" (l. 55) from a distance, all along intending to leave, by touching, his imprint or mark on his lady's body, making their book. In other words, the poem itself becomes a book metaphor associated with other "books" or poems belonging to Donne, their maker. So what has become of the Virgin Mary? Those tempted to complain that she has been left far behind in a "rabbit chase" should remark Donne's eye, the corner of which rests upon the thing she holds in her hand.

The book as image of a virtuous life was a commonplace during the Renaissance. Virtuous and learned women, as well as men, were often referred to as books. Renaissance ladies, who were well read in various fields, were naturally flattered when dedicatory verses associated them, sometimes, with Mary's study of sacred text and, more typically, with learning in general. The influence of Thomas More should not be forgotten here. He was among the first to advocate rigorous studies for women, including the Latin tongue practiced by his daughter Margaret, who may *indeed* have cowed Henry VIII by her fluency. William Roper, More's son-in-law, wrote that More brought up all three of his daughters, as well as his son, "to take virtue and learning for their meat and play for their sauce."[62] Elizabeth Donne, according to Dennis Flynn, perpetuated this tradition, nurturing her children in an environment of "gender-neutral humanism."[63]

One example of the Renaissance propensity to associate learned women with their books is a portrait recently identified as that of Princess Elizabeth (1596–1662).[64] It was painted by Robert Peake and possibly commissioned by Sir John Harington in 1606, when the princess was ten. In this portrait, now owned by the Metropolitan Museum of Art, Elizabeth is holding a book. The book's inscription reads:

> No Tablet
> For thy brest
> Thy Chr[ist]ian mo
> ther gives hir
> Dattere What
> Jewell Fits hir
> best A boke not
> big but yet ther
> in Some hidden
> Vertu is So christ
> So christ Procur. you
> grace with
> God And
> Give you
> endles [bliss?][65]

There is reason to believe that Donne knew about the portrait, along with its inscription.[66] Any understanding Renaissance reader, including Donne, would have recognized the allusions to the *Emerald Table* and to "hidden / Vertu." Adept readers know that the "Tablet" has been given by a mother to her daughter so that she can read it like a book, gleaning "hidden" secrets. "So christ Procur. you / grace with / God And / Give you / endles [bliss?]" is yet another indication of mingled codes. Grace, as we know, has its counterpart in alchemical theory, where it was designated as that power granted the adept as he or she entered the *sanctum sanctorum* (Figure 2). He or she (and there were female adepts) knew that without grace there was no hope of success. Whoever wrote the inscription to Princess Elizabeth's portrait seems to have had this in mind. Though the princess is dressed sumptuously in jewels, the "mother's" verse indicates that she is giving her daughter something more valuable in the form of a different tablet, wherein she can discover "some hidden Vertu." As a reference in Donne, *virtue*, Laurence Stapleton explains, may be a combination of ideas from Plato and Paracelsus.[67] Virtue combined with "tablet," however, indicates the occult sense of the efficacy or power of precious stones.[68]

In terms of church traditions, Elizabeth's mother is also saying, "I am giving my daughter a devotional book." Once we understand that Princess Elizabeth's mother was Queen Anne, the Catholic wife of James I (before whom, incidentally, Donne sometimes preached)

Figure 19: *Princess Elizabeth* (1596–1662), *Later Queen of Bohemia*, by Robert Peake the Elder (act. by 1576, d. 1619). The Metropolitan Museum of Art, Gift of Kate T. Davison in memory of her husband, Henry Pomeroy Davison, 1951. (51.194.1)

and that her grandmother was Mary, Queen of Scots, we are in a position to see the "devotional book" as a missal, which is indeed a book "not big" and fit for a "little" woman. Whatever else she meant, Queen Anne wanted this gift to encourage her daughter, reputed to be as lovely and winsome as her grandmother, to become a follower of the Virgin. At least here the image of book seems to include one or both of these Marys.

We can probably never know what part, if any, Donne played in the book in Princess Elizabeth's hand. However, we do know that one strong link between Donne and Princess Elizabeth was the Countess of Bedford, herself a model of virtue and learning. According to John Carey, "It was through the Countess that Donne came to the notice of Princess Elizabeth, daughter of James I."[69] Princess Elizabeth married Frederick, Elector Palatine, later king of Bohemia, on 14 February 1613. She was seventeen. The marriage settlement was made by Sir Robert Drury, Donne's current patron. Donne left his own record of the wedding celebration in the form of an epithalamium. He begins with a catalogue of birds, all "chirping Choristers," singing their wedding songs. This time Lady Elizabeth has no book in her hand, for she herself has become a phoenix.

The Hen

Yet another Donnean metonymy is the image of the brooding hen, which he sometimes uses to describe Christ, sometimes the Holy Spirit. The alchemists themselves had appropriated it from the New Testament.[70] Donne employs this image in a number of sermons, including one that he preached 15 September 1622 on Judges 5:20. In this sermon he envisions brooding God as the hatching hen. In the published version he wrote, "the seed of *God* hath remained in thee, *Incubat Spiritus,* the Holy Ghost hath sat upon that seed, and hatched a new Creature in thee."[71] Milton later appropriated the brooding hen as a way to represent "Creation as a birth-process."[72] Donne not only anticipates him here but also uses the metonymic reference in a slightly different way, even to depict the Holy Spirit as Womb or the Divine Mother. The seed of the male fertilizes this maternal womb, or egg, to produce new life, which is Donne's way of redefining, yet again, the Creator God as both He, "the seed of God," and She, the "*Incubat Spiritus,*" the "womb" of the Holy Spirit.

Other examples of Donne's excursions to the poultry yard can be culled from the sermons: "All egges are not hatched that the hen sits upon; neither could Christ himselfe get all the chickens that were hatched, to come, and to stay under his wings."[73] Even the early verse shows Donne experimenting with the hatching metaphor. In *La Corona*, possibly written in 1607, he had opened up the metaphor to include the classical reference to Minerva, hatched from Jupiter's head. Mary, he says here, was in God's mind from the beginning. Once she springs forth, he suggests, she becomes Wisdom.

Of course the "fiery hen" is Donne's alchemical analogue. Abraham's *Dictionary of Alchemical Imagery* defines the hen's role in alchemical transmutation thus:

> In order to keep the hermetically sealed vessel from breaking, the alchemist, when making his fire, attempts to emulate the gentle warmth of nature, like that of the hen or bird brooding on her eggs. The fire is the incubator which generates the kind of warmth necessary for hatching the chick (Stone) from the egg (vessel).[74]

Among Abraham's sources would be Roger Bacon's *The Mirror of Alchemy*, where he writes that basic materials for the opus are first drawn out of the vegetable world, from which is made *Argent-vive* and sulfur. Next, he says, materials are drawn from the animal kingdom: "And if wee should draw it from living creatures (of which sort is mans bloud, haire . . . hens egs, and what else proceede from living creatures) wee must likewise out of them extract Argent-vive and Sulphur by decoction."[75] Bacon's specific methodology is not so important here as the analogy proving that alchemical transmutation is somehow associated with the brooding hen. Emulating nature, adepts thought of themselves as brooding hens. The maternal warmth of their apparatus and their patient attention to the birthing of the Stone was compared to this natural phenomenon.

Grace

One of Donne's sermons provides a step-by-step analysis of what he thought to be the process of salvation. It also illustrates how codes from alchemy mingle with codes from medieval iconography to form his doctrine of grace. Grace, as cohesive agent, is central to the opus, which in this case is the work of salvation. In order to understand Donne's doctrine of grace, we shall attend to this sermon text, preached before the Prince and Princess Palatine (the Lady Elizabeth) at Heidelberg in June 1619.

One ordering principle behind his sermon is Augustine's theory of memory. Augustine wrote of the amazing power of memory, which he called a storehouse of images gathered from the past. These chambers of memory he likened to a treasure trove:

> There is treasured up [in the roomy chambers of memory] whatsoever likewise we think, either by enlarging or diminishing, or by varying in any way whatever those things which the sense hath arrived at; and whatever else hath been entrusted to it and stored up.... When I am in this storehouse, I demand that what I wish should be brought forth, and some things immediately appear; others require to be longer sought after.[76]

Donne, in his Heidelberg sermon, fixes upon grace as a concept to be "brought forth" by memory. His congregation is invited to rediscover in its own storehouse all aspects of grace already there, even those that must be "longer sought after." Among these are images of the Virgin.

Grace, Donne says, is imparted by the Holy Spirit, who acts as seed in the mother's womb. He repeats *grace*, knowing its polysemic value, especially as it has evolved in memory, throughout his sermon text. Each time it resurfaces it assumes various layers of meaning, including no doubt for some the Catholic memory of a Mary "full of grace."

Augustine had particularized collective memory as a means whereby any given text is enriched. The text is "complicated," he said, when individuals hearing or reading it add what their memories have already stored.[77] He addresses this matter in *The Confessions:*

> propterea inde per recordationem potuere depromi, forte ergo sicut de ventre cibus ruminando, sic ista de memoria recordando proferuntur.[78]

One translation reads:

> Perchance, therefore, even as meat is by chewing of the cud brought up again out of the belly, so by recalling are these [images] brought up again out of the memory.[79]

Donne's iteration of *grace* in the Heidelberg sermon demonstrates that he understood the power of memory as Augustine defines it. He does not refer directly to the Virgin, except at the end. (In fact, he shifts focus to the work of the Holy Spirit.) Nevertheless, his sermon is constructed so that numerous allusions to grace invite his congregation, and particularly Princess Elizabeth, to search their memories in order to create new meaning from these iterated "graces." For some this will be a way to rediscover what they may have otherwise forgotten, even the Virgin "full of Grace."

3: MNEMOTECHNICS IN THE SERMONS AND POEMS 115

He argues by analogy, beginning with the idea that corn, in order to grow, must be sown in the earth and *only* in the earth, which is its proper womb. Grace in the Christian, he says, is like corn. Donne explains the process of salvation through a series of alchemical codes, including the alchemist's seed of gold that germinates in the alembic until sublimation takes place.[80]

> Salvation is the inward means of salvation, the working of the spirit, that sets a seal to the eternal means: the *prope,* the nearness lies in this, that this grace which is this salvation in this sense, grows out of that which is in you already; not out of any thing which is in you naturally, but Gods first graces that are in you, grows into more and more grace. Grace does not grow out of nature; for nature in the highest exaltation and rectifying thereof cannot produce grace. Corn does not grow out of the earth, it must be sowd; but corn grows only in the earth; nature, and naturall reason do not produce grace, but yet grace can take root in no other thing but in the nature and reason of man.[81]

Salvation Donne defines as that "highest exaltation." This is an alchemical term familiar to many if not all among his congregation. Exaltation refers to the vaporization of the Stone, when it "is raised to a higher degree of purity and potency through a reiterated cycle of dissolution and coagulation of the Stone in its own mercurial blood."[82] Nature cannot produce this "inward means" of salvation, which is this exaltation. Rather grace must do it.

One does not have to be particularly astute to note that Donne has repeated *grace* numerous times (seven to be exact), likening it to corn. Adepts immediately understand that some degree of warmth is necessary for corn (or grace) to grow (Figure 2). Moreover, Donne's congregation would have recognized the familiar alchemical symbol of the husbandman scattering seeds in the ground, where they (whether the alchemical seeds of gold or the seeds of nature) will be warm. Grace, like corn, he says, is not naturally in the earth (womb). Someone must first put it there, either the farmer or the Holy Spirit. Naturally Donne's *ars memoria* invites his congregation to retrieve from the chambers of their treasurehouse the familiar icon of an inseminating Spirit hovering over the pure "Maiden's" head.

Repeated *graces* have invited Lady Elizabeth, whose memory, Donne knows, retains much on this subject, to discover the right linking verbs (*is, seems*) and to make her own sentences, whether declarations or questions. The diagram below indicates some of the variables available to her:

116   3: MNEMOTECHNICS IN THE SERMONS AND POEMS

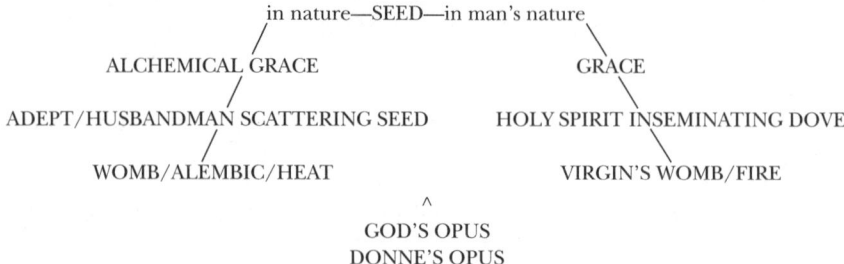

Though we can never know her response, it is logical to surmise that these *graces* jolted her memory back to the book in her earlier portrait, back to her mother's prayer that "Christ Procur. you grace."

Donne says that the Holy Spirit "sets a seal to the eternal means." Sealing, like stamping, involves joining, that is, pressing a particular emblem or character upon soft metal or wax so that the two are in effect "joined." The alchemical analogue for seal is *fixionem,* to make what was volatile permanent. Stamped on the face of the alchemical Child are the characters of both Parents. In alchemical theory, those parents are *Argent-vive* and Sulfur (or Sol and Luna). Whatever they are called, the matter of the Stone, the final product, is stamped with the character of both (Figure 15). The alchemical process is described in terms of human procreation, and the spiritual process is the same.

This is how Donne uses these codes in his Heidelberg sermon. The Holy Ghost places the seed of God in "the nature and reason of man," where it grows. Like *menstruum* the Holy Ghost serves as cohesive agent, becoming both the place and the means whereby Donne's version of organic-alchemic salvation occurs: "First then, salvation . . . is the internal operation of the holy Ghost, in infusing grace . . . now appropriated to thy particular soul."[83] How is this "infusing grace" appropriated? Donne's answer takes the form of another analogy. He compares spiritual union to earthly:

> In the constitution and making of a natural man, the body is not the man, nor the soul is not the man, but the union of these two makes up the man; the spirits in a man which are the thin and active part of the blood, and so are of a kind of middle nature, between soul and body, those spirits are able to doe, and they doe the office, to unite and apply the faculties of the soul to the organs of the body, and so there is a man.[84]

How this analogy compares with the Christian's salvation is not so simple: the spiritual body (which comes by way of the Covenant) and the soul (which comes by way of the sacrament of baptism) are united by a middle nature, which Donne distinguishes as "the thin and active part of the blood . . . a kind of middle nature, between body and soul."

It is tempting to think that Donne's perception of blood may have been influenced by William Harvey (1578–1657). Harvey had modified the Aristotelian view of spirits in the human body so that "animal" and "vital" became the same. Once these distinctions had disappeared, Harvey was able to speak of blood as "impregnated with spirits," meaning that the blood had the soul in itself.[85] By "soul" he meant the motive soul, along with the vegetative and sensitive soul. He eventually came to conclude that "the blood seems to differ in no way from the soul, or at least should be considered as a substance whose action is soul."[86]

Whether or not Donne knew or suspected this theory cannot be determined, though we do know that Donne was acquainted with Harvey's work when he wrote *The Anniversaries*. At any rate, Donne's description of blood in the Heidelberg sermon moves beyond Harvey, for he refines "spirits" in the blood so that they become the "middle nature" in the blood. Moreover, he attributes to this middle nature specific powers. Donne says that *grace*, because it is the *middle nature in Christ's blood* (neither male or female), is imbued with the power to join body and soul, making regenerate man.

Paracelsus's theory of the *tria prima* asserted that all matter was composed of sulfur, salt, and mercury, each of which has a spiritual analogue.[87] Sulfur (body) can only be combined with salt (soul) by means of mercury (pneuma). Though the Greek *pneuma* means "spirit" or "soul," Paracelsus redefined this word as mercury, a third element in the *tria prima*, the essence of which is its power to combine.[88] Mercury is hermaphroditic because it is composed of both salt and sulfur, of which all things consist (at least in some theories). Alchemists combine salt, sulfur, and mercury in the alembic hoping to create pure gold. The refining process is complicated by the fact that salt and sulfur are stable, but mercury active. In the sermon literature, as we have just seen, Donne calls this active agent, this mercury, *grace*.

According to Bernard, the Virgin is not the source of salvation but rather "the aqueduct through which the Source flows."[89] In order to explain her role in salvation, Bernard compares her to a channel or that "connecting portion" by which the body is joined to the head and by which the head exerts its power and its virtue: "For she is the neck of our Head by which He communicates to His Mystical body all spiritual gifts."[90] Donne revises Bernard's doctrine so that Mary becomes Mercury, or the "middle nature" in the blood, "between body and soul." Hence he mingles alchemical codes with Bernard's depiction of Mary as aqueduct.

Donne declares that "this Grace [this spiritual force analogous to alchemical Mercury] works powerfully in thee," compelling transformation from an external law, *jus ad rem*, to a personal possessing of it, *jus in re*. He also says that "This Grace is this Salvation," indicating a final stage or home. At this point, significantly, Donne launches into a rehearsal of the Magnificat, inviting his audience, including the Lady Elizabeth, to whom he is preaching, to reflect upon Gabriel's announcement to Mary:

> It shall be neer to thee, so as that thy reason shall apprehend it; and neerer then that, thy faith shall establish it; and neerer then all this, it shall create in thee a modest and sober, but yet an infallible assurance, that thy salvation shall never depart from thee: *Magnificabit anima tua Dominum,* as the B. Virgin speaks, *Thy soul shall magnifie the Lord.*[91]

This direct reference to Mary visited by Gabriel reestablishes birthing as the subject at hand. But those more adept members among Donne's congregation certainly picked up his alchemical references to "Conjunction" (Ripley's term) and establishment (what Ripley called "Projection") during the birthing of the Stone: "near to thee . . . shall apprehend it," "shall establish it," and "infallible assurance." The miracle Donne has just described places Mary, her womb, in the center, as "home," both the process and the place.

The Anniversaries

The First Anniversarie: An Anatomie of the World (1611) and *Of the Progres of the Soule: The Second Anniversary* (1612) were written to eulogize Sir Robert Drury's fifteen-year-old unmarried daughter. Though both are encomia, the tone of *The First Anniversarie* is more elegiac because its theme is mutability, the loss of the virgin soul on earth. In contrast, *The Second Anniversary* is more celebratory because its primary concern is the virgin's triumph in heaven. As Donne himself cautioned, both poems are concerned with a larger subject than that of the young girl now dead. He intimates as much when he writes, "Some moneths she hath beene dead (but being dead, / Measures of times are all determined) / But long shee'ath beene away, long, long . . ."

(*The First Anniversarie*, ll. 39–41). However, he was not willing to defile the mystery behind this "Shee," writing into the poem his own apology: "Nor could incomprehensiblenesse deterre / Me, from thus trying to emprison her" (*The First Anniversarie*, ll. 469–70).

Donne says he wants to try to understand his subject by fixing her in verse, even by anatomizing her: "I (since no man can make thee liue) will trie,/ What we may gaine by thy Anatomy" (*The First Anniversarie*, ll. 59–60). Several times throughout the poem he reminds us of this "anatomy," simultaneously reminding us that he is probing a difficult concept. The repeated line, "And learn'st thus much by our Anatomee" (ll. 185, 239, 327, 371, 429) serves to structure *The First Anniversarie*.

The refrain does not appear in *The Second Anniversary*. When Donne omitted the refrain, Louis Martz argues, he freed up transitions between sections, and ultimately created a more unified poem.[92] At any rate, the refrain of *The First Anniversarie* does serve as a reminder to Donne's readers that they are studying a "mystick book." In spite of the difficulties, he declares, he will undertake the task. Donne's Lullian sense of memory is that it should serve to investigate something otherwise left "incomprehensible." If he is also emulating the Lullian sense of "logic," then he is working backward, back from a "true conclusion," which *The Second Anniversary* represents. Here is the end:

> Immortall Maid, I might inuoque thy name.
> Could any Saint prouoke that appetite,
> Thou here shouldst make mee a french conuertite.
> But thou wouldst not; nor wouldst thou be content,
> To take this, for my second yeeres true Rent,
> Did this Coine beare any other stampe, then his,
> That gaue thee power to do, me to say this.
>
> (ll. 516–22)

These lines from *The Second Anniversary* represent the "final cause," in the Lullian sense, of Donne's poem(s). Since Lull himself defined reasoning as movement (*moviment*) in the mind, we shall begin to trace the motion of Donne's reasoning throughout both poems, trying to discover the causes leading to this true conclusion, which is "this Coine," which is "true Rent."[93] This coin, Donne says, bears no "other stampe, then his, / That gave thee power to doe." Following Donne's backward way may help us understand what he meant.

Ben Jonson's criticism of *The Anniversaries* is famous, but the implications have yet to be fully investigated. Jonson told Donne that if his praise "had been written of the Virgin Marie it had been something."[94] Donne's reply "that he described the Idea of a Woman, not as she was" is hardly a defense against Jonson's barb. In fact, it is Donne's way of telling Jonson that he was none too far from the mark. The theme of virtue in both *The Anniversaries* allows Donne to descant upon numerous ways of perceiving this "Idea," including Platonic and Paracelsian notions that virtue, being indivisible, means harmony, which in turn means health. Hence Donne is able to probe both classical and alchemical concepts of secret virtue as he refines his idea of the female soul into something extraordinary, including the "virtue" of the Virgin.[95]

Perhaps Jonson's criticism has prevented Donne's readers from scrutinizing the role of Mary in these poems, though the more general Christian references are frequently noted. John Shawcross observes that Donne's "Immortal Mayd" (of *The Second Anniversary*) alludes not only to the Virgin Mary but also to God the Father, to the Muse, "who chastely begets a child," and to Christ (a reference to the poem itself "leading mankind away from vice").[96] "Immortal Mayd" also refers to the Virgin Mary of medieval iconography, where she is sometimes depicted in swaddling clothes wrapped in the mind of God even before the Fall. Sometimes medieval artists showed her kneeling before the Father during the Creation of the World, in the very beginning.[97] This background, already committed to memory, is the page (or one of them) upon which Donne writes *The Second Anniversary*.

In the Lullian system one first discovers what Aristotle called the "final cause," which is the end or purpose for which something was made. Having isolated the final cause, one proceeds to discover by reasoning, defined as movement (*moviment*) in the mind, the other causes (whether material, formal, or efficient) that led to this end. So the Lullian system of "reason," which is more art than reason, works *backward* from an already established truth. Therefore, when Donne claims to be "anatomizing" Elizabeth Drury, he is really providing as background something other than (or in addition to) classical systems of thought. The various causes he (and/or his reader) will investigate are the material (remembered images and backgrounds), the formal (the Idea of Woman), and the efficient (specific images conveyed by language itself, including numbers and names).

In spite of current interest in the way religious controversy shaped Renaissance culture, scholars continue to exercise caution when interpreting references to the Virgin in these poems. Theresa M. DiPasquale's recent study has been most valuable in righting the balance between perceptions of Donne as Protestant and of Donne as Catholic. Though she makes no reference to Mary (neither does the poem), she defines Donne's subject as the "representation of women as conduits of grace."[98] This begins to probe issues concerning the value of the Virgin and the rosary in the poem. DiPasquale focuses on Eve's transgression and relegates what would ordinarily be the name of "Second Eve" (i.e., Mary) to "the Idea of Woman," which she says is Elizabeth Drury "transformed by a kind of transubstantiation . . . into pure unalloyed virtue."[99] The more overt alchemical references, she thinks, convey basically negative connotations (what *Romane Chymists* see), but she discovers different meanings, some of them versions of the "sacramentality of the feminine."[100] Instead of alchemy, she offers the body of Elizabeth Drury as "the transubstantiation of the Eucharistic elements."[101]

Louis Martz, writing fifty-five years ago, still comes closest to recognizing Mary as organizing principle throughout *The Anniversaries,* arguing that meditations on the Virgin were among the Counter-Reformation materials Donne chose for these poems.[102] Among the available devotional materials were fifteen meditations on the Joys of the Virgin, by Stephen of Salley, an English Cistercian of the early thirteenth century. As a Cistercian, Stephen owed much to his own "mother," St. Bernard of Clairvaux. Martz observes that Donne's treatment of Elizabeth Drury is very like the Cistercian practice of meditations on Mary, where "she is a 'Queene' ascended to Heaven, attended by Saints; [where] she is the Name above every name."[103] The implications of Donne's Catholic source materials, that which is in part a consequence of his harmonizing vision, are what I intend to explore below.[104]

That Donne is able to create associations between his Idea of Virtue, represented by Elizabeth Drury, and specific attributes of the Virgin is due, primarily, to his referentiality, which derives from many streams of thought, including Neoplatonism, Neopythagoreanism, Gnosticism, pseudo-Lullism, cabalism and, of course, Hermetism. For this reason we have addressed some of these subjects in Donne, also studying certain systems of memory he inherited. One example is Princess Elizabeth's portrait (Figure 19) and the occult sense of virtue attached to it. But Donne also relied upon classical systems of *ars memoria,* such as that developed by Augustine.

St. Augustine, as we know, thought of memory as a vast treasure-house with "roomy chambers," containing countless images stored by the senses.[105] The kinds of images Augustine cites range from the purely visual (light and colors) to the auditory to the less easily defined gustatory ("all flavors by that of the mouth"), and to the kinetic ("what is hard or soft, hot or cold"):[106]

> All these does that great receptacle of memory, with its many and indescribable departments, receive, to be recalled and brought forth when required; each entering by its own door, is laid up in it. And yet the things themselves do not enter it, but only the images of the things perceived are there ready at hand for thought to recall.[107]

Donne builds upon this theory by creating his own more mobile system of artificial memory, which is his store of particular images (some alchemical), all of which cooperate with similar images scattered throughout the canon. These references make Donne's language fluid, and it is this fluidity that resists confinement to a single poem, insisting instead upon association with other texts. Some we have already reviewed. These we will recognize when we encounter them in *The Anniversaries*. Others will be new to us. Tucked away in Donne's storehouse are such polysemic images as these: deluge/ark, coin, hen, poison, disease, cinder/ashes, womb, breast, song, fragment, book, cement/glue, memory, touch, and middle nature. For Donne and his readers, these become a powder keg ready to explode with new (and old) thoughts.

The concept of "middle nature" Donne assigns to *The Anniversaries* themselves. These are my poems, he says, the nature of which is *middle:* "Verse hath a middle nature: heauen keepes soules, / The graue keeps bodies, verse the fame enroules" (*The First Anniversarie*, ll. 473–74). By keeping Elizabeth Drury's fame alive, Donne's poems will rescue the ever-fading memory of that Woman now gone. So the middle nature of poetry, Donne argues, really functions as memory, the vital agent that reattaches the Original Image to what vestiges remain. Middle nature is the rainbow bridge connecting earthlings with Valhalla. As memory, *The Anniversaries* will help mankind get "home." As medicine, *The Anniversaries* will rectify failed memory. The "middle nature" of Donne's verse will bring back her image (who is this mysterious "Shee"?):

> Her Ghost doth walke; that is, a glimmering light,
> A faint weake loue of vertue and of good
> Reflects from her, on them which vnderstood
> Her worth; And though she haue shut in all day,
> The twi-light of her memory doth stay;
> (*The First Anniversarie*, ll. 70–74)

Donne argues that he will try to implement his own kind of corrective surgery, restoring mankind's memory through the vision of the poems.

It is impossible for readers who have studied Donne's Heidelberg sermon to ignore the variables of meaning in "middle nature," especially as he had there defined the middle nature in the blood as that agent that glues bodies to souls. It is indeed possible to read *The Anniversaries* without reference to Ramon Lull, but the more prudent course might be to consider how Lull's system of memory may be attached to Donne's avowed purpose. Lull's hope that his *Ars memorativa* could "heal the world" (accomplishing unity even among such diverse groups as Catholics, Jews, and Muslims) has been noted by Frances Yates and recently reaffirmed by others.[108] Donne's iterated concerns with fragmentation, which he defines as disease, seem related:

> 'Tis all in pieces, all cohaerence gone.
> (l. 213, *First Anniversarie*)

as well as his concern with motion:

> Know that all lines which circles doe containe,
> For once that they the center touch, do touch
> Twice the circumference.
> (ll. 436–438, *Second Anniversary*)

Touching the center is the way to all, achieving unity. Some readers will recognize here the alchemical symbol for salt, a line drawn through the center of a circle.[109] They will also remember that salt stands for the alchemical virgin. Significantly, Lull situates "A," the letter "reserved to indicate the totality of all nine [letters signifying the attributes of God]," in the center of his combinatory figure (Figure 17).[110] Anyone who can comprehend the center comprehends all. This is the way to achieve unity. Donne employs the circle image in *The Second Anniversary* because the poem moves "backward" toward this same Unity. Perhaps in some ways Donne's references are to the Lullian goal to bring "humans together" despite "doctrinal difference."[111] More important than any supposed influence is the fact that Donne himself declares the need to heal the world from fragmentation. But how does he accomplish or hope to accomplish this goal? I would submit that he works from the center out, that he begins with the Idea of Woman, which translates to Unity, and moves backward (or out) in order to discover true reasons for the Order she imposes.

Not all readers who encounter Donne's imagery in *The Anniversaries* will see the same things, nor will they form the same sentences out of the same linking verbs. However, such sentences must be made if the reader is to complete the opus (i.e., the interpretation of Donne's poem). As Mary Carruthers has observed, "A work is not truly read until one has made it part of oneself."[112] Memory, she says, is the only means whereby language and books make sense.[113]

Donne's associative imagery functions so that any given image from *The Anniversaries,* "*coin,*" for example, becomes a thread that unravels the sleeves of numerous other texts. Since we are looking for alchemical references to Mary in Donne's poems and since "coin" imagery is central to that matter (as well as to *The Anniversaries* themselves), we shall pull on that thread now.

Coin, we must remember, is among the final images in *The Second Anniversary* ("true Rent, / Did this Coine beare any other stampe," ll. 520–21). And the end of *The Anniversaries* is, we must remember, the beginning. Donne's final words remind us of the true reason for Robert Drury's "Rent money," Donne's Coin. For it is that which allows Donne to become I AM, which is the "Trumpet, at whose voice the people came" (l. 528). If we follow Ramon Lull's advice and work from this end (this final cause) backward, we may discover something that is worth its weight in gold.

Coins

We begin with Hugh of St. Victor's theory of memory and then move to the sermons. Hugh of St. Victor thought of memory as images stored, like coins, in the various compartments of a purse. As one needs or wants these coins, they are pulled out of their respective pockets.[114] The preface to Hugh of St. Victor's *Chronica* describes his mnemonic system as a method similar to that of images placed against backgrounds. However, numbers substitute for background and short pieces of text for images.[115] Since Donne too employs the coin image as reference to memory (which is his subject throughout the poems), it is tempting to think of Donne writing his own palimpsest, a metaphor of a metaphor of memory, suggesting numerous layers of memory, some almost gone.

Gold, what alchemists seek, becomes the subject of one of Donne's sermons. The alchemical symbol for gold is a circle, its exact center marked. This is the symbol of the Philosopher's Stone, which bears the stamp of both parent elements. Newly minted coins, Donne says, is what God would make of us. Moreover, God has provided man a way to pay his spiritual debt. The coin he has made is stamped in Mary's womb:

First, he [Christ] must pay it in such money as was lent; in the nature and flesh of man; for man had sinned, and man must pay. And then it was lent in such money as was coyned even with the Image of God; man was made according to his Image: That Image being defaced, in a new Mint, in the wombe of the Blessed Virgin, there was new money coyned; The Image of the invisible God, the second person in the Trinity, was imprinted into the humane nature. And then that there might bee *omnis plenitudo,* all fulnesse, as God, for the paiment of this debt, sent downe the Bullion, and the stamp, that is, God to be conceived in man, and as he provided the Mint, the womb of the Blessed Virgin, so hath he provided an Exchequer, where this mony is issued; that is his Church, where his merits should be applied to the discharge of particular consciences.[116]

Noteworthy is the way Donne develops his conceit so that bullion (God) is stamped in the mint (Mary), whom he is careful to distinguish from the exchequer (the Church). The Church is simply the treasury housing this coin. Just as parents imprint themselves upon the characters of their children, the "invisible" God is stamped upon the Virgin's sinless flesh. Between them they make a new image, a new coin.

John Carey has explained that "coins were much more human in Donne's day than they are now."[117] Because they were produced in a somewhat haphazard fashion (as people are), even sometimes restamped (as certain people are), they varied in size, shape, weight, and sometimes quality.[118] That Donne was attracted to coins is evidenced by his letters and poems, where he often compares them with human beings and human activities. His letter to Sir Henry Goodyer, for example, warns against changing sides in religion, arguing that restamped coins sometimes come out strange, looking "awry and squint." Obviously, the very idea of fixing a stamp upon precious metal (or conversely of stamping base materials in order to make them seem viable currency) has alchemical undertones.[119] We should not be surprised, therefore, to discover coins among the numerous collections of alchemical emblems and plates.[120]

Back to *The Anniversaries*

Numerous references to *gold* in *The First Anniversarie* are answered by *coin* in *The Second Anniversary*. So when Donne writes in *The First Anniversarie,* "had we chang'd to gold" (1.148) and "purifie / All, by a true religious Alchimy" (ll. 181–82), he is creating the conditions whereby we read or remember the next poem. He writes, for example, in *The First Anniversarie:*

> Shee that was best, and first originall
> Of all faire copies; and the generall
> Steward to Fate; shee whose rich eyes, and brest,
> Guilt the West Indies, and perfum'd the East;
> Whose hauing breath'd in this world, did bestow
> Spice on those Isles, and bad them still smell so,
> And that rich Indie which doth gold interre,
> Is but as single money, coyn'd from her:
>
> (ll. 227–34)

The catalogue of attributes associated with her include prophecy (her penetrating vision) and gold (a breast full of treasures). The breast imagery may compel Donne's readers to retrieve other texts from their memories. Among these is the Roman doctrine of transubstantiation, whereby blood (or in this case milk) becomes the sacred body fed to all. This is yet another example of Donne's confronting his readers with something like something else not the same, inviting them to make connections with linking verbs such as *is* or *seems*. Donne's own prefatory comments tell us that he means his readers to use *seems* rather than *is*.

Donne has joined "rich eyes" with "brest" in order to convey the idea of gold ("Guilt") and perfume ("perfum'd the East"). Adept readers cannot ignore this combination as an allusion to the dying Eastern phoenix, out of whose ashes exude that perfume soon to be followed by the resurrection of numerous birds, silver and gold. She contains all of this treasure ("Is but as single money, coyn'd from her"). Her breasts disseminate this wealth throughout the world, even to such far regions as the West Indies (renowned for precious ore). Her perfume wafts to the East (from which England was importing exotic spices). Her coin, of which she is the Original, is but small change compared to her.

Donne employs the same imagery in *The Second Anniversary*, its complement, knowing his readers will remember, adding this to that:

> ... remember then, that shee
> Shee, whose faire body no such prison was,
> But that a soule might well be pleas'd to passe
> An Age in her; shee whose rich beauty lent
> Mintage to others beauties, for they went
> But for so much, as they were like to her;
> Shee, in whose body (if wee dare prefer
> This low world, to so high a mark, as shee,)
> The Westerne treasure, Esterne spiceree,
> . . . .
> Shee, of whose soule, if we may say, t'was Gold,
> Her body was th'Electrum, and did hold

3: MNEMOTECHNICS IN THE SERMONS AND POEMS

>   Many degrees of that; we vnderstood
>   Her by her sight, her pure and eloquent blood
>   Spoke in her cheekes, and so distinckly wrought,
>   That one might almost say, her bodie thought,
>   Shee, shee, thus richly, and largely hous'd, is gone:
>   (ll. 220–28; ll. 241–47)

Hence he has given his readers special understanding, allowing them to add to the previous catalogue of riches (ore, spices, and gold) her body and her blood. Some adept readers will understand the source of all this wealth to be the Virgin whose womb is that mint, which dissolves, cleanses, and regenerates metals. Because she is gone, neither her body nor her blood remain visible, so that puny, half-blind men must crawl around unaware of how they were begotten in the first place:

>   Poore soule in this thy flesh what do'st thou know.
>   Thou know'st thy selfe so little, as thou know'st not,
>   How thou did'st die, nor how thou wast begot.
>   (*The Second Anniversary*, ll. 254–56)

Donne expects his readers to attach the first vision to the second in order better to comprehend the nature of this "Shee." The careful reader notices synecdoche functioning throughout; the breasts of the first vision and the blood (associated with the womb) of the second vision are meant to jolt the reader's memory when he or she eventually encounters "how thou wast begot." Later in *The Second Anniversary* Donne will jolt this memory yet again, this time adding the element of grace:

>   Who kept, by diligent deuotion,
>   Gods Image, in such reparation,
>   Within her heart, that what decay was growen,
>   Was her first Parents fault, and not her own:
>   Who being solicited to any Act,
>   Still heard God pleading his safe precontract;
>   Who by a faithfull confidence, was here
>   Betrothed to God, and now is married there,
>   . . . .
>   Who being heare fild with grace, yet stroue to bee,
>   Both where more grace, and more capacitee
>   At once is giuen: shee to Heauen is gone,
>   Who made this world in some proportion
>   A heauen, and here, became vnto vs all,
>   Ioye. . . .
>   (ll. 455–470)

128   3: MNEMOTECHNICS IN THE SERMONS AND POEMS

Donne's readers are not required to see the Virgin Mary here. However, many will. The Virgin, begotten by Adam and Eve (her first parents) has nevertheless overcome their fault. As Second Eve, she is full of grace. (At this point we try to recall that all this comes about by pulling on a thread called "coin.") That decay did not grow in her heart suggests an Immaculist view. Though the Virgin's mother and father were born in sin, she seems not to have been. Even now in heaven, she owns and disseminates more grace than she did when residing among men.

Obviously, the larger collective memory, which involves cooperation among various similar texts outside these poems, allows fullest comprehension, along with more variables. Those who attended St. Paul's on Christmas Day, 1622, and who had *also* read *The Anniversaries* were in a position to comprehend more fully Donne's vision of Mary:

> The Virgin Mary is full of Grace; and Grace is a fulnesse above both; above faith and works too, for that is the meanes to preserve both . . . Man was made according to his [God's] Image: That Image defaced, in a new Mint, in the wombe of the Blessed Virgin, there was new money coyned; The Image of the invisible God . . . he provided the Mint, the womb of the Blessed Virgin.[121]

Deep in the memories of such people among Donne's congregation were previous visions of the Virgin who was "first originall / Of all faire copies" so that all were "coyn'd from her" (*The First Anniversarie*). Also embedded in this collective memory was Donne's declaration that her "rich beauty lent / Mintage to others beauties" (*The Second Anniversary*). Furthermore, they would have added to other knowledge or remembrances his observation that she, when she was here, was "fild with grace" (*The Second Anniversary*). Those who knew *The Anniversaries* were able to read backward (from 1622 to 1611–12) in order to understand. They did this by studying revolving images and mnemonic devices that sometimes joined. They made meaning out of these by supplying linking verbs so that something like something else but not the same could be identified.

This is not to say that every time Donne reintroduces an image, especially an alchemical code, he means the same thing, for the very nature of Donne's cross-referencing demands a degree of ambivalence. One reader observes this phenomenon in *The Anniversaries*, especially when Donne employs alchemical codes "to stress delicate distinctions between degrees of virtue or between virtue and innocence."[122] Donne's variables are elastic, allowing the element of "degree" to enter, defying confinement to any fixed meaning or set of meanings, inviting what meaning there is to reside in the middle. Sometimes, as in the example of *coin,* the resurfaced image does represent progress, adding more to the same. Sometimes, however, the repeated image represents a sidestep or a modification, even a retraction.

When, for example, Donne names Elizabeth Drury "Microcosme" of the suburbs of the world (*The First Anniversarie,* l. 236), he allows her to remain human, expressing her as an example to others, the same as any virtuous man or woman would be. This idea is reinforced or sustained by the fact of her death, which Donne emphasizes in *The Second Anniversary,* explaining why this had to be. She was "Mithridate" (l. 127), an antidote to poison; yet she died. Though she was all health, he explains, she succumbed to disease, because "Death must vsher, and vnlocke the doore [to Heaven]" (l. 156). Thus Donne allows Elizabeth Drury the frailty that flesh is heir to.

When, however, the speaker envisions her in heaven among the saints and prophets, a certain degree of ambiguity is implied by the way Donne has manipulated cross-references. Having entered a state of ecstasy, the speaker expresses her as the "blessed Mother-maid," and celebrates "her interest, of mother-hood" above her goodness (ll. 341–44). The ambivalence created by disjunction between numerous offerings of Elizabeth Drury as "immortal maid," including the maid who "wouldst refuse / The name of Mother" (*The Second Anniversary,* ll. 33–34), and this specific image of the "blessed Mother-maid" is Donne's refusal to confine the analogy to what it ultimately suggests. This is an example of his thought sidestepping.

An example of his reversing the meaning of common images is the disjunction between Elizabeth Drury as Second Eve in *The First* and *Second Anniversaries* and Mary as Second Eve in Donne's sermon at St. Paul's Cross, delivered some five years later. In the poem he had written that "Shee tooke the weaker Sex, she that could driue / The poysonous tincture, and the stayne of *Eue,* Out of her thoughts" (*The First Anniversarie,* ll. 179–81). Donne's adept reader will understand that the Ouroboros is composed of two poisons, symbolic of the two parts of the cosmic cycle. One venom destroys, and one is the tincture or medicine that restores. He repeats this conceptual image in *The Second Anniversary,* when the speaker urges his own soul to try to remember:

> Poore soule in this thy flesh what do'st thou know.
> Thou know'st thy selfe so little, as thou know'st not,
> How thou did'st die, nor how thou wast begot.
> Thou neither knowst, how thou at first camest in,
> Nor how thou took'st the poyson of mans sin.
> Nor dost thou, (though thou knowst, that thou art so)
> By what way thou art made immortall, know.
> (ll. 254–60)

Associations between Eve's destructive "poyson," a reminder of "how thou did'st die," and the Second Eve's restorative "poyson," a reminder of "what way thou art made immortall," has become a significant construct in *The Anniversaries*. Donne's treatment of the images implies that *this* she, because she restores or heals mankind, is indeed Second Eve. However, against a very different background, his sermon at St. Paul's Cross, Donne will later declare that "nothing that she did entred into that, treasure, that ransom that redeemed us." This is an example of Donne reversing the implied meanings.

Ironically, Donne had prophesied this kind of "betrayal," or "switch-round," in *The Second Anniversary*. Referring to Heraclitus's doctrine of flux, whereby the river that flows today is not the same as yesterday, he envisions the image of the Virgin to men who have forgotten her:

> So flowes her face, and thine eies, neither now
> That saint, nor Pilgrime, which your louing vow
> Concernd, remaines; but whil'st you thinke you bee
> Constant, you'are howrely in inconstancee.
>
> (ll. 397–400)

The "loving vow" is broken because mankind's vision is impaired. Men prove inconstant, even on an hourly basis, because they fail to recognize "That saint," even while looking at her. Donne himself (in his first sermon at St. Paul's Cross) refused to grant Mary any intrinsic part in salvation. If he suffered any guilt because of this, he at least rectified that "fault" some ten years later when he retrieved her image, reinstating this Second Eve as that "new Mint" for God's Image, even "the wombe of the Blessed Virgin."

Language peculiar to the coining process seems to have intrigued Donne, particularly that part of the process in which the stamp presses down to produce an image, changing an otherwise "souless" and passive disc of metal into a precious and unique "child." In fact, he ends *The Second Anniversary* with a reference to this stamp and coin, implying that his poem is a coin bearing the stamp of Christ, who has given the Virgin the power "to doe" and Donne, therefore, the power "to say":

> Did this Coine beare any other stampe, then his,
> That gaue thee power to do, me, to say this.
> Since his will is, that to posteritee,
> Thou shouldest for life,and death,a patterne bee.
>
> (ll. 521–24)

That the Virgin's death is here associated with Christ's is significant. Donne makes them both a vital force in salvation and "a patterne" for all. *The Second Anniversary* is his coin, stamped by the poet himself, but not without the power of the Virgin, herself God's Maker.

Back to the Library

One other example illustrates the phenomenon of cross-referentiality in Donne's thought. *The Anniversaries* include numerous references to *book*, discussed above, as metonymy associated with Mary. The image of book is even more elastic than *coin* or *grace*, allowing Donne's reader to look at many other things besides Mary. Nevertheless, he sometimes, as in *The Second Anniversary*, compels that view.

"A Valediction of the booke" cannot be understood apart from the catalogue of other "books" to which he refers. That Donne was a great lover of learning is demonstrated by his verse letter to Edward Herbert (1610), where he had advised his friend to be a digester of many books, even to become a book himself that others might read. Now, two years later, Donne seems to manage another "switch-round," arguing that accumulating new learning (referring to Paracelsus, ll. 263–66 and Harvey, ll. 271–72) is not really worth the bother:

> Forget this world, and scarse thinke of it so,
> As of old cloaths, cast off a yeare agoe.
> To be thus stupid is Alacrity;
> Men thus lethargique haue best Memory.
> Looke vpward; that's towards her. . . .
>   (*The Second Anniversary*, ll. 61–65)

Where the madness of men is concerned, Donne has very little patience, even when that madness takes the form of new learning. Forget it, he says. Erase it from your minds. That is the "best Memory." Alluding to Plato, he had suggested to Edward Herbert that the philosopher can avoid thinking like foolish men by remaining ignorant of their ideas. Plato had written, "All these things the philosopher does not even know that he does not know; for . . . his mind, considering all these things petty and of no account, disdains them."[123] Donne reiterates this argument twice, both in his verse letter and in *The Second Anniversary*. Obviously he is intrigued by Plato's idea. However, his purpose in the poem is to offer a "better book" as antidote for the ever-growing body of "new learning" written by men who know little or nothing about her. Forget this world, he says, and go to heaven, where you will immediately understand all, mainly because she is the Original Book, full of all knowledge. Read her and your Memory will be restored:

> There thou (but in no other schoole) maist bee
> Perchance, as learned, and as full, as shee,
> Shee who all Libraries had throughly red
> At home, in her owne thoughts, And practised
> So much good as would make as many more:
> Shee whose example they must all implore,
> Who would or doe, or thinke well, and confesse
> That aie the vertuous Actions they expresse,
> Are but a new, and worse edition,
> Of her some one thought, or one action:
> Shee, who in th'Art of knowing Heauen, was growen
> Here vpon Earth, to such perfection,
> That shee hath, euer since to Heauen shee came,
> (In a far fairer print,) but read the same:
> Shee, shee, not satisfied with all this waite,
> (For so much knowledge, as would ouer-fraite
> Another, did but Ballast her) is gone,
> As well t'enioy, as get perfectione.
> And cals vs after her, in that shee tooke,
> (Taking herselfe) our best, and worthiest booke.
> (ll. 301–20)

Donne is inviting his readers to understand this passage alongside other images of books encountered elsewhere. If memory does its proper work, these readers will comprehend the importance of the Original Book, even the *Emerald Table*, which may restore their sight, if not their health.

When Donne reminds them that, whether in heaven or on earth, she should be "read the same" (l. 314), he is allowing "red" as a variable. Red is the color of the Stone when it is fixed. It is also the color of the outer circle of the Ouroboros, which represents "perfectione" (l. 318). Donne is telling his reader to "read" this "red." Because she is "all Libraries" (l. 303), those who read her—"who in th'Art of knowing Heauen . . . has growne . . . to . . . perfection" (ll. 311–12)—will learn true Wisdom. ("Valediction of the booke," if they have read it and remember, is among the variables offered.)

As one who kept to "her owne thoughts" (l. 304) they may recognize the Virgin. The apostle Luke, as every Christian knows, described Mary as one who "kept all these things, and pondered *them* in her heart" and again as one who "kept all these sayings in her heart."[124] Those who remember this will have her image restored to them. Those who do not will be satisfied with her Protestant substitute.[125]

When Donne's readers encounter that one whom "must all implore . . . and confesse," they are invited to see Mary apotheosized. ("The Canonization," if they know and remember it, helps them conclude this.) As the original "edition," they may understand how they themselves have come to represent a "worse edition / Of her some one thought, or one action." Memory, as Donne himself will say, is the key to understanding this elusive vision, which is also the key to getting home.

As in a palimpsest, Donne has deepened the texture of his writing by supplying layer upon layer without erasing any of them. In fact, *The Anniversaries* could be considered Donne's commonplace book. His subtext of recurring images and motifs serves as a network of imagery for the entire corpus. Those who complain about the forgotten subject, Elizabeth Drury, may profit by rereading the poems, for they offer a rich repository of associational imagery, much of which elucidates Donne's conception of the Virgin. If Elizabeth Drury serves to lead Donne's readers toward his vision of this elusive female, then *as metonymy* she becomes central to the entire canon, not just these dedicatory poems.

Before leaving *The Anniversaries* we need to return briefly to Donne's "good conclusion," to the "Immortall Maid" and to "this Coine," stamped by none other than Christ "That gaue thee power to do, me to say this." It is impossible, Donne knows, for this coin to be stamped by Christ alone. A coin is not genuine, is of no value, unless stamped by both parents on both the obverse and the reverse (Figure 15). Mary is the Mint in which this coin has been made. The Holy Spirit has pressed down upon her, thereby stamping Immortal Coin. This is the condition upon which Donne, the Christian poet, is empowered to speak, even these poems.

4
Ars Sacra Poetica

LA *CORONA* IS A GOOD PLACE TO BEGIN TO UNDERSTAND DONNE'S *ars sacra*. However, some of the backgrounds he employs have become so obscure to modern readers that I am compelled to attend to these matters as well as to the poem.

In *La Corona* Donne places memorized images against memorized backgrounds in order to express, vertically, the divine. In order to recognize some of the variables, we must know the background(s). The phoenix, symbolizing the *process* of *making*, is one such. The Ouroboros, symbolizing Eternity, is another. In fact, the Ouroboros (Figures 3 and 4) provides the very shape of Donne's poem.

The poem is a seven-sonnet sequence. Like beads on a necklace or a rosary, the sonnets are strung together by repetition of the last line of each poem as the first line of the next. This in itself suggests the shape of the Ouroboros. The final, seventh sonnet suggests Christ as the "red" Stone, as "the'uprising of this Sunne, and Sonne" (l. 86), who has been made by dissolution, ablution, and fire ("whose just teares, or tribulation / Have purely washt, or burnt your drossie clay," ll. 87–88). This last sonnet shows the Stone as fixed, *fixionem*, and it is this "Bright [red] Torch" (l. 95) that leads us back to the first sonnet's "All changing unchang'd Antient of dayes" (l. 4), also red. Thus the first sonnet swallows the last, and vice versa, making the outer red circle of the Ouroboros just.

Though the opening sonnet also contains the human element, in the form of the speaker's prayer, the second sonnet, "Annunciation," actually begins the second, more human, inner circle of the Ouroboros. It will be remembered that the outer circle is red, but that the inner circle, because it is in transition, is yellow or orange. This inner circle, in *La Corona*, is composed of the five remaining sonnets, beginning with "Annunciation."

The theme of this second sonnet, and the theme of the entire sequence, is *making*. The emblem for making is the phoenix, but some will see a particular phoenix in the poem, even the emblem of the Phoenix with Two Hearts, that is, the hearts of the Virgin Mother and her Son joined (Figure 9). Some of Donne's readers, confronting this Phoenix Riddle, "Whom thou conceiv'st, conceiv'd" (l. 25), recognize among the variables death, both alchemical and spiritual. He died in order to *make* her, as she represents all mankind. She, "Loe, faithful Virgin" (l. 19) died, submitting to her divine Spouse in order to conceive or *make*—"In prison, in thy wombe" (l. 20)—him.

The closing lines of the second sonnet so closely resemble another poem that it is possible Donne had it (or something like it, not the same) in mind. These lines contain the phoenix image:

> Ere by the spheares time was created, thou
> Wast in his minde, who is thy Sonne, and Brother,
> Whom thou conceiv'st, conceiv'd; yea thou art now
> Thy Makers maker, and thy Fathers mother.
>
> (ll.23–26)

This closely resembles a poem by Lactantius, among the most eloquent of church fathers (third century). Lactantius's *Carmen De Phoenice* ("Song concerning the Phoenix") reads thus:

> *Ipsa sibi proles, suus est pater, & hoeores:*
> *Nutrix ipsa sui, semper alumna sibi.*

[She to herself offspring is, and her own father, and her own heir: Nurse is she of herself, and ever her own foster daughter.][1]

The lines above were once attached to a picture, now lost. Undoubtedly, this picture depicted the Virgin and Son as phoenix. We know such images "existed before and during Shakespeare's time."[2] We have seen one example in Figure 9, an emblem of Mary and Christ as phoenix with two hearts joined.[3] This emblem, or something like it, is among Donne's variables in *La Corona*. He uses it in order to compel his readers to remember fading images from their pre-Reformation past. If they recognize the variables, both secular and sacred, they will be able to make meaning of the poem.

That past (to them fading, to us almost lost) is connected with pre-Reformation birthing rituals, a dangerous but sacred time for women. Because these too serve as background or context for *La Corona*, we shall review them now and then return to the poem.

Pre-Reformation Birthing Practices

Before the Reformation, women in childbirth turned to the protection of the Virgin, asking her to assist the child in the womb, as through a stormy sea, where it floats for nine months. Alchemists used this same idea, that is, of dangerous births, to explain their operations in the *sanctum sanctorum*. The emblem below was used to illustrate Paracelsus's explanation of the "mother's influence" upon the child in her womb. Even as its star and planet, he says, she creates and forms the child.[4] When Renaissance readers saw this emblem, they understood it not so much as the threatened ship but as the threatened child in the alembic or womb. Few modern readers can see this emblem in Donne's poem because it is not a part of their world. They only read, "Thy Makers maker, and thy Fathers mother, / Thou'hast light in darke; and shutst in little roome, / *Immensity*" (ll. 26–27). Donne's readers, however, remembered the mother's influence on her child, even while it struggled in the womb. Some may have remembered prayers to the Virgin during labor. Others may have remembered the adept anxiously hovering over the alchemical child.

David Cressy's survey of birthing rituals in early modern England helps us understand the human background of this poem, particularly from a woman's point of view. It also helps us see how alchemy attached itself to these rituals. "Every phase of the [birthing] process," he says, "was invested with . . . religious significance."[5] "[T]he miracle of reproduction was swathed in religious meaning."[6] The mystery of birthing was really "a series of transformations" that became "shared experiences" among women.[7]

Men were excluded from the mystery. "Very few men gained intimate entry to the birthroom or knew what happened behind the screen."[8] This observation helps us understand that, by making a poem about *making*, Donne himself is playing the role of midwife, probing the birth chamber for answers to questions only women knew. Among the secrets, which men were denied, were chants and charms, including prayers to the Virgin, amulets, stones, oils, and salt.[9] Central was the figure of Mary—her comfort, her protection, her intercession in the hour of need.

Naturally, Protestants sought to eliminate her, along with all forms of popery. In order to do this, they tried to control the midwives, for it was they who possessed secret knowledge, magic learned, not from men, but from other women before them.[10] Some of this magic was rooted in alchemy. Uroscopic analysis, for example, determined that "a reddish tinge" meant a boy would be born, and "a whitish colour"

Figure 20: "The Holy Virgin with the Child, as Patron Saint of Sailors." Woodcut. Reproduced as figure 18 in Paracelsus, *Selected Writings*, ed. Jolande Jacobi and trans. Norbert Guterman (New York: Pantheon, 1958). General Research Division, the New York Public Library, Astor, Lenox, and Tilden Foundations.

meant a girl.[11] Alchemy also influenced conditions in the birthing room, which was kept warm to resemble the alembic.[12] Even alchemical grace became an important factor, as "focus [was often] on [the woman's] spiritual preparation."[13] Like priests or adepts, midwives officiated during the entire process. Sometimes they even administered the sacrament of baptism and sprinkled the child with salt.[14] Everything, from regulating the temperature of the room to cleansing the child of the birthing fluids, was under their control. Theresa DiPasquale has noted that in *La Corona* the Virgin serves as Donne's model for making poetry.[15] I would add that Donne, when writing *La Corona*, also assumed the role of pre-Reformation midwife. DiPasquale comes close to saying the same thing when she observes, "*La Corona* itself—like Christ in the womb of the Virgin . . . is thus a child able to redeem its own parent, a work able to bestow redeemed identity on its maker [Donne]."[16]

Scholars generally assign *La Corona* an early date, perhaps as early as 1607.[17] Donne seems to have given it to Magdalen Herbert, mother of George and Edward.[18] So a female reader is among those making meaning. Those readers who attend to the woman's point of view when reading Donne's poem may discover meanings not otherwise apparent.

"The Annuntiation and Passion" was written about the same time. Since it is also patterned after the alchemical Ouroboros, we may be able to discover some cross-references between these two poems. Other background material is also pertinent. One of Donne's models, for example, is the secular "corona di sonetti" of Continental love poets, where the last line of one sonnet is repeated as the first line of the next. In this manner a crown of praise is woven by the poet for his mistress. Another of Donne's models is the "corona," a variant of the rosary. Though a Protestant variant was available to Donne, he seems to have chosen instead a form more closely associated with the Virgin herself.[19] Though both of these models help us understand Donne's poem, the motif they offer is that of one circle only. Studying the poem as a set of concentric circles helps us place it within the context of alchemical and Lullist theories, both of which profoundly influenced Donne's thought. This is what I propose to do.

The Inner Circle

The outer circle, composed of the first and last sonnets, represents eternity. Both form and function determine this. This outer circle should be viewed as stationary because it is the frame in which the other five revolve. Kate Gartner Frost has observed that the number *five* has various connotations, including the Virgin and circularity in marriage.[20] This helps us make sense of thematic concerns catalogued throughout the inner circle of *La Corona*. It helps us see this survey of human activity as a "marriage" between Christ and Mary.

Because this inner circle represents the progress of Christ's (and Mary's) sojourn in human history, it should be viewed as mobile. The subject is *making*. It takes the form of a narrative of Christ's earthly ministry. The third sonnet, for example, depicts him as an infant threatened by Herod, fleeing to Egypt, and so on. Subsequent sonnets continue to survey aspects of his earthly sojourn, for example, his first words, when he "sodenly speakes wonders" (l. 48), indicating that he understands, even from the beginning, "all which was, and all which should be writ" (l. 49). Such behavior results in envy, "envie in some begat" (l. 58), and the result is death, even alchemical death, where, like a tincture, Christ will draw the speaker, "draw mee" (l. 68), transmuting his "*dry soule*" into "*Moyst*" (l. 70). All of this activity on earth is attached to the Virgin. As human mother, cradling her newborn, she pities him, who, "helpless," needs her pity. But then this very Babe, in his wisdom, pities her: "Was not his pity towards thee wondrous high, / That would have need to be pittied by thee?" (ll. 39–40). This anticipates mutual pity at the Crucifixion, where her "faith" (l. 58) in him is answered by his "liberall dole" to her (l. 69). Color this inner circle, which traces the progress of her life with him, sometimes yellow, sometimes orange.

The Outer Circle

The element of alchemical grace appears in both the opening and closing sonnets. As mentioned above, adepts needed to be in a state of grace before entering the laboratory. Success or failure of the opus depended on this. In the first sonnet, therefore, the poet asks for grace to begin, "Reward my muses white sincerity" (l. 6). His desire to be rewarded with a crown, by "what thy thorny crowne gain'd" (l. 5) is complicated (in the Augustinian sense of complication) by other variables of crowns. Among these is that crown worn by the Queen of Heaven after her Assumption.[21] It is natural for the speaker to ask the Virgin Mary, full of grace, to be his Muse. The last sonnet repeats the Muse without the distinction, "And if thy holy Spirit, my Muse did raise" (l. 97), implying nonetheless that his request has been granted, that the circle is now complete. In fact, "All changing unchang'd Antient of dayes" (l. 4) echoes the motto usually attached to the

Ouroboros: "One is All through which is All and in it All."[22] Even the title, "Ascension," implies alchemical *fixionem*. The completed outer circle is stationary and, therefore, colored red.

"Annunciation"

Another model, other than the rosary or Roman Breviary, that may have influenced Donne to shape his poem as a circle is the meditative tradition of his pre-Reformation past. One feature of these devotional practices is that the final statement of one meditation becomes the dominant command of the next. Louis L. Martz's study of this phenomenon, especially as it pertains to structuring principles in *The Anniversaries,* helps us understand not only these poems but also Donne's participation in certain Counter-Reformation practices. "One should also recall," Martz writes, "that a renewal of devotion to the Virgin, especially encouraged by the Jesuits, was one of the strongest spiritual movements of the Counter-Reformation."[23] Referring to the introduction of Donne's *Anatomy,* Martz notes that "we find Elizabeth Drury treated in terms which seem to adumbrate the practice of meditating on Mary and Christ: she is a 'Queene' ascended to Heaven . . . she is the Name above every name."[24] I would suggest that we add to the above other features pertaining to Elizabeth Drury's role as protecting mother. "Being all color" (*The First Anniversarie,* l. 366), she is the Rainbow that guides us through dangerous floods. As Hen, she will "motherly sit on the earth" (*The First Anniversarie,* l. 383), protecting us at "birth-time" (*The First Anniversarie,* l. 382).

Martz's comments, and the features I have noted, provide a useful context for the second and last sonnets in *La Corona*—"Annunciation" and "Ascension." Because "Annunciation" is the first of fifteen meditations told in the rosary, it bears more attention than I have given it so far.[25] The Assumption of the Virgin, last of the glorious mysteries told by the rosary, is its complement. We shall therefore consider Donne's "Ascension" in this context.

The "Annunciation" sonnet in *La Corona* raises some of the same issues as "The Annuntiation and Passion," where Gabriel's announcement determines that Mary, in birthing, will likewise be bound to Passion or death. In this sense, "Annunciation" represents its own complete circle (a circle within a circle). Also significant is Donne's announcement of his *ars sacra poetica* (woven into the sonnet as he attaches it to the concept of "making"). He begins, according to the required form, with an echo of the previous sonnet's last line:

> *Salvation to all that will is nigh,*
> That All, which always is All every where,
> Which cannot sinne, and yet all sinnes must beare,
> Which cannot die, yet cannot chuse but die,
> Loe, faithfull Virgin, yeelds himselfe to lye
> In prison, in thy wombe; and though he there
> Can take no sinne, nor thou give, yet he'will weare
> Taken from thence, flesh, which deaths force may trie.
>
> (ll. 15–22)

"That All, which always is All every where" alludes to the Ouroboros, attached to which is often an inscription reading something like this: "All and through it is All, and to it All, and if it has not All, All is nothing."[26] Another version inserts the element of poison. Alchemically this may be understood positively, as a reference to healing: "One is the Serpent having the two compositions and the poison."[27] These variables allow some of Donne's adept readers to make meaning of the "snake" (possibly destructive, possibly restorative) woven into his poem.

Once we understand the reference to the Ouroboros, we see that "All, which always is All" applies to Mary as well as to Christ. Therefore, "All / . . . Which cannot sinne" seems to apply to her. The lines imply that neither Mary nor Christ can impart the poison of sin. This does not necessarily imply the doctrine of the Immaculate Conception. (Protestants and Catholics alike may understand that Mary was born as other children.)[28] However, this early poem hints that Donne is still developing his doctrine of Mary, shifting position sometimes along the way.

Here Donne seems more concerned with the process whereby the human egg is fertilized, "yields himselfe to lye / In prison, in thy wombe" (ll. 18–19). Adept readers already know that death or separation, "flesh, which deaths force may trie," (l. 22) must precede conjunction. As in "The Annuntiation and Passion," Donne yokes Christ's Passion, "yet cannot chuse but die" (l. 18), with Gabriel's announcement to Mary, "Loe, faithfull Virgin," (l. 19) in order to effect the collapse of time and to argue that death, at least in alchemical terms, is rebirth. Hence "Annunciation" (the second sonnet) and "Crucifying" (the fifth sonnet) represent the same moment in time.

Memory helps make this happen. Donne's system of memory, however, is not the classical *static* system whereby images rest side by side. Even backgrounds (also committed to memory) revolve, touching other backgrounds and images not ordinarily meant to be joined with them. Though the author of the *Ad Herennium* admonishes writers to keep backgrounds "in a series, so that we may never by confusion in their order be prevented from following the images,"[29] Donne does not follow this advice. The very fact that he has mixed the background of the occult Ouroboros with the background of the rosary indicates that he is introducing the concept of movement into memory. Because he has provided two different backgrounds, projecting particular images or mnemonic devices against them, his readers have to decide for themselves what meanings to attach to his poem.

Death is twice written into "Annunciation," "Which cannot die, yet cannot chuse but die" (l. 18). Adept readers will therefore recognize that "Resurrection" (the sixth sonnet) represents the later stage called *exaltation*, as natural consequence. Also from a Lullian point of view, that is, following the precepts of Lull's spiritual logic, the final seventh sonnet, "Ascension," is simply the "good conclusion" of "Annunciation." Depending upon their education and backgrounds, Donne's readers may choose to begin with "Ascension," which represents the stationary outer circle, in order to make meaning of "Annunciation." In this manner Donne's mnemotechnics invite some readers to discover "true reasons" for the "true conclusion," that is, "Ascension."[30]

Among those true reasons is the influence of the mother on her child during gestation (Figure 20). Now, finally, Paracelsus's observations can be brought to bear on Donne's poem. The emblem of the Virgin guiding her Child safely through the womb conveys, to some of Donne's readers, something like Paracelsus's idea of correspondence between mother and child, whereby she stamps her character upon it. To others, who know Lull's devotional arts, this correspondence takes on the quality of names, or rather attributes, that Mary gave her Son. These include Virtue, Truth, and Glory, which he gives to her and she back to him:

> That this Lord is within thee, O Queen, makes thee to be in great virtue and truth . . . Truth and Glory over all other creatures. . . . The Lord is in no creature so virtuously, truly and gloriously as in thee, for to no other creature has He given such power to receive His Virtue as to thee. Therefore, since by His Virtue thou canst receive greater virtue than any other creature, His Glory is more truly in thee than in any other.[31]

Lull's idea that reciprocity is written into the contract between Mother and Son is reflected in Donne's poem.[32] In fact, Donne's own position as maker is defined by her. Since Mary is now on *his* mind, he too will make her, even in a sonnet, that is, a "little roome":

> Ere by the spheares time was created, thou
> Wast in his minde, who is thy Sonne, and Brother,
> Whom thou conceiv'st, conceiv'd; yea thou art now
> Thy Maker's maker, and thy Fathers mother,
> Thou'hast light in darke; and shutst in little roome,
> *Immensity cloysterd in thy deare wombe.*

Some readers will recognize the androgyne (Figures 11 and 15) written as variable into "Brother." These will remember that "the Dragon is not killed, but by his Brother and his Sister; not by one of them alone, but by both together."[33] Some of Donne's readers also know that the features of these dragons differ. Nicolas Flamel has described *les deux dragons* as male (wingless) and female (winged and volatile). The male sits in the nest (*le mâle . . . est au-dessus*), and the female, because she is difficult to catch is dark and mysterious (*la femelle . . . est noire et obscure*).[34] Together they do the work. So Mary and Christ, Sister and Brother, do the great work. Christ is wingless. Like the alchemical fetus, he lies "In prison, in thy wombe," waiting to be tried.

While he waits, he must naturally submit to the formative powers of the Virgin. She stamps him with her own Image. According to Lull, She stamps him with Justice and Mercy: "Greater perfection, greater justice, greater liberality is given to thee than to any other woman soever—yea, than to all men."[35] According to Paracelsus, this stamping becomes the child's lodestar, guiding it through dangerous waters. "Her inner stars," he explains, "act powerfully and vigorously upon the fruit, so that its nature is thereby deeply and solidly shaped and forged."[36] If DiPasquale's insights are true (and I think they are), that the Mary Donne makes here is his own model, a model for the "priestly poet,"[37] then it follows that he also considers Elizabeth Heywood, his natural mother, when he writes the poem. As a Catholic mother, and especially as one whose line connected him with perhaps the greatest religious figure in England's history, this one stamped her character (and thereby More's) upon the fetus in her womb. As Donne, so Christ, whose Mother stamped her character upon him, even while "shutst in little roome," (l. 27).

William Harvey came to regard the fertilization of the egg as "an incorporeal process like the action of the magnet in passing on its own power of attraction to the iron it touches."[38] In *La Corona* Donne expresses Christ's conception not as "touching" but as "wearing." Christ will "wear" Mary's flesh and then that flesh will be "tried." Mary is necessarily involved in this "making" because she provides the alembic, her womb (Figure 12). Attached to this are several paradoxes and ironies.

Christ, who cannot sin, must bear it; Mary, who is sinless (presumably because she was sanctified in her own mother's womb), must bear Christ. The Virgin must be inseminated by the Holy Spirit, whose sword penetrates her ("Thou'hast light in darke," l. 27). As fetus, Christ also presses down upon her, contributing to the "*Immensity cloysterd in thy deare wombe*" (l. 28). As Savior, he will raise her up. As mother, Mary stamps (or impresses) her image of flesh upon one side of a "coin" called Christ. As husband, the Holy Spirit stamps the other side of that coin, making it divine. These images emerge from mingled traditions of Christian iconography and alchemical emblems. Light streams from heaven into the Virgin's womb.

Other medieval icons are embedded in the sonnet. When Donne writes, "Ere by the spheares time was created, thou / Wast in his minde," he is distinguishing Mary's unique place in eternity, when she was conceived by the mind of God. He thereby invites his readers to remember numerous images associated with the doctrine of the Immaculate Conception. According to exponents of this doctrine, Mary existed in the mind of God in the exact way in which she was to be born and to live. Therefore, she could be shown indiscriminately as mother, as maid, or even as infant. So it was not unusual to find in some Italian cathedrals an antiphonary showing the Virgin in swaddling clothes.[39] Neither was it unusual to see her depicted with the respective members of the Trinity, especially in scenes of the Coronation of Mary (Figure 1). Hence She becomes the model for all makers (and for all who are made), as well as paradigm for the Christian poet, who "makes" things ("yea thou art now / Thy Makers maker, and thy Fathers mother").[40] Together she and Christ constitute the Ouroboros symbolizing the great Work.

As maker, the Christian poet also participates, conceiving ideas and birthing this poem. The central problem of the first sonnet, how a Christian makes or even begins to make poetry, has been developed in this second sonnet. Unlike other mothers, Mary is chosen by her own Son, who "gave birth" to her himself when he "conceiv'd" her in his mind sometime before. In fixing his mind and his gaze upon her, he chose her from among all other women. In this sense he (her Sonne, her Brother, her Father) was also her Lover, and surely Donne, the Christian poet, understood the ramifications.

As creator, the poet conceives his subject, ponders or broods upon it, nurtures and develops it, eventually giving birth to a finished product.[41] As mentioned before, Donne seemed most intrigued with that alchemical process called *fixionem*, in which the purified product was stabilized so that it could not escape. Stamping, in fact, accomplishes that very thing, resulting in some permanent character. *La Corona* is an early example of Donne's interest in Mary's womb as the place where spiritual children are stamped. In human terms, during conception both parents' features are stamped upon the child so that he or she looks and behaves (more or less) like them. Christ and Mary make various children, all of whom (more or less) bear their stamp. For Donne the analogy extends to the act of "making" poetry. All of his poems are his children, for he has, or will, put his stamp upon them.

With Mary as model, Donne, as any mother, proceeds to make children. When Donne makes Mary in *La Corona*, she becomes one of his children. Furthermore, he demonstrates his child (the poem) to be a connecting link between man and God. The vision he imparts is difficult to define as either Maculist or Immaculist, and that is because a degree of ambivalence is written into her character. This ambivalence is the result of layers of metaphor, the poet acting as "god/creator," hatching in his mind a "child."

The relationship between poet and Mary is intriguing. In one respect, DiPasquale has demonstrated, *La Corona* itself "is thus a child able to redeem its own parent, a work able to bestow redeemed identity on its maker."[42] In fact, Mary, as model and Muse, *is* making the poet, even during the process of making the poem, for "yea thou art *now* [emphasis mine] / Thy Makers maker." She is also his Muse, and, as such, she is also his Husband. That radical thought he broached in a verse letter to the Countess of Bedford some two years later.[43] It is no accident that Donne left the letter unfinished.

"Resurrection" and "Resurrection, imperfect"

Because they make a useful comparison, it is convenient to discuss the *La Corona* sonnet entitled "Resurrection" alongside another poem by Donne, "Resurrection, imperfect."

"Resurrection" begins with that "*one drop of thy blood*" (left over from the last line of the previous sonnet) that works upon the "*dry soule*" (l. 71). Adept readers know that this "drop of . . . blood" is *menstruum*, one drop of which is sufficiently powerful to free what is "stony hard." This *menstruum* has several names, including perfect Mercury and "essentiall of Sunne and Moone,"[44] Sol and Luna, brother and sister. As such this "*one drop*" is the product of the mingled bloods of Christ and Mary. It is this that will, in "Resurrection," restore the "dry soule" (l. 71) no matter how "stony hard" (l. 73). Since tomb and womb are interchangeable metaphors for Christ and Mary, Donne offers *both* when he writes, "Flesh in that long sleep is not putrified, / But made that there, of which, and for which 'twas."

Rather than a place of putrefaction, the grave is a place of "making." Accordingly, Helen Gardner explains "that putrefaction is not the ultimate state of the body."[45] In fact, putrefaction, or dissolution, is a necessary step toward the reconstitution of elements in the alembic/grave. Donne's speaker in "Resurrection" declares something like the "Death be not proud" of the *Holy Sonnets:* "And life, by this death abled, shall controule / Death, whom thy death slue" (ll. 74–75). Moreover, the character of this death is alchemical. We know this when we read ahead to the final sonnet, "Ascension," which looks back upon the grave. Donne's theological alchemy works well here, for death, he writes, is passionate. "Tears" (l. 87) and "tribulation" (l. 87) have accompanied it. Also the process involved calcination ("burnt your drossie clay," l. 88) and ablution ("Have purely washt," l. 88). Resurrection, or alchemical exaltation, is the result of this death. What has not happened yet in this sonnet, what gives reason to "Feare" (l. 77) is that final stage called "projection," or *fixionem* or "establishment." The fear that brings the speaker misery ("bring miserie," l. 76) is that his name may not be written in the book of life ("If in thy little booke my name thou'enroule," l. 78).

Edgar Hill Duncan shows how Donne develops the idea of alchemical putrefaction or dissolution much further in "Resurrection, imperfect."[46] This poem, generally considered incomplete, has twenty-two lines.[47] However, those few lines define the process of spiritual regeneration in more overtly alchemical terms than the "Resurrection" sonnet, for they describe an Adept Christ making his own death in the womb:

> Hee was all gold when he lay downe, but rose
> All tincture, and doth not alone dispose
> Leaden and iron wills to good, but is
> Of power to make even sinfull flesh like his.
>
> (ll. 13–16)

Understanding these lines helps us understand the "Resurrection" sonnet where "Flesh in that long sleep is not putrified, / But made that there, of which, and for which 'twas; / Nor can by other meanes be glorified" (*La Corona*, ll. 79–81). In order to explain the "mortification-regeneration" process, Paracelsus employs this analogy:

> But the regeneration and renovation of metals takes place thus: As man can return to the womb of his mother, that is, to the earth from which the

first man sprang, and thus can be born again anew at the last day, so also all metals can return to quick mercury, can become Mercury, and be regenerated and clarified by fire, if they remain for forty weeks in perpetual heat, like a child in its mother's womb. Now they are born, however, not as common metals, but as metals which tinge: for if, as has been said, Luna is regenerated, it will afterward tinge all metals to Luna. So gold tinges other metals to Sol. . . .[48]

Mercury, as we know, is hermaphroditic. Because it is both hermaphroditic and volatile, it has the power to change other elements. Paracelsus is saying that this Mercury, regenerated and clarified, possesses the power to "tinge" or change other metals.

In "Resurrection, imperfect" Christ "was all gold when he lay downe, but rose / All tincture," implying that he fell as a male but rose, as Mercury, hermaphroditic. His regeneration took only three days (not the forty weeks Paracelsus recommends). However, he arose "All tincture," so that he could tinge other (human) metals. The "Resurrection" sonnet hints at the same thing. Here Donne employs the androgynous phoenix (rather than tincture) as his alchemical reference. When we put the two poems together, we understand that Donne's theological alchemy equates being washed in the blood of the Lamb with being washed in the blood of the tomb/womb, for they are essentially the same thing.

The final sonnet of *La Corona*, "Ascension," resides outside the inner circle. (Color it red.) As Easter celebration, it is eternal (stationary), for it represents the resurrected Stone, fixed forever in perfection. The opening lines portray Christ as the Sun, which is a Son sufficiently bright to lead men to salvation:

> Bright Torch, which shin'st, that I the way may see,
> Oh, with thy owne blood quench thy owne just wrath,
> And if thy holy Spirit, my Muse did raise,
> *Deigne at my hands this crowne of prayer and praise.*
>
> (ll. 95–98)

This same idea (of Christ as Light preparing man's way) is developed in the opening lines of "Resurrection, imperfect." Here Christ replaces the duller Sun (a reference to the eclipse at the Crucifixion), but he also replaces the duller fires of hell:

> Sleep, sleep old Sun, thou canst not have repast
> As yet, the wound thou took'st on friday last;
> Sleepe then, and rest; The world may beare thy stay,
> A better Sun rose before thee to day,
> Who, not content to'enlighten all that dwell

> On the earths face, as thou, enlightned hell,
> And made the darke fires languish in that vale,
> As, at thy presence here, our fires grow pale.
>
> (ll. 1–8)

The references to different kinds of fire (those that "enlighten all," those that are "darke" or "pale") are significant. For one thing, as fire, Christ is the Phoenix; and the nature of this Phoenix is necessarily androgynous. Readers of "Resurrection, imperfect," as of the sonnet, will recognize the familiar emblem of Christ and Mary as two hearts joined (Figure 9). It is impossible, especially given the context of Donne's poem, that the Phoenix be any other. But fire is important here for other reasons. The alchemists, as we have learned, are generally careful to distinguish among the kinds of fire employed in the great work. Those who preferred the "wet" method of transmutation (which was the slower way) preferred gentle heat. These practitioners argued that too much fire could destroy the work. Others preferred a special, more intense fire, sometimes called "philosophical fire," which they thought could accomplish miracles *without* destroying the opus. "Resurrection, imperfect" shows Christ conquering hell ("enlightned hell," l. 6) by his superior fire ("And made the darke fires languish," l. 7). Thereby, he conquered Satan's power ("our fires grew pale," l. 8), releasing multitudes of souls for salvation. At least this is Donne's argument.

In the "Ascension" sonnet of *La Corona* Donne writes that the "Sonne," now risen, has "purely washt, or burnt your drossie clay" (l. 4). Here his theological alchemy is expressed in essentially the same way: men are released from sin, are washed and refined ("burnt") by Christ. That burning, however, resolves in "Joy at the'uprising of this Sunne" (l. 86), which is the rising Eastern Sun, the Phoenix. In case there is any doubt of this, Donne provides his readers with further clues, distinguishing this Sun as "strong Ramme" (l. 93) and "Mild lambe" (l. 94).

Aries, or the Ram, was the alchemical symbol for the first stage in the process, called calcination, which is the breaking down of metals to ash by application of heat.[49] When Donne joined lamb with ram, he created other alchemical variables. Certain remarks by Edward Kelly, Donne's contemporary, may illuminate the allusion. Kelly uses color-coding to distinguish the aggressive red agent from the white during the process of putrefaction: "The red male must be digested in union with his white wife, till both become dry."[50] This indicates that Donne's "strong Ramme" and "Mild lambe" may originate in the alchemical idea of dissolution, which is the phoenix in its death throes.

If Lull's spiritual logic is brought to bear upon the poem, Mary and Christ translate into the attributes of Justice ("strong Ramme"?) and Mercy ("Mild lambe"?), which they share. As we know, Lull himself avoided corporeal images, substituting instead God's attributes. The attributes of Mary he defined in *Libre de sancta Maria,* which he organized into thirty chapters. According to one scholar examining this work, Lull "believed that her [Mary's] mercy put her above all men and allowed her to intercede between God and the sinner."[51] However, he adds, "Llull . . . attributed both justice and mercy to Mary, insisting that the two must coexist."[52] Lull's system of reasoning, which is movement in the mind, would have the "end take precedence over . . . its beginning."[53] Because God is the end and because God is both Justice and Mercy, Lull determined Mary's justice and Mary's mercy to correspond to his.[54]

We also know that later Lullists joined the corporeal with the abstract in order to depict various aspects of alchemical theory. Hence, a Lullist version of the heavenly Phoenix would substitute names, Justice/Mercy, for corporeal images (either that of the Ram/Lamb or that of the Phoenix as two hearts joined). In alchemical theory, Aries (the Ram) is symbolic of the initial fires during calcination, when elements are reduced by fire into a "calx." The Virgin's gentler fire, symbolic of distillation, accomplishes what the initial stage began. The image of Donne's "uprising . . . Sunne" (l. 86) in the "Ascention" sonnet is yet another image of the phoenix, of the marriage between the eagle and the dove. When we consider the connection between the sign of Aries and Easter, Donne's sun rising as Aries makes sense.[55]

Barry Spurr offers an interesting interpretation of the Ram/Lamb imagery in "Resurrection," attributing both names to Christ. He observes that "[w]hen Christ is finally addressed by name, in the sestet of the last sonnet, it is as the 'strong Ramme,' 'mild lambe' and 'bright torch' of devout metaphor, developed from scriptural titles, rather than by any of his biblical names of 'Jesus,' 'Christ,' 'Lord' and 'Master.'"[56] Spurr thinks that these metaphorical names illustrate Donne's balanced position, the careful via media noted by Jeanne Shami, Anthony Milton, and others, cultivated by the Church of England generally as it negotiated the dangerous waters between zealous Arminianism and zealous Calvinism.[57]

I agree that these metaphorical names, "stong Ramme" and "Mild lambe," show Donne's middle way. But this same evidence also shows

Donne using God's attributes as a way to restore to the Protestant religion some of the magic of its pre-Reformation past. For these names, the Ram and Lamb, depict attributes of the Phoenix. Mercy and Justice—*both*—combine as images of Christ and Mary, the "Bright Torch" (l. 95). The Phoenix image implied is attached to the Lullian concept of movement, which starts at the end (e.g., Donne's final sonnet, "Ascention") in order to rediscover the beginning. "*Deigne at my hands this crowne of prayer and praise*" (l. 98) leads back to "*Deigne at my hands this crowne of prayer and praise*" (l. 1). We should not be surprised, therefore, to see, lurking behind the structure of the whole, yet another image, even the Ouroboros that informs: "if it [Mercy] has not All [Justice], All [God *not* combined] is nothing." Only in combination can the Phoenix, God's Glory, live.

"A Litanie"

"A Litanie," to which Shawcross tentatively assigns a date of 1608,[58] employs the alchemical emblem of the flaming sword that pierces the Egg, assigning that role mainly to Christ. As an embellishment of the Egg imagery previously noted (Figure 13), "A Litanie" depicts him as the swordsman who miraculously pentrates the mysterious fifth element in the center. The opening stanzas, however, express each member of the Trinity as an Adept who somehow—in his own way—makes things.

> Father of Heaven, and him, by whom
> It, and us for it, and all else, for us
>   Thou madest, and govern'st ever, come
> And re-create mee, now growne ruinous:
>   My heart is by dejection, clay,
>   And by selfe-murder, red.
> From this red earth, O Father, purge away
> All vicious tinctures, that new fashioned
> I may rise up from death, before I'am dead.
>
> (ll. 1–9)

Donne has provided two backgrounds against which he projects familiar images. One is litanie, a form of spiritual exercise designed for public worship, and the other the *sanctum sanctorum*, a private place, where elements are first destroyed and then restored in some refined form (Figure 2). The familiar signs of formlessness are here: "growne ruinous" and "heart . . . by dejection [reduced to] clay" indicate the initial stages of calcination and dissolution that must precede ablution and coagulation, when the alchemical child is finally reconstituted and, eventually, born.[59]

This time God alone is the maker. The poet speaking as creature, asks the Adept to "re-create mee." The Father's re-making is defined in alchemical terms: "O Father, purge away / All vicious tinctures, that new fashioned / I may rise up from death, before I'am dead." Donne here distinguishes "vicious tinctures" from *tinctura*. "[V]icious tinctures" is attached to "selfe-murder, red" (l. 6), which is a reference to Adamic sin. Hence the speaker's prayer comes in the form of a familiar alchemical formula, which is also a kind of paradox, that is, dissolve "vicious" red with "rebis" red, and then the child will be born.[60] Paracelsus distinguishes the *rebis* as *tinctura* in the form of a bisexual creature. By tinging what is corrupt and incomplete, it removes the harmful parts, transforming what was naught into gold.[61]

The second member of the Trinity, addressed in the second stanza, is the bearer of two *new* things, which have somehow, slyly, "crept in" (l. 11). These are sin and death, "which were never made" (l. 11) before. Donne sustains both backgrounds, both the liturgical and the alchemical, in order to express the idea of making:

> O Sonne of God, who seeing two things,
> Sinne, and death crept in, which were never made,
>   By bearing one, tryed'st with what stings
> The other could thine heritage invade;
>   O be thou nail'd unto my heart,
>   And crucified againe,
> Part not from it, though it from thee would part,
> But let it be by'applying so thy paine,
> Drown'd in thy blood, and in thy passion slaine.
>   (ll. 10–18)

This time Christ is asked to be the Adept, even as the fiery swordbearer piercing the alchemical egg, "O be thou nail'd unto my heart," (l. 14). Some few observations will help us discover Donne's reference.

H. J. Sheppard's discussion of egg symbolism in alchemy includes a reference to Michael Maier's mystical symbol of the swordsman taking aim at the Egg.[62] Because heat is necessary to the opus, the sword illustrating Maier's text, *Atalanta fugiens* (1618), has just come out of the flames. Sheppard explains that the flaming sword "is intended to symbolize the production of the Philosopher's Stone from the Egg as a result of the application of heat (symbolized by the sword)."[63] The swordsman, having himself been tried by fire, has acquired sufficient wisdom and power to penetrate—even the mysterious center of—the Egg, which represents the soul.[64] Maier's theory coheres with Lull's idea that touching the center is a way to comprehend All.

Thus "A Litanie" depicts Christ as that One who is qualified to wield the fiery sword, "nail'd unto" hearts (l. 14), "applying so thy paine" (l. 17). The speaker proves this by listing Christ's qualifications. He has tested the power of death by bearing sin (ll. 11–12). Death could not, however, "with what stings" (l. 12), invade him. So now the Victor can, with his sword, invade death. Hence things "never made" (l. 11)—sin and death—are conquered, and Christ, now the Swordsman, applies fiery nails, "nail'd unto my heart" (l. 14) to the speaker's soul, making him anew. "Drown'd in thy blood, and in thy passion slaine" (l. 18), the human creature is reconstituted. Drawing upon a mystical moment in the Hermetic arts, Donne manages to restore, at least for some of his readers, some of the magic they yearn for but have been denied.

Another background (besides the *sanctum sanctorum*) for his sword imagery is the *Stabat Mater* of medieval iconography, another constant against which the variables can be tested. Here he continued a long pre-Reformation tradition, joining such artists as Masaccio and Piero and such religious theoreticians as Ramon Lull, all of whom were fascinated by the *Stabat Mater* as background for their compositions, whether in pictorial or in devotional form.[65] Lull's pilgrim, Blanquerna, for example, joins the Virgin at the foot of the cross:

> remembering. . . . how that Our Lady loved Him with wondrous love, and that, while men tormented Him, He looked upon her, and she upon Him. . . . How that Our Lady lamented over her Son when she saw Him die; how that she was sore afflicted, as she saw herself divided from Him by death.[66]

By placing Blanquerna, the pilgrim, beside Mary at the foot of the cross, Lull has added a variable to the constant. Donne, in the stanza entitled "The Sonne," accomplishes something like it, not the same, creating his own version of the variable. Depicting the speaker standing at the foot of the cross (a place usually reserved for Mary), he invites his readers to see (or at least identify with) her. The speaker, as Mary, gazes upon Christ, contemplating his torments and afflictions. This devotional act allows the speaker to rediscover union with God.

It should, therefore, be no surprise that alchemical symbolism informs the third stanza of "A Litanie," where the Holy Spirit inflames the speaker's heart, burning into him a new spirit:

> O Holy Ghost, whose temple I
> Am, but of mudde walls, and condensed dust,
> And being sacrilegiously
> Halfe wasted with youths fires, of pride and lust,
> Must with new stormes be weatherbeat;
> Double'in my heart thy flame,
> Which let devout sad teares intend; and let
> (Though this glasse lanthorne, flesh, do suffer maime)
> Fire, Sacrifice, Priest, Altar be the same.
>
> (ll. 19–27)

This early version of the Holy Spirit's role in spiritual regeneration stands in marked contrast to Donne's Heidelberg sermon of 1619. For one thing, there is no mention of grace per se nor of the gentle warmth accompanying it. Rather Donne's emphasis rests with the Spirit's office of baptism by fire. Perhaps we are meant to associate these fires with the Feast of Pentecost, when the Holy Spirit descended on Christ's disciples with a rush of wind and tongues of fire. (Though Donne could have alluded to the ancient tradition of baptizing neophytes at Pentecost, he refrained.)

Here, in "A Litanie," the Holy Spirit remakes man by converting his fires of lust to sacrifice and his fires of pride to tears of repentance. The process, in alchemical terms, is one in which superior fire destroys ordinary fire, allowing sublimation of the seed of gold.[67] This reading is compatible with the codes Donne has employed thus far. Whereas the Father "purge[s] away / All vicious tinctures" and the Son fixes his nails into the speaker's heart, the Holy Spirit's more intense "philosophical fire" acts more quickly, converting a slow process into an immediate effect.

One should not forget that the Holy Spirit is that One in the Trinity who planted the seed of God in Mary's womb. Donne's alchemical depiction of the Holy Spirit's procreative powers is probably as close as he comes to defining the mysteries of the Incarnation and of Mary's birth in the mind of God.

Significantly, "The Trinity," Donne's fourth stanza, depicts all three members of the Godhead joined to become "you distinguish'd undistinct" (l. 34).

> O Blessed glorious Trinity,
> Bones to Philosophy, but milke to faith,
> Which, as wise serpents, diversly
> Most slipperinesse, yet most entanglings hath,
> As you distinguish'd undistinct

> By power, love, knowledge bee,
> Give mee a such selfe different instinct,
> Of these let all mee elemented bee,
> Of power, to love, to know, you'unnumbred three.
>
> (ll. 28–36)

The reference to "Bones to Philosophy" suggests masculine systems of thought, certainly something more rigid than the "milke to faith," which suggests the fluid, hence female, attributes of the Godhead. This dichotomy seems analogous to the "strong Ramme" and "Mild lambe" of *La Corona*. At least it is a hint of Donne's developing thought.

The main point of this stanza is to argue for the sublimation of sexual identities, the Godhead having become so slippery and so entangled that it is "distinguish'd undistinct." The speaker, desiring to join with their "all," asks that he be given different instincts. Since Donne's drive as poet (and later as priest) seems to have been toward identity with his Maker, we should not overlook the speaker's prayer: "As you distinguish'd undistinct / . . . Give mee a such selfe different instinct" (l. 32 and l. 34).

That they are the "unnumbred three" argues for complete entanglement, pure androgyny. These first four stanzas of "A Litanie" almost complete Donne's conceptual image of God, almost but not quite. For lurking behind this image of the Trinity is a fourth Presence very often included in the iconography of medieval and Renaissance times.

Patrick O'Connell's study of "A Litanie" notes the importance of the Virgin in the redemptive process but also in the act of intercession: "the stanza on the Virgin Mary (V) stresses the idea of the dependence of all believers . . . on Mary for their redemption. . . . Since men are dependent on her for redemption, they can likewise consider themselves dependent upon her for prayer."[68] When O'Connell observes the role of Mary in redemption and in intercession, he links Donne's poem with a very long church tradition and specifically with St. Bernard's perception of Mary as Second Eve.

That Donne wants his reader to see Mary as intercessor for all mankind is indicated by his pronoun shift from the "I/me" of the first four stanzas to the "we" of the fifth stanza.[69] However, his emphasis remains on the subject of salvation, specifically on the place or home where salvation occurs. This home is described as the "she-Cherubin," who "made / One claime for innocence."

> For that faire blessed Mother-maid,
> Whose flesh redeem'd us; That she-Cherubin,

> Which unlock'd Paradise, and made
> One claime for innocence, and disseiz'd sinne,
>   Whose wombe was a strange heav'n, for there
>   God cloath'd himselfe, and grew,
> Our zealous thankes wee poure. As her deeds were
> Our helpes, so are her prayers; nor can she sue
> In vaine, who hath such titles unto you.
>
> (ll. 37–45)

The alchemical references are not so overt in this stanza, though *wombe* cooperates with earlier codes to become the *alembic,* wherein "God cloath'd himselfe, and grew." As we know, various alchemical theories appropriated the language of nature in order to define the formation of the alchemical "child" in the alembic or "womb."

Paracelsus, for example, was fascinated by the natural process of birth and studied how this analogue pertained to alchemical regeneration. He began with the forty-week term required, during which time the seed develops according to nature's ordering. The seed of the head, he says, moves to its proper place. Likewise the seed of the arms, and so on. "When everything is in its right place, the matrix rests."[70] During this time the fetus grows. During this time the fetus is subject to "God's grace."[71] However, the mother also plays her part:

> For the child in the mother's womb is exposed to the mother's influence, and is as though entrusted to the hand and will of its mother, as the clay is entrusted to the hand of the potter, who creates and forms out of it what he wants and what he pleases.[72]

If Donne had anything like this in mind when he celebrated Mary in "A Litanie," then he provides his own answer to the question: "How was it that the Virgin 'disseiz'd sinne'?"

Mary, who was innocent of sin, "disseiz'd sinne" when her imagination acted upon the already divine Fetus, thereby making a "strange heav'n" for Christ in her womb (Figure 20). "*Disseise,*" as a legal term, means to put out of actual possession or inheritance, but it can also mean to deliver (from something) or, in Donne's time, to expel. Donne thereby argues that Mary's possession of Christ has dispossessed sin. When she delivered him out of her "strange heav'n," she delivered the entire world from Satan.

Though Helen Gardner warns that Mary "cannot make the further claim of being innocent of original sin," Donne's language is elusive, not limited to this more Protestant interpretation.[73] He says her "flesh redeem'd us." He says she "unlock'd Paradise." He calls her womb "a strange heav'n." As alembic, her womb is the place where "God cloath'd himselfe, and grew." Those who know the alchemical equivalent know that she was a volatile force in that growing. In order to understand the Mary of "A Litanie," we need to understand her *active* role in the making of the Christ child.

The titles Donne indicates in the final line of this stanza on "The Virgin Mary" are left to his readers' memories to conjure. Such titles as "Holy Mother," "Mother of Sorrows," "Blessed Virgin," and "Queen of Heaven" become her credentials as intermediary. (One recalls Bernard's analogy of Mary as "aqueduct" through which the Source flows.) Because the opening lines of the fifth stanza were more concerned with her credentials as Maker, Donne's readers are compelled to consider among her titles her status as "home." She is the place where "God cloath'd himselfe," where his nature was combined with hers through the properties of her blood. Hence her womb, like the alchemist's alembic, proves a perfect heaven wherein God could dwell during his own remaking. Thanks to Donne's more careful analysis of the process elsewhere, we have more than a vague idea of how this occurred.

Letter to Edward Tilman

Donne was ordained in 1615. Between 1618 and 1620 he wrote a letter to Edward Tilman, advising him concerning the priestly office.[74] Edward Tilman was ordained deacon in 1618 and two years later priest of the Church of England. Donne's verse letter, "To Mr. Tilman after he had taken orders," contains his definition of the priest's role: bringing men to heaven, or heaven to men, he says, is not easy. But if we look at earth as our mother, bearing the children that our Father in heaven begets, we shall understand our role as priest.

He begins with the need to be restamped *in substance*, rather than in the normal way, when "new crowned Kings alter the face, / But not the monies substance" (ll. 15–16). Central to the priest's vocation is the matter of being restamped with Christ ("so hath grace / Chang'd onely Gods old Image by Creation, / To Christs new stampe, at this thy Coronation," ll. 16–18). Better than kings, who cannot "keepe heavens doore" (l. 39) is the priest, who (like Mary) can "open life" (l. 39). "*Maries* prerogative was to beare Christ" (l. 41). Following her example, priests convey Christ from their pulpits. The priest, therefore, is called to be both mother and father, "a blest Hermaphrodite" (l. 54). His commission is to knit these two identities. As father, he begets spiritual children; and as mother, he bears them. If he is able to accomplish this pure union, then he will have become a maker of spiritual children, whom he will continue to nourish throughout their earthly lives.[75]

Bernard's precepts seem to be the background Donne has chosen for his letter to Edward Tilman. When separated from his brothers at Clairvaux, Bernard had written, "My children are snatched from my breast before it is time. Those whom I have 'begotten' in the Gospel . . . I am not allowed to rear."[76] But Donne has written this letter against another page as well. We know this when he writes, "And so the heavens which beget all things here, / And the'earth our mother, which these things doth beare, / Both these in thee, are in thy Calling knit" (ll. 51–53).

Theoretical alchemists thought that things below reflect things above; moreover, that things below are imbued with the spirits of the divine. Those who are able, by grace, to discover these secrets are able to transform the world. Whatever the particular theory, all adepts considered the work of the hermaphrodite central to the process of transmutation, for it represents that middle nature, that link between the earthly and the divine. This bisexual agent, Paracelsus says, transmutes base metal, "removing its harmful parts, its crudity, its incompleteness . . . transform[ing] everything into a pure, noble, and indestructible being."[77] When Donne defined Edward Tilman's priestly office as that of "blest Hermaphrodite," he was combining Bernard's views with alchemical theory in order to express his own evolving theological alchemy. It can be no accident that this was also his vision of the Christian poet.

The *hermaphrodite*, as image, is polysemic, reminding those readers who encounter it to think of something like something else but not quite the same. Certainly, Donne intended his adept readers to interpret the image vertically, as a representative of higher things. His earlier reference to Mary ("*Maries* prerogative was to beare Christ," l. 41), especially as he combines her role in Christ's making with the priestly role that Edward Tilman has assumed, indicates that she is somehow attached to this hermaphrodite—if nothing else, as the pelican vessel (Figure 16) to which alchemical theorists attributed so much power. Working backward, as the spiritual logic of Lull would have us do, we discover the "true reason" for this attachment. Donne had noted earlier that "Christs new stampe" (l. 18) on "Gods old Image by Creation" (l. 17) has transmuted "the monies substance" (l. 15), even "by grace" (l. 15), reconstituting the old as something new and eternal. No adept reader could ever miss the point.

Conclusion: *Schekhina*

OUT OF THE RELIGIOUS CONTROVERSY OF EARLY MODERN ENGLAND arose the burning question: What shall we do with residual Catholicism? This study has shown how Donne answered the question, writing England's pre-Reformation culture into his sermons and poems. Generally, Anthony Milton tells us, the various art forms of the Jacobean and Caroline periods—music, architecture, painting, and so on—expressed ideas both Roman Catholic and Protestant.[1] People still "read" the Catholic iconography of stained glass windows left intact. They also enjoyed the music of Dowland and Byrd, neither of whom worried too much about adhering to Protestant forms. Although magic itself had been banished from the land, Donne discovered a way to restore it, at least for some of his readers, through alchemical discourse. Like a good husbandman, he scattered seeds of gold throughout his texts, hoping the ground was good, letting others reap the harvest.

Alison Shell, addressing the issue of residual Catholicism, remarks the special place reserved for poetry over prose. "A poem," she says, "may transcribe doctrine, reflect doctrine or reflect upon doctrine."[2] Whereas writers of prose are compelled to construct "definitive theological argument,"[3] poets enjoy greater freedom of expression. Milton concurs, remarking that the poetry of early modern England includes a "degree of cross-confessionalism."[4] Poets, musicians, and painters enjoyed freedom of expression partly because Rome was still considered "a Church of Christ. . . . Rome was *in a sense* a Church."[5] His investigation indicates a somewhat uneasy coexistence of potentially contradictory cultures, that is, Roman Catholic and Protestant, a cultural phenomenon resulting from the Protestant humanist drive to accommodate different faiths. Somewhat connected, perhaps, was the concomitant, ecumenical drive of certain intellectuals toward language reform.

THE LANGUAGE OF PARADISE

The seventeenth-century effort to compile an international sign language could be viewed as a response to the Protestant print culture.

We have studied how certain thinkers—Francis Bacon, Elias Ashmole, John Wilkins, Sir Robert Cotton, and Jan Amos Comenius—were inspired to construct "a system whereby scholars throughout the world could read their own tongue from a single set of characters."[6] We know that these "tinkerers" in language contrived combinatory systems based upon one of two models, the numbers and names of the cabala and the corporeal images of Chinese cryptography. Naturally, Donne, who enjoyed the friendship, and probably the library, of Sir Robert Cotton, was aware of the project.

David S. Katz observes that Cotton corresponded with numerous linguists interested in new theories of language reform.[7] Among these was Francis Bacon. Bacon preferred the Chinese model of "Characters Real, which express neither letters nor words in gross, but Things or Notions."[8] That was because he thought that *all* people could understand this system of writing. Naturally, Donne was encouraged to combine this system of sign language with the cabalistic mnemotechnics he had already acquired from Pico and Lull.

We have seen evidence that he was intrigued by shapes. He used, for example, the alchemical (or Gnostic) Ouroboros as the organizing principle in "The Annuntiation and Passion" and in *La Corona*. He had already learned from models like Giovanni Pantheo, whose *Theoria Transmvtationis Metallicae cum Voarchadúmia* (1550) combined certain linguistic features of the cabala and alchemy, the value of *gematria* and *notarikon*, or the use of mystical numbers, letters, and names.[9] Like Pantheo, Donne uses alchemical discourse and cabalistic methodologies to express the middle ground between fact and faith. And, like the seventeenth-century linguists with whom he was aligned, he also hoped that these combinations would restore the magic to religion.[10]

According to Katz, it was the "magical element which was important for early modern Englishmen, especially the language planners and linguistic theorists."[11] Donne's own peculiar method of restoring this "magical element" is best illustrated by his sonnet beginning "Show me deare Christ, thy spouse." That is why this chapter is devoted mainly to it. I begin with a brief review of how cabalistic methodology worked.

Background for Donne's Sonnet on the Church

According to Katz, "the universal language planners hoped to return to linguistic innocence, and hoped that the Jewish kabbalists could show them the way."[12] One Hebrew specialist explains cabalistic investigative practice as a combinatory system in which the meaning derived exceeds the sum of the parts:

> From the very beginning of Kabbalistic doctrine these two manners of speaking [letters and names] appear side by side. The secret world of the godhead is a world of language, a world of divine names that unfold in accordance with a law of their own. The elements of the divine language appear as the letters of the Holy Scriptures. . . .Each one of them represents a concentration of energy and expresses a wealth of meaning which cannot be translated, or not fully at least, into human language.[13]

Christian cabalists like Pantheo thought that studying letters and names "side by side" (Figure 6) would lead to the secrets of God.[14] Linguists who tried to follow such models as his eventually became frustrated. "At some point," Katz writes, "the projectors came to see that what they were really working on was a sort of shorthand which almost created more problems than it solved."[15] The project was abandoned. By this time, however, Donne had already used this enterprise to great advantage.

His interest in cabalistic investigative methodology is very great indeed. He says so when he calls the cabalists "the Anatomists of words . . . [who] have a Theologicall Alchimy to draw sovereign tinctures and spirits from plain and grosse literall matter, [who] observe in every variety some great mystick signification."[16] When he praised "the Anatomists of words," he aligned himself with Christian cabalists (like Pico, Ficino, Pantheo, and, especially, Reuchlin) and against radical Calvinists, who denied the Church her magic.[17] But his interest in Lull's system of divine names is also suggested. "Names," he says, "are to instruct us, and express natures and essences. This *Adam* was able to do."[18] Lull, of course, believed that God's attributes, for which he devised nine names, expressed his very nature. Moreover, the purpose of Lull's combinatory system of names was medicinal. He wanted "to heal the world's cultural wounds, [and] . . . to make the world a place marked by religious and cultural unity."[19] Donne's sonnet reflects the influence of Lull's healing art.

Lull's aim, as Yates has noted, was to train an army of missionaries to convert both Jews and Muslims.[20] His version of Utopia was a world where diversity is celebrated, where tolerance prevails.[21] Donne's idea of the universal church may have been influenced by Lull's "burning desire to change the world"[22] as well as by More's dream of a utopia where men tolerated each other's different views. As a means to this end, Lull studied the cabala. (He seems not to have known Hebrew.)[23] He also studied Sufi mysticism, which "attaches great importance to meditating on the Names of God."[24] According to Mark D. Johnston, this is how "the Islamic *hadras* (Divine Attributes)" was written into his *Principia*.[25] Lull designed his *ars combinatoria* to correspond "with various Christian, Jewish and Islamic precedents,"[26] expecting it to express a "catholique" faith.

Lull thought that a fragmented world could be healed by reading all the variables in the Divine Book, reattaching them to the One. That is why his art includes *all*. Donne's claim that "every variety" of Divine Spirit has "mystick signification"[27] and his admonition that man should draw into himself "All his faith can swallow, 'or reason chaw"[28] is equally optimistic and perhaps equally naive. Because "every" and "all" contain elements of the divine, Donne wants to investigate everything.

This is his answer to Calvin's doctrine of total depravity, which asserted "the whole" to be thoroughly corrupt, "the whole man is overwhelmed . . . so that no part is immune from sin."[29] Perhaps it is significant that Calvin emphasizes Adam as the origin of sin: "Adam, by sinning, . . . plunged our nature into like destruction. . . . Adam so corrupted himself that infection spread from him to all his descendants. . . . when Adam was despoiled, human nature was left naked and destitute."[30] The "doctrine of total depravity" is one of five tenets embraced by radical Calvinists which, still today, distinguish them from Arminians, who believe, like Luther, that "God is present in all creatures."[31]

A commonly used acronym for Calvin's five tenets is TULIP, signifying the doctrines of total depravity, unconditional election, limited atonement, irresistible grace, and perseverance of the saints. These five doctrines are reciprocal, meaning that it is impossible to adhere to one, for example, perseverance, and not to the others. They all comprise a perfect Dutch tulip. Total depravity, based upon Adam's sin, is the bulb, or to use Calvin's phrase, the "rotten root,"[32] out of which all the others grow. In other words, when Calvin looked at the World Egg (Figure 13), he thought it to be rotten.

Reciprocity is also the basis of Lull's spiritual logic, except the "seed" of his system is belief in man's essential goodness. It is significant, therefore, that Lull attributed much of this good nature to Second Eve: "And that this Lord is within thee, O Queen, makes thee to be in great virtue and truth, who after thy Son art pre-eminent in Virtue, Truth and Glory over all other creatures."[33] All aspects of creation, thought Lull, are essentially good. Because of the coessentiality of God's attributes—Truth, Virtue, Wisdom, and so on—all of creation, including man, reflects all of him.[34] When Lull looked at the World Egg, he thought it to be the wholesome product of Second Eve (Figures 12 and 14).

CONCLUSION: *SCHEKHINA*

The problem with mankind, from Lull's point of view, is that their memories, not they, are bad. Because they have forgotten many of God's Attributes, that is, his Names, their religions are mere fragments of the original faith. Remembering these will restore mankind to Unity, which both the Egg and the Circle signify. Possibly Donne's Spanish motto, remarked by Joseph Hall, is a page from Lull's book.

In his own hand, Hall says, Donne wrote in Spanish, "Blessed be God that he is God, divinely like himself."[35] Circle imagery, we know, captured Donne's imagination, and we see it here in his Spanish motto. Like the inscriptions for the Ouroboros,—"One is the Serpent" and "One is All and through it is All"—the "logic" of Donne's motto is circular. His Spanish motto testifies that God's very name bears all his attributes. Hence One contains All.

We have evidence that Donne sometimes thinks in such ways. The sermons provide one example: "Fixe upon God any where and you shall find him a Circle."[36] The devotions provide another: "If I depart from thee, my centre, all is imperfect. This proceeding to action, therefore, is a returning to thee."[37] *The Second Anniversary* provides one more:

> Then, soule, to thy first pitch worke vp againe;
> Know that all lines which circles doe containe,
> For once that they the center touch, do touch
> Twice the circumference; and be thou such.
> . . . Onely who haue enjoyd
> The sight of God, in fulnesse, can thinke it;
> For it is both the object, and the wit.
>
> (ll. 435–38; 440–42)

Lull's *Principia*, which Donne owned, argues that the Divine Dignities are not only reciprocal but equal.[38] As symbol, the circle aptly depicts the kind of harmony this reciprocity, God's "fulnesse," suggests. Hence, Lull's spiritual "logic," itself circular, begins by investigating the attributes of God as he is perceived by "the three great religions."[39] Jews, Muslims, and Christians—all understand that the circle signifies the heavens.[40] Lull's allegory, *Arbor scientiae*, depicts the Circle as "the figure most like to God, with no beginning or end," defended by Aries, the Ram.[41] He was convinced that Jews, Muslims, and Christians—all three—would see their own God in this circle.

Others have noted the ecumenical spirit in Donne.[42] Perhaps he was caught up in the contagion spread by the international sign language project. More likely a combination of influences—Lull, the Christian cabalists, Thomas More, and so on—worked upon him. Among these would be Sir Robert Cotton, Francis Bacon, Elias Ashmole, and other seventeenth-century linguists trying to recover the language of paradise, some determining it to be Hebrew.[43] So when Donne spoke of the cabalists as "the Anatomists of words," he was referring not only to their quest for the perfect language, but also to *his* quest for true religion: "Where is true religion to be found?" This question is the subject of his sonnet on "the true Church,"[44] which has troubled so many for so long.

"Show me deare Christ, thy spouse"

This sonnet is found only in the Westmoreland MS, now in the Berg Collection at the New York Public Library.[45] Like "The Annuntiation and Passion," its subject is Christ's true spouse, and it contains references to the Ouroboros and the phoenix. It begins, "Show me deare Christ, thy spouse, so bright and cleare." John Carey thinks that it may have been written around 1620, "following the defeat . . . of the Protestants (under James I's son-in-law the Elector Palatine) by the Catholics."[46] "This disaster," he says, "prompts Donne to ask God to reveal the True Church."[47] Carey is one among many who use historical context as a way to identify Donne's "bright and cleare" spouse.

During this period, we know, James I was considering a Spanish match for Prince Charles. When Frederick, the Elector Palatine, was defeated by the Roman Catholic Ferdinand, people already nervous about the proposed marriage became more deeply upset. Some readers see Donne's poem as his response to this historical moment. Some think that the poem reflects his desire "for the reunion of Christendom."[48] If this is so, then Donne was not alone. In fact, Peter Lake observes, some divines were turning their attention away from the visible Church, which they considered "a this-worldly institution," and toward "the invisible church, conceived as a spiritual body whose existence transcended the confines of everyday human society and history."[49] This is the thesis of Donne's poem. If we study the vertical as well as the horizontal relationships among his references, we discover a spiritual logic that transcends any earthly institution.

Donne's *Essays in Divinity* argue that the invisible Church has one (nameless) name. The cabalists, Donne says, study "the variation of names in the Scripture" in order to identify "one Name."[50] *Esau, Seir,* and *Edom,* for example, are all one name. ("Show me . . . thy spouse" illustrates this phenomenon as it surveys "the variation of names" of the Church, none of which is the *one.*) The Church, Donne says, is a body marked by "convulsions, distraction, rents, schisms, and wounds, by the severe and unrectified Zeal of many."[51] These rents and wounds will heal, he says, when we rediscover the origin of our faith. We begin by studying names. Let "this variety of Names," he says, teach us that "Salvation is in this unity and no where else."[52] Like Lull, Donne states his belief that studying the attributes of God is a way to bring the followers of "strange doctrines" into Christ's fold.

The sonnet opens with a picture of the Church in fragments. Instead of Christ's "spouse," the speaker sees only her rags and tags here and there:

> Show me deare Christ, thy spouse, so bright and cleare.
> What, is it she, which on the other shore
> Goes richly painted? or which rob'd and tore
> Laments and mournes in Germany and here?
> Sleepes she a thousand, then peepes up one yeare?
> Is she selfe truth, and errs? now new, now'outwore?
>
> (ll. 1–6)

As in "Satyre III," some of the allusions are fairly easy to understand. Gaudy Roman Catholicism is on the Continent, and drab Calvinism is both here and there. Some allusions are more complicated. Erring "selfe truth," especially during the later Caroline era, would come to characterize various factions detached from the Anglican Church. These would include the Independents and Dissenters—the Presbyterians, Baptists, and Quakers—all of whom, Nicholas Tyacke says, eventually gained the right to worship freely under the Anglican system.[53] Of course, some of Donne's readers will remember that Henry VIII, erring in "selfe truth," severed England (along with More's head) from Rome. As individual exegetes, his readers must interpret these variables, deciding for themselves what hill Christ's "spouse" might occupy.

> Doth she, 'and did she, and shall she evermore
> On one, on seaven, or on no hill appear?
> Dwells she with us, or like adventuring knights
> First travaile we to seeke and then make love?
>
> (ll. 7–10)

Helen Gardner, some decades ago, identified these three hills as specific religions: "The 'one hill' is Mount Moriah, where Solomon built the Temple. . . . The Church on seven hills is the Roman Church, and the Church on no hill is the Genevan."[54] Lukas Erne thinks that her interpretation is too restrictive.[55] Of course, specifying the variables of any given text necessarily restricts it. Nevertheless, that is what readers *do*.

Gardner identifies the spouse of the opening lines as "the desolate Virgin of Zion, once beloved, now, for her sins, abandoned by her Lord and left to be the prey of her enemies."[56] This is a useful insight not only because it helps us see the poem as Donne's response to the Protestant defeat in 1620 but also because it begins to articulate the subject of his poem. Mount Moriah, Gardner says, best represents "the Church Universal, at present hidden from our sight by the divisions which obscure her unity in her Lord."[57] Hence, it represents the Jerusalem of Lamentations:

> I would suggest that Donne has seen a parallel between the captivity of Israel and the total collapse of the Protestants after the defeat of the Elector in the battle of the White Mountain, outside Prague, on 29 October 1620.[58]

Gardner's insight that "the Church Universal" is Donne's theme is supported by his references to Israel. But it is also supported by the fact that he gives no names to the hills.

Alison Shell defines Gardner's interpretations as those of an "Anglican apologist" seeking to prove "that the intellect and poetical ability of Donne and Herbert helped validate Anglicanism."[59] I rather think that Gardner's reading of Donne's poem comes closer than most to discovering something other than the Anglican via media. Though she notes the end, the Church Universal, not the means, Donne's alchemical codes and Lullian logic, she does at least suspect the vertical relationships that these references imply.

Alchemy, we know, mediates between fact and faith. It begins with natural facts but then moves to something higher. Donne gives his readers geographical *and* alchemical references so that they are invited to move beyond investigating the natural world (trying to decide whether the "hills" referred to are those of Rome, Geneva, Mount Moriah, etc.) in order to investigate the relationship between these natural phenomena and the divine principle. Unless modern readers learn how Renaissance Lullists read Donne's poem, they will always be condemned, it would seem, to ask forever the same questions in order to come up with the same questions.

One sign that Donne means us to look up, above the rather serpentine movements of religious institutions on earth, is the intrusion of the phoenix image in the fifth line: "Sleepes she a thousand, then peepes up one yeare?" Others, who study the arithmology of Donne's poems, may provide useful insights here. Kate Gartner Frost, for example, observes the importance of "androgynous five."[60] Obviously, we are not meant to infer that every "fifth line" in Donne will contain an androgynous figure.[61] It is intriguing, though, that this particular line 5, often ignored by readers of the poem, suggests such a figure in the "sleeping" and the "waking" of Christ's Spouse.[62]

The phoenix was thought to be an Arabian bird, hence a phenomenon from Eastern culture. According to legend, it "slept" for many years, no less than five hundred but often longer.[63] In Donne's sonnet it sleeps a thousand years. Though modern readers may not remark this sign, many of Donne's contemporaries, used to seeing the Phoenix as Christ and Mary—two hearts joined (Figure 9)— connected "this," the allusion to sleeping and waking (in the fifth line) with "that," the allusion to Christ and His Spouse (in the first line). Anyone who remembered Hawkins's poem remembered "a Phoenix with a twin-like hart. / These are the harts of Jesus and his Mother / So linkt in one, that one without the other / Is not entire."[64] Those who matched "this" with "that" necessarily investigated the vertical relationship between Christ's spouse "so bright and cleare" and "the Phoenix Riddle in Heaven."

These adept readers also understood certain variables attached to it. As a symbol of renewal and resurrection, the phoenix signifies the Unity of all matter. As representative of the rubedo, it is red. Those who recognize the phoenix in Donne's poem will compare its red with the "richly painted" alternative offered in the third line. Some will recognize the androgynous figure, her sex no longer significant because she/it has achieved power. All will construct sentences, for example, "The phoenix is . . ." "The spouse seems . . . ," that articulate the possible vertical relationships between them. Because the phoenix dies and is resurrected in fire, it is "so bright," but that it is *not* "cleare"—that is the problem.

Once the alchemical background is recognized, new meanings become available. The opening lines describing the fragments of the Church, only pieces here and there, may now be seen as a depiction of calcined matter, the first stage of the opus, when matter is reduced to an ashy calx. Adept readers will understand this otherwise bleak picture as one that is full of hope. They know that calcination leads to dissolution, which leads, eventually, to the resurrection of unified matter.

Perhaps this is a good time to review certain observations from the introduction. Sir Joshua Reynolds, it may be remembered, employed classical models in order to transfer vertically the human element into the divine.[65] Manipulating the background allowed him to superimpose divinity upon man. "Show me deare Christ" is an example of this same phenomenon, except that Donne's subject is a human institution, not a man.

As one of his backgrounds—an alternative to those otherwise problematic hills—he has provided a familiar scene from the Bible, a place where "no hill" is. The variable he offers is Moses's prayer: "And he said, I beseech thee, shew me thy glory" (Exodus 33: 18). Since Donne's prayer, "Show me deare Christ, thy spouse, so bright and cleare," alludes to Moses's prayer, "shew me thy glory," we should study the biblical reference.

Donne's prayer is never answered, but Moses's is. In fact God's instructions to Moses provide the frame for Donne's poem:

> Behold, there is a place by me, and thou
> shalt stand upon a rock: And it shall
> come to pass, while my glory passeth by,
> that I will put thee in a clift of the
> rock, and will cover thee with my hand
> while I pass by: And I will take away
> mine hand, and thou shalt see my back
> parts: but my face shall not be seen.
> (Exodus 33: 21–23)

Like Moses, Donne's speaker has asked to see God. God's answer to Moses is that he shall never see his face, "Thou canst not see my face: for there shall no man see me, and live" (Exodus 33:20). Donne knew, of course, that there was a precedent for this among the Christian cabalists, who attached Mary's name to God's *Schekhina,* or Wisdom that cannot be seen.[66] But *Schekhina* also means "Jehovah dwells."[67] So *Schekhina* in Donne's poem may be both a *place* where God dwells and an *attribute,* which cannot be seen.

The matter is complicated by Lull's coessentiality of Divine Attributes, which makes Wisdom concomitant with Mercy, Justice, Glory, and so on. Donne's background draws upon all of these, that is, the cabalistic references, Lull's spiritual logic, and the biblical story where Moses, because "no hill appear," stands upon a rock. His readers, who cannot see God's face and live, can anticipate a similar experience. Significantly, Donne gives them a glimpse of God, not the "back parts" but the breasts.

How do we know this? In the *Essays,* Donne uses breasts as metonymic reference for unity among the Church's various factions. The Christian cabalists, he says, dare not omit anything just because it "be not . . . at unity with us, nor it self."[68] In the end, every religion "sucks her vegetation from one and the same ground."[69] Hence Donne begins a series of metonymic signs, all of which imply the female principle as the source of God's power. Such is the reference in the sestet of his sonnet, which dwells on the female body:

> Dwells she with us, or like adventuring knights
> First travaile we to seeke and then make love?

> Betray kind husband thy spouse to our sights,
> And let myne amorous soule court thy mild Dove,
> Who is most trew, and pleasing to thee, then
> When she'is embrac'd and open to most men.
>
> (ll. 9–14)

The image, as many readers see it, is troublesome. Saurat explains such responses as typical among "the uninitiated," who are scandalized by "the sexual relations between God and the *Schekhina*."[70] Most of Donne's readers are concerned with the way these lines offer, or do not offer, resolution.

Erne, for example, says that "the sonnet's ending is disturbing on several counts."[71] For one thing, "embrac'd," even when revised to mean some sort of chastity, resolves as "multiple adultery."[72] In this context, he says, the word "betray" in the eleventh line "records a kind of apostasy."[73] David Chanoff interprets the final lines in a similar way, observing that they are "a product of Donne's ongoing attempt to rationalize his membership in the Anglican Communion."[74] Helen Gardner refrains from explication, offering instead a précis: "Lord, do not thus hide thy Bride from our sight, but let me woo the gentle spouse of thy marriage song, who is most faithful to thy will and most pleasing to thee, when the greatest number of men seek and receive her embraces."[75] Ultimately, she understands these lines in quasi-human terms.[76] All of these readings, though useful up to a point, naturally proceed from reluctance to look upon Donne's naked, hence "bright," Spouse.

John T. Shawcross, however, defines "betray" as "reveal."[77] This insight is worth further investigation. There is evidence that this meaning was available to Donne, even in its refined form, "to reveal, disclose . . . to exhibit, show signs of (a thing which there is no attempt to keep secret)."[78] To initiates of the *Zohar*, Donne's sonnet reveals the very sensuality that most refuse to see, even "the desire of the One on high . . . aroused in love for the *Schekhina*, like to the desire of the male for the female."[79] But Donne's *ars combinatoria* allows other options.

Adept readers want to *see* Christ's Spouse in some recognizable form. When and if they see the phoenix ("amorous soule" combined with "mild Dove"), they are not troubled, for this image coheres with the familiar riddle introduced earlier in the poem (l. 1 and l. 5). The word "embrac'd," which troubles so many readers, is actually a hinge upon which multiple meanings move. Its literal sense could be "to clasp in the arms as a sign of fondness," but its figurative senses range far: "to worship (a deity)," "to adopt (a course of action)," "to take (a road or course in travelling)," or "to adopt (a doctrine, opinions, religion)."[80] No one need be bothered by these figurative connotations. As in the *Essays*, the image of the last line, "When she is embrac'd and open to most men," refers, in a metonymic sense, to the breasts of Christ's Church.

Donne, in the *Essays*, describes England as his own "Pasture," where he sucks "milk from the brests of this [Anglican] Church."[81] But he also states his belief that "disunited" parts continue to belong to the body, not as Christ's Sister perhaps, nevertheless as his "little sister." Here he quotes Solomon: "We have a little sister, and she hath no brests."[82] We cannot, he warns, "tempestuously and ruinously demolish and annull her; but rather cherish and foment her vitall and wholsome parts."[83] After all, she will grow up. Whether Hebrew or Muslim, her breasts will develop, and many will, eventually, be nourished by her. This is Donne's way of arguing the ethic of mutual interdependence of parts. His sonnet is, among other things, an argument against cultural xenophobia. All parts of the body—including Catholics, Muslims, and Jews—are necessary for the health of the whole.

As metonymic reference, Albert H. Tricomi reminds us, breasts can signify power, both political and spiritual. His discussion of the Duchess of Malfi as pelican mother, nourishing even her enemies, illustrates how power can be invested in the female body.[84] Those who destroy her are compelled to feed elsewhere or die. Donne uses breast imagery in a similar way. The breasts of Christ's spouse, especially in an alchemical sense, signify power (Figure 16).

Lullist readers would naturally translate this metonymic reference, "embrac'd and open," into God's Attributes, including Power but also Mercy and Justice. All three express One. To the Lullist, Christ, who is Mercy *and* Justice, is also Mary.[85] Hence Tricomi's argument reiterates the Lullist theory that Christ's breasts and the breasts of Christ's spouse are the same coessential and reciprocal Mercy, Beauty, and Power. Though ages apart, they argue a similar thing.

Trinity

As mentioned above, Lull thought that the Circle is "most like to God."[86] The triangle, however, was also important in his art. His allegory, *Arbor scientiae*, depicts Triangle as a reflection of "the soul of man and . . . God the Trinity."[87] This is compatible with Luther's belief that "all creatures are a declaration and a signification of the Holy Trinity."[88] Most readers will look for signs of the Trinity in devotional verse. M. Thomas Hester, for example, when he studies "Satyre III," looks for the three faculties of the rational soul, that is, memory, understanding, and will.[89] Like so many others, he works from scholastic formulations of the Trinitarian structure in man, the microcosm. Here I shall work from another point of view, nevertheless applying this same principle to Donne's poem.

Yates explains the Trinitarian structure of Lull's art. "As *intellectus*, it was an art of knowing or finding out truth; as *voluntas* it was an art of training the will towards loving truth; as *memoria*, it was an art of memory for remembering truth."[90] Lull knew that if he hoped to persuade Jews and Muslims, he had to establish common ground. As we know, he began by formulating the Divine Dignities to cohere with their own "spiritual logic." (Johnston notes the "remarkable affinities" between Lull's art and the theories of his Muslim contemporary, Ibn Sab'in.)[91] But Lull recognized that common concepts of the Trinity were another means of persuasion.[92] Peter Lombard (ca. 1100–ca.1160) had already based his "famous proof of the Trinity" upon the cabala.[93] Later Christian cabalists used his argument, "that the second word of the Hebrew version of Genesis is an acronym for Father, Son, and Holy Spirit,"[94] to restore the magic to religion. In spite of the fact that Calvin had rejected Lombard's cabalistic proof, certain seventeenth-century linguists repeated it as a rationale for restoring the "magic" to language.

Lull's *ars combinatoria* is a movement between horizontally and vertically arranged things. The nine *Principia* reside on a horizontal plane above the other levels of Creation (the Angels, the Elements, and so on), all of which reflect the same Dignities. This idea seems to have developed alongside the medieval chain of being. However, it is more scientific and works by the principle of motion. Also it functions according to Trinitarian principles. In order to do Lull's art, Mark D. Johnston observes, one must exercise "the three faculties of the human mind—the Intellect, Will, and Memory—whose primary tasks are, respectively, to know, to love, and to recall God."[95] Because Donne's sonnet, "Show me deare Christ," is devotional reenactment, we should consider how these three faculties are implemented by it.

BACK TO THE POEM

Memory, or rather loss of it, informs the whole. The speaker, who has lost sight of Christ's Spouse, sues for mercy, asking that his vision be corrected. Everywhere he looks, he sees fragments, shards, and shreds of what once might have been something like Christ's Spouse. In Lullian terms, Christ represents the attribute of Mercy. He is the one asked to perform corrective surgery, to restore the speaker's vision or memory. Christ, not his Spouse, plays the role of intercessor. Justice, the coessential of Mercy, is the Spouse. But she refuses to pacify the human creature, hence exercising her right to impose a judgment against him. She is also Power because she is what all men *need*. Finally, she is Glory because she is so bright and clear.

So the subject of the poem is loss of memory, but it is also understanding, which in Lull's art means finding the *Principia* reflected on some lower plane. The speaker's task is to study the fragments in order to determine where Christ's Spouse might reside. He reasons inductively, investigating categories and places, all of which lead him to the conclusion that she *seems* not to be "this," *seems* not to be "that," and *seems* not to reside "here" or "there." But the poem is also about love, about *voluntas*, about the speaker's need to love Christ's Spouse and Christ's need to have his Spouse loved by others: "Who is most trew, and pleasing to thee, then / When she'is embrac'd and open to most men."

We begin to unravel these lines with the observation that the marriage between Christ and his Spouse resides on a higher plane. Donne himself helps us see this when he comments upon human marriages: "Marriage is but a continuall fornication, sealed with an oath: And marriage was not instituted to prostitute the chastity of the woman to one man, but to preserve her chastity from the tentations of more men."[96] Clearly the subject of Donne's poem is not this. Rather, "Betray kind husband" carries the sense of disclosure.

Wishing to join the Heavenly Phoenix, Donne's speaker asks "let myne amorous soule court thy mild Dove." *Voluntas* or love drives toward the same kind of union we have observed in *La Corona*, where the "strong Ramme" and "Mild lambe" signify the resurrected Philosopher's Stone. This kind of Union is also the subject of Donne's sonnet on the Church.

Mary Carruthers has commented on how medieval memories worked: "It is my contention that medieval culture was fundamentally memorial, to the same profound degree that modern culture in the West is documentary."[97] As mentioned above, modern interpretations of "Show me deare Christ" tend to be just that, documentary. Fortunately, and paradoxically, modern film theorists have managed to rescue some of the older concepts of memory for us. As conceptual metaphor, montage helps us understand the mnemotechnics of Lull and Donne. Because we understand, somewhat, how to read films, we begin to understand how to read Renaissance texts.

When we recognize images or names or shapes projected against different backgrounds, we are compelled to make meaning. The process is dynamic. Sometimes an image clashes with the background, sometimes it coheres. With memory actively engaged, we are in a position to decide whether "this is like that" or "this *seems* like that" or "this is not the same." Not all Renaissance texts are as fluid as Donne's, but *when* they are, knowing the language of film helps us appreciate the Lullian art they employ. It helps us resist the temptation to pin, with documentation, their butterflies, created to move, on a static wall.

SCHEKHINA

One image some of Donne's readers may have seen in "Show me deare Christ" is an elaborate emblem used to illustrate Robert Fludd's *Utriusque Cosmi Historia* (1617). The editors of *The Riverside Shakespeare* have included it (plate 17, vol. 1) as a depiction of the chain of being, familiar to every student of English Renaissance literature. E. M. W. Tillyard has credited Raymond of Sebond as the original source of the concept this emblem illustrates. Sebond, a famous Lullist of the fifteenth century, was among the many Spanish authors Donne often cited.[98] Sebond's *Natural Theology* takes the form of a dialogue between teacher and pupil and was translated by Montaigne, eventually becoming, Tillyard says, "the common property of western Europe in the sixteenth century."[99]

As a Lullist, it is no accident that Sebond's account of the great chain of being emulates Lull's own *Liber de ascensu et descensu intellectus*. Like Lull, Sebond used the ladder to refer to the various levels of creation. Lull's main interest in the schema was to show how the intellect apprehended truth. Yates explains "The Ladder of Ascent and Descent" as mental activity based upon the Divine Names written into the art:

> [W]e see Intellectus, holding one of the figures of the Art, ascending the scale of creation, the various steps of which are illustrated with, for example, a tree on the plant step, a lion on the brute step, a man on the step *Homo,* stars on the step *coelum,* an angel on the angel step, and on reaching the summit with *Deus,* the Intellect enters the House of Wisdom.[100]

The detail of the female figure in Fludd's illustration shows the chain of being, attached to her wrist, making her a link between man and the Name of God. In Sebond's Lullist theory, it is this figure that connects Intellectus with Wisdom. This same female appears in

Figure 21: Detail of female figure from Robert Fludd, *Utriusque Cosmi Historia* (1617). Glasgow University Library, Department of Special Collections.

"Show me deare Christ" as one who dwells in the House of Wisdom. As mental traveler, the speaker attempts to discover *where*.

Christ's Spouse in Donne's sonnet is Wisdom and Glory, even God's *Schekhina* glory. Later she will become the Wisdom that assists Creation in Milton's *Paradise Lost*. Both poets had precedents for her in rabbinical treatments of the subject of *Schekhina*. Harris F. Fletcher, for example, observes that Milton had for models various rabbinical personifications of Wisdom that made "her at once an idea in the mind of God, and a sort of separate aspect of his Spirit emanating from God's will to create."[101] Giovanni Pantheo, the priest turned cabalist-alchemist, wrote her, as the Tetragrammaton, into his system of thought.[102] Working from such precedents, both Milton and Donne were able to conceive a sexually ambivalent God.[103] *The Essays in Divinity*, one subject of which is Christ's Spouse, illustrate this.

Christ's Spouse in the Essays

Donne's discussion of Creation falls into three parts. Part 1 considers things *before* Creation. Part 2 considers the Hebrew names of God. Part 3 announces God's "most glorious worke . . . the *Creation*."[104] At this point Donne introduces the female principle:

> [H]e that hath refin'd all the old Definitions, hath put this ingredient *Creabile*, (which cannot be absolutely *nothing*) into his Definition of Creation: And that *Nothing* which was, we cannot desire; for mans will is not larger then Gods power; and . . . Nothing was not a pre-existent matter, nor mother of this All, but onely a limitation when any thing began to be.[105]

She existed before Creation: "Nothing was not a pre-existent matter." Because she was in the beginning, she became "mother of this All."

Donne's sources, already noted, include one that he cites himself, that is, Pico's *Heptaplus*, which John Chamberlin describes as "a multilayered and luxuriant commentary on the verses of Genesis that relate the divine acts of Creation."[106] Whatever his sources, the importance of the passage to this study is Donne's reference to the "mother of this All." This single phrase is important because it is attached to the Tetragrammaton. It can be no accident that Donne describes Creation in this way.

Another source, this time *literary*, for Donne's "mother of this All" seems to have been Edmund Spenser, who wrote a cabalistic version of *Sapience* into his *Hymnes*. Appropriating the *Schekhina* of cabalistic lore, Spenser managed to render the character of Sapience more sensuous.[107] In the cabala, sexual relations between God and the *Schekhina* are evident.[108] Saurat observes that they "are certainly the highest expression of the sensuality which fills the *Zohar.*"[109] Moreover, he adds, "it is probably this trait which forms the chief difference between the Schekhina of the *Zohar* and the Wisdom of the Bible."[110] When Spenser's voluptuous and richly ornamented *Schekhina* crowns herself, "the blessings of heaven are poured forth everywhere."[111]

As variables, Donne's "mother of this All" in the *Essays* and his "spouse so bright and cleare" in the sonnet allude to Spenser's *Schekhina*. Fludd's allegorical figure is a good illustration of both the essay and the poem. As personification of Wisdom, she becomes part of Creation, "emanating from God's will to create."[112] So when Donne alludes to "mother of this All," he means some of his readers (those who know Pico, whose source was the *Zohar*), to understand *Schekhina*. According to the *Zohar,* creation began with her:

> At the beginning of Genesis there is none but Elohim which denotes the Schekhina, because all which was created, from the Hayoth and the Seraphim down to the smallest earth worm, live in Elohim and through Elohim . . . for the creation is the work of the *Schekhina,* and she watches over it as a mother watches over her children.[113]

The subtitle in Donne's essay is *"Elohim."* It is no accident, therefore, that he chooses this moment to mention a female principle within the Divine (*"Elohim* which denotes the Schekhina"). Numerous times throughout this study we have seen Donne toy with the idea of *Schekhina,* "the feminine part of the Deity (a part necessary to creation, since the creation is represented as a cosmic act corresponding to the sexual act)."[114] He defines Creation as a moment "when any thing began to be." This moment involved our "mother," without whom there would be "Nothing." "One is All and through it is All, and to it All, and if it has not All, All is nothing."[115]

At this point we might pause to consider what Mary is *not*. Actually, Donne himself has told us, in a sermon preached at St. Paul's on Christmas Day, 1627:

> *What is your Gods name?* [The heathen nation asks Moses.] you pretende a necessity of worshipping a new God, your God, but what shall we call your God, what is your Gods name?[116]

Donne's question invites his congregation to come up with a name. As Protestants, they may choose the name of Christ or the Holy Spirit. The Christian-cabalist may choose the Tetragrammaton or *Schekhina*.

The Lullist may choose among nine attributes, including Mercy or Justice, both of which are associated with Mary. What name will Donne choose?

> You who worship many Gods, need many names to distinguish your Gods by; we, who know but one God, need no other name of God, but God; wee who worship the onely true God, need not the semi-gods, nor the sesqui-gods of the Romane Church; not their semi-gods, their halfe-gods, men beatified, but not sanctified . . . nor any sesqui-god, any that must be more then God, and receive appeales from God, and reverse the decrees of God, which they make the office of the Virgin *Mary*, whom no man can honour too much, that makes her not God, and they dishonour most, that make her so much more.[117]

This is not what we have come to expect of Donne. Or is it? We have seen him earlier speak of Mary on Christmas Day, 1622. Then he had declared her "full of Grace . . . a fulnesse above . . . faith and works too, for that is a means to preserve both."[118] Now five years later, again on Christmas Day, Donne seems to have switched his position, saying that "the office of the Virgin *Mary*" is not that of God. When he says *not*, he means something else.

She is not, at least as she evolved in Donne's doctrine, the Mary of medieval tradition, that is, Mary immaculately conceived. That Mary, according to one Immaculist, is "link'd to all the Trinitie."[119] We have seen Donne say the same, but that was when her image was yet evolving in his mind. To the medieval mind, Mary is inextricably bound with a Triune God, who has conceived her in his own mind. We have seen Donne express this point of view in *La Corona* and "A Litanie." But the Mary we see or do not see in Donne's Christmas sermon of 1627 is not that. Rather she has been translated into abstract principle, so that she transcends sexual limitation, so that she has no human form.

As abstraction, she cannot be seen. No more than as that pneuma linking things below with heaven. The Mary we see, or rather do not see, in Donne's sermon is to be discovered in the *Name of God*. What has happened, in terms of Donne's *ars memoria*, is a switch from corporeal similitudes (both those deriving from classical models and those deriving from Hermetism) to the more abstract principles of the cabala, those names and numbers that Ramon Lull was convinced would lead all to the otherwise inexpressible God. Her attributes—goodness, eternity, power, wisdom, and so on—combine and recombine with the other names of God.

In order to make Mary this, Donne had to smash many otherwise convenient corporeal images, compelling his congregation, at least those who were awake, to revise and review their perceptions of what Mary should mean on this particular day. By seeming to say something radically different from what he had said before, Donne was creating a clash between familiar icons and this new text, which focuses on God's *name*.

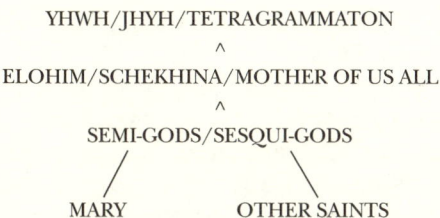

Donne has said that "Mary is *not* God," thereby smashing her image. Though he denies "her" her office as "sesqui-god," he also "denies" God's "other names," that is, the Father, Son, and Holy Spirit: "You who worship many Gods, need many names to distinguish your Gods by; we, who know but one God, need no other name of God, but God." His focus here is YHWH and that alone. All the familiar corporeal images, not just of Mary but of each member of the Trinity, seem to have gone. All that remains is a name.

What Donne is doing here is to shift attention from one "mary" to Another. This sermon shows Donne, toward the end of his career as Anglican priest, saying something like something else (his first sermon at St. Paul's Cross, when he had denied Mary any intrinsic part in the process of redemption) but not the same. If we think of these two sermons as parentheses in his career, we may begin to understand the evolution of his thought by the "between" times. Leaving the rags of "mary" to fall—or remain—where the Reformation left them, Donne in this later sermon demonstrates that he understands the female principle in God. He now discards the name "Mary" because he has learned that "she" is "*Schekhina,* and she watches over it [Creation] as a mother watches over her children."[120] Finally, "Nothing that she did . . . redeemed us" can translate to a vision of God as Mother. By focusing on *The Name of God* alone, Donne reconstituted "mary" as attribute of God, as abstract principle subsumed by the name that cannot be uttered.

* * *

There is much about this study that is not new. Those who are familiar with the critical history of the period recognize here insights from many decades ago. This is especially true where the influence of cabalistic thinking is concerned. In 1930 both Saurat and Fletcher published studies proving the influence of the cabala upon Spenser and Milton. Fletcher has shown how *Paradise Lost* depicts "a feminine personification of the idea of Wisdom, the abstract quality" as co-partner with the Son during the Creative Act.[121] Milton's source, he said, was the original Hebrew which represented "Creation as a birth-process, and the Act of Creation as an impregnation-process."[122] Seventy-five years later, I have studied how the same phenomenon informs the poetry of Donne.

The Phoenix Riddle, investigated here, also has its precedents. Green's important discovery of Henry Hawkins's *The Virgin* (1633), with the phoenix emblem attached, was published in 1870. The emblem, he said, antedates Shakespeare. Certainly it was alive in seventeenth-century memories. Perhaps unwittingly, N. J. C. Andreasen applied the *concept*, not the emblem that expresses it, to Donne's thought: "According to Platonic tradition, Renaissance lovers could also be two-in-one and one-in-two in another sense as well. Not only might they unite with one another physically, but they could also achieve a spiritual or intellectual union. . . . their reward for their *imitatio Dei.*"[123]

I have tried to show how Donne, inspired by the desire to know God, put the phoenix under the microscope. Three hundred years later some of his fellows would do the same, probing the atom, past the surface phenomena into the essence, where they discovered things strangely beautiful, things heretofore unknown. These modern alchemists eventually discovered the glue, the binding energy, behind matter. Once they understood that, they could perform a true "alchemical work," the first artificial transmutation of the atom.[124] Like Edward Teller, J. Robert Oppenheimer, and Enrico Fermi, Donne tried to penetrate the strangely beautiful Phoenix-God. Employing the methodologies of Lull's spiritual logic, alchemical theories, and cabalistic investigative practices, he struggled to make sense of the Riddle in Heaven.

Which brings me to yet another aspect of this study, not new. It is the ladder metaphor, which signifies spiritual and intellectual ascent. I have suggested that some of Donne's poems and sermons function as ladders, allowing his readers to ascend, memory by memory, toward spiritual truth. Andreasen notes the ladder as conceptual metaphor in Ficino's Platonism, that is, "the lover climbs a ladder on three rungs, rising from the body to the soul to the Angelic Mind, ultimately reaching God Himself."[125] My study shifts and refines the conceptual metaphor from Platonism per se to Lull's *ars combinatoria*, which includes Platonism and more. Thus I have been able to investi-

CONCLUSION: *SCHEKHINA*

gate the dynamics of metaphysical poetry from a new, or Lullian, perspective.

The ideological context for this study has been provided by certain new historicists (Tyacke, Katz, Lake, Milton, Davies, Cressy, Sharpe, etc.), who help us understand why Donne wrote as he did. Cressy has shown how the Protestant attempt to erase certain popish icons was undermined by the very rituals installed to replace them.[126] This study has particularized that observation by looking at the ways alchemy kept images of the Virgin alive in the poetry of early modern England.

New historicist studies have shown that, in spite of various policies of practical toleration toward the Church of Rome and the Puritans at home, England continued to be plagued by religious strife until the Toleration Act of 1689.[127] This gives us a new context for two of the most pressing issues confronted by Donne: fragmentation and isolation. Now we can better understand why he, like Francis Bacon and William Laud, wanted to see Christendom united. We can reread Donne's sonnet, "Show me deare Christ," as a quest for the invisible Church. Now, Richard Strier observes, we can understand Donne's "No man is an island" to mean "No island is an island."[128] Such insights go beyond reaffirmation of what critics have long noted—"that Donne 'is more aware of disintegration than of comprehensive harmony.'"[129] They are rather the fruits of new investigations that provide new insights concerning the ethos underlying Donne's harmonizing vision. Now we can see that restoring the world to health, the subject of *The Anniversaries*, means, for Donne, reconstituting its fragments so that it is restored to "wholesomeness."

This same harmonizing vision drove Donne to employ the Ouroboros as structuring principle in his poems, arguing that "All" included her, for without her "All is Nothing." We have seen him cooperate in the Reformation effort to provide acceptable substitutes for what many considered "unacceptable" Roman images. By emphasizing mutual interdependence of sometimes conflicting parts, he hoped to see the Church of England as Jerusalem *renewed*, that is, as healed of strife.

One other matter not new is Donne's knowledge of the movement toward an international sign language. David Katz's work has been most useful in providing this context for his poems.[130] Some linguists, he observes, "tinkered with Arabic numerals, others with alchemical symbols or signs of the zodiac"[131] in order to realize "the mystical qualities of the Adamic vernacular."[132] I have argued that Donne—in his own way—engaged in some form of language reform, striving toward the language of paradise, even the names Adam first used, in order to express God. Like a true linguist, he too tinkered with "forrain wisdome." Unlike other linguists, who tended to fall into opposing camps, he combined two very different models—one corporeal, the other abstract—in order to "express natures and essences."[133]

Finally, I have tried to make sense of the copy of Lull's *Principia* in Donne's library. For a long time we have known it was there. For a long time we have heard Frances Yates remind us of Lull's profound influence on early modern England. Now I have applied Lull's theories to Donne's poems, showing how Lull's spiritual logic, which emphasizes Unity, and Lull's *ars combinatoria*, which emphasizes memory that moves, allowed him to rescue residual Catholicism, reconstituting it as an "altared" form of Mary. This was Donne's unique contribution to English culture.

Epilogue

Donne died a slow death, probably from cancer. Approximately one month before, on 25 February 1631, he preached his last sermon, posthumously published as *Deaths Duell*. About the same time, he ordered an artist to draw him with a shroud about his head, his eyes closed. This picture he kept at his bedside during the remaining three weeks of his life. It was subsequently transferred to sculpture.[134]

Donne bequeathed his portrait of Mary, which he kept in his dining room, to the Earl of Carlisle. After he died 31 March 1631, he left another legacy, not yet declared. In 1666 the Great Fire of London totally destroyed St. Paul's Cathedral. Donne's marble effigy, mounted on an urn, fell through the floor and was inundated by debris. Perhaps that is why it survived intact. The only evident damage is a brown scorch mark on the urn upon which Donne's figure stands. Rarely do life and art cohere. This phoenix is a notable exception.

Notes

Preface

1. "A Qualified Intolerance: The Limits and Ambiguities of Early Stuart Anti-Catholicism," in *Catholicism and Anti-Catholicism in Early Modern English Texts*, ed. Arthur F. Marotti (New York: St. Martin's Press, 1999), 95.
2. John Calvin, *Institutes of the Christian Religion*, vol. 20, ed. John T. McNeill, trans. Ford Lewis Battles (Philadelphia: Westminster Press, 1960), 250.
3. Ibid., 251.
4. Ibid., 253 and 265.
5. *The Table Talk of Martin Luther*, trans. William Hazlitt (London: Bell & Daldy, 1872), 74.
6. Tyacke, *Anti-Calvinists: The Rise of English Arminianism c. 1590–1640* (Oxford: Clarendon Press, 1987), 182.
7. "John Donne in Meditation: *The Anniversaries*," *A Journal of English Literary History* 14 (1947): 251.
8. Letter to the author, 24 February 2001.

Introduction

The term "theological alchemy," used as the title of the introduction, is from John S. Chamberlin's *Increase and Multiply: Arts-of-Discourse Procedure in the Preaching of Donne* (Chapel Hill: Univ. of North Carolina Press, 1976), 105. Citing Donne's interest in the correlation between words and meanings, including *gematria* (the cabalistic habit of assigning numbers to letters of the alphabet), Chamberlin argues that Donne's sermons were profoundly influenced by such Christian cabalists as Pico della Mirandola and Johann Reuchlin. The term "theologicall alchymy" is Reuchlin's and probably alludes, Chamberlin says, to cabalistic "devices of occultist interpretation . . . matching one word with another by means of mathematical equivalence," 105. Rarely do I investigate the arithmetical subtext of Donne's poems. Nevertheless, Reuchlin's idea of "theologicall alchymy" is an important context for this study of Donne.

1. For a discussion of Counter-Reformation influences, see Martz's *The Poetry of Meditation: A Study in English Religious Literature of the Seventeenth Century* (New Haven: Yale Univ. Press, 1954). See also his article on *The Anniversaries* in *A Journal of English Literary History* 14 (1947): 247–73. The words, "that Donne's Catholic background shines through most of his writings," are from his letter to the author (24 February 2001), part of which is quoted in the preface above.

2. Studies that survey the social and historical context include Alison Shell, *Catholicism, Controversy, and the English Literary Imagination, 1558–1660* (Cambridge Univ. Press, 1999) and Dennis Flynn, *John Donne and the Ancient Catholic Nobility* (Indiana Univ. Press, 1995). One collection of essays that illustrates the way religion shaped poetic sensibilities during this period is *Catholicism and Anti-Catholicism*, ed. Arthur Marotti. John Carey's psychobiography, *John Donne: Life, Mind, and Art* (New York: Oxford Univ. Press, 1981) studies the way Donne's apostasy influences specific poems. R. V. Young examines poems by other poets, besides Donne, in order to discover how doctrine influenced imagination. See his *Doctrine and Devotion in Seventeenth-Century Poetry: Studies in Donne, Herbert, Crashaw, and Vaughan* (Rochester, N.Y.: D.S. Brewer, 2000). Other recent studies include James Doelman, *King James I and the Religious Culture of England* (Rochester, N.Y.: D.S. Brewer, 2000); Jeffrey Johnson, *The Theology of John Donne* (Rochester, N.Y.: D.S. Brewer, 1999); James Loxley, *Royalism and Poetry in the English Civil Wars: The Drawn Sword* (New York: St. Martin's Press, 1997); and Jeanne Shami, *John Donne and Conformity in Crisis in the Late Jacobean Pulpit* (Rochester, N.Y.: Boydell & Brewer, 2003).

3. O'Connell, "*'La Corona'*: Donne's Ars Poetica Sacra," in *The Eagle and the Dove: Reassessing John Donne*, ed. Claude J. Summers and Ted-Larry Pebworth (Columbia: Univ. of Missouri Press, 1986), 124. Already mentioned in my preface is DiPasquale's *Literature and Sacrament* (1999). Concerning *La Corona*, she observes, "In imitating the Virgin's creative role, the poet assumes a sacerdotal function," 69. Also pertinent is her article, "'to good ends': The Final Cause of Sacramental Womanhood in *The First Anniversarie*," *John Donne Journal* 20 (2001): 141–50. Here she argues that Donne implements a Protestant version of the Catholic doctrine of transubstantiation in order to transform Elizabeth Drury into "unalloyed essence," 147.

4. Klawitter, "John Donne and the Virgin Mary," in *John Donne's Religious Imagination: Essays in Honor of John T. Shawcross*, ed. Raymond-Jean Frontain and Frances M. Malpezzi (Conway: Univ. of Central Arkansas Press, 1995), 138.

5. Frontain, "Donne's Protestant *Paradiso*: The Johannine Vision of the *Second Anniversary*," in *John Donne and the Protestant Reformation: New Perspectives*, ed. Mary Arshagouni Papazian (Detroit: Wayne State Univ. Press, 2003), 123.

6. See, for example, John Shawcross, *Intentionality and the New Traditionalism: Some Liminal Means to Literary Revisionism* (University Park: Pennsylvania State Univ. Press, 1991). Although Shawcross does not refer to memory per se, he implies as much when he acknowledges the importance of the reader's experience during the act of reading. He distinguishes three kinds of texts: 1) the text per se, which he defines as "the specific words as they appear on the page," 2) the reader's text, which he defines as "the understanding the reader derives from reading that text," and 3) the author's text, which is "the text the author has provided for the reader to read, with all its potentialities," 4. Interaction between the author's text and the reader's text, he says, depends partly upon the devices and allusions the author provides: "The author's text . . . may embody device and allusion, and indeed any allusion or device becomes evidence of the author's text," 5. Obviously, the reader's memory, what he or she has experienced of these devices and allusions, is crucial in creating the reader's text.

7. For further discussion of Ficino's contribution to *memoria*, or the systems of memory influencing Renaissance culture, see Frances Yates, *The Art of Memory* (Chicago: Univ. of Chicago Press, 1966), 160–65.

8. See Susan Haskins, *Mary Magdalen: Myth and Metaphor* (New York: Harper-Collins, 1993). She traces the concept of the female principle in God from the Old Testament, where Wisdom was personified as a woman, called Hokhmah. Between

the third and second centuries BC, however, the word *hokhmah* was exchanged for *sophia*. *The Wisdom of Solomon*, for example, depicted Sophia as "the emanation of God's glory, the Holy Spirit, the immaculate mirror of his energy, *and* spouse of the Lord," 43.

9. See Diana Fernando, *Alchemy: An Illustrated A to Z* (New York: Sterling, 1998). She distinguishes St. Bernard as the spiritual alchemist whose order took as its motto the alchemical "Laborare est Orare" [of the Benedictines], 24. The Benedictines, from which Bernard originated, were attached to Hermetic theories concerning the Virgin. Bernard himself believed that the Virgin once answered his prayers by suckling him with "several drops of milk from her breast," 23. This vision was somehow connected with the revival of Bernard's monastery as "a Hermetic paradise," 24.

10. See Kevin Sharpe and Steven N. Zwicker, "Introduction: Discovering the Renaissance Reader," in *Reading, Society and Politics in Early Modern England*, ed. Kevin Sharpe and Steven N. Zwicker (New York: Cambridge Univ. Press, 2003). "The reformed experience centred on the individual conscience, the heart of each believer; the journey to faith was a continuous process of interiorizing the word. And that interiorization often involves strenuous acts of writing and reading," 11.

11. See Gareth Roberts, *The Mirror of Alchemy: Alchemical Ideas and Images in Manuscripts and Books from Antiquity to the Seventeenth Century* (Toronto: Univ. of Toronto Press, 1994). Another source, mentioned above, is Fernando's *Alchemy* (1998). For a broader context see Stanton J. Linden, *Darke Hierogliphicks: Alchemy in English Literature from Chaucer to the Restoration* (Lexington: Univ. Press of Kentucky, 1996). Linden argues that works by Donne, Herbert, Crashaw, and Vaughan evidence their interest in alchemy. In contrast, he says, Milton's interest seems slight. Especially useful is Lyndy Abraham's *A Dictionary of Alchemical Imagery* (Cambridge: Cambridge Univ. Press, 1999); hereafter referred to as *Dictionary*. Still pertinent as a comprehensive research tool is Lynn Thorndike's, *A History of Magic and Experimental Science*, 8 vols. (New York: Columbia Univ. Press, 1923).

12. Rosamund Tuve, *A Reading of George Herbert* (London: Faber & Faber, 1952), 134.

13. Among the most frequently cited studies is Anthony Milton, *Catholic and Reformed: The Roman and Protestant Churches in English Protestant Thought, 1600–1640* (New York: Cambridge Univ. Press, 1995). Also pertinent is the work of Peter Lake, David Cressy, Kevin Sharpe, and Nicolas Tyacke. See, for example, David Cressy's *Literacy and the Social Order: Reading and Writing in Tudor and Stuart England* (New York: Cambridge Univ. Press, 1980), which examines how the reader's experience was influenced by images, both secular and religious, which often substituted for literacy, that is, reading and writing. Cressy observes that Thomas More, Donne's great-granduncle, did not consider an English translation of the Bible essential for the salvation of English souls. "Many," More wrote, "shall with God's grace, though they never read word of scripture, come as well to heaven," 44. See also Kevin Sharpe, "'An Image Doting Rabble': The Failure of Republican Culture in Seventeenth-Century England," in *Refiguring Revolutions* (above), 25–56. Sharpe argues the important role images played in shaping, or rather failing to shape, the Protestant world. Finally, see Nicholas Tyacke, *Aspects of English Protestantism, c. 1530–1700* (New York: Manchester Univ. Press, 2001). Tyacke demonstrates ways that visual elements controlled English society.

14. The reference is to Nicholas Tyacke, *Anti-Calvinists: The Rise of English Arminianism* (New York: Oxford Univ. Press, 1987).

15. See Julian Davies, *The Caroline Captivity of the Church: Charles I and the Remoulding of Anglicanism, 1625–1641* (New York: Oxford Univ. Press, 1992). Davies observes,

"Certainly the application of Arminianism could be as loose and as indiscriminate as other terms of denomination or abuse," 92. Generally, he says, "'Arminianism' was looked upon as a bridge to popery," 90.

16. For discussion of a tenuous alliance between the Arminians and papists during the Caroline era, see Nicholas Tyacke, *Aspects*, 230–38. But Davies (*The Caroline Captivity*, above) cautions against perceiving the religious conflicts of this period (1625–41) "in terms of a simplistic polarity between Arminian and Calvinist," 95. Laud himself, he notes, "had no 'arminian' confidence in man's nature or in his innate ability," 97.

17. See David Cressy, *Bonfires and Bells: National Memory and the Protestant Calendar in Elizabethan and Stuart England* (Berkeley: Univ. of California Press, 1989).

18. For a similar view of a different phenomenon, see Anthony Milton, "The Creation of Laudianism: A New Approach," in *Politics, Religion, and Popularity in Early Stuart Britain: Essays in Honour of Conrad Russell*, ed. Thomas Cogswell, Richard Cust, and Peter Lake (New York: Cambridge Univ. Press, 2002), 162–84. Milton observes that England eventually became "a country united in its rejection of a small group of people called Laudians," 183. He suggests that we view the events that led to the fall of Laudianism in 1640 as "events occurring in a country which was trying to wipe out its own recent past, with people seeking to redefine themselves," 183.

19. Sharpe and Zwicker, "[T]he enemies of Protestantism had warned [against] . . . an assertion of each believer as determinant of meaning," 11.

20. Ibid.

21. Ibid. The authors make no reference to alchemical discourse. Rather, they emphasize the importance of "personal reading."

22. See David Cressy, *Birth, Marriage and Death: Ritual, Religion, and the Life-Cycle in Tudor and Stuart England* (New York: Oxford Univ. Press, 1997).

23. Sharpe and Zwicker, 4.

24. For discussion of revisions of the liturgical calendar, see Cressy, *Bonfires and Bells*, 2–12.

25. See Kevin Sharpe, "'An Image Doting Rabble': The Failure of Republican Culture in Seventeenth-Century England," in *Refiguring Revolutions*, 25.

26. See Cressy, *Birth, Marriage and Death*. He shows how "[r]itual performance, in practice, revealed frictions and fractures that everyday local discourse attempted to hide or to heal," 2. He concludes that "full reformation was slow to take root . . . and unreformed catholic practices were never entirely suppressed," 137. Even during the new ceremonialism of the 1620s and 1630s, many, he says, "feared that all manner of discredited substances [the vestiges of Roman Catholicism] were creeping back into favour," 137. See also *Bonfires*. "Corpus Christi day," Cressy observes, "was dropped from the Protestant ecclesiastical calendar because it reeked of the rejected doctrine of transubstantiation, but it was harder to eliminate from popular culture," 25. Other examples of rituals difficult to erase were bellringing, the sign of the cross during baptismal ceremonies, and the use of candles at Candlemas.

27. See Stanton J. Linden, "Expounding George Ripley: A Huntington Alchemical Manuscript," *Huntington Library Quarterly* 61 (2000): 411–28. Linden writes, "In addition to manuscripts, early printed versions of the *Compound* and other works by Ripley clearly suggest that his works were highly regarded in England—even as Francis Bacon, the new philosophy, and eventually the Royal Society were calling into doubt the theory and practice of alchemy and related bodies of knowledge," 413.

28. See Cressy, *Bonfires and Bells: National Memory*. Paranoia and anti-Catholic sentiment, he argues, resulted in a rich vocabulary of ritual, a mixture of contending

forces. "While a powerful minority of high ceremonialists insisted on strict and elaborate observances, another minority of godly precisians sought to safeguard the advances of the Reformation, and then to take them further," 35. Memory, he says, played a part. For example, "[m]emories of 1588 . . . served to inflame anti-Catholicism and hatred and fear of the Spaniards," 122. Later Arminian attempts to reinstate rituals previously dropped resulted in a Puritan revival (39). During the Caroline regime, for example, Puritans burned popish effigies and thereby offended the Catholic queen. Ultimately, Cressy argues, memory became "a weapon as well as a salve and balsam," 168.

29. Mazzeo, 113.

30. Linden, *Darke Hierogliphicks*, 154.

31. Ibid., 155.

32. See *Darke Hierogliphicks*. Linden describes how the alchemical image works in Herbert and Donne, saying, "It is placed in a poem in such a way that only its root meaning of *change and transformation* and its *energizing potential* are initially present and visible. . . . Although seemingly dormant, its potential vitality and energy can be channeled in a number of different directions, wherever the poetic situation calls for the idea of change and transformation: e.g., the dawning of the emotion of powerful love, the transforming power of God's grace, or the devastating effects of human loss. Within the same poem this core of meaning may, in fact, be released in several directions, sometimes simultaneously, more often in a close chronological progression. Typically, then, as it functions within a given poem, the alchemical image moves from a state of potentiality to one of actuality," 155.

33. See John Shawcross, *Intentionality and the New Traditionalism: Some Liminal Means to Literary Revisionism* (University Park: Pennsylvania State Univ. Press, 1991), 4. The three kinds of texts he distinguishes were cited above, n. 6.

34. Ibid., 18.

35. Shawcross explains that the author uses variables in order "to illuminate those constants, to put them into perspective, to make them meaningful and different," 18.

36. My task—to show how Donne managed to "preserve and make culture"—is similar to that of Albert H. Tricomi, who attempts "to revise the dominant new-historicist proposition that texts reproduce culture and to demonstrate the more complex proposition that they simultaneously make and reproduce culture," 1. See his study, *Reading Tudor-Stuart Texts Through Cultural Historicism* (Gainsville: Univ. Press of Florida, 1996). He notes that "the entire *process* [emphasis mine] whereby change occurs within cultural systems" is too often ignored, 15.

37. Tricomi writes, "The past we recover may not be and never was *the* past, but it can be for all that a historicized past," 6.

38. Cressy, *Bonfires*, 6–7.

39. St. Anselm of Aosta, bishop of Canterbury (1093–1109) believed that Mary was sanctified at the moment of her birth but did not become completely pure until the moment of the Annunciation. The theory of Sanctification put Mary on the same level with John the Baptist, also sanctified in the womb of his mother. Hence her role in salvation was minimal. Because St. Thomas Aquinas embraced this doctrine, the Dominicans were vigorous proponents.

40. The theory of Mary's sanctification seems to be similar to that of the Immaculate Conception. However, according to one source, "it is actually in conflict with it because it includes Mary in the law by which every human being is *naturaliter* subject to the consequences of Original Sin." See Mirella Levi D'Ancona, *The Iconography of the Immaculate Conception in the Middle Ages and Early Renaissance: Monographs on*

Archaeology and Fine Arts, vol. 7 (The College Art Association of America, 1957). The citation is from page 9.

41. Fernando, 23.

42. Ibid., 24. She does not note that it was also the motto of the Benedictine Order.

43. St. Bernard, "Sermon 41," in *Sancti Bernardi Opera,* 1:139–40. Quoted by Caroline Walker Bynum, *Jesus as Mother: Studies in the Spirituality of the High Middle Ages* (Los Angeles: Univ. of California Press, 1982), 118.

44. Bernard, "To the Brothers at Clairvaux," in *Selected Works,* trans. G. R. Evans (New York: Paulist Press, 1987), 284–86. The citation is from 284.

45. Probably Bernard's especial devotion to the Virgin has led to the popular misconception that he supported the theory of the Immaculate Conception, which held Mary to be one with God. Thus, by a strange irony, Bernard has come to be associated with a "doctrine" that in his lifetime he adamantly opposed.

46. In 1488 the Mass of the Conception was celebrated for the first time. Susan Haskins's comments on the doctrine of the Immaculate Conception are curious, for she does not distinguish between the Maculist and Immaculist views. Rather she cites Bernard of Clairvaux as "the Virgin Mary's most fervent champion" during a time when "churchmen . . . were unable to agree that Joachim and Anne had not coupled naturally, and that the Virgin herself had not been conceived in angelic *apatheia* rather than in human 'mire'; the theory was to become dogma in the Roman Catholic Church only as late as 1854," 140.

47. See, for example, Moshe Idel, "Ramon Lull and Ecstatic Kabbalah," *Journal of the Warburg and Courtauld Institutes* 51 (1988): 170–74. Idel observes that "similarities between the Kabbalistic Sefirot and Lull's *dignitates* . . . may be the result of the influence of common sources and Scotus Eriugena [*sic*] may indeed be considered just such a source," 170.

48. See Lina Bolzoni, *The Gallery of Memory: Literary and Iconographic Models in the Age of the Printing Press* (Toronto: Univ. of Toronto Press, 2001), 81. Bolzoni's source suggests that, by the Renaissance, a connection had been established between Giulio Camillo's famous *Idea del theatro* and the theories of Lull. Evidently the cabala and the art of Lull were already combined.

49. Frances Yates, "The Art of Ramon Lull: An Approach to it through Lull's Theory of the Elements," *Journal of the Warburg and Courtauld Institutes* 17 (1954): 166.

50. Ibid. She says that Lull's manuscripts were disseminated throughout Italy and "may have been known to Dante," 166. She adds that Lullian geometry may have influenced Italian architectural theory.

51. For further discussion, see *The Art of Memory,* 175.

52. Though there were many pseudo-Lullian alchemical works being read and printed during the Renaissance, only one short treatise by Lull himself provides the basis for understanding, firsthand, his theory of memory. See Yates's review of *Liber ad memoriam confirmandam* in *The Art of Memory,* 191–97. For discussion of Lull's relationship with the Dominicans, see Anthony Bonner, "Ramon Llull and the Dominicans," *Catalan Review* 4.1–2 (1990): 377–92.

53. Yates, *Memory,* 193.

54. Ibid., 196.

55. Among Donne's sources for the *Essays in Divinity* were several Franciscans. These included Alfonso Castrensis (1495–1558), a Spanish Franciscan; Petrus Galatinus, who after his conversion from Judaism to Christianity became a Franciscan friar; Franciscus Georgius Venetus, or F. Zorgi, whose *De Harmonia Mundi totius cantica* (1525) was rife with cabalistic ideas. Also Sebastian Münster (1489–1552), a

Franciscan monk, whose *Cosmographia Universalis* (Basil, 1578) was in Donne's library. See Evelyn Simpson's edition of *Essays in Divinity*, "Sources," 101–108. Also see R. C. Bald, *John Donne: A Life*, 52n and 558–59. According to Bald, "At some time, probably between 1597 and 1601, Donne presented a copy of an edition (1578) in German of Münster's *Cosmographia* to Edward Parvish," 52n.

56. This phenomenon is discussed by Levi D'Ancona, 19.

57. One illustration Levi D'Ancona offers is *Virgin Immaculate with Trinity* (fig. 16, page 85). Discovered in a Carmelite missal from the end of the fourteenth century, it is now in the British Museum (Add. MS 29704, fol. 193v).

58. The latter reference to Lull's Neoplatonism is from Yates, *Memory*, 187. See also David Katz, *Philo-Semitism and the Readmission of the Jews to England, 1603–55* (Oxford: Clarendon, 1982). Cabalists believed, Katz observes, "The Torah scroll was written without vowels, punctuation, or cantillation marks because, in the words of one seventeenth-century kabbalist, it originally formed a *tel shel'othyyoth bilty mesuddaroth*, a heap of unarranged letters," 73.

59. Yates, *Memory*, 176.

60. For discussion of the Trinity as Pico della Mirandola and other Christian cabalists appropriated it from Lull's theories, see R. J. Zwi Werblowsky, "Milton and the *Conjectural Cabbalistica*," *Journal of the Warburg and Courtauld Institutes* 18.1–2 (January–June 1955): 92–93. "Two main trends," he says, "are to be discerned in Christian Kabbalah. The specifically 'Christian' one in its narrowest sense is mainly concerned with adducing proof from kabbalistic texts for the Trinity and other Christological dogmas. This tradition was founded by Pico and Reuchlin, and though it was based on genuine kabbalistic learning, it had little in common with the fundamental interests of Kabbalah proper," 92. See also David Katz, *Philo-Semitism*. According to him, John Wilkins (who published the first English textbook on cryptography in 1641) "rehearsed the famous proof of the Trinity from Christian kabbalah . . . that the second word of the Hebrew version of Genesis is an acronym for father, son, and Holy Spirit," 82.

61. For discussion of the philo-Semitic movement in early seventeenth-century England, see *From Persecution to Toleration: The Glorious Revolution and Religion in England*, ed. Ole Peter Grell, Jonathan I. Israel, and Nicholas Tyacke (Oxford: Clarendon, 1991). The editors note that "a philo-Semitic movement had been gathering strength since the early seventeenth century. Motives, however, were extremely mixed, including a very important millenarian component. . . . a major ambition of those in favour of readmission was the *conversion* of the Jews to Christianity," 7.

62. Katz, 79. He notes that the English language reformers sought to create "a system whereby scholars throughout the world could read their own tongue from a single set of characters," 45. They debated whether Francis Bacon (1561–1626), who had become intrigued with the Chinese language, or Jan Amos Comenius (1592–1670), who was devoted to the Christian cabala, should be credited as "father" of this movement (44).

63. According to Katz, Ashmole thought to use signs for the planets, metals, minerals, and weights (47).

64. Katz quotes Bacon (*Works*, ed. J. Spedding, 3:399–401): "it is the use of China and the kingdoms of the high Levant to write in Characters Real, which express neither letters nor words in gross, but Things or Notions," 46.

65. Donne, *Essays*, 48.

66. Katz, 82.

67. Though Donne died before William Laud became archbishop of Canterbury (1633–45), he nevertheless felt the growing presence of a radical Calvinist minority

that sought to remove certain elements of ceremonialism. It is in this context that Cressy distinguishes the opposing factions as "a powerful minority of high ceremonialists [which] insisted on strict and elaborate observances, [and] another minority of godly precisians [who] sought to safeguard the advances of the Reformation, and then to take them further." See *Bonfires*, 35.

68. Donne, *Essays*, 23.

69. See Cecil Roth, *A History of the Jews in England* (Oxford: Clarendon, 1949). He cites evidence of a Jewish cemetery in London during the Middle Ages, observing that "licence was given for putting under the ban those who failed to pay the amounts promised for the upkeep of the cemetery in London, with the proviso that any eventual profits should accrue to the king," 117. Cromwellian policy generally urged toleration of the Jews, albeit for the purpose of conversion. This policy continued during the reign of Charles II, although the motive seems to have shifted to include economic issues. For discussion of this issue, see *From Persecution to Toleration: The Glorious Revolution and Religion in England*, ed. Ole Peter Grell, Jonathan I. Israel, and Nicholas Tyacke, 7.

70. Katz, 108.

71. For discussion of Renaissance birthing practices, see Cressy, *Birth*. The citation is from 15.

72. Cressy reports an incident of cross-dressing whereby a man disguised himself as a woman in order to enter the birth room. See *Travesties and Transgressions in Tudor and Stuart England* (New York: Oxford Univ. Press, 2000), 92–97.

73. Cressy, *Birth*, 15.

74. Cressy observes that "social and economic differences . . . were dissolved in the primal activity of birth," *Birth*, 15.

75. The term "re-Catholicization" is from Peter Lake and Michael Questier, "Prisons, Priests and People," in *England's Long Reformation, 1500–1800*, ed. Nicholas Tyacke (London: University College London, 1998), 195.

76. See my article, "Alchemical Augmentation and Primordial Fire in Donne's 'The Dissolution,'" in *Studies in English Literature, 1500–1900* 45. no. 1 (Winter 2005): 95–115. I argue here that the origin of Donne's alchemy is the pre-Socratic Greeks. Both Heraclitus "the Dark" and Hippocrates were fascinated by riddles, so much so that they sought to obscure what otherwise might seem too clear. Both avoided clear-cut answers in favor of mind-teasers. Naturally Donne and certain of his contemporaries were drawn to them.

77. See Joseph Mazzeo, "John Donne's Alchemical Imagery," *Isis* 48 (June 1957): 113. John Dee was an English mathematician and occultist. He became a favorite of Elizabeth. His interest in divination led to an alliance with the alchemical theorist, Edward Kelly, with whom he traveled abroad.

78. For discussion of John Dee's influence upon Edward Kelly, see Lyndy Abraham's article, "Edward Kelly's Hieroglyph," in *Emblems and Alchemy* ed. Alison Adams and Stanton J. Linden, vol. 3, Glasgow Emblem Studies (Sherborne, Dorset: Remous Ltd., Milborne Port, 1998), 95–108.

79. See Kevin Sharpe, *Sir Robert Cotton, 1586–1631: History and Politics in Early Modern England* (New York: Oxford Univ. Press, 1979). Sir Robert Cotton's famous library, widely circulated, included both works by Dee and works from his personal library, part of which Cotton was able to acquire. According to Sharpe, "Priceless pieces from John Dee's library came to Sir Robert only indirectly, as an exchange with D'Ewes who had acquired them," 60. Cotton had connections with the poets and playwrights in the literary circle of his kinswoman, Lucy Harrington, Countess of

Bedford. Among these was Donne (200). Donne seems to have sought the patronage of Sir Robert Cotton, hoping to secure from him a place at court (207).

80. Yates, "The Art of Ramon Lull," 166.

81. Yates, *The Art of Memory*, 183.

82. For more information on Giovanni Pantheo (Johannes Augustinus Pantheus), see Thorndike, 5:537–40. According to Thorndike, Pantheo was a priest of Venice, who was given special permission by the Council of Ten and an edict of Pope Leo X to print his work, in spite of "the reported prohibition of the practice of alchemy by the Venetian government in 1468 or 1488," 537.

83. An excellent review of this phenomenon is H. J. Sheppard's article, "Gnosticism and Alchemy," *Ambix* 6 (1957): 86–101.

84. For a review of Dee's pseudo-Solomonic magic and the inspection of figures, see Stephen Clucas, "'Non est legendum sed inspicendum solum': Inspectival knowledge and the visual logic of John Dee's *Liber Mysteriorum*," in *Emblems and Alchemy*. ed. Alison Adams and Stanton J. Linden, vol. 3, Glasgow Emblem Studies (Sherborne, Dorset: Remous Ltd., Milborne Port, 1998), 109–31.

85. See H. J. Sheppard, "Gnosticism and Alchemy," *Ambix* 6 (1957): 89–101.

86. For a review of the history of the Ouroboros, see H. J. Sheppard, "The Ouroboros and the Unity of Matter in Alchemy: A Study in Origins," *Ambix* 10 (June, 1962): 83–96. The reference is to 95.

87. Ibid., 95.

88. Haskins, 42.

89. Yates, "The Art of Ramon Lull," 166.

90. Abraham, *Dictionary*, 210.

91. *The Hermetic and Alchemical Writings of Paracelsus the Great*, ed. Arthur Edward Waite (London: James Elliott, 1894), 1:66.

92. Christian humanists such as Pico della Mirandola attempted to distinguish between "spiritual" and "demonic" magic. Pico's nephew Giovanni, for example, wrote a treatise, *Strix*, which explored the relationship between God's miracles and Satan's magic. Among the issues confronted were the miracles of the Roman Catholic Church and whether or not it was possible for miracles to occur in a postapostolic age. Some humanist scholars distinguished between operative magic and contemplative magic, condemning the agents of operative magic as diabolical and destructive. Others refused to admit the possibility of either, explaining away the powers of Pharoah's magicians and indiscriminately attacking papists, witches, alchemists, and any credulous enough to believe witch-related tales. Generally speaking, however, there was some confusion among demonologists concerning "white" and "black" magic and concerning the hierarchy of individuals involved with the black arts.

93. Naturally, such men as Donne and Herbert, intrigued by alchemy and by the writings of the Christian cabalists, took notice. The cabalists, for example, interpreted Scripture on the basis of the "magic" invested in each word, letter, and number. They eventually began to wear amulets as secret signs and to employ "sacred" emblems in magical practices.

94. For Augustine's discussion of memory, see chapters 8–26 in *The Confessions: Basic Writings of St. Augustine*, ed. Whitney J. Oates (New York: Random House, 1948). The citation is from 153.

95. Ibid., 153.

96. Ibid.

97. See David Cressy, *Literacy and the Social Order: Reading and Writing in Tudor and*

Stuart England (New York: Cambridge Univ. Press, 1980). Cressy observes that "Religious conservatives of the mid-Tudor period saw little reason for people to trouble themselves with literacy, and viewed with disdain the early protestant effort to spread the vernacular Bible. Thomas More, for example, denied that 'the having of the scripture in English be a thing so requisite of precise necessity that the people's souls should needs perish. . . . Many . . . shall with God's grace, though they never read word of scripture, come as well to heaven [by means of reading an image],' " 2. The context for these remarks, Cressy notes, is that "More guessed 'far more than four parts of all the whole divided into ten could never read English yet', suggesting that possibly up to 60% of the population could read," 44. See also Lina Bolzoni, *The Gallery of Memory: Literary and Iconographic Models in the Age of the Printing Press* (Toronto: Univ. of Toronto Press, 2001). Discussing various types of alphabets and word games, Bolzoni cites the imaginary alphabet of More's *Utopia* (1518). Having invented this alphabet, the inhabitants of Utopia demonstrate the importance of word games that blend script and ciphers with magic or "useful secrets," 88–89.

98. *The Sermons of John Donne*, ed. George R. Potter and Evelyn M. Simpson, 10 vols. (Berkeley: Univ. of California Press, 1953–62). This citation from 8:261. All citations of Donne's sermons, unless otherwise noted, are from this edition.

99. Some of the recent studies of the function of memory in Renaissance texts seem to have been inspired by Frances Yates, *The Art of Memory* (1966) and by John S. Chamberlin, *Increase and Multiply* (1976). See for example, Mary Carruthers, *The Book of Memory: A Study of Memory in Medieval Culture* (New York: Cambridge Univ. Press, 1993). Also Achsah Guibbory's "John Donne and Memory as 'the Art of Salvation,'" *The Huntington Library Quarterly* 63 (1980): 261–74. Guibbory argues the importance of memory to Donne's doctrine of salvation. "Whereas sin separates man from God," she says, "memory leads him back," 269. Also Noralyn Masselink's "Memory in John Donne's Sermons: 'Readie'? or Not?" *South Atlantic Review* 63 (Spring 1998): 99–107. Masselink argues that Donne's epistemology accommodates the classical mnemonic devices *loci et imagines*. His reliance on *loci*, she says, "may be read as evidence both of his desire to teach men through an appeal to memory as well of his recognition that the memory has been seriously marred by the fall," 103. Ultimately, she argues, Donne's epistemology owes more to Thomistic sense-oriented theories than to Augustinian precepts. Both Jeffrey Johnson and Jeanne Shami think that the Holy Ghost represents memory, transferring spiritual wisdom from God to man. Since Donne himself had urged this: "Study all the history, and write all the progres of the Holy Ghost in thy selfe . . . thou wilt find an infinite comfort in this particular tracinge of the Holy Ghost, and his working in thy soule" (2:159), it is natural for critics to fix upon the Holy Ghost as agent. See Jeanne Shami, "Anatomy and Progress: The Drama of Conversion in Donne's Men of Middle Nature," *University of Toronto Quarterly* 53.3 (Spring 1984): 221–35. See also Jeffrey Johnson, *The Theology of John Donne* (Rochester, N.Y.: D.S. Brewer, 1999).

100. The reference is to Reynolds's painting, *Augustus Viscount Keppel.*

101. In alchemical theory the seven planets correspond with seven minerals: the moon is silver, Mercury mercury, Venus copper, sun gold, Mars iron, Jupiter tin, and Saturn lead.

102. The author of the *Ad Herennium* says, "The backgrounds are very much like wax tablets or papyrus, the images like the letters, the arrangement and disposition of the images like the script, and the delivery is like the reading," 209.

103. See "Sources of the Essays in Divinity," in *Essays in Divinity*, ed. Evelyn Simpson (Oxford: Clarendon, 1952), 101–8. Simpson cites Pico della Mirandola as "a

brilliant Italian scholar and Platonist, a friend and pupil of Ficino, who studied oriental languages and the Jewish Cabala." He is quoted also in *Biathanatos*, 49, and in the *Sermons*, 107. According to David S. Katz, *Philo-Semitism* (1982), Pico is "the father of Christian kabbalah . . . Pico had a large body of kabbalistic literature translated into Latin for him by a Jewish convert known as Flavius Mithridates. Pico believed that Christian doctrines such as the Trinity and Reincarnation could be proven through the use of kabbalah, and his works were enormously influential in the Christian world," 75.

104. Katz cites Johann Reuchlin as a follower of Pico who "helped to integrate kabbalah with contemporary Christian intellectual developments," 75.

105. Chamberlin studies the influence of Pico della Mirandola and Johann Reuchlin upon Donne. Yates also offers a lengthy survey of how Christian humanism attached itself to cabalistic theory. The vision, she says, was to realize some sort of spiritual unity. See, *The Occult Philosophy in the Elizabethan Age* (London: Routledge & Kegan Paul, 1979). Yates concludes that the "Hermetic-Cabalist movement failed as a movement of religious reform, and that failure involved the suppression of the Renaissance Neoplatonism which had nourished it," 92–93.

106. Simpson describes Reuchlin as "a great German humanist and student of Hebrew. He was interested in the Jewish cabala, and wrote *De Verbo Mirifico* (1494) and *De Arte Cabbalistica* (1517). Donne alludes to him also [in addition to the *Essays*] in *Catalogus Librorum*, *Biathanatos*, and the *Sermons*," 107.

107. Yates, *Occult*, 61. Two more recent studies of this phenomenon are David Cressy's *Birth* (1997) and *Bonfires* (1989). Both are cited above.

108. See Lyndy Abraham's *Marvell and Alchemy* (Brookfield, Vt.: Scolar Press, 1990). She discusses the "visual alphabets, associated with contemporary occult memory systems," 170.

109. For further discussion of the importance of *memoria* to ancient and medieval minds, see Mary Carruthers's *The Book of Memory* (1993). She writes, "The idea that language, as a *sign* of something else, is always at a remove from reality is one of the cornerstones of ancient rhetoric. This idea gives to both books and language a subsidiary and derivative cultural role with respect to *memoria*, for they have no meaning except in relation to it. A work is not truly read until one has made it part of oneself," 10.

110. Yates, *Occult*, 55.

111. Ibid.

112. Ibid.

113. Thorndike, 7:599.

114. See Lyndy Abraham, *Marvell and Alchemy*. Abraham cites as examples Boncompagno (thirteenth century), Lodovico da Pirano (fifteenth century), and Rosellius (sixteenth century).

115. Ibid., 170.

116. Ibid.

117. Ibid.

118. For further discussion see Allen G. Debus, *The Chemical Philosophy: Paracelsian Science and Medicine in the Sixteenth and Seventeenth Centuries* (New York: Science History Publications, 1977), 1:35–36. Debus observes that Pantheo "assigned numbers to Latin, Greek, and Hebrew letters," giving "each letter a number according to its place in the alphabet, added the total, and multiplied by eight," 35. This is a form of *gematria*, a cabalistic investigative technique.

119. Abraham, *Marvell*, 231.

120. Yates, "The Art of Ramon Lull," 166.

121. Yates notes that the Dominicans, who "had their own art of memory," resisted Lull. See *The Art of Memory*, 175.
122. Ibid., 176.
123. Ibid.
124. Stephen Clucas, "John Dee's *Liber Misteriorum*," in *Emblems and Alchemy*, ed. Alison Adams and Stanton J. Linden, vol. 3, Glasgow Emblem Studies (Sherborne, Dorset: Remous Ltd., Milborne Port, 1998), 115.
125. Clucas cites Dee's directions for the practice of inspecting images: "The operator must not move from the place where he is seated when he inspects these figures, until he has recited all the orations which pertain to the figures, and until he has finished inspecting the figure [. . .] once the figure has been inspected in the prescribed manner he can move and walk around, until the time appointed for the inspection of the second figure," 120. Of course, this represents the initial stage in "memorizing." Thereafter, Dee instructs seers to contemplate four figures simultaneously.
126. See my article, "Montage, *Mise en Scène*, and Miserable Acting: Feminist Discourse in Donne's *Holy Sonnet X*," *ELN* 29 (June 1992): 23–32. Also my article, "Coining and Conning: Alchemical Motifs in Donne's 'Oh my blacke Soule!'" *ELN* 42 (December 2004): 1–10.
127. Yates, *The Art of Memory*, 176.
128. *Ad Herennium*, book 3, section 17, 210–11.
129. Chamberlin, 118.
130. Augustine, *The Confessions*, Book 10, trans. William Watts (Cambridge: Harvard Univ. Press, 1997), in Loeb Classical Library. The citation is from page 112.
131. Watts's translation of Augustine, 113.
132. Carruthers explains, "The ruminant image is basic to understanding what was involved in *memoria* as well as *meditatio*, the two being understood as the agent and its activity," 165.
133. Ibid., 165–66.
134. For an example of how people may understand the same code differently, see Julian Davies, *The Caroline Captivity of the Church* (New York: Oxford Univ. Press, 1992). In 1627, when some people heard certain beneficed lecturers "speaking irreverently about the Virgin Mary," each had to decide how to understand the reference. The bishop's response, in this case, was to revoke their licenses (154). Evidently, the bishop remembered differently.
135. John T. Shawcross, *Intentionality and the New Traditionalism*, 3.
136. Ibid.
137. Bolzoni, 90.
138. See Stanton J. Linden, *Darke Hierogliphicks*. Linden says Donne, Herbert, and Milton used alchemy in order to express spiritual truths. Their contemporaries, however, were beginning to employ it satirically. He observes, "In both Donne and Herbert nonsatirical uses outweigh those that are satirical in nature, pointing the direction to be followed in the alchemical imagery of Milton . . . ," 155. For two earlier studies of Milton's use of the cabala see H. F. Fletcher, *Milton's Semitic Studies* (Chicago: Univ. of Chicago Press, 1926) and his *Milton's Rabbinical Readings* (Urbana: Univ. of Illinois Press, 1930). See also Denis Saurat, *Milton: Man and Thinker*, 2nd ed., trans. Dorothy Bolton (London: Dent, 1944; repr., 1946). When Saurat published his discovery of cabalistic doctrines in *Paradise Lost*, C. S. Lewis was among the first to celebrate his research, saying, "One of Professor Saurat's great contributions has been to discover the doctrine of the *Zohar* which was almost certainly present in Milton's mind when he wrote those verses [book 7, ll. 166ff.]," (*A Preface to Paradise*

Lost, 87). The doctrine in question, the *Zohar*, Lewis defines as "God . . . infinitely extended in space (like ether), and therefore in order to create—to make *room* for anything to exist which is not simply Himself—he must contract, or retire, His infinite essence," 87.

139. Katz, 77.
140. Thorndike, 8:14.
141. Fernando, 133.
142. Sheppard, "Gnosticism," 91.
143. Ibid., 92. Sheppard is citing G. Verbeke, *L'Évolution de la Doctrine du Pneuma des Stoiciens à S. Augustin* (Paris & Louvain, 1945), 142.
144. Jeffrey Johnson, *The Theology of John Donne* (Rochester, N.Y.: D.S. Brewer, 1999), 62–66.
145. Pamela H. Smith, *The Business of Alchemy: Science and Culture in the Holy Roman Empire* (Princeton: Princeton Univ. Press, 1994), 269.
146. Ibid., 270.
147. *The Works of George Herbert*, ed. F. E. Hutchinson (Oxford: Clarendon, 1941).
148. For further discussion of "swallowing" as alchemical concept see John Read's *Prelude to Chemistry: An Outline of Alchemy* (Cambridge: MIT Press, 1966), 133.
149. Examples of such illustrations can be found in C. A. Burland's *The Arts of the Alchemists* (New York: Macmillan, 1968), 51.
150. Donne gave a copy of Münster's *Cosmographia* (1578) to Edward Parvish. Bald says his purpose may have been "an acknowledgement of kindness experienced during his travels abroad," 52n.
151. The story is found in the Old Testament book of Jonah.
152. Schoenfeldt, "Reading Bodies," in *Reading, Society and Politics in Early Modern England*, ed. Kevin Sharpe and Steven N. Zwicker, 222.
153. Ibid. In the case of cultural "disease," Schoenfeldt says, the Galenic physiology could work one of two ways: "[O]ne can stress either the mutual interdependence of parts or the necessary purgation of deleterious matter."
154. The reference is to Donne's *Essays*, 48.
155. The reference is to *Paradise Lost*, bk. 5. Raphael explains that angels too need food ("and food alike those pure / Intelligential substances require," ll. 7–8). Though he explains angel digestion as the same as mankind's, he nevertheless employs alchemical terms (concoctive heat / To transubstantiate . . . by fire / Of sooty coal the Empiric Alchemist / Can turn, or holds it possible to turn / Metals of drossiest Ore to perfet Gold," [ll. 437–42]).
156. The citation is from Donne's verse letter "To Sr. Edward Herbert. At Julyers." All citations of Donne's poetry, unless otherwise noted, are from *The Complete Poetry of John Donne*, ed. John T. Shawcross (Garden City: Doubleday/Anchor Books, 1967). Rpt. New York: New York Univ. Press, 1968.
157. Thorndike, 7:212.
158. I cite from *Selections from Ralph Waldo Emerson*, ed. Stephen E. Whicher (Boston: Houghton Mifflin, 1960). Concerning beauty (in *Nature*) Emerson writes, "Nothing is quite beautiful alone; nothing but is beautiful in the whole." The process whereby individual beauties are reconstituted into a beautiful whole Emerson describes as mental. This opus takes place in the alembic of the poet's mind: "A single object is only so far beautiful as it suggests this universal grace [wholeness]. The poet, the painter, the sculptor, . . . seek each to concentrate this radiance of the whole on one point, . . . Thus is Art, a nature passed through the alembic of man," 30–31. Emerson sometimes cites Donne, for example, *The Second Anniversary* (ll. 244–46) in "Love," and he sometimes emulates his prose style. For elab-

oration, see *The Early Lectures of Ralph Waldo Emerson* (Harvard Univ. Press, 1964), xiv.

159. See Nicholas Tyacke, *Aspects of English Protestantism, c. 1530–1700* (New York: Manchester Univ. Press, 2001). Tyacke notes that Lord Herbert's *De Veritate* was inspired by Grotius and Daniel Tilenus, "the leading French defender of Arminius' teachings," 233. Among the issues confronted, he says, is "'free will [which] has been given us for our benefit that we may devote ourselves by our free choice to the means which lead to happiness' . . . [and a warning against the] 'doctrines of predestination' which issue in 'a kind of Stoic fate,'" 233.

160. Sharpe and Zwicker, 14–15. The context is Schoenfeldt's thesis that body and book are interconnected.

161. See Nicholas Tyacke, *Anti-Calvinists: The Rise of English Arminianism, c. 1590–1640* (Oxford: Clarendon, 1987). After the accession of Charles I, "by November 1629 Donne had became much bolder in attacking Calvinist predestinarian teaching from the pulpit," 261.

162. For discussion of Donne's Protestant and Catholic poetics see Heather L. Meakin, *John Donne's Articulation of the Feminine* (New York: Oxford Univ. Press, 1998). When Meakin discusses what she calls Elizabeth Drury's "sexual textualization" in *The Anniversaries*, she refers to the "Catholic (closed) and Protestant (dilatory) conceptions of the female body," 205. "Donne," she writes, "makes use of Elizabeth's paradoxically chaste and fertile body which aligns her with the Virgin Mary to arrive finally at a fully Protestant position from which to preach: that of mediator between heaven and earth. Elizabeth is his first sermon, in other words," 205–6. Meakin's dichotomy is based upon the idea that the Virgin, because perfect, must be "closed." My study of Donne indicates that he considered the Virgin a vital or active force. Therefore, I would not attach the label "closed" to Catholic "textualization" or discourse; rather, I believe that both Catholics and Arminians (if that is what Meakin means by "Protestant" discourse, in which case she excludes radical Calvinists) should be categorized as "open."

163. See Tyacke, *Anti-Calvinists*. He cites one example of Donne's "Arminian preaching . . . at Paul's Cross," 182. Referring to the Puritans as those who "despise others as men whom nothing can save. . . . [as] Men that think no sinne can hurt them because they are elect," Donne places himself firmly in the Arminian camp. "His words," Tyacke writes, "almost certainly had the approval of higher authority, for we know that Laud, as Bishop of London, required to see copies of Paul's Cross sermons before they were preached," 182.

164. One useful survey of Protestant tolerance in early modern England is Peter Lake, *Moderate Puritans and the Elizabethan Church* (New York: Cambridge Univ. Press, 1982). He argues that the language of gesture was used to resolve, rather than exacerbate, disputes among Protestants.

165. For a discussion of the Laudian attitude toward Roman Catholic recusants, see Anthony Milton, *Catholic and Reformed: The Roman and Protestant Churches in English Protestant Thought, 1600–1640* (New York: Cambridge Univ. Press, 1995). Milton observes that "Roman Catholic recusants represented a denial of the legitimacy and integrity of the Laudian church. However moderate their position might be towards the Roman Church, the Laudians would therefore still have had little sympathy for recusants who were ultimately just another type of native separatist, rejecting the authority and communion of their native established church," 88. One Laudian warned, "Babylons Brats [Catholics] must not be dandled, but dasht against the stones," 88.

166. For discussion of the Puritan rise to power, see Tyacke, "Puritan Politicians and King James VI and I, 1587–1604," in *Politics, Religion, and Popularity in Early Stuart Britain: Essays in Honour of Conrad Russell,* ed. Thomas Cogswell, Richard Cust, and Peter Lake (New York: Cambridge Univ. Press, 2002), 21–44. One link between James VI of Scotland and the Puritan faction in England was Robert Devereux, second Earl of Essex (under whom Donne had served against Spain in 1596). Essex was in contact with Scotland during the 1590s and up until the time of his rebellion in 1601. When Elizabeth ordered his arrest, he was incarcerated for a time in the home of Sir Thomas Egerton, Lord Keeper of the Great Seal, and Donne's employer. According to Tyacke, after the execution of Essex, Sir Henry Bromley, who had raised support for his rebellion, went with Sir Oliver Cromwell (Bromley's brother-in-law and MP) to Scotland to confer with James VI, then about to become James I of England. Cromwell, Tyacke observes, "entertained the new king at Hinchingbrooke, in Huntingdonshire, between 27 and 29 April [1603]," 37. Having discussed Puritan preparations for attaching themselves to the center of power, Tyacke proceeds to discuss their "puritan blueprint" for cleansing the Commonwealth and the Church (38–39). The administrative practices of Sir Thomas Egerton were among those cited as needing reform, as one "singled out, along with Sir Walter Raleigh, either as pluralists or vendors of office," 40. At the Hampton Court Conference of 1604 these Puritans were rebuffed (43). All that this evidence suggests is that Donne was well aware of growing tensions and of the need to discover a center or centers of power that would assure his political survival.

167. For a discussion of antipapal polemics during the 1630s in England, see Anthony Milton's *Catholic and Reformed.* He argues that Laudian pamphlets attempted to confront "the dangerous extremes to which anti-papal overreaction had driven Protestantism," 67. One example is Anthony Stafford's *The Female Glory* (1635), written to restore the Blessed Virgin to her place of honor (67).

168. The citation is from Donne's "'Sermon LXII,' Preached Upon the Penitential Psalms," in *The Works of John Donne,* ed. Henry Alford (London: John W. Parker, 1839), 3:100–101.

169. This observation is made by Joseph A. Mazzeo, "Notes on John Donne's Alchemical Imagery," *Isis* 48.2 (June 1957): 114.

170. Shawcross, *Intentionality,* 6.

171. See Edward Kelly, *The Englishman's Two Excellent Treatises on the Philosopher's Stone,* trans. from the Hamburg edition of 1676 by A. E. Waite (1893, London: Stuart and Watkins, 1970). Kelly describes the coagulated solution as "a mass of clear snow-white colour . . . the white transforming into yellow and saffron, and at last into a deep ruby colour," 142. He also says, "The philosophers agree in this, that the white colour must precede the red," 143.

172. See Linden's article, "Expounding George Ripley: A Huntington Alchemical Manuscript," *The Huntington Library Quarterly* 61. 3–4 (2000): 411–28. The citation is from 424. Ripley's outline of the process is conventional. Diana Fernando, for example, cites Antoine Joseph Pernety (1716–1801), whose *Dictionnaire Mytho-Hermétique* lists twelve steps, each represented by a sign of the zodiac: calcination (Aries), congelation (Taurus), fixation (Gemini), solution (Cancer), digestion (Leo), distillation (Virgo), sublimation (Libra), separation (Scorpio), ceration (Sagittarius), fermentation (Capricornus), multiplication (Aquarius), and projection (Pisces). Mylius and Valentine, she notes, also divided "the processes leading to the Philosopher's Stone into 12," (*Alchemy,* 126).

173. Ripley cited by Linden, 424–25.

Chapter 1: Emblems of Making

1. The persistence of this image in human memory is argued by John Steinbeck's *The Grapes of Wrath*, which ends with Rose of Sharon suckling a starving man.

2. The label "devices" is from John Shawcross. For a discussion of variables, among which is allusion, see *Intentionality*, where he observes that content "is a variation upon the known, it presents a different set of constants, perhaps, with a different set of tendencies, yielding a different focus, and all within a literary form reveling in its own constants and variables. The author's content works out of these sets of constants, highlighting, diminishing, foregrounding, skewing them to achieve a different angle of vision (that is, different from some other author's or some other work's); the author includes variables to illuminate those constants, to put them into perspective, to make them meaningful and different. And some of these variables I label devices; among these literary devices are . . . allusions," 18.

3. Ben Jonson makes satirical reference to virgin's milk, or *lac virginis*, in *The Alchemist* (2.3.87–196). This virgin's milk, made from various ingredients (including horse manure) was considered a wonder-working formula believed to have restorative power. Heraclitus may be among the earliest sources for belief in the restorative virtues of manure. See *Heracleitus*, introduction, *On the Universe*, trans. W. H. S. Jones in *Hippocrates*, vol. 4, Loeb Classical Library, (Cambridge: Harvard Univ. Press, 1992), 469–509. According to this account, Heraclitus "buried himself in a cowshed, expecting that the noxious damp humour would be drawn out of him by the warmth of the manure," 462. The early alchemists seem to have concocted virgin's milk from the same recipe. Mazzeo points out that Donne refers to the use of horse dung as a source of heat, evidence that he is familiar with this alchemical phenomenon. See "John Donne's Alchemical Imagery," *Isis* 48 (June 1957): 103–23. The reference is to Donne's verse letter, "*To the Countesse of Bedford*" (ll. 10–12): "For when from herbs the pure part must be wonne / From grosse, by Stilling, this is better done / By despis'd dung, then by the fire of Sunne." Edward Kelly focuses on the end product, rather than the process, defining "virgin's milk" as the "white tincture, or elixir . . . the everlasting water, and water of life, because it is as brilliant as white marble; it is also called the White Queen, who by increasing the fire becomes the Mighty King, the white transforming into yellow and saffron, and at last into a deep ruby colour," 142. The progression from Queen/white to King/red implies transformation to the androgynous state.

4. "Introductions," in *Sermons*, 1:114.

5. *Sermons*, 1:200. The sermon, entitled, "A Sermon Preached at Pauls Cross to the Lords of the Council, and other Honorable Persons," was preached 24 March 1616/17. Donne's text was Proverbs 22:11: "He that loveth pureness of heart, for the grace of his lips the king shall be his friend." All citations of Scripture are from the King James version.

6. "Introductions," in *Sermons*, 1:125. The editors are citing John Chamberlain's letter to Dudley Carleton. Chamberlain's testimony is interpreted as something to be taken seriously, for other letters by him indicate that he could be very critical of sermons preached at St. Paul's Cross.

7. "Introductions," in *Sermons*, 1:127.

8. *Sermons*, 4:287. The sermon text cited is an explication of Colossians 1:19–20: "For it pleased the Father that in him should all fulness dwell; And, having made peace through the blood of his cross, by him to reconcile all things unto himself; by him, I say, whether they be things in earth, or things in heaven." This sermon was preached at St. Paul's on Christmas Day, 1622.

9. For a discussion of Donne's reservations about Christmas observances see Dayton Haskin's, "John Donne and the Cultural Contradictions of Christmas," *John Donne Journal* 11.1–2 (1992): 133–57. Haskin observes that "by the 1580s Christmas had become a charged subject for debates about the national religion and the nature of English society," 138.

10. Henry Green, *Shakespeare and the Emblem Writers* (London: Trübner, 1870), 383.

11. Ibid.

12. Huston Diehl, "Discovering the Old World: The Renaissance Emblem Book as Cultural Artifact," in *Approaches to Teaching the Metaphysical Poets,* ed. Sidney Gottlieb (New York: Modern Language Association, 1990), 68–74. The citation is from page 70.

13. Quoted by Green, 384.

14. For a discussion of fire in alchemy see Joseph A. Mazzeo, "Notes on John Donne's Alchemical Imagery," *Isis* 48.2 (June 1957): 103–23. He observes that, "The alchemists are generally careful to state that a special kind of fire must be employed in the great work, although they are seldom very explicit about it and shroud it in the general secrecy that covered all the important phases of the alchemical process," 112. For the significance of the phoenix in alchemy see John Read, *Prelude to Chemistry: An Outline of Alchemy* (Cambridge: MIT Press, 1966). According to Read, "Fire was the common agent used in this [alchemical] process [of sublimation]: the adepts held that while 'ordinary fire' destroyed the seeds of substance, the germinative power was unaffected by the action of various forms of 'philosophical fire,'" 138. Read furthermore associates the alchemical phoenix with philosophical fire as well as with alchemical principles of augmentation and multiplication (219). A more recent discussion of the phoenix can be found in Lyndy Abraham's *Dictionary of Alchemical Imagery,* 152.

15. Diehl, "Picture and Word," 73.

16. For a discussion of the alchemist's need to prepare him or herself (women sometimes performed or assisted in the work), see Eluned Crawshaw, "Hermetic Elements in Donne's Poetic Vision," in *John Donne: Essays in Celebration,* ed. A. J. Smith (London: Methuen, 1972), 324–48. The citation is from 332–33.

17. See John Watkins's essay, "'Out of her Ashes May a Second Phoenix Rise': James I and the Legacy of Elizabethan Anti-Catholicism," in *Catholicism and Anti-Catholicism in Early Modern English Texts,* ed. Arthur F. Marotti (1999), 116–36. A translation of Owen's epigram and commentary is found on 120.

18. See *Sermons,* vol. 7. Donne refers to the Wings of God as "denotation of Power," but he also distinguishes this power as twofold: 1) a power like England's once great navy (Donne skirts this troublesome issue, stating instead that this power "hovers over the world, and intimidates it with her sailes and ships") and 2) the power of the protecting wings of the mother hen, who, in the person of Christ, "would have gathered Jerusalem, as a henne gathers her chickens under her wings," 67–68. Of course the idea of the protecting "hen" is connected with that of the gentle dove. Hence Donne's text, providing the constants, allows his reader to discover among the variables an eagle and dove joined as phoenix.

19. Susan Haskins, *Mary Magdalen,* 49.

20. *Sermons,* 5:186. This churching sermon was delivered either in 1621 or in 1623. For an argument for the earlier date (based upon evidence concerning Jewish prophecies) see N. I. Matar, "The Date of John Donne's Sermon 'Preached at the Churching of the Countess of Bridgewater,'" *Notes and Queries* 39 (December 1992): 447–48. The constant Donne provides, that is, ashes to ashes, reads, "Whither can

Man, derived from earth before his life, enamored of the earth, embracing it, and maried to it in his life, destined to the earth, betrothed to it for a second mariage after this life, whither can he fall? It is true of us all, *I shall say to corruption, Thou art my father,"* and so on.

21. *Sermons*, 2:260–62.

22. Here Donne distinguishes "the thin and active part of the blood" as "a kind of middle nature, between soul and body" (*Sermons*, 2:262). In this same sermon he will define *grace* as the *middle nature in Christ's blood,* implying this nature to be androgynous.

23. *Sermons*, 2:260–61.

24. Gareth Roberts observes, "God prepares one to whom the secret may be handed on. The secrets of alchemy are never merely to be found out by human labour, but 'bi teching or revelacion' and the Stone is to be obtained by grace, rather than reading," 79. Roberts's citation is from Sir Edward Kelly's work in Ashmole (1652).

25. Much controversy surrounds the problem of the ordering of Donne's "Holy Sonnets." Altogether there are nineteen sonnets and scholars tend to agree that sixteen of these belong to some sort of successive arrangements. The sonnet cited above begins "Oh my blacke Soule!" and is the second sonnet in the most authoritative texts.

26. See Albert H. Tricomi, *Reading Tudor-Stuart Texts Through Cultural Historicism* (Gainsville: Univ. Press of Florida, 1996), 154. The context for Tricomi's term, "metonymic transposition," is the "mothering body" of the Duchess of Malfi. Tricomi is among those who have described the figurative natures of historical and literary discourse as "unavoidably tropological," 161. However, he distinguishes "imaginative literature" from historical, observing that it is not necessarily "bound" by the past, 161. This is compatible with his own version of cultural historicism, which he defines as "an understanding of history as an ongoing cultural, not merely event-based, process," 2. Tricomi defines this concept of cultural historicism as an examination of "the ways texts situated in the past make claims on us by engaging our feelings, thereby subtly informing our present values," 8. Thus, like John Shawcross, he shows how the reader's experience and knowledge, brought to bear upon the author's text, cooperate in making his or her own present meaning. My work joins both in that it demonstrates how Donne developed a language system that makes and reproduces culture. Alchemical discourse, which looks back and forth, is naturally part of the process.

27. All quotations from the *Anniversaries* are taken from volume 6 of *The Variorum Edition of the Poetry of John Donne,* ed. Gary A. Stringer et al. (Bloomington and Indianapolis: Indiana Univ. Press, 1995). Other poems are quoted from John T. Shawcross's edition.

28. Yates, preface, in *Art,* xii.

29. See Yates, *Art,* 135–36.

30. The reference is to Sandford's translation of Agrippa (1569): "*Sephiroth,* which is called *Hochma,* that is to say, wisdome."

31. The citation is from Joseph Leon Blau, *The Christian Interpretation of the Cabala in the Renaissance* (New York: Columbia Univ. Press, 1944), 28.

32. Ibid.

33. Sometimes this four-letter word is written *YHWH* or *JHYH* and vocalized YaHWeH. Hence Tetragrammaton is sometimes substituted for *YaHWeH,* the mysterious name of God and used as the title of the Deity. Jeremy Taylor, for example, writes of the "adoreable Mystery of the Patriarchs" (1649). According to Babington

(*Catholic Faith*, 1610) it is the "name that cannot bee expressed! O name truly tetragrammaton!"

34. Blau, 82. As noted above, John Wilkins published the first English textbook on cryptography in 1641. Though Wilkins's publication followed Donne's death, there is no reason to believe that Donne was unaware of this project, a cooperative effort during the early years of the century.

35. For a discussion of Eve, including Second Eve, see Gertrude Grace Sill, *A Handbook of Symbols in Christian Art* (New York: Macmillan, 1975), 53–54. "When Adam and Eve are shown with the apple," she writes, "it is a symbol of their disobedience and of original sin. . . . Conversely, when near or held by Mary or the Christ Child, the apple signifies acceptance of man's sins and salvation," 54. The illustration provided is Crivelli's *Madonna and Child* (fifteenth-century Italian), which depicts Mary holding the apple.

36. One example, a silver stamp seal kept in the Musée du Louvre, Départment des Antiquités Orientales (catalogue no. 261) depicts a goddess seated on a dragon. Its origin is western central Asia, and it comes from the Bactria Margiana Archaeological Complex. This item was included in the Metropolitan Museum of Art's exhibit, "Art of the First Cities: The Third Millennium B.C. from the Mediterranean to the Indus," 2003. Though the goddess rides the dragon, there is no indication that it is evil.

37. David Katz distinguishes between the "Lurianic kabbalah," with its emphasis on last things and the "kabbalah," "with its emphasis on the doctrine of the *sefiroth* and Creation," 73. The latter "believed that when the divine light surged forth in Creation, the first being who emanated from the light was *Adam Kadmon*, primordial man, from whose head burst a tremendous light that took on a variety of intricate and complex patterns," 74. Agrippa's theory reverses this order, making Eve closer to God than Adam.

38. The observation is made by H. J. Sheppard, "Egg Symbolism in Alchemy," *Ambix: Journal of the Society for the Study of Alchemy* 6 (August 1958): 140–48. The reference is to 140.

39. See, for example, Lyndy Abraham's "Edward Kelly's Hieroglyph," in *Emblems and Alchemy*, ed. Alison Adams and Stanton J. Linden, vol. 3, Glasgow Emblem Studies (Sherborne, Dorset: Remous Ltd., Milborne Port, 1998), 95–108. She calls attention to the egg symbol as Kelly employs it in his *Theatre of Terrestrial Astronomy* (Hamburg, 1676). The figure she is studying is that of the three-headed Deity standing over the egg or "little globe," 101.

40. Not all alchemists appropriated the four-element theory, but those who did assigned to the Egg these respective parts. Accordingly, the shell of the Egg is Earth, the white is Water, the skin between is Air, and the yolk is Fire. See Sheppard, "Egg Symbolism," 144.

41. The *Turba philosophorum* is an imagined conversation wherein adepts from the ancient world discuss details of the Great Work.

42. For discussion of the phenomenon whereby the Yolk of Fire hatches a chick, see Sheppard, "Egg Symbolism," 144.

43. Ibid., 147.

44. See *Sermons*, vol. 4. The reference is to Donne's sermon on Judges 5:20: "They fought from heaven; the stars in their courses fought against Sisera." The context was that of Deborah's prophecy and of Jael's execution of Sisera by driving a nail into his head. Donne observes that, "*God* would effect his purpose by so weake an instrument by a woman," 181.

45. Ibid., 185.

46. For discussion of World Egg, see Sheppard, "Egg Symbolism." The term "picture-thinking" is his. Picture-thinking, he says, "has been of inestimable value in aiding man to comprehend what cannot be reproduced as precepts but only imagined by constructing a picture out of concepts. Reason expresses itself here by imagination; and in the comprehension of the cosmic process imagination seized upon the creative process commonly observed within the animal world. By this means the World Egg most probably arose as a universal symbol of creation," 141.

47. Sheppard observes, "The Philosopher's Egg takes its place in an interpretation of alchemy as a symbolic redemption of the soul of man according to Orphic-inspired Gnostic conceptions of regeneration," 141.

48. In the Islamabad Museum, Department of Archaeology and Museums, Pakistan, is a standing terracotta figure, the nature of which is androgynous. From Baluchistan, Nausharo, it is identified as "Nausharo" (ca. 2600–2500 BC), catalogue no. 268b. The figure wears a headdress typical of female figures and holds an infant, but it has the chest and clothing of a male.

49. The reference is to Henry Green, *Shakespeare and the Emblem Writers*, above.

50. Whitney's comment from *The Riverside Shakespeare*, plate 22.

51. One reference is to Laertes' attempt to mollify Claudius, who fears revenge. "To his good friends thus wide I'll ope my arms, / And like the kind life-rend'ring pelican, / Repast them with my blood" (4.5.146–48). The other is Lear's comment on his two eldest children. "Judicious punishment: 'twas this flesh begot / Those pelican daughters" (3.4.70–71). For commentary, see *The Arden Edition of the Works of William Shakespeare: King Lear*, ed. Kenneth Muir (New York: Methuen, 1975). Muir cites *Batman uppon Bartholome* (1582) as a possible source: "The Pellican loueth too much her children. For when the children bee haught, and begin to waxe hoare, they smite the father and the mother in the face, wherfore the mother smiteth them againe and slaieth them. And the thirde daye the mother smiteth her selfe in her side that the bloud runneth out, and sheddeth that hot bloud vppon the bodies of her children. And by virtue of the bloud the birdes that were before dead, quicken againe," 111.

52. Kelly's letter to Edward Dyer (14 September 1595) quoted by Abraham: "I was wont with the spirit of wine in glasses, and especially in such vessels as they commonly call pelicans, by the means of the gentle vapour of the bath, to elevate the calces of metals" (Bodleian, Ashmolean MS 1420,328). See *Dictionary*, 143.

53. Roberts, 86.

54. Edward Kelly, *The Englishman's Two Excellent Treatises on the Philosopher's Stone*, trans. from the Hamburg edition of 1676 by A. E. Waite (1893; London: Stuart and Watkins, 1970), 136–37.

55. Ibid., 135.

56. For Tricomi's discussion of the mothering body, see *Reading Tudor-Stuart Texts*, chapter 7, "Affectivity and New Historicism," 136–56.

57. Ibid., 137.

58. John Webster, *The Duchess of Malfi*, in *English Drama, 1580–1642*, ed. C. F. Tucker Brooke and Nathaniel Burton Paradise (Lexington, Mass.: D.C. Heath, 1933).

59. An intriguing reversal of this trope in Christian tradition is the story of Saint Nicholas, who in his infancy refused his mother's breast, hence making the saint an exemplum for fasting and abstinence, whence came his power. An illustration of this story comes in the form of a cameo owned by the Metropolitan Museum of Art. The pendant depicts the saint refusing his mother's attempt to suckle him by grasping her hand. The cameo (1200–1250) is southern Italian (catalogue no. 2000.347).

60. Tricomi, 149.

61. Brooke and Paradise (n. 58) cite Donne's *Anatomy of the World* (1611) that is, *The First Anniversarie*, among the sources of *The Duchess of Malfi* (646).

62. *Dictionary*, 143. Abraham notes that the shape of a pelican with its beak in its breast resembled that of a circulatory still. In Jonson's *The Alchemist* Face informs Subtle that "the Retort brake, / And what was sau'd was put into the *Pelicane*" (2.3.77–78).

63. Ibid., 144.

64. *Sermons*, 3:196.

65. Ibid., 10:248.

66. My concept of metaphysical mnemotechnics is primarily based upon those of Ramon Lull, though the reference here is to classical systems of memory. See, for example, Mary Carruthers's *The Book of Memory* (New York: Cambridge Univ. Press, 1990). Part of her study examines Augustine's idea of how the mind attaches present images to past, organizing and classifying those already stored in memory alongside those currently on the page or currently viewed. She picks up Augustine's thread to explain how those who preach and those who paint, even those who construct cathedrals, employ mnemonic devices in order that their viewers or listeners may understand: the technique they employ, she says, "serves essentially as a coding and filing system for the orderly and ready recollection of the material," 100.

67. The cabalistic idea of *Schekhina*, or glory, was appropriated by Ramon Lull as one of the names of God in his *ars combinatoria*.

Chapter 2: Donne's Doctrice of Mary

1. Frances Yates, *Giordano Bruno and the Hermetic Tradition* (Chicago: Univ. of Chicago Press, 1964), 186.

2. Anthony Milton, "A Qualified Intolerance: The Limits and Ambiguities of Early Stuart Anti-Catholicism," in *Catholicism and Anti-Catholicism in Early Modern English Texts*, ed. Arthur F. Marotti (New York: St. Martin's, 1999), 107. Milton studies various reasons for Protestant tolerance toward Catholics, including practical matters such as politics and economics. For example, Roman Catholics penalized for nonconformity became an important source of revenue. Milton observes that "the Exchequer was more keen to exploit them [Catholics] as a source of state revenue . . . than to use the laws to secure their permanent religious conformity," 101. Other issues addressed are aesthetics—including poetry, music, and art—and scholarship, including devotional literature and Bible commentaries. Ultimately, Milton says, "the semantic associations of 'tolerance' in this period were almost entirely negative ones," 107.

3. Ibid., 103.

4. C. S. Lewis, *The Allegory of Love* (1936; New York: Oxford Univ. Press, 1975), 296n.

5. Ibid., 74.

6. Yates, *Bruno*, 186.

7. Ibid., 90.

8. Evelyn M. Simpson, "Sources," in *Essays in Divinity by John Donne* (Oxford: Clarendon, 1952), 107.

9. Yates, *Bruno*, 187.

10. See Eamon Duffy, "The Long Reformation: Catholicism, Protestantism and

the Multitude," in *England's Long Reformation, 1500–1800*, ed. Nicholas Tyacke (London: Univ. College London Press, 1998), 33–70. Duffy quotes George Herbert, "at sermons and prayers men may sleep or wander; but when one is asked a question, he must discover what he is," 44.

11. John Carey studies the way Donne's apostasy influenced his work. See *John Donne: Life, Mind, and Art* (New York: Oxford Univ. Press, 1981). Describing the terrors and persecutions endured by Catholics during Donne's time, Carey compares his dilemma to that of any "young Jewish writer in Germany in the 1930s" (18).

12. David Hickman, "From Catholic to Protestant: The Changing Meaning of Testamentary Religious Provisions in Elizabethan London," in *England's Long Reformation, 1500–1800*, ed. Nicholas Tyacke (London: Univ. College London Press, 1998), 134.

13. Cressy, *Birth*, 10.

14. Ibid., 135.

15. Ibid.

16. Ibid., 109.

17. Donne, "Sermon LXII, Preached Upon the Penitential Psalms," in *The Works of John Donne*, ed. Henry Alford, vol. 3 (London: John W. Parker, 1839), 100–101.

18. Cressy, *Birth*, 107.

19. *Dictionary*, 210.

20. Salt and the sign of the cross were also important in birthing rituals. According to David Cressy, "Traditional catholicism encouraged the practice of crossing the child after swaddling, sprinkling it with protective salt, and placing a coin in the baby's cradle or hand," *Birth*, 81–82. This leads to the conclusion that medieval images depicting the Virgin in swaddling clothes (noted above in the introduction) encouraged the viewer to contemplate the variable salt.

21. Arthur F. Marotti, preface, in *Catholicism and Anti-Catholicism in Early Modern English Texts*, ed. Arthur F. Marotti (New York: St. Martin's Press, 1999), xiii.

22. Yates, *The Occult Philosophy in the Elizabethan Age* (London: Routledge and Kegan Paul, 1972), 55.

23. Milton, "Qualified Intolerance," 86.

24. Ibid., 104.

25. Milton, *Catholic and Reformed*, 206.

26. Katz, 70.

27. Ibid.

28. Ibid., 78.

29. For discussion of the social side of practical toleration, see Milton, "Qualified Intolerance," 100–101. Milton observes, "There were precious few puritanically inclined families in the Elizabethan or early Stuart period which were entirely free of Roman Catholics," 100. Also he writes, "A significant percentage of the higher nobility of England also remained Roman Catholic or crypto-Catholic," 101.

30. Quoted in Cressy, *Literacy and the Social Order: Reading and Writing in Tudor and Stuart England* (New York: Cambridge Univ. Press, 1980), 2.

31. Cressy discusses how customs concerning Mary were transferred to altered forms. See *Bonfires*, 50 and 58.

32. David Hickman notes the "diminishing place of the Virgin and saints" in funeral practices. See, "From Catholic to Protestant," in *England's Long Reformation*, ed. Nicholas Tyacke, 118.

33. Julian Davies, *The Caroline Captivity of the Church: Charles I and the Remoulding of Anglicanism, 1625–1641* (New York: Oxford Univ. Press, 1992), 154. In 1627, Davies observes, complaints were issued "against the lecturers of the Ampthill combination

for speaking irreverently about the Virgin Mary and for being in some points nonconformist," 154.

34. Hickman, 118.

35. Ibid.

36. Ibid., 125.

37. For review of the ways religious practices were revised during the English Reformation, see Cressy, *Bonfires*. Cressy argues that Protestants revised the English calendar in order to accommodate the new religion but also in order to assure continuity. For example, the calendars of 1552 and 1561 had the same number of holy days. Catholics, he says, still had access to publications "which featured the traditional monthly array of saints," 12. Ironically, the ecclesiastical courts kept the pre-Reformation calendar. Thus, Cressy says, Protestants inadvertently managed to "perpetuate the memory of saints whose days had ceased to be festivals," 11. The uneasy transition Cressy studies is intriguing. Some Puritan centers, for example, "still adhered to pre-Reformation patterns," even in the early seventeenth century (16).

38. See Cressy, *Bonfires*. "In 1628 the Arminian prebend of Durham, John Cosin, scandalized more austere Protestants by flooding the cathedral with Candlemas candles, tapers and torches," 17.

39. Hickman, 119.

40. My source is James S. Baumlin's catalogue of anti-Catholic legislation taken from the Ellesmere manuscripts. See Baumlin's "From Recusancy to Apostasy: Donne's 'Satyre III,'" *Explorations in Renaissance Culture* 16 (1990): 67–85.

41. For distinctions between the Reformation on the Continent and the Reformation in England, see Nicholas Tyacke, introduction, in *England's Long Reformation, 1500–1800*, 1–32. Tyacke observes that continental historians tend to view the Reformation as a religious movement resisted by Catholics with some degree of success. English historians, however, tend to treat it as a political movement, as "a succession of legislative enactments—culminating under Elizabeth I and followed by a fairly rapid collapse of Catholicism," 1. This succession of new laws supports the view that Donne had reason to be anxious for his political (if not his spiritual) survival.

42. The references are two: Milton, *Catholic and Reformed*, 251–60, and Milton, "Qualified Intolerance," 105.

43. The term "re-Catholicization" is from Peter Lake and Michael Questier, "Prisons, Priests and People," in *England's Long Reformation, 1500–1800*, ed. Nicholas Tyacke (1998), 195–234. The authors discuss various Protestant attempts to curtail or exploit the activities of Catholic clergy in prisons. Prisons and the staging of public executions, they argue, "provided an arena where both sides could make a pitch to a wider public," 196.

44. For dicusssion of the way the Oath of Allegiance countered Protestant fears about "*unseen*" Roman Catholics lurking about the land, see Milton, "Qualified Intolerance," 105–6. He writes, "The Oath was in a sense a tangible manifestation of the pragmatic assumption of most people that there were indeed politically loyal Roman Catholics, even if theoretically this was impossible," 105–6.

45. For discussion of Bruno's system of "magic memory," see Frances Yates, *Giordano Bruno*. Yates surveys the dialogue of Bruno's *De umbris idearum*, which makes reference to "a wheel divided into thirty lettered divisions, with a sun at the centre of it," 195. This is a Lullian element.

46. Lake and Questier, 197. In some cases, they say, laypersons came "to regard the gaols as substitutes for religious houses," 200.

47. Ibid.

48. Dennis Flynn, "Donne and the Ancient Catholic Nobility," *English Literary Renaissance* 19.3 (1989): 310.
49. Ibid., 314.
50. See Flynn, "'Awry and Squint': The Dating of Donne's Holy Sonnets," *John Donne Journal* 7.1 (1988): 40–41.
51. Flynn, "Donne and the Ancient Catholic Nobility," 311.
52. Ibid., 313.
53. Ibid.
54. Geoffrey Keynes, *A Bibliography of Dr. John Donne, Dean of Saint Paul's,* 4th ed. (Oxford: Clarendon, 1973), 271. Keynes lists this work by Lull among Donne's library, saying it bears his signature and motto.
55. For Lull's influence during Donne's time, see Manuel Duran, "Ramon Llull: An Introduction," *Catalan Review: International Journal of Catalan Culture* 4.1–2 (July–December 1990): 11–18. Duran remarks, "The impact of Llull's works upon Renaissance thought was considerable. Pico della Mirandola, the great Italian humanist, attempted to harmonize the Lullian Art with the Kabbalah. Giordano Bruno and Nicolas of Cusa were also influenced by Llull, Philip II of Spain was an admirer of Llull," and so on, 17.
56. Keynes says "pencil markings in margins" (271) indicate "the care with which Donne read his books" (260).
57. Ibid., 258.
58. Duran, 12.
59. Duran observes Lull's "indebtedness to Sufi poetry for some of his ideas about love and the mystical union with God" and "the basic ideas of the Kabbalah," 17. See also Mark D. Johnston, *The Spiritual Logic of Ramon Llull* (Oxford: Clarendon, 1987). Johnston says that Lull's *Principia,* which Donne owned, "posits nine Relative *Principia* by means of which the Dignities mutually communicate their natures and diffuse them throughout all creation. . . . The writings of John Scotus Erigena, Algazel, the Jewish *sephiroth,* and Islamic *hadras* . . . have all been proposed as direct sources for Llull's scheme of Dignities," 19.
60. See Gregory B. Stone, "Ramon Llull vs. Petrus Alfonsi: Postmodern Liberalism and the Six Liberal Arts," *Medieval Encounters: Jewish, Christian and Muslim Culture* 3.1 (March 1997): 70–93. The citation is from 70. Petrus Alfonsi was born a Jew and spent his youth in Muslim Spain. Stone studies the differences between Alfonsi, a proponent of "that great project known as Scholasticism" (71) and Lull, an exponent of his own peculiar system of spiritual logic, which complements Aristotelian logic in that it works backward from a "true" conclusion in order to discover the reasons for the already established "end." Alfonsi, Stone writes, converted to Christianity but then "turned into a most formidable enemy of his former religion . . . [and even] initiated the modern tradition of anti-Semitism" (71). In comparison, Ramon Lull (who sensed that Aristotelian logic and Scholasticism in general had failed) developed his own more tolerant system of thought.
61. Duran, 11–18. Duran observes, "According to a tradition that has been accepted for a long time he [Ramon Llull] dies in North Africa a martyr's death. Most modern researchers, however, think Llull managed to return to Majorca an [sic] died soon afterwards" (16).
62. One example is the work of George Ripley, *The Compound of Alchymy* (1591). See Stanton J. Linden, "Expounding George Ripley: A Huntington Alchemical Manuscript," *Huntington Library Quarterly* 61.3–4 (2000): 411–28. According to Linden, "The *Compound*'s popularity in early modern England may be demonstrated

through brief reference to manuscript versions located at the British Library. The Sloane collection, for example, includes at least eight manuscripts of the *Compound*, all of which are complete or nearly so and date from the sixteenth and seventeenth centuries," 413. Ripley frequently refers to Lull. In fact, Linden says, "Lull . . . [is] Ripley's most frequently cited source," 109n13. See George Ripley, *The Compound of Alchemy*, ed. Stanton J. Linden (Brookfield, Vt.: Ashgate, 2001).

63. Yates, *The Art of Memory*, 188–89.
64. John S. Chamberlin, *Increase and Multiply*, 106.
65. Yates, *The Art of Memory*, 177–78.
66. *Essays*, 24.
67. Ibid.
68. See Yates, *The Art of Memory*, 193.
69. Haskins, 48. The references in the Gnostic myth sometimes confuse Mary with Mary Magdalen.
70. Tyacke, *Aspects of English Protestantism, c. 1530–1700* (New York: Manchester Univ. Press, 2001), 254.
71. Yates, *The Art of Memory*, 188.
72. Ibid., 176.
73. For one recent example of scholarship investigating the influence of Ramon Lull upon Pico, see Paola Zambelli, *L'apprendista stregone: Astrologia, cabala e arte lulliana in Pico della Mirandola e seguaci* (Venice: Marsilio Editori, 1995).
74. See Kevin Sharpe, *Sir Robert Cotton, 1586–1631: History and Politics in Early Modern England* (New York: Oxford Univ. Press, 1979).
75. Sharpe says that Cotton's library included "the collections of Nowell, Lambarde, Parker, and Dee," 56. The "exchange" was negotiated "with D'Ewes who had acquired them," 60.
76. Sharpe writes that "Dr. Bainbridge, the physician and astronomer, wrote to his old Oxford friend, Ussher, to tell him that he had been searching for Dee's papers; so, 'I resorted to Sir Rob. Cotton (with very warm welcome)'," 70.
77. Quoted by Sharpe, 82.
78. Sharpe cites Gosse as his source for a reference of Donne's meeting with Cotton (206). He also notes that "John Donne thought his friend Cotton might assist him to a place at court in 1614," 207.
79. See Evelyn Simpson, "Donne's Spanish Authors," *Modern Language Review* 43 (1948): 184. Variants of Raymond's name include "Sebond" and "Saibunde," as well as "Sebund," which Simpson uses. Other pseudo-Lullist or cabalistic sources (other than Spanish) Simpson lists in Donne's *Essays*, 103–8. They are Archangelus, author of *Cabalistarum selectiora obscuraque dogmata* (1569) and *Apologia pro defensione doctrinae caballae* (1600); Buxdorfius, author of *Synagoga Judaica* (1603); Franciscus Georgius Venetus (or F. Zorgi), author of *De Harmonia Mundi totius cantica* (1525); Pico della Mirandola, author of *Heptaplus* (which Donne quotes in his *Essays in Divinity*); and Johann Reuchlin, author of *De Verbo Mirifico* (1494) and *De Arte Cabbalistica* (1517). Also included are Paracelsus and Galileo. Three of these cabalists—F. Zorgi, Pico, and Reuchlin—Donne frequently cited.
80. Mark D. Johnston, letter to the author, 4 January 2003.
81. Mark D. Johnston, *The Spiritual Logic of Ramon Llull* (Oxford: Clarendon, 1987), 21. Johnston distinguishes other specific components of Lullian logic to be "the writings of John Scotus Erigena, Algazel, the Jewish *sephiroth*, and Islamic *hadras* (Divine Attributes)," 19. Another source study suggests that an anonymous thirteenth-century cabalistic text may have been among Lull's sources. A figure

consisting of three concentric circles, each containing an alphabet, seems to correspond with Lull's (and Pico's version of Lull's) *ars combinatoria*. See Moshe Idel, *Journal of the Warburg and Courtauld Institutes* 51 (1988): 170–74.

82. Flynn, "'Awry and Squint,'" 45n. William Stanley was admitted to Lincoln's Inn on 13 August 1594.

83. For discussion of William Stanley's interest in alchemy, see "'Awry and Squint,'" 41. Flynn bases his remarks partly upon a reference from George Chapman. In a prefatory letter to "Poeticall Hymnes" Chapman mentions the "ingenious Darbie" as one member of "the School of the Night," a group of students interested in alchemy.

84. Introduction, in *Biathanatos*, ed. and intro. Michael Rudick and M. Pabst Battin (New York: Garland, 1982), xiv. (Professor Rudick assumes primary responsibility for x–xli.)

85. See Susanne K. Langer, *Feeling and Form: A Theory of Art Developed from Philosophy in a New Key* (New York: Charles Scribner's Sons, 1953). Langer writes, "When this [life] rhythm is disturbed, all activities in the total complex are modified by the break; the organism as a whole is out of balance . . . or . . . it adapts itself to the situation," 328.

86. *Sermons*, 4:238, 242, and 247.

87. Anthony Martin, *An Exhortation, To stirre up the minds of all her Maiesties faithfull subjects* (1588), quoted by Cressy, *Bonfires*, 117.

88. Cressy, *Bonfires*, 50.

89. Ibid., 124.

90. Ibid., 125–26.

91. Ibid., 58.

92. The midsummer rite of bonfires was, Cressy says, "derived from ancient rituals designed to drive away dragons," 3. Along with these were parades and pageants featuring the banishing of dragons (26). "At Burford, Oxfordshire," he says, "the parade of giants and dragons continued until well into the seventeenth century," 27. Probably the origin of these festivals was Druidic.

93. *Sermons*, 4:246.

94. *Dictionary*, 59.

95. *Sermons*, 4:245.

96. Milton, "Qualified Intolerance," 97. His source is Jeanne Shami, "The Stars in their Order Fought against Sisera," *John Donne Journal* 14 (1995): 1–58.

97. For a review of the marriage negotiations between England and Spain/France, see Kevin Sharpe, "The Earl of Arundel, His Circle and the Opposition to the Duke of Buckingham, 1618–1628," in *Faction and Parliament: Essays on Early Stuart History*, ed. Kevin Sharpe (New York: Oxford Univ. Press, 1978), 209–44.

98. John Carey, *John Donne: Life*, 90.

99. Sharpe, "The Earl of Arundel," 230.

100. Nicholas Tyacke, "Puritan Politicians and King James VI and I, 1587–1604," in *Politics, Religion, and Popularity in Early Stuart Britain: Essays in Honour of Conrad Russell*, ed. Thomas Cogswell, Richard Cust, and Peter Lake (New York: Cambridge Univ. Press, 2002), 39.

101. The "puritan blueprint," as noted, meant to cleanse all levels of administration, not just the Church. Even Donne's former employer, Lord Keeper Egerton, was singled out as among those "pluralists or vendors of office." See Tyacke, "Puritan Politicians," 39–40.

102. Tyacke, *Aspects of English Protestantism*, 238.

103. Donne quoted by Tyacke, *Anti-Calvinists: The Rise of English Arminianism, c. 1590–1640*, 182.
104. Ibid.
105. See Anthony Milton, *Catholic and Reformed*. Milton cites the example of a Calvinist archbishop who "had felt it important to compile a detailed list of all the errors which medieval writers had committed in their worship of the Virgin in order to dissuade possible converts to popery," 67. As a way of confronting such assaults, Anthony Stafford "published his life of the Blessed Virgin, *The Female Glory*, in 1635," 67. Milton explains, "Stafford's main concern was to counteract 'the Puritans' neglect of the Virgin's honour, which undermined the worship of Christ," 67.
106. The reference is to Stafford's treatise noted above.
107. For discussion of Laudian practices during the reign of Charles I, see Austin Warren, *Richard Crashaw: A Study in Baroque Sensibility* (Ann Arbor: Univ. of Michigan Press, 1957), 5–40.
108. Ibid.
109. The reference is to Donne's last sermon, *Death's Duel*.
110. Milton, "Qualified Intolerance," 104.
111. Paul R. Sellin remarks the influence of Thomas More upon his great-grandnephew. See *"So Doth, So Is Religion": John Donne and the Diplomatic Contexts in the Reformed Netherlands, 1619–1620* (Columbia: Univ. of Missouri Press, 1988), 166.
112. David Cressy, *Literacy and the Social Order*, 2.
113. Quoted by Cressy, *Literacy*, 2.

Chapter 3: Mnemotechnics in the Sermons and Poems

1. *Sermons*, 1:200. The sermon was preached 24 March 1616/17.
2. *Sermons*, 4:287. This sermon was preached at St. Paul's on Christmas Day, 1622.
3. John Carey, "Donne and Coins," in *English Renaissance Studies: Presented to Dame Helen Gardner in honour of her Seventieth Birthday* (Oxford: Clarendon, 1980), 151–63. The citation is from 157. Of Donne's mind Carey says, "Once a relationship intrigues him, he feels impelled to probe it, modify it, reverse it, and try it out in different concentrations and in various matrices. His mind advances not forward but sideways, spreading out through parallels which are never quite parallel, and analogies which alter what they illustrate," 157.
4. The reference is to Mary Ann Radzinowicz, "The Politics of John Donne's Silences," *John Donne Journal* 7 (1988): 1–19. Radzinowicz studies four areas where Donne cultivates silence: America, Ireland, exceptional women, and other poets. She also offers four interpretative paradigms: the coterie, censorship, class, and the literary system.
5. Quoted by Simpson in "Introduction to Volumes Seven and Eight," in *Sermons*, 52.
6. H. J. Sheppard, "The Ouroboros," 94.
7. Ibid., 96.
8. Ibid.
9. Ibid.
10. For the Catholic contribution to English literary culture, see Alison Shell's *Catholicism, Controversy and the English Literary Imagination, 1558–1660* (New York:

Cambridge Univ. Press, 1999). Shell explores apostasy (or loyalism) as referent in the writings of such figures as Sidney, Spenser, Webster, and Middleton. Ignoring John Carey's earlier thesis (*Life,* 71–76) that Donne's Catholic sympathies influenced his work, Shell implies that Donne should be contrasted with Robert Southwell, whose verse, she says, was "more characteristically Catholic than Protestant," 60. She elicits support from both T. S. Eliot and Helen Gardner, both of whom maintain that Donne "helped to validate Anglicanism," 101. For biographical discussion of Donne's Catholicism, see Dennis Flynn's *John Donne and the Ancient Catholic Nobility* (Bloomington: Indiana Univ. Press, 1995). Also see his series of articles: "Donne's Catholicism: I," *Recusant History* 13 (1975): 1–17, and "Donne's Catholicism: II," *Recusant History* 13 (1976): 178–95. Flynn offers a fuller account of Donne's early life and family background than either R. C. Bald (*John Donne: A Life,* 1970) or John Carey. See, for example, Bald, 128–54. See also James S. Baumlin's "From Recusancy to Apostasy: Donne's 'Satyre III' and "Satyre V,'" *Explorations in Renaissance Culture* 16 (1990): 67–85.

11. See Yates, 174.
12. David J. Viera, "Exempla in the *Libre de Sancta Maria,*" *Catalan Review* 4.1–2 (July–December 1990): 222.
13. Ibid.
14. Ibid., 223.
15. Ibid., 224.
16. Ramon Llull, *The Art of Contemplation,* ed. and trans. from the Catalan by E. Allison Peers (London: The Society for Promoting Christian Knowledge, 1925), 75–76.
17. See Yates, "The Art of Ramon Lull," *Journal of the Warburg and Courtauld Institutes* 17 (1954): 115–73. Yates argues Lull's influence upon Paracelsus, noting, "The Lullian medical theories were known to Paracelsus," 166.
18. Paracelsus, *Aureolus Philippus Theophrastus Bombast, of Hohenheim, Called Paracelsus the Great* or *Hermetic Medicine and Hermetic Philosophy,* ed. Arthur Edward Waite, 1:66.
19. Ibid.
20. Ibid.
21. Ibid.
22. See "Addition to Calid's *Secret of Secrets,*" appendix 2, in Roger Bacon's *The Mirror of Alchemy,* ed. Stanton J. Linden (New York: Garland, 1992). This treatise describes Mercury as "a better Spirit than all others . . . [because] it is much subtiler, clearer, and penetrative, so it is joyned to the Metals, and changed into them," 114. The writer adds that Mercury, called *Argent-vive,* "is the Father of all the Wonderful things of this our Magistery, and is congealed, and is both Spirit and Body: This is the *Argent Vive* which . . . is the very matter which does make perfect," 112.
23. See Denis Saurat, *Literature and the Occult Tradition* (London, 1930), 222–37. Saurat notes that one edition of Spenser's *Hymnes,* "picks out points of resemblance between *Sapience* and the Virgin of the Catholic religion," 222.
24. *Sermons,* 1:239.
25. *Sermons,* 3:196.
26. The epigram is contained in the *Viridarium.* Mermaidlike, Aphrodite is shown with a golden crown and twin tails. See John Read, *Prelude to Chemistry: An Outline of Alchemy* (Cambridge: MIT Press, 1966), 270. According to Read, Aphrodite was a favored symbol of the alchemists.
27. *Sermons,* 10:248.
28. H. J. Sheppard's article, "Egg Symbolism," begins to explain this phenomenon in Donne's theological alchemy. The Philosopher's Egg, he says, "takes its place

in an interpretation of alchemy as a symbolic redemption of the soul of man," 141. By the late Middle Ages, this alchemical emblem had become polysemic, specifically Christian symbolism having been transferred to it.

29. Lyndy Abraham observes that "the alchemist's vessel of transmutation in which the birth of the philosopher's stone takes place [is] . . . also known as the griffin's or gripe's egg . . . the alchemist, when making his fire, attempts to emulate the gentle warmth of nature, like that of the hen or bird brooding on her eggs," 66. See *Dictionary*.

30. Levi D'Ancona discusses one such image, the *Virgin Immaculate with Trinity* (fig. 85). Discovered in a Carmelite missal (late fourteenth century), it is now in the British Museum (Add. MS 29704, fol. 193v).

31. Both the Feast of the Annunciation and the Feast of the Passion fell on 25 March 1608.

32. Sheppard, "The Ouroboros," 84.

33. Ibid., 87.

34. The significance of green varies from theory to theory. One treatise says that "Greeness is all that is perfect therein, and all that is perfect, is in that Greeness only . . . For that Greeness, by our Magistery is in a very little time transmuted into the most fine Gold." See "Calid's *Secret of Secrets*," appendix 2, in Roger Bacon's *The Mirror of Alchemy*, ed. Linden, 110–11.

35. F. Sherwood Taylor, *The Alchemists: Founders of Modern Chemistry* (New York: Henry Schuman, 1949), 111. Tail-eating dragons, he cautions, "play . . . but the smallest part [in Lullian works]," 111.

36. Sheppard, "Ouroboros," 84.

37. Ibid., 96.

38. Ibid., 87.

39. *Dictionary*, 127.

40. John Dee's "*Monas Hieroglyphica*" (Antwerp, 1564), cited by C. H. Josten, *Ambix* 12 (1964): 177. The entire issue is devoted to this subject.

41. *Dictionary*, 124.

42. Ibid.

43. Yates, *Art*, 189.

44. Ibid.

45. Sergei Eisenstein was developing his theory of montage in the 1920s. He and the German Expressionists defined montage as a process of synthesis, so that the film is actually constructed (rather than edited) as a dialectical process that creates a third meaning when two images join or collide.

46. Stanton Linden, Introduction, in Roger Bacon's *The Mirror of Alchemy* (New York: Garland, 1992), xi–xii.

47. Ibid, xvi.

48. Ibid., xvii.

49. *Dictionary*, 128.

50. George Ripley, *The Compound of Alchemy*, ed. Stanton J. Linden (Brookfield, Vt.: Ashgate, 2001), 23.

51. Sir Edmund Gosse, *Life and Letters of John Donne*, 2 vols. (London: Heinemann, 1899), 109–10. Simpson, the editor of Donne's sermons, did not believe that Donne's picture constituted evidence for his Catholic affinities, arguing that there was "nothing secret or furtive, as Gosse suggests, about [Donne's homage to the Virgin]," 5:23.

52. For a discussion of scriptural texts and narratives appropriated by the alchemists, see Gareth Roberts, *The Mirror of Alchemy: Alchemical Ideas and Images in Manu-*

scripts and Books from Antiquity to the Seventeenth Century (Toronto: Univ. of Toronto Press, 1994). Roberts notes that "the life of the Virgin [along with the life of Christ] . . . found parallels in alchemy. In the emblem for cibation in *Symbola aureae mensae* we see the Virgin suckling her child, and the accompanying chapter compares the birth of the Stone to the Nativity, sublimation to the Passion, the black stage to Christ's death on Calvary and of course the red stage to the Resurrection," 79.

53. *Sermons*, 8:77.

54. Roberts, 79. Concerning adepts, Roberts observes, "God prepares one to whom the secret may be handed on. The secrets of alchemy are never merely to be found out by human labour, but 'bi teching or revelacion' and the Stone is to be obtained by grace, rather than reading," 79. Roberts is citing Edward Kelly's work in Ashmole (1652).

55. Quoted by John Carey, "Donne and Coins," 156. Donne's letter to Sir Henry Goodyer warns his friend against any inclinations to switch religions. He writes, "You shall seldom see a Coyne upon which the stamp were removed, though to imprint it better, but it looks awry and squint." Restamped coins look wrong, Donne implies.

56. For discussion of Mary's intercessory role, see David J. Viera, "Exempla in the *Libre de Sancta Maria*," 221–25. He observes that "Llull confirmed Mary's power to interecede [sic] between God, the just or sinners. She derived this role from her motherhood of Christ," 222.

57. For a review of the way Catholic interests became a political issue at the end of Elizabeth's reign, see Nicholas Tyacke, "Puritan Politicians and King James VI and I, 1587–1604," in *Politics, Religion, and Popularity in Early Stuart Britain: Essays in Honour of Conrad Russell*, ed. Thomas Cogswell, Richard Cust, and Peter Lake (New York: Cambridge Univ. Press, 2002), 21–44.

58. Ibid., 33–36.

59. George Ripley, probably incorrectly, attributes to Ramon Lull this notion of Mercury, of the third "essentiall" sort, joining sulfer and salt to create the Philosopher's Stone in *The Compound of Alchemy*, 23 and 92.

60. "Calid's *Secret of Secrets*," appendix, in Roger Bacon's *The Mirror of Alchemy*, ed. Linden, 110.

61. This tenuous date has been established on the basis of internal evidence, namely Donne's reference to going abroad (with the Drurys) in line 55.

62. William Roper, from *The Life of Sir Thomas More, Knight* (?1557), in *The Renaissance in England* (Lexington, Mass.: D.C. Heath, 1954), 48.

63. See Dennis Flynn, "Donne and a Female Coterie," *LIT* 1 (1989): 32.

64. Katharine Baetjer, *British Portraits in The Metropolitan Museum of Art. The Metropolitan Museum of Art Bulletin* 57.1 (Summer 1999): 9–13. For identification of the portrait see page 10.

65. Ibid., 11.

66. Lucy, Countess of Bedford, was Donne's patroness. She also supported him by standing godmother to his daughter Lucy and by taking this child into her household at Twickenham Park. Donne himself associated the Countess of Bedford with books, writing in his elegy for her that there was "no such booke as shee." Her mother, Lady Harrington, was guardian to Princess Elizabeth.

67. See Stapleton's "The Theme of Virtue in Donne's Verse Epistles," *Studies in Philology* 55 (1958): 187–200.

68. The *Oxford English Dictionary* (*OED*) defines *virtue* as 1) a mighty work; a miracle but also 2) the particular power or efficacy of precious stones (occult).

69. See Carey's introduction to the Oxford Authors edition of Donne (New York: Oxford Univ. Press, 1990), xxvii.

70. See Luke 13:34 and Matthew 23:37.

71. *Sermons*, 4:185.

72. Harris F. Fletcher, *Milton's Rabbinical Readings* (Urbana: Univ. of Illinois Press, 1930; repr., Archon, 1967), 126. Though the idea of Creation as a birth-process is common to every history of the world, Fletcher says that Milton appropriated "the 'dove-like' brooding" because "he wanted and needed a representation . . . of his complete idea of Creation, which thought of it as not only being instantaneous so far as God was concerned, but which also occupied the time of Six Days," 126–27.

73. Quoted from "Introductions," in *Sermons*, vol. 1, 95.

74. *Dictionary*, 66.

75. Roger Bacon, *The Mirror of Alchemy*, ed. Stanton Linden, 7.

76. *Basic Writings of Saint Augustine*, ed. Whitney J. Oates (New York: Random House, 1948), 153–54.

77. For a discussion of this Augustinian precept see Chamberlin, who writes "Complication . . . involves the memory, for the mind draws out these implications and associations by ruminating upon the words of the text, recalling similar but different instances of them elsewhere in Scripture, and distinguishing multiple significations," 118.

78. Augustine, *The Confessions*, Book 10, trans. William Watts (Cambridge: Harvard Univ. Press, 1997), Loeb Classical Library, 112.

79. Ibid., 113.

80. For discussion of the supposed seed of gold see John Read, *Prelude to Chemistry*, 138. A common alchemical symbol was that of the husbandman scattering seeds.

81. *Sermons*, 2:260–61.

82. *Dictionary*, 72.

83. *Sermons*, 2:261.

84. Ibid., 261–62.

85. Thorndike is quoting Harvey, saying he "no longer distinguished between vital and animal spirits in the human body [but] he at least spoke of the blood as 'impregnated with spirits and, it might be said with balsam' (a Paracelsan touch)" (7:515).

86. Harvey, *Exercitationes de generatione animalium* (1651), quoted by Thorndike (7:516–17). Donne may have anticipated this later development in Harvey's thought.

87. Donne was ambivalent concerning the *tria prima*. By 1619, the date of his Heidelberg sermon, he seems to have come to accept Paracelsus's "new" theory.

88. For the importance of pneuma as principle of alchemy see Taylor, *The Alchemists*, 11–16. Curiously, Abraham omits pneuma from her *Dictionary*. The alchemists appropriated their versions of pneuma from Aristotle, who seems to have been among the first to discuss it, associating it with heat but (unlike certain alchemists) disassociating it from fire. Aristotle defines pneuma as part of semen, making it a vital creative force. In *On the Generation of Animals*, he writes: "all [souls] have in their semen that which causes it to be productive; I mean what is called vital heat. This is not fire nor any such force, but it is the breath [pneuma] included in the semen and the foam-like, and the natural principle in the breath, being analogous to the element of the stars" (1:1143). See *The Complete Works of Aristotle*, ed. J. Barnes (Princeton: Princeton Univ. Press, 1984).

89. Bernard, *Selected Works*, 31.

90. Ibid, 290.

91. *Sermons*, 2:262.

92. See Louis L. Martz, "John Donne in Meditation: *The Anniversaries*," *ELH* 14 (December 1947): 247–73.

93. See Gregory B. Stone, "Ramon Llull vs. Petrus Alfonsi: Postmodern Liberalism and the Six Liberal Arts," *Medieval Encounters in Confluence and Dialogue: Jewish, Christian, and Muslim Culture* 3.1 (March 1997): 70–93. Stone distinguishes the difference between Aristotelianism and Lullism (between what he calls "Logic" and "Art"). "The difference," he says, "lies in the difference between reasoning and the right intention, between *ratio* and *intentio*, between rationality and goodwill," 79. He explains how this concept is developed in Lullian art. Though scholars studying Donne usually consider his logic only within the classical frame, I hope that this study will persuade some to consider the influence of Lullian "logic" upon Donne's thought. For contrasting views, see Theresa M. DiPasquale, "'to good ends': The Final Cause of Sacramental Womanhood in *The First Anniversarie*," *John Donne Journal* 20 (2001): 141–50. DiPasquale considers the argument of Donne's poem to have been constructed according to Aristotelian causal-analysis. As support she elicits the work of Elizabeth L. Wiggins, "Logic in the Poetry of John Donne," *Studies in Philology* 42 (1945): 56. Wiggins's study, which had pinpointed the "assisting efficient cause," allows DiPasquale to study Elizabeth Drury's function in *The First Anniversarie* as various forms of "cause."

94. See *Ben Jonson: Selected Works*, ed. David McPherson (New York: Holt, Rinehart and Winston, 1972). The conversation between Donne and Jonson was reported by William Drummond, whose full entry reads: "That Donne's *Anniversary* was profane and full of blasphemies; that he told Mr. Donne, if it had been written of the Virgin Mary it had been something; to which he answered that he described the Idea of a Woman and not as she was; that Donne for not keeping of accent deserved hanging" (quoted by McPherson, 420).

95. For a discussion of the word *virtue* in Donne's *Letters to Severall Personages*, see Laurence Stapleton's "The Theme of Virtue in Donne's Verse Epistles," *Studies in Philology* 55 (1958): 187–200. Stapleton believes that Donne somehow derived his understanding of *virtue* by combining Plato's ideas with those of Paracelsus. He observes that "pondering on Plato's arguments for the unity of virtue, and the way in which Paracelsian doctrines interact gave Donne a fine sequential harmony to develop in his 'Letter to the Lady Carey and Mrs. Essex Riche, from Amyens,'" 199.

96. *Complete Poems*, 407.

97. Shawcross reviews the various readings of "Shee" in *The First Anniversarie*, observing that "Shee" is a symbol of the Church, of Christ and Astraea, and of Wisdom (*Complete Poems*, 405). In *The Second Anniversary* Shawcross interprets lines 33–44 to include, among the list cited, "the Virgin Mary" (407). See also Mirella Levi D'Ancona, *The Iconography of the Immaculate Conception in the Middle Ages and the Early Renaissance* (1957). Levi D'Ancona remarks that some early believers thought that "the Virgin Mary existed from the beginning of time, and, therefore, also before the Fall of Man," 7. This idea, she says, was "defended by theologians and occasionally depicted by artists," 7. Among the latter is an illustration for a Book of Hours (Morgan Library, MS M 69, fol. 59v) dated 1546. It shows the Virgin kneeling before God, who is creating the world.

98. See DiPasquale, "'to good ends'." The citation is from 141.

99. Ibid., 147.

100. Ibid., 149.

101. Ibid., 147.

102. Louis L. Martz, "John Donne in Meditation: The *Anniversaries, ELH* 14 (December 1947): 247–73. Martz's discussion of Donne's Counter-Reformation materials is found on 251–53. More recent studies have argued that the "Mary" of these poems becomes but a vehicle whereby Donne can express his Protestant views. See, for example, Maureen Sabine's *Feminine Engendered Faith* (Worcester: Billing and Sons, 1992). Sabine says that Donne in *The Anniversaries* had begun to restamp Mary's face on the now Protestant coin. However, she argues, he ultimately decided to print instead "the masculine image which bought him admission to a Christian fraternity where the female had lost face," 105. See also H. L. Meakin's *John Donne's Articulations of the Feminine* (1998). Meakin argues that Donne in *The Anniversaries* opts for an invisible, hence Protestant, Mary. Whereas Meakin is able to see Donne's references to Eve as a source of mankind's woe, she is (for whatever reason) unable to see or recognize Donne's references to Mary as *Second* Eve. (These references allow Donne to make a more comprehensive and unified statement concerning Mary's role in salvation.) Meakin concludes that Donne "retained the especially negative view of Eve, proportional to the Catholic faith's positive view of Mary, yet out of all proportion when she is left standing alone in the Protestant landscape," 178. By leaving the Catholic Mary out of his poem, Meakin argues, Donne forces a division of the sacred persona, preparing the way for the poet himself to serve as "mediator between Elizabeth Drury and the reader," 206.

103. Martz, "John Donne," 253.

104. Some recent scholars insist that the Virgin Mary in *The Anniversaries* is made to serve the Protestant cause. Maureen Sabine admits Donne's "involuntary Catholic instinct to honour the Virgin Mary" in these poems, but concludes that Elizabeth Drury's "deficiency [is] the *modus operandi* of the *Anniversaries*," xii. Donne realized too late, she says, that "he had squandered the praises of the Virgin on unworthy noblewomen," 233. See *Feminine Engendered Faith* (note 102 above). H. L. Meakin (also note 102 above) offers a particular version of Sabine's view. Focusing on Elizabeth Drury's body, she drives a wedge between Donne's "Catholic (closed) and Protestant (dilatory) conceptions of the female body," concluding that "Elizabeth's paradoxically chaste and fertile body . . . aligns her with the Virgin Mary to arrive finally at a fully Protestant position," 205–6. Also see Raymond-Jean Frontain, "Donne's Protestant *Paradiso:* The Johannine Vision of the *Second Anniversary*," in *John Donne and the Protestant Reformation: New Perspectives*, ed. Mary Arshagouni Papazian (Detroit: Wayne State Univ. Press, 2003): 113–42. He argues that "Donne is clearly writing a reformist revelation to meet the challenge of the Roman Catholic Mary," 123. The most successful argument (to date) for Donne's harmonizing vision is Jeanne Shami's "Anatomy and Progress: The Drama of Conversion in Donne's Men of 'Middle Nature'," *University of Toronto Quarterly* 53.3 (Spring 1984): 221–35. Ignoring Catholic/Protestant polarities in *The Anniversaries*, Shami understands Elizabeth Drury to be exemplary of those who "are struggling to rectify God's image in themselves," 221. Shami is able to construct a convincing argument for this by focusing on memory as operative device throughout the poems. However, she sees the speaker's memory, not Elizabeth Drury, as the subject of the poems; his memory allows "transcendental escape" from this corrupt world (224). I agree that the harmonizing vision of Donne's poems is one of remembrance that "Shee," once dead now alive, is the Phoenix, which, once remembered, will restore the world.

105. Augustine, chapters 8–25, in *The Confessions: Basic Writings of St. Augustine*, ed. Whitney J. Oates (New York: Random House, 1948), 152–66. The citation is from 153.

106. Ibid.

107. Ibid.

108. See Gregory B. Stone, "Ramon Llull vs. Petrus Alfonsi: Postmodern Liberalism and the Six Liberal Arts," *Medieval Encounters in Confluence and Dialogue* 3.1 (March 1997): 70–93. The citation is from 70.

109. See James Elkins, *What Painting Is: How to Think about Oil Painting, Using the Language of Alchemy* (New York: Routledge, 1999), 65.

110. Mark D. Johnston, *The Spiritual Logic of Ramon Llull,* 20–21.

111. Stone, 70. He observes that Lull's thinking was "marked by its celebration of diversity and its liberal tolerance," 76.

112. Carruthers, 10.

113. Ibid.

114. According to Carruthers, Hugh of St. Victor (twelfth century) "likens the making of a memory image to a coin stamped by the coiner with a likeness which gives it value and currency . . . books as well as coins [were considered] very precious things, useful for nourishing memories," 39. His favorite image, she says, is the "image of the trained memory as an orderly moneybag," 92.

115. Ibid., 81.

116. *Sermons,* 4:288.

117. Carey, "Donne and Coins," 152.

118. Carey reviews the process of coining during the sixteenth century. "Most European currency in the late sixteenth and early seventeenth centuries was struck by the traditional method of hammering. Discs were stamped out of thin bars of precious metal, placed between two dies, and hammered, so that the image on the dies was transferred to the coin. So primitive a technique produced irregular results. . . . Fat, thin, lop-sided, or vague-looking coins resulted. They were almost as various in their expressions as people, and their precise physiognomy was as worth studying, if not more so," 152–53. The Commonwealth, Carey says, initiated production of machined coins.

119. For a discussion of the way alchemy has influenced culture, see Pamela H. Smith, *The Business of Alchemy: Science and Culture in the Holy Roman Empire* (Princeton: Princeton Univ. Press, 1994). Smith argues that during the baroque period, seeds of distrust toward alchemical charlatanry were sown. The men of the Enlightenment, she says, "denounced deception, rejected metaphor and enigma, and ridiculed the scholarship of the seventeenth century as charlatanry perpetuated by learned pedants," 270. Rejecting the seventeenth-century emblem books that professed the "polysemic nature" of an image as a fuller expression of truth than any single statement, men of the Enlightenment, she says, rejected alchemy for science, which represented visible truth.

120. One such example is the collection of emblems compiled by Michael Ruprecht Besler, the Republic of Nürnberg and senior inspector of apothecary shops. Besler's emblems and plates are references to the three kingdoms: animal, vegetable, and mineral. The plates for the mineral kingdom include ancient coins, gems, and seals. For a description of Besler's book see Thorndike (8:14). Coins were also associated with "illicit magic," defined as prohibited secrets such as relics of paganism or popery. The use of certain words or characters, figures or images, and amulets were sometimes classified as "illicit" (8:539). Paracelsus made images that were considered to be security against plague (7:305).

121. *Sermons,* 4:288.

122. See Eluned Crawshaw, "Hermetic Elements in Donne's Poetic Vision," in *John Donne: Essays in Celebration,* ed. A. J. Smith (London: Methuen), 324–48. The citation is from 345.

NOTES

123. Plato, *Theaetetus*, trans. Harold North Fowler, Loeb Classical Library (Cambridge: Harvard Univ. Press, 1996), 119–21.
124. The references are to Luke 2:19 and Luke 2:51.
125. See Raymond-Jean Frontain, "Donne's Protestant *Paradiso*." He argues that Donne wanted "to replace Dante's Virgin Mary, the penultimate figure of his revelation, with the Protestant image of any regenerate Christian soul," 123.

CHAPTER 4: *ARS SACRA POETICA*

1. Translation by Henry Green, *Shakespeare and the Emblem Writers* (London: Trübner, 1870), 383. His source is *Lactantii Opera, studio Galloei* (Leyden, 1660).
2. Ibid.
3. Ibid., 384. The reference is to Henry Hawkins's *The Virgin*.
4. Paracelsus, *Selected Writings*. He observes that "The child in the mother's womb is exposed to the mother's influence, and is as though entrusted to the hand and will of its mother, as the clay is entrusted to the hand and will of the potter, who creates and forms out of it what he wants and what he pleases. Thus the child requires no stars or planets: its mother is its star and its planet," 32.
5. Cressy, *Birth*, 15.
6. Ibid., 16.
7. Ibid., 15.
8. Ibid.
9. Cressy says the Reformation tried to purge birthing rituals of the superstitions of "[t]raditional Roman Catholicism," 22. Among these were "an armoury of comforts to the childbearing woman [who] . . . could call on . . . the Virgin . . . and could supplement this saintly intercession by clutching religious relics, girdles, amulets, and fragments of the consecrated host," 22.
10. Ibid., 23. "Bishop Barnes of Durham instructed his clergy in 1577 to discipline 'all such women as shall . . . at the child's birth use superstitious ceremonies, orisons, charms.' . . . Midwives were put on oath not to 'use any kind of sorcery or incantation' and to inform against any who so offended."
11. Ibid., 43.
12. Ibid., 53–54. The "childbed woman 'must be kept from the cold air because it is an enemy of the spermatical parts . . . and therefore the doors and windows of her chamber in any wise are to be kept close shut'," 53. "The room became a womb, warm, dark, and comfortable, restricting entry to evil spirits," 54.
13. Ibid., 51.
14. Ibid., 61. "Ministers sometimes looked upon midwives with suspicion because alone among women they occasionally performed a priest-like function, administering the sacrament of baptism *in extremis* to a child who seemed likely to die."
15. Theresa DiPasquale, *Literature and Sacrament* (1999), 69. Concerning the "metapoetic implications" of the second sonnet in *La Corona*, she writes, "As a 'maker' privileged to be the vessel of divinity, the Virgin is the poet's model; as she 'conceiv'd' Christ in the 'little room' of her womb, he will seek to conceive a Eucharistic reincarnation of Christ in his sonnets' little rooms."
16. Ibid., 84.
17. See David Novarr, "The Dating of Donne's *La Corona*," *Philological Quarterly* 36 (1957): 259–65. Novarr speculates that the letter accompanying the *La Corona* sonnets was sent some time after 25 March 1608. See also Patrick O'Connell, "The

Successive Arrangements of Donne's 'Holy Sonnets,'" *Philological Quarterly* 60 (1981): 323–42. O'Connell argues that the letter and sonnets could have been sent some time after 27 February 1609, adding "that this sequence is the only group of sonnets which could plausibly have been written as early as July 1607," 337. However, he cautions that Gardner's assignment of a date of July 1607, or shortly before, is probably too early. See also Shawcross, "The Arrangement and Order of John Donne's Poems," 130. He dates the poem July 1607.

18. For discussion of the supposed allusion to Magdalen Herbert in *La Corona*, see Barry Spurr, "The Theology of *La Corona*," *John Donne Journal* 20 (2001): 121–39.

19. See Maureen Sabine, *Feminine Engendered Faith*, 47. She observes that two models were available to Donne. The "three-sonnet chaplet which could be read as a corona intended exclusively for Our Lord," was a Reformation depiction of the presumably masculine Trinity. Significantly, she notes, Donne chose instead "a distinctively feminine, seven-sonnet division corresponding to the rosary attributed to St Bridget and honoured as the *Crown of Our Lady*."

20. See Kate Gartner Frost, "'Preparing Towards Her': Contexts of *A Nocturnall upon S. Lucies Day*," in *John Donne's "desire of more": The Subject of Anne More Donne in His Poetry*, ed. M. Thomas Hester (Newark: Univ. of Delaware Press, 1996), 162.

21. The opening sonnet catalogues several crowns, some offered, some requested. In the first line the speaker requests that God accept his gift of verse. "Deigne at my hands," John Shawcross observes, implies that the speaker is holding the Rosary as he speaks (*Complete Poems*, 334). Helen Gardner thinks that the main ideas of this first sonnet (even much of the phrasing) comes from the Advent Offices in the Roman Breviary. She says, "Any Breviary Donne used would be a Roman one, since the Sarum Use fell into desuetude after the Reformation" (*Divine Poems*, 57). Donne's speaker asks for a crown of praise attached to which is immortality, a crown "which doth flower alwayes" (l. 8). He also asks for a crown specifically intended for poets, that is, the "bayes" or laurel wreath. Christian poets, however, seek heavenly rewards, perhaps even sainthood. The variables in this sonnet, if considered as a collection of crowns, include those worn by all the apostles, by Christ, by his Bride (the Church), and by Mary, Queen of Heaven.

22. Sheppard, "Ouroboros," 87.

23. Martz, "John Donne in Meditation: The *Anniversaries*," *Journal of English Literary History* 14.4 (December 1947): 251.

24. Ibid., 252–53.

25. The Catholic Rosary is a series of meditations celebrating events in the lives of Jesus and Mary. The sequence of *La Corona* is an abbreviated form of the series of mysteries told in the Rosary: 1) the joyful mysteries (the Annunciation, the Visitation, the birth of Jesus, the Purification of the Virgin, the finding of the Christ child among the doctors); 2) the sorrowful mysteries (the agony in the garden, scourging and crowning with thorns, bearing the cross to Calvary, the Crucifixion); and 3) the glorious mysteries (the Resurrection, the Ascension, the descent of the Holy Ghost or Pentecost, the Assumption of the Virgin, her Coronation as Queen of Heaven). For a study of how these events figure in *La Corona*, see Maureen Sabine, *Feminine Engendered Faith* (1992). She observes that the sequential sonnets of *La Corona* evidence "the seven sorrows of Mary [as well as Christ's pain]," 54.

26. See H. J. Sheppard, "The Ouroboros," 87. He records several versions of the inscription.

27. Ibid.

28. Thomas Aquinas (1125–74) seems to have been an opponent of the doctrine of Mary's sinless conception. He embraced instead that theory of sanctification,

which held that she was conceived in sin but, when her sanctified soul joined her body in the womb of her mother Anne, it freed her body from impurity and restored it to a state of grace.

29. [Cicero, M. Tullius], *Rhetorica ad Herennium (Ad c. Herennium libri IV De ratione dicendi)*, ed. and trans. Harry Caplan, Loeb Classical Library (Cambridge: Harvard Univ. Press, 1954), 210–11.

30. The allusions ("true conclusions," "good conclusion," and "invent true reasons") are from Gregory B. Stone's "Ramon Llull," 80–81.

31. Ramon Lull, *The Art of Contemplation*, trans. from the Catalan by E. Allison Peers (London: Society for Promoting Christian Knowledge, 1925), 76.

32. There is no evidence that Donne knew Lull's *The Art of Contemplation*, certainly not as a primary source.

33. "Calid's *Secret of Secrets*," appendix 2, in Roger Bacon's *The Mirror of Alchemy*, ed. Stanton Linden (New York: Garland, 1992), 110.

34. *Nicolas Flamel: His Exposition of the Hieroglyphicall Figures (1624)*, trans. from Latin to French by P. Arnauld (Paris: Société d'édition Les Belles Lettres, 1993), 41.

35. Lull, *Contemplation*, 76.

36. Paracelsus, *Selected Writings*, 32.

37. DiPasquale, *Literature and Sacrament*, 76.

38. Thorndike quoting Harvey's *Exercitationes de generatione animalium* (London, 1651), 7:514–15. Actually, Harvey came to believe that conception did not occur in the womb but in the ovary. Thorndike cites his famous statement "that all animals, even the viviparous and man himself, are produced from an egg" (514).

39. Levi D'Ancona, *Iconography of the Immaculate Conception in the Middle Ages and Early Renaissance*, 19. She offers as example an antiphonary, *Virgin Predestined* (Pienza: Cathedral Museum).

40. For a discussion of Mary as paradigm for the Christian poet, see Patrick O'Connell, "'Both Adams Met in Me': A Reading of the *Divine Poems* of John Donne," diss., Yale University, 1978, 79–82.

41. See Anthony Russell, "'Thou seest mee striue for life': Magic, Virtue, and the Poetic Imagination in Donne's *Anniversaries*," *Studies in Philology* (1998): 347–410. He cites Donne's defense of his poems in a letter written from France: "[I]t became me to say, not what I was sure was just truth, but the best that I could conceive," 376. He interprets this as Donne's confession that his poems were "not determined or guided by some preexisting Form or Idea," 377. My study, on the contrary, shows how Lullian and Hermetic principles, both "preexisting" forms, influenced Donne's thought.

42. DiPasquale, *Literature and Sacrament*, 84. She argues that the Eucharistic sacrament (Christ in the womb of the Virgin, the poem in the womb of the poet) redeems him.

43. The unfinished letter was written while Donne was in France with Robert Drury (1611–12). Donne hints that the countess has begotten in him inspiration; hence he has been raised up by her so that his "verses bud" (l. 10).

44. George Ripley, preface, in *The Compound of Alchemy*, ed. Stanton Linden, 23.

45. Gardner, ed., The *Divine Poems*, by Donne, 63.

46. For a discussion of Donne's alchemical thinking in "Resurrection, imperfect," see Edgar Hill Duncan, "Donne's Alchemical Figures," *ELH* 9 (1942): 257–85.

47. For another view, see Kate Gartner Frost, "Magnus Pan Mortuus Est: A Subtextual and Contextual Reading of Donne's 'Resurrection, imperfect,'" in *John Donne's Religious Imagination: Essays in Honor of John T. Shawcross*, ed. Raymond-Jean Frontain and Frances M. Malpezzi (Conway: Univ. of Central Arkansas Press, 1995), 231–61.

Frost argues that "Resurrection, imperfect" "is a finished poem concerned with unfinished time," 231.

48. Quoted by Duncan, 278.

49. For symbols associated with each stage of the alchemical opus, see Diana Fernando, *Alchemy* (1998), 126. Since the number of steps in the process is often cited as twelve, and since there are twelve signs of the zodiac, it follows that this connection would be made. Aries, the Ram, she notes, symbolizes calcination, the first step. Stanton Linden defines calcination in his notes to George Ripley's poem, *The Compound of Alchymy:* "*Calcination* is the purgation. Ripley begins his account of the first stage of the twelve-stage process with definitions and instructions for proceeding correctly. Calcination, the reduction of a metal to an ashy calx through heat for the purpose of purification, must be achieved without loss of its 'radicall humiditie' (which would destroy the body) and only through the use of appropriate materials," 111. Elsewhere, Linden remarks the popularity of Ripley's work during Donne's time. See, for example, "Expounding George Ripley: A Huntington Alchemical Manuscript," *Huntington Library Quarterly* 61. 3–4 (2000): 411–28. Here he notes that "early printed versions of the *Compound* and other works by Ripley clearly suggest that his works were highly regarded in England—even as Francis Bacon, the new philosophy, and eventually the Royal Society were calling into doubt the theory and practice of alchemy and related bodies of knowledge," 413.

50. Edward Kelly, *The Englishman's Two Excellent Treatises on the Philosopher's Stone*, trans. from the Hamburg edition of 1676 by A. E. Waite (1893; London: Stuart and Watkins, 1970), 140.

51. David J. Viera, "Exampla in the *Libre de Sancta Maria* [of Ramon Llull] and Traditional Medieval Marian Miracles," *Catalan Review* 4.1–2 (July–December 1990): 223.

52. Ibid.

53. Gregory B. Stone, "Ramon Llull vs. Petrus Alfonsi: Postmodern Liberalism and the Six Liberal Arts," *Medieval Encounters: Jewish, Christian and Muslim Culture* 3.1 (March 1997): 70–93. Stone defines "Llullian reasoning" as "a movement (*moviment*) in the mind in which the first principle and primary intention is one's purpose," 80.

54. Viera, 224. "Mary's justice must correspond to God's justice. In addition, the Christian looks upon Mary as the Mother of Mercy rather than the Mother of Justice."

55. My reading is not incompatible with John Shawcross's note in *Complete Poetry:* "Christ is identified with Aries since under that sign comes the return of spring with the vernal equinox. It is, of course, roughly around the time of Easter," 337.

56. Barry Spurr, "The Theology of *La Corona*," *John Donne Journal* 20 (2001): 124.

57. Ibid., 137–39. Spurr argues that *La Corona* is "a text of the *via media* of the English Church," 136–37. "Donne's thought and the corpus of his writing, with its complexities and contrariety, cannot be definitely consigned to either side of the great theological divide of the Reformation," 138.

58. *Complete Poetry*, 414. Also see Shawcross, "The Arrangement and Order of John Donne's Poems," in *Poems in Their Place: The Intertextuality and Order of Poetic Collections*, ed. Neil Fraistat (Chapel Hill: Univ. of North Carolina Press, 1986), 119–63. He lists "A Litanie" among the earliest divine poems, those dated between July 1607 (*La Corona*) and "Good Friday" (April 1613), 130.

59. For another reading see Scott R. Pilarz, S.J., "'Expressing a Quintessence Even from Nothingness': Contextualizing John Donne's 'A Litanie,'" *Christianity and Literature* 48.4 (Summer 1999): 399–424. Though the title implies an explication of alchemical references, there are none. Pilarz approaches the poem as the product of

Donne's difficult Mitcham years when he felt "diminished in terms of both spiritual aridity and worldly usefulness," 402. The second stanza of "A Litanie" is understood in terms of Donne's identity with the primordial Adamic state. This, Pilarz argues, is the context for "re-create mee, now growne ruinous," 402. Concerning Christ's nails, he says, "Donne's own heart becomes the site of the Crucifixion," 414. Though Pilarz does not distinguish it as such, the nails of Christ in the heart is a standard motif within the *Stabat Mater* tradition, which Donne has chosen as one of the backgrounds for "A Litanie."

60. For discussion of how symbolic red functions between correspondents in the *Holy Sonnets,* see my article, "Coining and Conning: Alchemical Motifs in Donne's 'Oh my blacke Soule!'" *English Language Notes* 42.2 (December 2004): 1–10.

61. See Paracelsus, *Selected Writings.* He defines *tinctura* as a kind of *arcanum,* of which there are four. "The first arcanum is the *prima materia,* the second the *lapis philosophorum,* the third the *mercurius vitae,* and the last *tinctura.* . . . *Tinctura,* the last arcanum, is like the *rebis*—the bisexual creature—which transmutes silver and other metals into gold; it 'tinges,' i.e., it transforms the body, removing its harmful parts, its crudity, its incompleteness, and transforms everything into a pure, noble, and indestructible being," 148.

62. Sheppard, "Egg Symbolism," 147.

63. Sheppard's survey of the origins of this symbol, that is, the flaming sword, "recalls a similar theme in the *Tractatus Micreris,* wherein an allegory attributed to Ostanes requires that the Egg be pierced with a fiery sword," 147.

64. Sheppard says that "the structure of the Egg as it appears in the *Turba*" included, in addition to the four outer layers of the soul (representing earth, air, fire, and water), a fifth mysterious center, the element that cannot be named, 146.

65. Schubert employed the *Stabat Mater* as background for lieder. Haydn and Caldara situated some of their masses at the foot of the cross. For Ramon Lull's version of *Stabat Mater,* see *The Art of Contemplation,* devotion 9, 80–81.

66. Lull, *The Art of Contemplation,* 80.

67. For a discussion of the way the seed of gold is germinated by "philosophical fire" see John Read, *Prelude to Chemistry* (1966), 138.

68. For discussion of "A Litanie" see Patrick O'Connell, "'Both Adams Met in Me': A Reading of the *Divine Poems* of John Donne," diss., Yale University, 1978, 118.

69. This is O'Connell's observation, not mine.

70. Paracelsus, *Selected Writings,* 30.

71. Ibid.

72. Ibid., 32.

73. Helen Gardner, ed., "Commentary," in *The Divine Poems,* by Donne, 84. In spite of the protests of Bernard, Aquinas, and Bonaventure, the Roman Church eventually established the Immaculate Conception as doctrine. Duns Scotus (1266–1308) was undoubtedly the most influential force behind this trend. On 28 February 1476 and again on 4 September 1483, Pope Sixtus IV gave his approval by condemning as heretics those who believed otherwise. In 1546 the Council of Trent qualified their declaration on original sin to exclude the Virgin. In 1567 Pope Pius V condemned Baius's proposition that only Christ was free from original sin. In 1617 Pope Paul V and in 1622 Gregory XV forbade the denial of the Immaculate Conception in public sermons. On 8 December 1854, Pius IX pronounced the doctrine an article of divine-Catholic faith that in the first instance of her conception Mary was pure.

74. Concerning the dating of Donne's verse letter to Mr. Tilman, see Shawcross, "Arrangements," where he observes, "For the first time we encounter 'Tilman' . . .

written perhaps in December 1618, or more likely in March 1620 when Tilman became an Anglican priest," 132.

75. For a discussion of Christ and Adam as androgynous beings, see Frances M. Malpezzi, "Adam, Christ, and Mr. Tilman: God's Blest Hermaphrodites," *The American Benedictine Review* 40.3 (1989): 250–60. Malpezzi finds examples in Donne, Spenser, Du Bartas, Crashaw, Bunyan, and Herbert. Malpezzi observes the tradition of Jesus as mother, including Crashaw's "Blessed be the paps," which envisions "Mary nursing at her son's bloody breast," 258.

76. Bernard, "To the Brothers at Clairvaux," in *Selected Works*, trans. G. R. Evans (New York: Paulist Press, 1987), 284.

77. Paracelsus, *Selected Writings*, 148.

Conclusion

1. Anthony Milton, "A Qualified Intolerance," in *Catholicism and Anti-Catholicism in Early Modern English Texts*, ed. Arthur F. Marotti (New York: St. Martin's Press, 1999), 85–115. Concerning conditions in early modern England, Milton observes that "works of foreign Roman Catholics in all these fields [poetry, music, painting, sculpture, and architecture] were admired, and musicians such as Byrd, Bull and Dowland observed only minimal conformity to Protestantism. The works of Rubens and Bernini were famously admired in Charles I's court," 95.

2. Alison Shell, *Catholicism, Controversy and the English Literary Imagination, 1558–1660* (New York: Cambridge Univ. Press, 1999), 2.

3. Ibid.

4. Milton, "A Qualified Intolerance," 95.

5. Ibid., 88.

6. David S. Katz, *Philo-Semitism and the Readmission of the Jews to England 1603–1655* (Oxford: Clarendon, 1982), 45.

7. Katz observes that Richard [Rowlands] Verstegan, a printer in Antwerp, was one among several who "corresponded with Sir Robert Cotton," 56. Verstegan was interested in using Dutch as the Adamic vernacular, 57.

8. Ibid., 46.

9. Katz defines *notarikon, sairuf,' albam,* and *' atbash* as "variants of *gematria,*" 82. For the influence of Christian cabalists on fifteenth- and sixteenth-century writers, see Allen G. Debus, *The Chemical Philosophy: Paracelsian Science and Medicine in the Sixteenth and Seventeenth Centuries* (New York: Science History Publications, 1977). Debus observes, "Christian scholars found a new stimulus for mystical numerical and geometrical studies in their fascination with the Hebrew Cabala and the Lullian system. . . . Because these studies were quickly applied to alchemical thought, they are of importance for an understanding of Paracelsian mathematics. Thus J. A. Pantheus discussed the art and theory of metallic transmutation in a Cabalistic system which assigned numbers to Latin, Greek, and Hebrew letters," 35n.

10. For a discussion of magic in early modern England, see Debus, *The Chemical Philosophy*, 34–36. He observes, "The Renaissance interest in natural magic [as opposed to "evil or demonic magic"] raised an unavoidable theological conflict," 35.

11. Katz, 70.

12. Ibid., 71.

13. Quoted by Katz, 72.

14. The reference is to the priest, Giovanni Agostino Pantheo, *Theoria Transmvta-*

tionis Metallicae cum Voarchadúmia: Proportionibus, numeris, & iconibus rei accommodis illustrata (Milan, 1550). His cabalistic-alchemical system gave numerical values to letters in the Latin, Greek, and Hebrew alphabets. Concerning Pantheo, Thorndike observes, "After the manner of the Lullian alchemical treatises he sets letters for stages in the process of transmutation," 5:538. But Pantheo also used names in the same manner as numbers. Thorndike notes that "[t]here is a pageful of names which he says all signify the same thing," 5:538.

15. Katz, 48.

16. *Essays*, 48.

17. Concerning the Reformation aversion to magic, Katz observes that Peter Lombard's cabalistic "proof" of the doctrine of the Trinity was "repeated throughout the Middle Ages until Calvin and others began to reject it," 82.

18. *Essays*, 23.

19. Gregory B. Stone, "Ramon Llull vs. Petrus Alfonsi: Postmodern Liberalism and the Six Liberal Arts," *Medieval Encounters: Jewish, Christian and Muslim Culture* 3.1 (March 1997): 70.

20. See Yates, *The Art of Memory:* "He believed that if he could persuade Jews and Muslims to do the Art with him, they would become converted to Christianity," 176.

21. Stone describes Lull's thought as "thinking . . . marked by its celebration of diversity and its liberal tolerance," 76.

22. Manuel Duran, "Ramon Llull: An Introduction," *Catalan Review* 4.1–2 (July–December 1990): 11.

23. See Michela Pereira, *The Alchemical Corpus Attributed to Raymond Lull* (London: The Warburg Institute, University of London, 1989): "[Vicente] Mut . . . maintained that Hebraic terms were used in the alchemical works, although Lull knew no Hebrew," 51.

24. Yates, *The Art of Memory*, 177.

25. Mark D. Johnston, *The Spiritual Logic of Ramon Llull* (Oxford: Clarendon, 1987), 19.

26. Ibid.

27. *Essays*, 48.

28. "To Sr. *Edward Herbert*. At *Julyers*" (l. 38).

29. *Institutes of the Christian Religion*, vol. 20, ed. John T. McNeill and trans. Ford Lewis Battles (Philadelphia: Westminster Press, 1960), 253. Calvin's analogy for the spiritual condition of mankind, including infants, is rot: "Hence, rotten branches came forth from a rotten root, which transmitted their rottenness to the other twigs sprouting from them," 250.

30. Ibid., 249–50.

31. *The Table Talk of Martin Luther*, trans. William Hazlitt (London: Bell and Daldy, 1872), 74.

32. *Institutes*, 250.

33. *The Art of Contemplation*, trans. E. Allison Peers (London: Society for Promoting Christian Knowledge, 1925), 75–76.

34. Johnston observes one problem with Lull's "logic": "The need to posit this reciprocity of Dignities in the Godhead as a paradigm for the interrelations of *Principia* in creatures leads to certain difficulties regarding God's absolute simplicity," 116.

35. Quoted by Keynes, 259. The reference is to Hall's *The Remedy of Prophaneness* (1637). This motto has not yet been found on any of Donne's books. More familiar is Donne's motto, "For Rachel have I served, not for Leah." This is usually regarded as Donne's way of choosing the contemplative life over the active. Duran observes

that Lull himself, long after his death, was regarded as "a model, a guide, an intellectual hero: a man who knew how to harmonize . . . contemplation and heroic action," 11.

36. Quoted by Evelyn Simpson, introduction, in *Sermons*, 7:52.

37. *Devotions Upon Emergent Occasions* (Ann Arbor: Univ. of Michigan Press, 1959), 135.

38. Johnston quotes from the Latin Lull's argument that God's will and his being are equal. Answering Aquinas, Lull "posits equality or *aequiparantia* as such a relation," 116. This principle, *aequiparantia*, concerns mainly "the Divine nature, and thus serves pre-eminently in his [Lull's] work as a kind of special theological logic," 116.

39. Yates, *Art of Memory*, 176.

40. Ibid., 182.

41. Ibid.

42. See, for example, Elena Levy-Navarro, "Breaking Down the Walls That Divide: Anti-Polemicism in the *Devotions Upon Emergent Occasions*," in *John Donne and the Protestant Reformation: New Perspectives*, ed. Mary Arshagouni Papazian (Detroit: Wayne State Univ. Press, 2003), 273–92. Levy-Navarro concludes, "Donne revels in imagining the moment of the final consummation as one that breaks down all the walls currently maintained and erected in the church by strident polemicists. In the last moment, 'puritan' will be united with 'avant-garde conformist,' Catholic with Protestant, and all with Jesus Christ," 287.

43. Katz says that many people thought that native Americans "might be Israelites," 138.

44. Shawcross, *Complete Poetry*, 349n. He defines "spouse" as "the true Church."

45. The editors of the forthcoming variorum edition of the *Holy Sonnets* have renamed the manuscript NY3.

46. *John Donne: The Oxford Authors*, ed. John Carey (New York: Oxford Univ. Press, 1990), 474. John Shawcross dates the sonnet "after Jan. 1615," "After ordination," 415.

47. Carey, *Authors*, 474.

48. Gardner, appendix, in *Divine Poems*, 121.

49. Peter Lake, *Moderate Puritans and the Elizabethan Church* (New York: Cambridge Univ. Press, 1982), 104.

50. *Essays*, 48.

51. Ibid., 49.

52. Ibid., 48–49.

53. Nicholas Tyacke, "The Legalizing of Dissent, 1571–1719," in *From Persecution to Toleration: The Glorious Revolution and Religion in England*, ed. Ole Peter Grell, Jonathan I. Israel, and Nicholas Tyacke (Oxford: Clarendon, 1991), 41.

54. Gardner, ed. *The Divine Poems*, by Donne, 80.

55. See Lukas Erne, "Donne and Christ's Spouse," *Essays in Criticism* 51 (April 2001): 208–29. Erne argues that Helen Gardner's reading, that Donne's sonnet "could hardly have been written by anyone but an Anglican" (*Divine Poems*, 122), is too restrictive and reveals "the critical effects of such biographical assumptions," 215. Instead he insists that "Donne's 'one hill' refers to Geneva rather than to Gardner's far-fetched 'Mount Moriah'," 217.

56. Gardner, ed., *Divine Poems*, by Donne, 125.

57. Ibid., 122.

58. Ibid., 124.

59. Shell, 101.

60. Frost, "'Preparing Towards Her': Contexts of *A Nocturnall upon S. Lucies Day*," in *John Donne's "desire of more": The Subject of Anne More Donne in His Poetry*, ed. M. Thomas Hester (Newark: Univ. of Delaware Press, 1996), 163.

61. Other meanings Frost says are attached to "five" include "circularity in potential, justice, marriage . . . [and] the Virgin," 162.

62. John Carey takes the question to simply mean, "Was the True Church in abeyance for centuries prior to the Protestant Reformation?" See *Authors*, 474. John Shawcross does not comment on the line.

63. For the tradition that has the phoenix sleep five or six hundred years, see note appended to the phoenix emblem (Whitney, 1586) in *The Riverside Shakespeare*, vol. 2 (New York: Houghton Mifflin, 1997), 1890. According to *The Encyclopedia Britannica* (1973), "It is very long-lived; no ancient authority gives it a life span of less than five hundred years; some say it lives for 1,461 years (an Egyptian Sothic Period): an extreme estimate is 97,200."

64. Quoted by Henry Green, *Shakespeare and the Emblem Writers* (London: Trübner, 1870), 384.

65. The reference is to Reynolds's portrait, *Augustus Viscount Keppel*. The artist paints the naval officer in the same posture as *The Apollo Belvedere*.

66. Denis Saurat, *Literature and the Occult Tradition: Studies in Philosophical Poetry*, trans. Dorothy Bolton (New York: L. MacVeagh, Dial Press, 1930). Saurat writes, "The Bible texts which speak of wisdom form naturally the basis of the [cabalist] conception of the Schekhina, who is Wisdom," 225–26.

67. "Dictionary of Scripture Proper Names" in *The Scofield Reference Bible*, ed. C. I. Scotfield, D. D., 4th ed. (New York: Oxford University Press, 1945), 41.

68. *Essays*, 50.

69. Ibid.

70. Saurat, 228.

71. Erne, 221.

72. Ibid., 222.

73. Erne's explanation is, "Whereas 'kind husband' implies the maximum intimacy and presupposes belonging to the Church, the need for Christ to betray his spouse to the speaker implies that the latter has unchurched himself," 222.

74. David Chanoff, "The Biographical Context of Donne's Sonnet on the Church," *The American Benedictine Review* 32 (1981): 386.

75. Gardner, ed., *Divine Poems*, by Donne, 127.

76. Gardner's note on the final lines does not connect Donne's references to any particular historical moment. She simply observes, "He prays that we may see the Spouse of Christ appear to men, as a wife who delights to welcome all her husband's friends, and whose husband, unlike earthly husbands, delights in her approachability," 122.

77. John T. Shawcross, *The Complete Poetry of John Donne*, 350.

78. *OED*. The illustration offered is from Dryden's translation of Virgil's *Georgics*, 4:426: "Betray no Wound on his unbroken Skin." The story itself concerns the capture of Proteus, the shape-shifter, by Aristaeus. Caught unawares and fettered in his grot, Proteus is compelled to reveal his shape. Donne, we know, carefully studied Virgil. His personal copy of *La Eneide tradotta in Terza Rima per M. Giovanpaolo Vasio* (Venice, 1538) bears his signature and motto on the title page (Keynes, 277). E. E. Duncan-Jones argues that the second book of Virgil's *Georgics* (ll. 69–70) is a source

for "The Autumnall." See his article, "The Barren Plane-Tree in Donne's 'The Autumnall,'" *Notes and Queries* 7 (1960): 53.

79. Saurat, 228.
80. *OED.*
81. *Essays,* 51.
82. Ibid., 50.
83. Ibid.
84. Albert H. Tricomi, *Reading Tudor-Stuart Texts Through Cultural Historicism* (Gainsville: Univ. Press of Florida, 1996). Especially see chapter 7, "Affectivity and New Historicism: The Mothering Body Surveilled in *The Duchess of Malfi* and *The Duchess of Suffolk.*"
85. For discussion of Mary's attributes of Mercy and Justice (assigned by Lull), see David Viera, "Exempla in the *Libre de Sancta Maria,*" *Catalan Review* 4.1–2 (July–December 1990): 221–31. The rabbinical texts also assume that the world was ordained by Mercy and Justice. See H. F. Fletcher, *Milton's Rabbinical Readings* (Urbana: Univ. of Illinois Press, 1930; repr., Archon, 1967). Fletcher observes that "Creation was originally effected in Justice; but Justice alone was not enough, and Mercy was added," 164.
86. Yates, *The Art of Memory,* 182.
87. Ibid., 183.
88. *Table Talk,* 74.
89. M. Thomas Hester, "'All our Soules Devotion': Satire as Religion in Donne's *Satyre III,*" *Studies in English Literature, 1500–1900* 18 (1978): 36–37.
90. Yates, *The Art of Memory,* 174.
91. Johnston, *Spiritual Logic,* 23.
92. Yates, *The Art of Memory,* 176.
93. Katz, 82.
94. Ibid.
95. Johnston, 26.
96. *Sermons,* 2:346–47. The editors note that this "is the earliest we possess of several sermons that Donne preached at marriages," 42. The date of this sermon concurs with John Carey's dating of Donne's sonnet (ca. 1620), for it was preached "shortly before the 12th of February, 1619/20," 42.
97. Mary Carruthers, *The Book of Memory: A Study of Memory in Medieval Culture* (New York: Cambridge Univ. Press, 1993), 8.
98. See Evelyn Simpson, "Donne's Spanish Authors," *Modern Language Review* 43 (1948): 182–85. Simpson observes that Donne was "familiar with the philosophical work of Raymond of Sebund," 184. Mark Johnston elaborates, noting that "Raymond of Sebond (or Saibunde, and other alternate spellings) was a well-known Lullist of the fifteenth century and if Donne was familiar with his work, then he certainly knew of Llull's ideas. . . . As it happens, Llull's *ars universalis* was really far more popular outside Spain in the sixteenth and seventeenth centuries than it was there, so it's entirely possible that Donne knew of Llull's ideas from other European sources" (letter dated 4 January 2003). That Sebond was one among many Spanish authors in Donne's library is indicated by a letter he sent to the Duke of Buckingham in Madrid in 1623: "I can thus far make myself believe that I am where your Lordship is, in Spain, that, in my poor library, where indeed I am, I can turn mine eye towards no shelf, in any profession from the mistress of my youth, Poetry, to the wife of mine age, Divinity, but that I meet more authors of that nation than of any other," Edmund Gosse (2:176) quoted by Keynes, 262.

99. E. M. W. Tillyard, *The Elizabethan World Picture* (1943; repr., New York: Random House, 1959), 27.

100. Yates, *The Art of Memory*, 180–81.

101. Harris Francis Fletcher, *Milton's Rabbinical Readings*, 313.

102. Thorndike remarks Pantheo's use of "charts, diagrams and columns of letters and numbers as well as the *Tetragrammaton* and Greek and Hebrew characters. After the manner of the Lullian alchemical treatises he sets letters for stages in the process of transmutation and gives diagrams of the four elements and primary qualities," 5:538. The function of the female agent is understood.

103. Fletcher notes that "Milton thought of the contact of the Spirit of God with the elements of Chaos as an impregnation," 124. The source of this representation, he says, is "the original Hebrew of the first chapter of Genesis," 126.

104. *Essays*, 27.

105. Ibid., 31.

106. Chamberlin, *Increase and Multiply*, 106. See also Pico della Mirandola, "Heptaplus," in *De hominis dignitate, Heptaplus, De ente et uno*, ed. E. Garin (Florence: Vallecchi, 1942).

107. See Saurat, *Literature and Occult Tradition*, 222–37.

108. Ibid., 228.

109. Ibid.

110. Ibid.

111. Saurat quoting the *Zohar*, 229.

112. Fletcher, 313.

113. Saurat quoting the *Zohar*, 230.

114. Ibid., 233.

115. Sheppard, "The Ouroboros," 87.

116. *Sermons*, 8:143.

117. Ibid.

118. Ibid., 4:287. Donne's text was Colossians 1:19–20.

119. The reference is to the sonnet entitled "On the blessed Virgin Mary," attributed to Henry Constable. It appears in the John Marriot edition of Donne's *Holy Sonnets* (1635). The reference to God's "sole-borne daughter" implies a female Soul born out of God himself long before her human birth. Mary, the poet says, did not need "grace" in her "mothers wombe." (This, of course, distinguishes her from John the Baptist, who did need this grace.) Instead the poet implies that she is equal with her Spouse: "To match thee like thy births nobilitie." This Immaculist position is reaffirmed with the line, "And so was link'd to all the Trinitie."

120. Saurat, 230.

121. Fletcher, *Milton's Rabbinical Readings*, 111. Milton's innovation, Fletcher says, was to create "a companion or sister Spirit," who was present during Creation. "According to the text of Proverbs, Wisdom appears to have been alone with God at Creation. The text of Scripture, therefore, could not have suggested to Milton the strange idea of having two, apparently equal Spirits present with the Son on his mission of Creation."

122. Ibid., 126.

123. Andreasen, *John Donne: Conservative Revolutionary* (Princeton: Princeton Univ. Press, 1967), 72–73.

124. Ernest Rutherford discovered the nucleus of the atom in 1919. Though it was said that he had "split" the atom, he had really transmuted the nucleus, forming an isotope out of the resultant disintegration.

125. Andreasen, 74.

126. See *Bonfires and Bells: National Memory and the Protestant Calendar in Elizabethan and Stuart England* (Berkeley: Univ. of California Press, 1997). According to Cressy, "Pre-Reformation England followed a calendar that drew on celestial, pagan and ecclesiastical elements," 1. After the Reformation, this calendar was "purged." Evidently, public demand was so great that in 1541 some of the feast days were reinstated. "Official observance of the feasts of Saints Luke, Mark, and Mary Magdalene crept back into the calendar in 1541," 5–6. Ironically, the ecclesiastical courts continued to "adhere to the pre-Reformation calendar," 11. Hence the courts, "whose tasks included enforcing the discipline of the reformed religion," managed to "perpetuate the memory of saints whose days had ceased to be festivals," 11.

127. The Toleration Act of 1689 granted freedom of religion to almost everyone. Ironically, this freedom was gained at Catholic expense. According to Tyacke, "Catholics were the losers" ("The Legalizing of Dissent, 1571–1719," 41).

128. Quoted by Richard Strier, "Donne and the Politics of Devotion," in *Religion, Literature, and Politics in Post-Reformation England, 1540–1688* (New York: Cambridge Univ. Press, 1996), 108.

129. Joseph H. Summers, *George Herbert: His Religion and Art* (Cambridge: Harvard Univ. Press, 1968), 25.

130. Katz cites Donne's *Essays*, not the poems. See 50 and 79.

131. Ibid., 46.

132. Ibid., 70.

133. *Essays*, 23.

134. The artist was Nicholas Stone the Elder (d. 1647).

Glossary of General and Specialized Alchemical Terms

ablution: See "women's work."

albedo: The white stage in the alchemical process following "digestion," or the initial black stage, when elements are broken down by some sort of menstruum or solvent. Successful achievement of the white stage is sometimes associated with Hercules' cleansing of the Augean stables.

alembic (or **limbeck**): An apparatus used in distilling. It consists of a gourd-shaped vessel containing the substance to be distilled and is surmounted by a *head*, the beak of which conveys vapors to a *receiver*, where they are condensed.

Aphrodite: A favorite emblem in alchemical theory. Mermaidlike Aphrodite is born from the sea, origin of all things. One emblem in the *Viridarium* includes an epigram: "I am a goddess exceeding fair, born from the depths of the sea, which in its course washes and surrounds all the dry land. Let my breasts pour forth to thee twin streams of blood and milk, which thou canst well know" (Read, *Prelude*, 270). These twin streams are references to virgin's milk or *lac virginis*. See "virgin's milk" below.

ark: Synonym for the "alembic" (above), where contrary elements are joined and resolved as one.

Assumption (or Coronation) **of the Virgin:** Understood by the alchemists as glorification of matter. The crowned virgin symbolized purity and was associated with Sapientia (wisdom) and salt, which cleanses, purifies, and regenerates metals.

augmentation (or **multiplication**): That penultimate stage in the process, identified with cibation, when the potency and quantity of the elixir are augmented through reiterated dissolution and coagulation of matter. This quality of abundance occurs as the opus is achieving culmination. Augmentation is symbolized by the burning phoenix, out of whose ashes fly numerous chicks.

balm or **balsam:** Any substance imbued with restorative virtue or healing power. Adepts sought to find and to multiply this indestructible and regenerative spirit that preserved and strengthened matter.

black stage: Also called the "nigredo," when putrefaction in the alembic is described as "black as hell." The profundity of this blackness is said to influence the psyche of the adept himself. Sometimes the nigredo is referred to as "Passion" or "Crucifixion."

blood: Thought to be the habitation of animal and vital spirits in the human body (Aristotle). William Harvey (1578–1657) modified this view so that "animal" and "vital" became the same phenomenon in the blood, composed of the motive, vegetative, and sensitive soul. Harvey later concluded that blood differed in no way from soul, "or at least should be considered as a substance whose action is soul." Alchemical theorists adopted a similar view, considering blood analogous to the solvent *menstruum* but also to the volatile spirit, called *pneuma*, that joins things. Harvey himself thought blood to be impregnated with balsam, implying its restorative powers. When Donne defines "grace" as the "middle nature" in the blood, he expresses a similar idea.

calcination: Subjecting any infusible substance to a roasting heat so that it is reduced to a "calx" or powder.

Calvary, Crucifixion (or **Passion**): Associated with calcination and the black stage (above). Because the female element was thought to "die" with her husband in the alembic, alchemists appropriated the "*nigra sed formosa*" bride of Christ from the *Song of Songs* to symbolize the chemical "wedding." See "dissolution" below.

cibation: That stage in the process called "feeding the matter." See also "augmentation."

Diana: A reference to the cold, white, moist feminine nature of the Stone. Also symbol of the albedo (above). As the "virgin huntress," Diana was naturally associated with the pure Virgin.

dissolution: Putrefaction following the alchemical marriage, when male and female elements rot in their "marriage bed" or "grave," also called the alembic or tomb. See "Calvary," above, and "marriage," below.

distillation: See "sublimation."

dove: Symbol for the albedo. Also the symbol for that "Mercurius" who unites male and female elements in order to bring peace to quarreling factions. Its counterpart in Christian iconography is the Holy Spirit, the "brooding" Dove of Creation.

dragon: Symbol for dual-natured Mercury. The dragon is often distinguished as two sexes. The wingless dragon (sulfur) is male. Considered a stable force, he never leaves the fire or "nest." The winged dragon (quicksilver) is female. Considered more volatile, she flies through the air, sometimes evaporating. The union of these two dragons is necessary to creation. See also "eagle."

eagle (or **flying eagle**): Symbol for "white Mercury" or "virgin's milk." When a series of sublimations was implemented, these stages were referred to as "eagles." The "flying white eagle" indicates Mercury in its most volatile state.

egg: Alchemical emblem symbolizing the work born out of chaos. Hence, the alembic, shaped like its gestatory function, is sometimes called "the egg." Sometimes the birth of the Philosopher's Stone is compared to the hatching of a chick from its egg. Since the gentle warmth of their apparatus emulated maternal heat and since their patient attendance completed the task, adepts often thought of themselves as brooding hens. The alchemical emblem corresponds with Christian depictions of Christ as hen and of the Holy Spirit as brooding hen or dove. See also, "sword."

elixir (or **quintessence**): Another name for the Philosopher's Stone. Because it is the purest of substances, immortal and incorruptible, it is the great transmuting agent in alchemy. In order to find it, adepts must first understand principles of unity.

fire: The underlying substance of the universe, all other elements being mere transformations of it (Heraclitus). Alchemists considered fire (or warmth) necessary to all important phases of transmutation and sublimation. Later Paracelsian theory developed the idea that mercury, sulfur and salt were the basic constituents of matter. Paracelsus perceived sulfur as fire uniting the other two elements (salt and mercury). This theory was known as the *tria prima*. Adepts sometimes distinguished between ordinary fire, with its destructive power, and philosophical fire, with its germinative power. See also "sword" and "seeds."

fixionem (or **establishment**): The final stage of the opus when purified matter, the nature of which is volatile or "fugitive," is stabilized. This stage can only occur after the processes of calcination, dissolution, ablution, cibation, and so on, have been completed. Also the process of converting a volatile spirit or essence, like gas, into a permanent bodily form. An example would be the conversion of mercury to solid matter by amalgamating or combining it with another element.

grace: Power granted the adept as he entered the laboratory. It was thought that the success or failure of the opus directly corresponded to the adept's state of grace. See also "blood."

hen: Sometimes depicted as the burning hen. See "egg."

marriage: Symbol for the union of male (sulfur) and female (salt) elements in the alembic, where "husband and wife," melting with ardor, finally "die" (in the Renaissance sense of experiencing sexual orgasm), breaking down into pieces. Hence, the alembic is both marriage bed and grave. This stage in the alchemical process came to be known as dissolution. See also "menstruum."

materia prima: First matter, symbolized in numerous ways: as the pure Virgin and Adam before his corruption; as the sea, thought to contain all forms of life; as mother earth; as seed; as sperm; as menstrue containing the seeds of all things; and as the Philosopher's Stone. Extraction of materia prima was the alchemist's goal. See also "virgin."

menstruum: Solvent in the alembic, used by the alchemists to dissolve the earthly metallic body into a more noble elixir. The base metal undergoing transmutation into gold was compared to the seed developing in the womb by the agency of menstrual blood. Some alchemists thought that the human fetus consisted of a spermatic and a menstrual part, derived from the two parents. Sometimes they associated menstruum with saliva, especially as it figured in the process of digestion. During the fourteenth century some adepts considered the best menstruum to be mercury purged of earth and phlegm. See also the "mercury alone doctrine" (below).

Mercury (or **Mercurius**): Androgynous figure symbolizing transformation, without which the opus cannot be performed. Mercury is the bearer of life and change, for it is the guide of souls. Hence, it is the mother of all metals and the substance from which all other metals are created. Its volatile nature renders it powerful in uniting male and female elements.

"Mercury alone" theory: Fourteenth-century theory that the Philosopher's Stone could best be made from mercury only (rather than from a combination of mercury and sulfur, as previously thought).

mint: See "virgin" and "womb."

multiplication: See "augmentation."

Ouroboros: See "Uroboros."

Passion: See "Calvary."

pelican: Alchemical symbol of revivification, or cibation, when the infant Stone is fed with mercurial blood. Certain vessels were called *pelicans*, presumably because of their resemblance to the bird.

Philosopher's Stone: An imaginary substance thought to be capable of transmuting lesser metals into gold. Other properties include the power to restore health and youth. See also "elixir."

phoenix: Mythical bird symbolizing renewal and resurrection, especially that of the Philosopher's Stone at the rubedo. It also serves as the symbol for multiplication or augmentation, where the quality and quantity of the elixir are infinitely multiplied by dissolution and coagulation. As symbol of augmentation, it is seen perched on a globe, hatching numerous chicks, silver and gold. In some versions of the original myth, the bird burns itself on the altar of the temple at Heliopolis, fanning the flames with its wings, thereby producing aromatic ashes, from which fiery nest a worm appears. Hence, in alchemical theory the worms in the alembic signify a "new phoenix" or resurrection of the Stone.

pneuma: From the original Greek, breath or that principle of life that is the reservoir of the world soul. This breath was believed to be distributed through the body by means of the lungs and blood vessels. Yet, according to Aristotle, it could also be transformed into things. The alchemists appropriated *pneuma* as the breath or soul to be extracted from base matter. Hence, they affirmed their belief that this subtle but not wholly immaterial pneuma could aid in making new forms.

rainbow: Occurs when the dry principle acts upon the moist so that "all the colours of a Peacock's Tail begin to spring up in the Sage's vessel" (Edward Kelly, *Alchemical Writings*, 140). When the moisture of the nigredo finally disappears, these shifting colors resolve in the whiteness of the albedo. Christian alchemists associated the rainbow of the biblical flood story with the ark, that is, the virgin's womb.

rebis: According to Paracelsus, "the bisexual creature—which transmutes silver and other metals into gold" (*Selected Writings*, 148). He associates it with *tinctura*, that step in the alchemical process that "transforms the body, removing its harmful parts, its crudity, its incompleteness, and transforms everything into a pure, noble, and indestructible being" (148).

red stage (or **rubedo**): Final stage in the opus associated with Resurrection, when the Stone is crowned king, emerging from his glassy "sepulchre" or alembic as glorified matter.

Resurrection: See "red stage" and "phoenix."

retort: A vessel made of glass, metal, or earthenware and provided with a long neck, bent downward, in which liquids, subjected to distillation, are heated.

rosary: From the Roman Catholic prayer (or beads) organized as a series of fifteen meditations on the lives of Jesus and Mary. These were the joyful, sorrowful, and glorious mysteries (including the Annunciation, the Visitation, the birth of Jesus, the Purification of the Virgin, the Crucifixion, the Resurrection, the Assumption of the Virgin, and her Coronation as Queen of Heaven). Various stages in the prayer were appropriated by alchemical theorists in order to designate certain steps in the opus, culminating in the nativity and maturation of the Stone.

rubedo: See "red stage."

Sapientia: The crowned virgin, or wisdom, associated with salt, the purifying agent. As Sapientia, the virgin dissolved, cleansed, and regenerated metals.

seeds: From agriculture and human sexuality, an apt analogy for the alchemical process. The seed buried deep in the warm earth was thought to be like the alchemist's seeds in the alembic. Certain theorists identified "seeds of fire." Sometimes these seeds were distinguished as male or female and signified the conception, gestation, and birth of the Stone. Once the Stone was born, it had to be nourished until it grew to maturity.

semen: The primary elements contained in the alchemical worm. The theory derives from Hippocrates, who believed that *prima materia* exists in male and female semen in separation until recombined. Alchemical theorists sometimes propose that a little worm is present in the semen of the male and, sometimes, that female semen contains the worm of generation.

sublimation (or **distillation**): The processes whereby impure matter is clarified. The goal is extraction of the spirit or essence of any substance by means of an alembic, retort, and receiver. Distinctions between the two are generally based upon the nature of the matter clarified. In the process of sublimation, matter begins as solid. In the process of distillation, matter may be in any form except vapor. In sublimation, applied heat produces rapid vaporization that transforms matter from a solid to a gaseous state without becoming liquid. This is followed by cooling and condensation, which resolidifies the matter. In distillation, applied heat produces a vapor, which is then condensed by some version of refrigeration into liquid form. The purpose of both is to free the volatile substance (considered pure) from its baser source.

sword: Symbol for the application of heat during the alchemical process. The figure of a swordsman taking aim at the Egg with his sword of fire represented the birth of the Philosopher's Stone. In some theories the sword first penetrated the shell (representing earth), then the thin membrane between shell and white (representing air), then the white (representing water), and finally the yolk (representing fire).

tincture: See "rebis."

tria prima: Sulfur, salt, and mercury, each of which has its analogue (Paracelsus). Sulfur (body) can only be combined with salt (soul) by means of mercury (pneuma). Though the original Greek meaning of pneuma is *spirit* or *soul*, Paracelsus redefines this word as a third element in the tria prima, or Trinity. Because mercury is composed of both salt and sulfur, it is considered hermaphroditic. The refining process is complicated by the fact that salt and sulfur are stable, but mercury active.

Uroboros: Alchemical symbol depicting a serpent eating its own tail. It represents the process of transmutation and is the symbol of eternity.

Venus: See "Aphrodite."

virgin: Symbol of original matter; also the receptive, that is feminine aspect of dual-natured Mercurius. The analogue in Christian theology was thought to be God's stamping original Matter with all things during the Creative Act. Hence the Virgin Mother (also called materia prima) was origin of All and thought to be Mint of God's first Creation. In alchemy the receptive feminine aspect of Mercurius is known as *argent-vive* and is symbolized by the virgin. See also "womb."

Virgin suckling her Child: Emblem for cibation, when the infant Stone is fed with mercurial blood. Hence, the alchemists compare Christ's birth with the "nativity" and maturation of the Philosopher's Stone. See also "augmentation" and "cibation."

virgin's milk: *Lac virginis*, a wonder-working concoction possessing restorative powers. Horse manure (and time) were important ingredients in the making of virgin's milk. Heraclitus may be among the earliest sources for belief in the virtues and restorative powers of manure. He reputedly "buried himself in a cowshed, expecting that the noxious damp humour would be drawn out of him by the warmth of the manure" (*Heracleitus*, 461). So convinced was he of the healing powers of manure, that he had his servants "plaster him over with cow-dung while he lay in the sun" (462). Virgin's milk has been described as May-dew, distilled with *aqua fortis*, mixed with sublimated mercury, and putrified for a month in warm horse-dung (Read, 157). Various alchemical treatises note the importance of virgin's milk in preparation of either the Philosopher's Stone or medicine. Basilius, for example, writes, "When the Medicine and Stone of all the Sages has been perfectly prepared out of the true virgin's milk, take one part of it to three parts of the best gold . . . ," and so on (Read, 205–6). Jonson's play, *The Alchemist* (1610), also includes virgin's milk among a list of secret powers: " . . . your elixir, your *lac virginis*, / Your stone, your med'cine, and your chrysosperm, / Your sal, your sulphur, and your mercury" (2.3:87–89).

Wisdom: See "Sapientia."

womb: Alchemical symbol for the alembic or vessel, where the "chemical wedding" is performed. Comparing the process with the Christian doctrine of the Virgin Birth, alchemists propagated the idea that the "alchemical King" must enter again his virgin mother's womb. The growth of the fetus in the womb was thought to be controlled by heat that emulated human generative fires. Hence, Donne's reference to Mary as "mint," a place where money is coined, is also a reference to the alchemical womb. See also "menstruum."

women's work: The work of cleansing and purifying matter. It is associated with that stage in the process called laundering or ablution.

worm: Alchemical symbol for corruption leading to generation. As the devouring worm of death, it consumes all. As the nourishing worm of life, it feeds the alchemical chick. Emblems depicting the worm in the vessel argued that new life would come from alchemical death. In the Renaissance *worm, serpent,* and *dragon* were used interchangeably. See also "phoenix," "semen," and "dragon."

Selected Bibliography

Primary Sources

Alsted, Johann Heinrich. *Clavis artis Lullianae, et verae logices duos in libellos tribvta. Opera & studio Johannis Henrici Alstedi. Accessit novum specvum logices minime vulgaris.* Imprint Strasbourg: Sumptibus Lazari Zetzneri, Bibliopol, 1609 and 1652.

Aquinas, Thomas, Saint. *The Summa Theologica.* Translated by L. Shapcote. 22 vols. London: Burns, Oates, 1912–36.

Aquinas, Thomas, Saint [Pseudo]. *Aurora Consurgens: A Document Attributed to Thomas Aquinas on the Problem of Opposites in Alchemy.* Edited by Marie-Louise von Franz. Translated by R. F. C. Hull and A. S. B. Glover. New York: Pantheon, 1966.

Ashmole, Elias. *Theatrum Chemicum Britannicum.* 1652. Edited by Allen G. Debus. New York: Johnson Reprint, 1967.

Augustine, Saint. *Basic Writings of Saint Augustine.* Edited by Whitney J. Oates. New York: Random House, 1948.

———. *The Confessions: Books IX–XIII.* Translated by William Watts. Loeb Classical Library. Cambridge: Harvard University Press, 1997.

Bacon, Francis. *The Works of Francis Bacon.* Edited by James Spedding, Robert L. Ellis, and Douglas D. Heath. 14 vols. 1857–74. Reprint, London: Longmans, 1963.

Bacon, Roger. *The Emerald Table.* In *The Mirror of Alchemy, Composed by the Thrice-famous and Learned Frye, Roger Bachon,* edited by Stanton J. Linden. New York: Garland, 1992.

Bernard of Clairvaux. *Selected Works.* Translated by G. R. Evans. Introduction by Jean Lecleroq, O.S.B. New York: Paulist Press, 1987.

———. *On the Song of Songs I: The Works of Bernard of Clairvaux.* Translated by Kilian Walsh OCSO. Vol. 2. Spencer, Mass.: Cistercian Publications, 1971.

Bruno, Giordano. *The Expulsion of the Triumphant Beast.* Translated with introduction by Arthur D. Imerti. New Brunswick: Rutgers University Press, 1964.

Calvin, John. *Institutes of the Christian Religion.* Edited by John T. McNeill. Translated by Ford Lewis Battles. Vol. 20, Library of Christian Classics. Philadelphia: Westminster, 1960.

[Cicero, M. Tullius]. *Rhetorica ad Herennium (Ad C. Herennium libri IV De ratione dicendi).* Edited and translated by Harry Caplan. Loeb Classical Library. Cambridge: Harvard University Press, 1954.

Cradock, Edward. "A Treatise Touching the Philosopher's Stone (c. 1575)". In *Alchemical Poetry, 1575–1700: From Previously Unpublished Manuscripts,* edited by Robert M. Schuler, 3–48. Vol. 5, English Renaissance Hermeticism. New York: Garland, 1995.

Crashaw, Richard. *The Poems English, Latin and Greek of Richard Crashaw.* Edited by L. C. Martin. Oxford: Clarendon, 1927.

———. *The Complete Poetry of Richard Crashaw.* Edited by George Walton Williams. New York: New York University Press, 1972.

Dee, Arthur. *Fasciculus Chemicus.* Translated by Elias Ashmole. Edited by Lyndy Abraham. English Renaissance Hermeticism. New York: Garland, 1997.

Donne, John. "The Anniversaries." *The Variorum Edition of the Poetry of John Donne.* Edited by Gary A. Stringer et al. 7–37. Vol. 6. Bloomington and Indianapolis: Indiana University Press, 1995.

———. *The Complete Poetry of John Donne.* Edited by John T. Shawcross. Garden City, N.Y.: Doubleday/Anchor Books, 1967. Reprint, New York: New York University Press, 1968.

———. *Devotions Upon Emergent Occasions Together with Death's Duel.* Ann Arbor: University of Michigan Press, 1982.

———. *The Divine Poems.* Edited by Helen Gardner. 2nd ed. Oxford: Clarendon, 1978.

———. *Essays in Divinity.* Edited by Evelyn M. Simpson. Oxford: Clarendon, 1952.

———. *John Donne's 1622 Gunpowder Plot Sermon: A Parallel-Text Edition.* Edited by Jeanne Shami. Pittsburgh: Duquesne University Press, 1999.

———. *The Life and Letters of John Donne, Dean of St. Paul's.* Edited by Edmund Gosse. 2 vols. London: Heinemann, 1899. Reprint, Gloucester, Mass.: 1959.

———. *The Sermons of John Donne.* Edited by George R. Potter and Evelyn M. Simpson. 10 vols. Berkeley: University of California Press, 1953–62.

———. *The Works of John Donne.* Edited by Henry Alford. 6 vols. London: John W. Parker, 1839.

Emerson, Ralph Waldo. *Natural History of the Intellect and Other Poems.* Edited by Edward W. Emerson. Boston: Houghton Mifflin, 1904.

———. *Selections from Ralph Waldo Emerson.* Edited by Stephen E. Whicher. Boston: Houghton Mifflin, 1960.

Ficino, Marsilio. *Three Books on Life.* Edited and translated by Carol V. Kaske and John R. Clark. Vol. 57, Medieval and Renaissance Texts and Studies. Renaissance Society of America. New York: Binghamton, 1989.

———. *Commentary of Plato's "Symposium" on Love.* Translated by Jayne Sears. Rev. ed. Dallas: Spring Publications, 1985.

Flamel, Nicolas. *Écrits Alchimiques* (1624). Edited by Didier Kahn. Translated by P. Arnauld. Paris: Société d'édition Les Belles Lettres, 1993.

Harrison, G. B., ed. *The Elizabethan Journals: Being a Record of Those Things Most Talked of During the Years 1591–1603.* Ann Arbor: University of Michigan Press, 1955.

Heracleitus. "On the Universe." In *Hippocrates,* edited and translated by W. H. S. Jones, 469–509. Vol 4, Loeb Classical Library. Cambridge: Harvard University Press, 1992.

Herbert, Edward. *The Life of Edward, First Lord Herbert of Cherbury.* Edited by J. M. Shuttleworth. London: Oxford University Press, 1976.

Hermes Trismegistus. *Hermetica: The Ancient Greek and Latin Writings Which Contain Religious or Philosophic Teachings Ascribed to Hermes Trismegistus.* Edited and translated by Walter Scott. 4 vols. Oxford: Clarendon, 1924–36. Reprint, Boston: Shambhala, 1985.

Heywood, Jasper. "Easter Day." In *The Renaissance in England,* edited by Hyder E. Rollins and Herschell Baker, 213. Lexington, Mass.: D.C. Heath, 1954.

Hippocrates. "Regimen in Health." In *Hippocrates: Heracleitus "On the Universe,"* edited and translated by W. H. S. Jones, 44–59. Vol. 4, Loeb Classical Library. Cambridge: Harvard University Press, 1992.
Jonson, Ben. *The Alchemist.* In *English Drama, 1580–1642,* edited by C.F. Tucker Brooke and Nathaniel Burton Paradise, 573–623. Lexington, Mass.: D.C. Heath, 1933.

———. *Selected Works.* Edited by David McPherson. New York: Holt, Rinehart and Winston, 1972.

Jung, C. G. *Psychology and Alchemy.* Translated by R. F. C. Hull. 2nd ed. New York: Princeton University Press, 1953.
Kelly, Edward. *The Englishman's Two Excellent Treatises on the Philosopher's Stone.* 1676. Translated by A. E. Waite (1893). London: Stuart and Watkins, 1970.
Linden, Stanton J., ed. *The Alchemy Reader: From Hermes Trismegistus to Isaac Newton.* New York: Cambridge University Press, 2003.
Llull, Ramon. *The Art of Contemplation.* Edited and translated by E. Allison Peers. London: Society for Promoting Christian Knowledge, 1925.

———. *Opera ea Qvae ad Adinventam ab Ipso Artem Vniversalem, Scientiarvm Artivmove Omnivm.* Imprint Strasbourg: Sumptibus Lazari Zetzneri, 1609.

———. *Selected Works of Ramon Llull.* Edited and translated by Anthony Bonner. 2 vols. Princeton: Princeton University Press, 1985.

Luther, Martin. "The Magnificat: Translated and Expounded by Dr. Martin Luther, Augustinian." In *Luther's Works,* edited by Jaroslav Pelikan and translated by A. T. W. Steinhaeuser, 295–355. Vol. 21. Saint Louis: Concordia Publishing House, 1956.

———. *The Table Talk of Martin Luther.* Translated and edited by William Hazlitt. London: Bell & Daldy, 1872.

Maier, Michael. *Symbola aurea Mensa.* Frankfurt, 1617.
Marvell, Andrew. *Complete Poetry.* Edited by George de F. Lord. New York: Random House, 1968.
Milton, John. *John Milton: Complete Poems and Major Prose.* Edited by Merritt Y. Hughes. Indianapolis: Bobbs-Merrill, 1976.
Mirandola, Pico della. "Heptaplus." In *De hominis dignitate, Heptaplus, De ente et uno,* edited by E. Garin. Florence: Vallecchi, 1942.
Münster, Sebastian. *Cosmographia Universalis.* Basel, 1614.
Pantheo, Giovanni Agostino. *Theoria Transmvtationis Metallicae cum Voarchadúmia: Proportionibus, numeris, & iconibus rei accommodis illustrata.* Milan, 1550.
Paracelsus. *Aureolus Philippus Theophrastus Bombast, of Hohenheim, Called Paracelsus the Great or Hermetic Medicine and Hermetic Philosophy.* Edited by Arthur Edward Waite. Vol. 1. London: James Elliott, 1894.

———. *Selected Writings.* Edited by Jolande Jacobi. Translated by Norbert Guterman. New York: Pantheon, 1958.

Plato. *The Republic.* Translated by Paul Shorey. In *The Collected Dialogues of Plato Including the Letters,* edited by Edith Hamilton and Huntington Cairns, 575–844. Princeton: Princeton University Press, 1961.

———. *Theaetetus.* Translated by Harold North Fowler, 1–257. Vol. 7, Loeb Classical Library. Cambridge: Harvard University Press, 1996.

Ripley, George. *The Compound of Alchemy.* Edited by Stanton J. Linden. Brookfield, Vt.: Ashgate, 2001.

Roper, William. From *The Life of Sir Thomas More, Knight*. In *The Renaissance in England*, edited by Hyder E. Rollins and Herschell Baker, 48–52. Lexington, Mass.: D.C. Heath, 1954.

Waite, Arthur Edward, ed. *The Hermetic Museum, Restored and Enlarged*. 2 vols. London: James Elliot, 1893.

Secondary Sources

Abraham, Lyndy. Introduction. In *Arthur Dee Fasciculus Chemicus*, edited by Lyndy Abraham, xi–xcii. Translated by Elias Ashmole. English Renaissance Hermeticism. New York: Garland, 1997.

———. *Dictionary of Alchemical Imagery*. Cambridge: Cambridge University Press, 1999.

———. "Edward Kelly's Hieroglyph." In *Emblems and Alchemy*, edited by Alison Adams and Stanton J. Linden, 95–108. Vol. 3, Glasgow Emblem Studies. Sherborne, Dorset: Remous Ltd., Milborne Port, 1998.

———. "'The Lovers and the Tomb': Alchemical Emblems in Shakespeare, Donne, and Marvell." *Emblematica* 5 (Winter 1991): 301–20.

———. *Marvell and Alchemy*. Brookfield, Vt.: Scolar Press, 1990.

Albrecht, Roberta. "Alchemical Augmentation and Primordial Fire in Donne's 'The Dissolution.'" *Studies in English Literature, 1500–1900* 45.1 (Winter 2005): 95–115.

———. "Conning and Coining: Alchemical Motifs in Donne's 'Oh my blacke Soule!'" *English Language Notes* 42 (December 2004): 1–10.

Allen, D. C. "John Donne's Knowledge of Renaissance Medicine." *Journal of English and Germanic Philology* 42 (1943): 322–42.

Andreasen, N. J. C. *John Donne: Conservative Revolutionary*. Princeton: Princeton University Press, 1967.

Auerbach, Erich. *Literary Language and its Public in Late Latin Antiquity and in the Middle Ages*. Translated by Ralph Mannheim. Princeton: Princeton University Press, 1965.

Baetjer, Katharine. *British Portraits in the Metropolitan Museum of Art*. The Metropolitan Museum of Art Bulletin 57.1 (Summer 1999): 9–13.

Bald, R. C. *John Donne: A Life*. New York and Oxford: Oxford University Press, 1970.

Baumlin, James S. "From Recusancy to Apostasy: Donne's 'Satyre III' and 'Satyre V.'" *Explorations in Renaissance Culture* 16 (1990): 67–85.

Blau, Joseph Leon. *The Christian Interpretation of the Cabala in the Renaissance*. New York: Columbia University Press, 1944.

Bolzoni, Lina. *The Gallery of Memory: Literary and Iconographic Models in the Age of the Printing Press*. Toronto: University of Toronto Press, 2001.

Bonner, Anthony. "Ramon Llull and the Dominicans." *Catalan Review* 4.1–2 (July–December 1990): 377–92.

Briggs, John C. *Francis Bacon and the Rhetoric of Nature*. Cambridge: Harvard University Press, 1989.

Burland, C. A. *The Arts of the Alchemists*. New York: Macmillan, 1968.

Burrow, John A. *Medieval Writers and Their Work*. New York: Oxford University Press, 1982.

Bynum, Caroline Walker. "The Female Body and Religious Practice in the Late Middle Ages." In *Fragments for a History of the Human Body*, edited by Michel Feher et al., 175–82. Cambridge: MIT Press, 1989.

———. *Jesus as Mother: Studies in the Spirituality of the High Middle Ages*. Publications of the Center for Medieval and Renaissance Studies, no. 16. Los Angeles: University of California Press, 1972.

Camden, Carroll. "Memory, the Warder of the Brain." *Philological Quarterly* 18 (1939): 52–72.

Carey, John. "Donne and Coins." In *English Renaissance Studies: Presented to Dame Helen Gardner in honour of her Seventieth Birthday*, 151–63. Oxford: Clarendon, 1980.

———. Introduction. In *John Donne: The Oxford Authors*, xix–xxxii. New York: Oxford University Press, 1990.

———. *John Donne: Life, Mind, and Art*. New York: Oxford University Press, 1981.

Carruthers, Mary. *The Book of Memory: A Study of Memory in Medieval Culture*. New York: Cambridge University Press, 1993.

Chamberlin, John S. *Increase and Multiply: Arts-of-Discourse Procedure in the Preaching of Donne*. Chapel Hill: University of North Carolina Press, 1976.

Chambers, A. B. "The Fly in Donne's 'Canonization.'" *JEGP* 65 (1966): 252–59.

Chanoff, David. "The Biographical Context of Donne's Sonnet on the Church." *The American Benedictine Review* 32 (1981): 378–86.

Clark, Donald Lemen. *Rhetoric and Poetry in the Renaissance*. New York: Columbia University Press, 1922.

Clucas, Stephen. "'Non est legendum sed inspicendum solum': Inspectival Knowledge and the Visual Logic of John Dee's *Liber Mysteriorum*." In *Emblems and Alchemy*, edited by Alison Adams and Stanton J. Linden, 109–31. Vol. 3, Glasgow Emblem Studies. Sherborne, Dorset: Remous Ltd., Milborne Port, 1998.

Clulee, Nicholas H. *John Dee's Natural Philosophy*. New York: Routledge, 1988.

Coffin, Charles Monroe. *John Donne and the New Philosophy*. 1937. Reprint, New York: Humanities Press, 1958.

Colish, Marcia L. *The Mirror of Language*. New Haven: Yale University Press, 1968. Reprint, Lincoln: University of Nebraska Press, 1983.

Copenhaver, Brian. "Astrology and Magic." In *The Cambridge History of Renaissance Philosophy*, edited by Charles B. Schmitt, 264–300. Cambridge: Cambridge University Press, 1988.

Corbett, M. K. "Ashmole and the Pursuit of Alchemy: The Illustrations to the *Theatrum Chemicum Britannicum, 1652*." *Antiquaries Journal* 63 (1983): 326–36.

Crawshaw, Eluned. "Hermetic Elements in Donne's Poetic Vision." In *John Donne: Essays in Celebration*, edited by A. J. Smith, 324–48. London: Methuen, 1972.

Cressy, David. *Birth, Marriage and Death: Ritual, Religion, and the Life-Cycle in Tudor and Stuart England*. New York: Oxford University Press, 1997.

———. *Bonfires and Bells: National Memory and the Protestant Calendar in Elizabethan and Stuart England*. Berkeley: University of California Press, 1989.

———. *Literacy and the Social Order: Reading and Writing in Tudor and Stuart England*. New York: Cambridge University Press, 1980.

———. *Religion and Society in Early Modern England: A Sourcebook*. Edited by David Cressy and Lori Anne Ferrell. London; New York: Routledge, 1996.

———. *Travesties and Transgressions in Tudor and Stuart England.* New York: Oxford University Press, 2000.

Croll, Morris W. *Style, Rhetoric and Rhythm.* Edited by J. Max Patrick et al. Princeton: Princeton University Press, 1966.

Cunnar, Eugene R. "Donne's 'Valediction: Forbidding Mourning' and the Golden Compasses of Alchemical Creation." In *Literature and the Occult: Essays in Comparative Literature,* edited by Luanne Frank, 72–110. Arlington: University of Texas Arlington Press, 1977.

Daemmrich, Ingrid D. *Enigmatic Bliss: The Paradise Motif in Literature.* New York: Peter Lang, 1997.

Daly, Loyd W., and B. A. Daly. "Some Techniques in Medieval Latin Lexicography." *Speculum* 39 (1964): 229–39.

Davies, Julian. *The Caroline Captivity of the Church: Charles I and the Remoulding of Anglicanism, 1625–1641.* New York: Oxford University Press, 1992.

———. *Revival House.* New York: Viking Penguin, 1991.

Debus, Allen G. *The Chemical Philosophy: Paracelsian Science and Medicine in the Sixteenth and Seventeenth Centuries.* 2 vols. New York: Science History Publications, 1977.

———. *The English Paracelsians.* New York: Franklin Watts, 1966.

De Rola, Stanislas Klossowski. *The Golden Game: Alchemical Engravings of the Seventeenth Century.* London: Thames and Hudson, 1988.

Diehl, Huston. "Discovering the Old World: The Renaissance Emblem Book as Cultural Artifact." In *Approaches to Teaching the Metaphysical Poets,* edited by Sidney Gottlieb, 68–74. New York: Modern Language Association of America, 1990.

DiPasquale, Theresa. *Literature and Sacrament: The Sacred and the Secular in John Donne.* Pittsburgh: Duquesne University Press, 1999.

———. "'to good ends': The Final Cause of Sacramental Womanhood in *The First Anniversarie.*" *John Donne Journal* 20 (2001): 141–50.

Dobbs, Betty Jo Teeter. *Alchemical Death and Resurrection: The Significance of Alchemy in the Age of Newton.* Washington, D.C.: Smithsonian Institution Libraries, 1990.

Doelman, James. *King James I and the Religious Culture of England.* Rochester, N.Y.: D.S. Brewer, 2000.

Doerksen, Daniel W. *Conforming to the Word: Herbert, Donne, and the English Church before Laud.* Lewisburg, Pa.: Bucknell University Press, 1997.

———. "Polemist or Pastor? Donne and Moderate Calvinist Conformity." In *John Donne and the Protestant Reformation: New Perspectives,* edited by Mary Arshagouni Papazian, 12–34. Detroit: Wayne State University Press, 2003.

Doherty, M. J. "Beyond Androgyny: Sidney, Milton and the Phoenix." In *Heirs of Fame: Milton and Writers of the English Renaissance,* edited by Margo Swiss and David Kent. 34–65. Lewisburg, Pa.: Bucknell University Press, 1995.

Dubrow, Heather. "Tradition and the Individualistic Talent: Donne's 'An Epithalamion, Or mariage Song on the Lady Elizabeth . . .'" In *The Eagle and the Dove: Reassessing John Donne,* edited by Claude J. Summers and Ted-Larry Pebworth, 106–16. Columbia: University of Missouri Press, 1986.

Duffy, Eamon. "The Long Reformation: Catholicism, Protestantism and the Multitude." In *England's Long Reformation, 1500–1800,* edited by Nicholas Tyacke, 33–70. London: University College London Press, 1998.

Duncan, Edgar Hill. "The Alchemy in Jonson's *Mercury Vindicated.*" *Studies in Philology* 39 (1942): 625–37.

———. "Donne's Alchemical Figures." *ELH* 9 (1942): 257–85.
Duran, Manuel. "Ramon Llull: An Introduction." *Catalan Review* 4. 1–2 (July–December 1990): 11–29.
Elkins, James. *What Painting Is: How to Think about Oil Painting, Using the Language of Alchemy.* New York: Routledge, 1999.
Erne, Lukas. "Donne and Christ's Spouse." *Essays in Criticism* 51.2 (April 2001): 208–29.
Falk, Ruth E. "Donne's *Resurrection, Imperfect.*" *Explicator* 17 (1958). Item 24.
Feingold, Mordechai. "The Occult Tradition in the English Universites of the Renaissance: A Reassessment." In *Occult and Scientific Mentalities in the Renaissance,* edited by Brian Vickers, 73–94. Cambridge: Cambridge University Press, 1984.
Ferguson, John. "Some English Alchemical Books." *Journal of the Alchemical Society* 2 (1913): 2–16.
Fernando, Diana. *Alchemy: An Illustrated A to Z.* New York: Sterling, 1998.
Fletcher, Harris Francis. *Milton's Rabbinical Readings.* Urbana: University of Illinois Press, 1930. Reprint, Hamden, Conn.: Archon, 1967.
———. *Milton's Semitic Studies and Some Manifestations of Them in His Poetry.* Chicago: University of Chicago Press, 1926.
Flynn, Dennis. "'Awry and Squint': The Dating of Donne's Holy Sonnets," *John Donne Journal* 7 (1988): 35–46.
———. "Donne and the Ancient Catholic Nobility." *English Literary Renaissance* 19.3 (1989): 305–23.
———. "Donne and a Female Coterie." *Literature, Interpretation, Theory* 1.1–2 (1989): 127–36.
———. "Donne's Catholicism: I." *Recusant History* 13 (1975): 1–17.
———. "Donne's Catholicism: II." *Recusant History* 13 (1976): 178–95.
———. "Donne, the Man, the Legend." In *The Wit to Know: Essays on English Renaissance Literature for Edward Tayler,* edited by Eugene D. Hill and William Kerrigan, 41–56. Fairfield, Conn.: *George Herbert Journal,* 2000.
———. *John Donne and the Ancient Catholic Nobility.* Bloomington: Indiana University Press, 1995.
Frecerro, John. "Donne's 'Valediction: Forbidding Mourning.'" In *Essential Articles for the Study of John Donne's Poetry,* edited by John R. Roberts, 279–304. Hamden: Archon, 1975.
Frontain, Raymond-Jean. "Donne's Imperfect Resurrection." *Papers on Language and Literature* 26 (Fall 1990): 539–45.
———. "Donne's Protestant *Paradiso:* The Johannine Vision of the *Second Anniversary.*" In *John Donne and the Protestant Reformation: New Perspectives,* edited by Mary Arshagouni Papazian, 113–44. Detroit: Wayne State Univeristy Press, 2003.
Frost, Kate Gartner. *Holy Delight: Typology, Numerology, and Autobiography in Donne's "Devotions Upon Emergent Occasions."* Princeton: Princeton University Press, 1990.
———. "The Lothian Portrait: A Prologomenon." *John Donne Journal* 15 (1996): 95–125.
———. "Magnus Pan Mortuus Est: A Subtextual and Contextual Reading of Donne's 'Resurrection, imperfect.'" In John Donne's Religious Imagination: Essays in Honor of John T. Shawcross, edited by Raymond-Jean Frontain and Frances M. Malpezzi, 231–61. Conway: University of Central Arkansas Press, 1995.

———. "'Preparing Towards Her': Contexts of *A Nocturnall upon S. Lucies Day*." In *John Donne's "desire of more": The Subject of Anne More Donne in His Poetry*, edited by M. Thomas Hester, 149–71. Newark: University of Delaware Press, 1996.

Gardner, Helen, ed. *The Divine Poems*. 2nd ed. Oxford: Clarendon, 1978.

Gilman, Ernest B. "'To adore, or scorne an image': Donne and the Iconoclastic Controversy." *John Donne Journal* 5 (1985): 62–100.

Gombrich, E. H. *Art and Illusion: A Study in the Psychology of Pictorial Representation*. 2nd ed. Princeton: Princeton University Press, 1972.

———. "Botticelli's Mythologies: A Study in the Neoplatonic Symbolism of his Circle." *Journal of the Warburg and Courtauld Institutes* 8 (1945): 7–60.

———. "*Icones Symbolicae:* The Visual Image in Neo-Platonic Thought." *Journal of the Warburg and Courtauld Institutes* 11 (1948): 163–92.

———. *Meditations on a Hobby Horse and Other Essays on the Theory of Art*. New York: Phaidon, 1963.

González-Casanovas, Roberto J. "Llull's *Blanquerna* and the Art of Preaching: The Evolution Towards the Novel-Sermon." *Catalan Review* 4.1–2 (July–December 1990): 233–58.

Green, Henry. *Shakespeare and the Emblem Writers*. London: Trübner, 1870.

Gregory, Joshua C. "Chemistry and Alchemy in the Natural Philosophy of Sir Francis Bacon, 1561–1626." *Ambix* 2 (1938): 93–111.

Guibbory, Achsah. *Ceremony and Community from Herbert to Milton: Literature, Religion, and Cultural Conflict in Seventeenth-Century England*. Cambridge; New York: Cambridge University Press, 1998.

———. "Donne, Milton, and Holy Sex." *Milton Studies* 32 (1995): 3–21.

———. "Donne's Religion: Montagu, Arminianism, and Donne's Sermons, 1624–30." *English Literary Renaissance* 31.1 (2001): 412–39.

———. "John Donne and Memory as 'the Art of Salvation.'" *The Huntington Library Quarterly* 63 (1980): 261–74.

———. "'The Relique,' *The Song of Songs*, and Donne's *Songs and Sonnets*." *John Donne Journal* 15 (1996): 23–44.

Guss, Donald. *John Donne, Petrarchist*. Detroit: Wayne State University Press, 1966.

Haeffner, Mark. *Dictionary of Alchemy*. London: Aquarian Press, 1991. Reprint, San Francisco: Harper, 1995.

Haller, William. *The Rise of Puritanism*. New York: Columbia University Press, 1938.

Harland, Paul W. "Donne's Political Intervention in the Parliament of 1629." *John Donne Journal* 2.1–2 (1992): 21–37.

Haskin, Dayton. "John Donne and the Cultural Contradictions of Christmas." *John Donne Journal* 11.2 (1992): 133–57.

Haskins, Susan. *Mary Magdalen: Myth and Metaphor*. London: HarperCollins, 1993.

Hester, M. Thomas. "'All our Soules Devotion': Satire as Religion in Donne's *Satyre III*." *Studies in English Literature, 1500–1900* 18 (1978): 35–55.

Hickman, David. "From Catholic to Protestant: The Changing Meaning of Testamentary Religious Provisions in Elizabethan London." In *England's Long Reformation, 1500–1800*, edited by Nicholas Tyacke, 117–139. London: University College London, 1998.

Hill, John Spencer. *Infinity, Faith, and Time: Christian Humanism and Renaissance Literature*. Montreal: McGill-Queen's University Press, 1997.

Hopkins, Arthur John. *Alchemy: Child of Greek Philosophy.* New York: Columbia University Press, 1934.

Howell, Wilbur S. *Logic and Rhetoric in England, 1500–1700.* Princeton: Princeton University Press, 1956.

Idel, Moshe. "Ramon Lull and Ecstatic Kabbalah: A Preliminary Observation." *Journal of the Warburg and Courtauld Institutes* 51 (1988): 170–74.

Iser, Wolfgang. *The Act of Reading: A Theory of Aesthetic Response.* Baltimore: Johns Hopkins University Press, 1978.

Johnson, Jeffrey. *The Theology of John Donne.* Rochester, N.Y.: D.S. Brewer, 1999.

Johnston, Mark D. *The Spiritual Logic of Ramon Llull.* Oxford: Clarendon, 1987.

Josten, C. H. "John Dee's *Monas Hieroglyphica* (Antwerp 1564)." *Ambix* 12 (1964).

Jung, C. G. *Psychology and Alchemy.* Translated by R. F. C. Hull. 2nd ed. Princeton: Princeton University Press, 1968.

Katz, David S. *Philo-Semitism and the Readmission of the Jews to England, 1603–1655.* Oxford: Clarendon, 1982.

Keister, D. A. "Donne and Herbert of Cherbury: An Exchange of Verses." *Modern Language Quarterly* 8 (1947): 430–34.

Keynes, Geoffrey. *A Bibliography of Dr. John Donne: Dean of Saint Paul's.* 4th ed. Oxford: Clarendon, 1973.

———. "John Donne's Sermons." *The Times Literary Supplement* 28 (May 1954): 351.

Kirk, G. S. et al, eds. *The Presocratic Philosophers: A Critical History with a Selection of Texts.* 2nd ed. New York: Cambridge University Press, 1983.

Klawitter, George. "John Donne's Attitude toward the Virgin Mary: The Public versus the Private Voice." In *John Donne's Religious Imagination: Essays in Honor of John T. Shawcross,* edited by Raymond-Jean Frontain and Frances M. Malpezzi, 122–40. Conway: University of Central Arkansas Press, 1995.

Kristeller, Paul O. *Medieval Aspects of Renaissance Learning: Three Essays.* Durham, N.C.: Duke University Press, 1974.

Labriola, Albert. "Donne's 'Hymne to God My God in My Sicknesse': Hieroglyphic Mystery and Magic in Poetry." *The Ben Jonson Journal: Literary Contexts in the Age of Elizabeth* 2 (1995): 1–7.

Lake, Peter. *Anglicans and Puritans?: Presbyterianism and English Conformist Thought from Whitgift to Hooker.* Boston: Allen and Unwin, 1988.

———. *The Antichrist's Lewd Hat: Protestants, Papists and Players in Post-Reformation England.* New Haven: Yale University Press, 2002.

———. "The Laudian Style: Order, Uniformity, and the Pursuit of the Beauty of Holiness in the 1630s." In *The Early Stuart Church,* edited by Kenneth Fincham, 161–85. Stanford, Calif.: Stanford University Press, 1993.

———. *Moderate Puritans and the Elizabethan Church.* New York: Cambridge University Press, 1982.

———. "Moving the Goal Posts? Modified Subscription and the Construction of Conformity in the Early Stuart Church." In *Conformity and Orthodoxy in the English Church, c. 1560–1660,* edited by Peter Lake and Michael Questier, 179–205. Woodbridge, Suffolk: Boydell, 2000.

———. [and Michael Questier] "Prisons, Priests and People." In *England's Long Reformation, 1500–1800,* edited by Nicholas Tyacke, 195–233. London: University College London Press, 1998.

Langer, Susanne K. *Feeling and Form: A Theory of Art Developed from Philosophy in a New Key.* New York: Charles Scribner's Sons, 1953.

Larson, Deborah Aldrich. "John Donne and Biographical Criticism," *South Central Review* 4.2 (Summer 1987): 93–102.

Lederer, Josef. "John Donne and the Emblematic Practice." *Review of English Studies* 22 (1946): 182–200.

Lepage, John Louis. "Eagles and Doves in Donne and Du Bartas: 'The Canonization.'" *Notes and Queries* 30 (October 1983): 427–28.

Levi D'Ancona, Mirella. *The Iconography of the Immaculate Conception in the Middle Ages and Early Renaissance: Monographs on Archaeology and Fine Arts.* Vol. 7. New York: College Art Association of America, 1957.

Levine, Jay Arnold. "'The Dissolution': Donne's Twofold Elegy." *ELH* 28 (1961): 301–15.

Levy-Navarro, Elena. "Breaking Down the Walls That Divide: Anti-Polemicism in the *Devotions Upon Emergent Occasions.*" In *John Donne and the Protestant Reformation: New Perspectives,* edited by Mary Arshagouni Papazian, 273–92. Detroit: Wayne State University Press, 2003.

Lewalski, Barbara Kiefer. *Protestant Poetics and the Seventeenth-Century Religious Lyric.* Princeton: Princeton University Press, 1979.

Lewis, C. S. *The Allegory of Love.* New York: Oxford University Press, 1975.

———. *English Literature in the Sixteenth Century.* Oxford: Clarendon, 1954.

———. *A Preface to Paradise Lost.* New York: Oxford University Press, 1961.

Linden, Stanton J. "Alchemy and Eschatology in Seventeenth-Century Poetry." *Ambix* 31 (November 1984): 102–24.

———. *Darke Hierogliphicks: Alchemy in English Literature from Chaucer to the Restoration.* Lexington: University Press of Kentucky, 1996.

———. "Expounding George Ripley: A Huntington Alchemical Manuscript." *Huntington Library Quarterly* 61.3–4 (2000): 11–28.

———. "Francis Bacon and Alchemy: The Reformation of Vulcan." *Journal of the History of Ideas* 35 (October–December 1974): 547–60.

———. General Introduction. In *Alchemical Poetry, 1575–1700: From Previously Unpublished Manuscripts,* edited by Robert M. Schuler, xi–xiii. Vol. 5, English Renaissance Hermeticism, general editing by Stanton J. Linden. New York: Garland, 1995.

———. "The Ripley Scrolls and *The Compound of Alchemy.*" In *Emblems and Alchemy.* edited by Alison Adams and Stanton J. Linden, 73–94. Vol. 3, Glasgow Emblem Studies. Sherborne, Dorset: Remous Ltd., Milborne Port, 1998.

Low, Anthony. "Love and Science: Cultural Change in Donne's *Songs and Sonnets.*" *Studies in the Literary Imagination* 22.1 (1989): 5–16.

———. *Love's Architecture: Devotional Modes in Seventeenth-Century English Poetry.* New York: New York University Press, 1978.

Loxley, James. *Royalism and Poetry in the English Civil Wars: The Drawn Sword.* New York: St. Martin's Press, 1997.

Madsen, William G. *From Shadowy Types to Truth.* New Haven: Yale University Press, 1968.

Malcolm, Norman. *Memory and Mind.* Ithaca: Cornell University Press, 1977.

Malpezzi, Frances M. "Adam, Christ, and Mr. Tilman: God's Blest Hermaphrodites." *The American Benedictine Review* 40.3 (1989): 250–60.

Manning, John. "The Eagle and the Dove: Chapman and Donne's 'The Canonization.'" *Notes and Queries* 33 (September 1986): 347–48.

Marotti, Arthur F. "Alienating Catholics in Early Modern England: Recusant Women, Jesuits and Ideological Fantasies." In *Catholicism and Anti-Catholicism in Early Modern English Texts*, edited by Arthur F. Marotti, 1–34. New York: St. Martin's Press, 1999.

———. *John Donne, Coterie Poet.* Madison: University of Wisconsin Press, 1986.

———. Preface. In *Catholicism and Anti-Catholicism in Early Modern English Texts*, edited by Arthur F. Marotti, xiii–xvii. New York: St. Martin's Press, 1999.

Martz, Louis. "Donne and Herbert: Vehement Grief and Silent Tears." *John Donne Journal* 7 (1988): 21–34.

———. "John Donne in Meditation: *The Anniversaries*." *A Journal of English Literary History* 14 (1947): 247–73.

———. *The Poetry of Meditation.* New Haven: Yale University Press, 1962.

———. "Voices in the Void: The Action of Grief in Proust and Herbert." In *George Herbert in the Nineties: Reflections and Reassessments*, edited by Jonathan F. S. Post and Sidney Gottlieb, 90–104. Fairfield, Conn.: *George Herbert Journal*, 1995.

Masselink, Noralyn. "Donne's Epistemology and the Appeal to Memory." *John Donne Journal* 8.1 (1989): 57–88.

———. "A Matter of Interpretation: Example and Donne's Role as Preacher and as Poet." *John Donne Journal* 2.1–2 (1992): 85–98.

———. "Memory in John Donne's Sermons: 'Readie'? or Not?" *South Atlantic Review* 63 (Spring 1998): 99–107.

Matar, N. I. "The Date of John Donne's Sermon 'Preached at the Churching of the Countesse of Bridgewater.'" *Notes and Queries* 39 (1992): 447–48.

Matchinske, Megan. *Writing, Gender, and State in Early Modern England: Identity Formation and the Female Subject.* New York: Cambridge University Press, 1998.

Mauer, Margaret. "The Real Presence of Lucy Russell, Countess of Bedford, and the Terms of John Donne's 'Honour is so Sublime Perfection.'" *ELH* 47 (Summer 1980): 205–34.

Mazzeo, Joseph A. "Notes on John Donne's Alchemical Imagery." *Isis* 48 (June 1957): 103–23.

Meakin, H. L. *John Donne's Articulations of the Feminine.* New York: Oxford University Press, 1998.

Mebane, John S. *Renaissance Magic and the Return of the Golden Age: The Occult Tradition and Marlowe, Jonson, and Shakespeare.* Lincoln: University of Nebraska Press, 1989.

Merritt, J. F. "The Pastoral Tightrope: A Puritan Pedagogue in Jacobean London." In *Politics, Religion and Popularity in Early Stuart Britain: Essays in Honour of Conrad Russell*, edited by Thomas Cogswell, Richard Cust, and Peter Lake, 143–61. New York: Cambridge University Press, 2002.

Metz, Christian. *Film Language: A Semiotics of the Cinema.* New York: Oxford University Press, 1974.

Milton, Anthony. "Canon Fire: Peter Heylyn at Westminster." In *Westminster Abbey Reformed: Nine Studies, 1540–1642*, edited by C. S. Knighton and R. Mortimer, 207–31. Burlington, Vt.: Ashgate, 2003.

———. *Catholic and Reformed: The Roman and Protestant Churches in English Protestant Thought, 1600–1640.* New York: Cambridge University Press, 1995.

———. "The Creation of Laudianism: A New Approach." In *Politics, Religion, and Popularity in Early Stuart Britain: Essays in Honour of Conrad Russell*, edited by Thomas Cogswell, Richard Cust, and Peter Lake, 162–84. New York: Cambridge University Press, 2002.

———. "A Qualified Intolerance: The Limits and Ambiguities of Early Stuart Anti-Catholicism." In *Catholicism and Anti-Catholicism in Early Modern English Texts*, edited by Arthur F. Marotti, 85–115. New York: St. Martin's Press, 1999.

Monaco, James. *How to Read a Film: The Art, Technology, Language, History, and Theory of Film and Media*. New York: Oxford University Press, 1977. Reprint 1981.

Murray, W. A. "Donne and Paracelsus: An Essay in Interpretation." *RES* 25 (1949): 115–23.

Nash, Ronald H. *The Light of the Mind: St. Augustine's Theory of Knowledge*. Lexington: University Press of Kentucky, 1969.

Nicholl, Charles. *The Chemical Theatre*. London: Routledge & Kegan Paul, 1980.

Nicolson, Marjorie Hope. *The Breaking of the Circle: Studies in the Effect of the 'New Science' upon Seventeenth Century Poetry*. New York: Columbia University Press, 1960.

Novarr, David. "The Dating of Donne's *La Corona*." *Philological Quarterly* 36 (1957): 259–65.

O'Brien, Gordon W. "Milton, Hermes, and the Rhetoric of Mental Flight." *Cauda Pavonis: Studies in Hermeticism* 7 (Spring 1988): 1–8.

O'Connell, Patrick. "'Both Adams Met in Me': A Reading of the *Divine Poems* of John Donne." Dissertation, Yale, 1978.

———. "'La Corona': Donne's *Ars Poetica Sacra*." In *The Eagle and the Dove: Reassessing John Donne*, edited by Claude J. Summers and Ted-Larry Pebworth, 119–29. Columbia: University of Missouri Press, 1986.

Oliver, P. M. *Donne's Religious Writing: A Discourse of Feigned Devotion*. Harlow: Longman, 1997.

Oppenheimer, Paul. *The Birth of the Modern Mind: Self, Consciousness, and the Invention of the Sonnet*. New York: Oxford University Press, 1989.

Orgel, Stephen. *The Illusion of Power: Political Theater in the English Renaissance*. Berkeley: University of California Press, 1975.

Papazian, Mary Arshagouni. "John Donne and the Thirty Years' War." *John Donne Journal* 19 (2000): 235–60.

———. Introduction. In *John Donne and the Protestant Reformation: New Perspectives*, 1–11. Detroit: Wayne State University Press, 2003.

Parker, William Riley. *Milton: A Biography*. 2 vols. Oxford: Clarendon, 1968.

Patridge, Edward B. *The Broken Compass*. New York: Columbia University Press, 1958.

Payne, Robert O. *The Key of Remembrance*. New Haven: Yale University Press, 1963.

Pelikan, Jaroslav. *Mary through the Centuries: Her Place in the History of Culture*. New Haven: Yale University Press, 1996.

Pereira, Michela. *The Alchemical Corpus Attributed to Raymond Lull*. Warburg Institute Surveys and Texts. London: Warburg Institute, 1989.

Pilarz, Scott R., S.J. "'Expressing a Quintessence Even from Nothingness': Contextualizing John Donne's 'A Litanie.'" *Christianity and Literature* 48.4 (Summer 1999): 399–424.

Pocock, J. G. A. "Texts as Events: Reflections on the History of Political Thought." In *Politics of Discourse: The Literature and History of Seventeenth-century England*, edited by

Kevin Sharpe and Steven N. Zwicker, 21–34. Berkeley: University of California Press, 1987.

Questier, Michael. "Conformity, Catholicism and the Law." In *Conformity and Orthodoxy in the English Church, c. 1560–1660*, edited by Peter Lake and Michael Questier, 237–61. Woodbridge, Suffolk: Boydell, 2000.

Radzinowicz, Mary Ann. "The Politics of John Donne's Silences." *John Donne Journal* 7.1 (1988): 1–19.

Randall, Lilian M. C. *Images in the Margins of Gothic Manuscripts*. Berkeley: University of California Press, 1966.

Rattansi, P. M. "Paracelsus and the Puritan Revolution." *Ambix* 11 (1963): 24–32.

Read, John. "Alchemy Under James IV of Scotland." *Ambix* 2 (September 1938): 60–67.

———. *Prelude to Chemistry: An Outline of Alchemy*. London: Bell, 1936. Reprint, Cambridge: MIT Press, 1966.

Revard, Stella P. "Donne and Propertius: Love and Death in London and Rome." In *The Eagle and the Dove: Reassessing John Donne*, edited by Claude J. Summers and Ted-Larry Pebworth, 69–79. Columbia: University of Missouri Press, 1986.

Rhodes, Richard. *The Making of the Atomic Bomb*. New York: Simon and Schuster, 1986.

Richardson, John T. E. *Mental Imagery and Human Memory*. London: Macmillan, 1980.

Roberts, Gareth. *The Mirror of Alchemy: Alchemical Ideas and Images in Manuscripts and Books from Antiquity to the Seventeenth Century*. Toronto: University of Toronto Press, 1994.

———. "Women and Magic in English Renaissance Love Poetry." In *Representing Women in Renaissance England*, edited by Claude J. Summers and Ted-Larry Pebworth, 59–75. Columbia: University of Missouri Press, 1997.

Rosenblatt, Louise M. *The Reader, the Text, the Poem: The Transactional Theory of the Literary Work*. Carbondale: Southern Illinois University Press, 1978.

Ross, Thomas W. "Five Fifteenth-Century 'Emblem' Verses from Brit. Mus. Addit. MS. 37049." *Speculum* 31 (1957): 274–82.

Rossi, Paolo. *Francis Bacon: From Magic to Science*. Translated by Sacha Rabinovitch. Chicago: University of Chicago Press, 1968.

Roth, Cecil. *A History of the Jews in England*. 2nd ed. Oxford: Clarendon, 1949.

Rovang, Paul R. "Donne's Holy Sonnet XVIII." *The Explicator* 57.1 (Fall 1998): 11–14.

Rudick, Michael. Introduction. In *Biathanatos*, edited and introduction by Michael Rudick and M. Pabst Battin, x–xli. New York: Garland, 1982.

Russell, Anthony Presti. "Magic, Virtue, and the Poetic Imagination in Donne." *Studies in Philology* 95.4 (1998): 374–410.

Sabine, Maurine. *Feminine Engendered Faith: The Poetry of John Donne and Richard Crashaw*. Houndmills, Basingstoke, Hampshire: Macmillan, 1992.

Saurat, Denis. *Literature and Occult Tradition: Studies in Philosophical Poetry*. Translated by Dorothy Bolton. New York: L. MacVeagh, Dial Press, 1930.

Schoenfeldt, Michael C. "Reading Bodies." In *Reading, Society and Politics in Early Modern England*, edited by Kevin Sharpe and Steven N. Zwicker, 215–43. New York: Cambridge University Press, 2003.

Schuler, Robert M. "Introduction: Renaissance Alchemical Poetry in Context." In *Alchemical Poetry 1575–1700: From Previously Unpublished Manuscripts*, edited by

Robert M. Schuler, xv–lviii. Vol. 5, English Renaissance Hermeticism, general editing by Stanton J. Linden. New York: Garland, 1995.

———. "Some Spiritual Alchemies of Seventeenth-Century England." *Journal of the History of Ideas* 41 (April–June 1980): 293–318.

Sellin, Paul. *"So Doth, So Is Religion": John Donne and the Diplomatic Contexts in the Reformed Netherlands, 1619–1620.* Columbia: University of Missouri Press, 1988.

———. "The Proper Dating of John Donne's 'Satyre III.'" *The Huntington Library Quarterly* 43.4 (1980): 275–312.

Sessions, W. A. "'Child of Time': Bacon's Uses of Self-Representation." In *Betraying Our Selves: Forms of Self-Representation in Early Modern English Texts*, edited by Henk Dragstra, Sheila Ottway, and Helen Wilcox, 94–104. New York: St. Martin's, 2000.

Shami, Jeanne. "Anatomy and Progress: The Drama of Conversion in Donne's Men of 'Middle Nature.'" *University of Toronto Quarterly* 53.3 (Spring 1984): 221–35.

———. *John Donne and Conformity in Crisis in the Late Jacobean Pulpit.* Rochester, N.Y.: Boydell & Brewer, 2003.

———. "'Speaking Openly and Speaking First': John Donne, the Synod of Dort, and the Early Stuart Church." In *John Donne and the Protestant Reformation: New Perspectives*, edited by Mary Arshagouni Papazian, 35–65. Detroit: Wayne State University Press, 2003.

Sharpe, Kevin. "The Earl of Arundel, His Circle and the Opposition to the Duke of Buckingham, 1618–1628." In *Faction and Parliament: Essays on Early Stuart History*, edited by Kevin Sharpe, 209–44. New York: Oxford University Press, 1978.

———. "'An Image Doting Rabble': The Failure of Republican Culture in Seventeenth-Century England." In *Refiguring Revolutions: Aesthetics and Politics from the English Revolution to the Romantic Revolution*, edited by Kevin Sharpe and Steven N. Zwicker, 25–56. Berkeley: University of California Press, 1998.

———. "Introduction: Discovering the Renaissance Reader." In *Reading, Society and Politics in Early Modern England*, edited by Kevin Sharpe and Steven N. Zwicker, 1–37. New York: Cambridge University Press, 2003.

———. *The Personal Rule of Charles I.* New Haven: Yale University Press, 1992.

———. *Politics and Ideas in Early Stuart England: Essays and Studies.* New York: Pinter, 1989.

———. *Sir Robert Cotton, 1586–1631: History and Politics in Early Modern England.* New York: Oxford University Press, 1979.

Shawcross, John T. "The Concept of *Sermo* in Donne and Herbert." *John Donne Journal* 6.2 (1987): 203–12.

———. *Intentionality and the New Traditionalism: Some Liminal Means of Literary Revisionism.* University Park: Pennsylvania State University Press, 1991.

———. "The Meditative Path and Personal Poetry." *John Donne Journal* 19 (2000): 87–97.

Shell, Alison. *Catholicism, Controversy, and the English Literary Imagination, 1558–1660.* New York: Cambridge University Press, 1999.

Sheppard, H. J. "Egg Symbolism in Alchemy." *Ambix* 6 (August 1958): 140–48.

———. "Gnosticism and Alchemy." *Ambix* 6 (1957): 89–101.

———. "The Ouroboros and the Unity of Matter in Alchemy: A Study in Origins." *Ambix* 10 (June 1962): 83–96.

Sherman, William H. *John Dee: The Politics of Reading and Writing in the English Renaissance.* Amherst: University of Massachusetts Press, 1995.

Shumaker, Wayne. *The Occult Sciences in the Renaissance: A Study in Intellectual Patterns.* Berkeley: University of California Press, 1972.

———. *Renaissance Curiosa: John Dee's Conversations with Angels,* etc. Vol 8. Center for Medieval and Renaissance Texts and Studies. Binghamton, N.Y.: State University of New York at Binghamton Press, 1982.

Simanos, Peggy Munoz. "'Love is a spirit all compact of fire': Alchemical *Coniunctio* in *Venus and Adonis.*" In *Emblems and Alchemy,* edited by Alison Adams and Stanton J. Linden, 133–56. Vol. 3, Glasgow Emblem Studies. Sherborne, Dorset: Remous Ltd., Milborne Port, 1998.

Simpson, Evelyn. "Donne's Spanish Authors." *Modern Language Review* 43 (1948): 182–85.

Smith, David L. "Catholic, Anglican or Puritan? Edward Sackville, Fourth Earl of Dorset, and the Ambiguities of Religion in Early Stuart England." In *Religion, Literature, and Politics in Post-Reformation England, 1540–1688,* edited by Donna B. Hamilton and Richard Strier, 115–37. New York: Cambridge University Press, 1996.

Spurr, Barry. "The Theology of *La Corona.*" *John Donne Journal* 20 (2001): 121–39.

Stanwood, Paul G. "Time and Liturgy in Donne, Crashaw, and T. S. Eliot." *Mosaic* 12 (Winter 1979): 91–105.

Stapleton, Laurence. "The Theme of Virtue in Donne's Verse Epistles." *Studies in Philology* 55 (April 1958): 187–200.

Stein, Arnold. "Structure of Sound in Donne's Verse." *Kenyan Review* 13 (1951): 20–36, 256–78.

Stewart, Stanley. *"Renaissance" Talk: Ordinary Language and the Mystique of Critical Problems.* Pittsburgh: Duquesne University Press, 1997.

Stone, Gregory B. "Ramon Llull vs. Petrus Alfonsi: Postmodern Liberalism and the Six Liberal Arts." *Medieval Encounters: Jewish, Christian and Muslim Culture* 3.1 (March 1997): 70–93.

Strier, Richard. "Donne and the Politics of Devotion." In *Religion, Literature, and Politics in Post-Reformation England, 1540–1688,* edited by Donna B. Hamilton and Richard Strier, 93–114. New York: Cambridge University Press, 1996.

Stull, William L. "Sacred Sonnets in Three Styles." *Studies in Philology* 79 (1982): 78–99.

———. "'Why Are Not *Sonnets* Made of Thee?': A New Context for the 'Holy Sonnets' of Donne, Herbert, and Milton." *Modern Philology* 80 (1982): 129–35.

Summers, Joseph H. *The Muse's Method: An Introduction to Paradise Lost.* Cambridge: Harvard University Press, 1962.

Swiss, Margo. "Lachrymae Christi: Tears in Lycidas and Donne." In *Heirs of Fame: Milton and Writers of the English Renaissance,* edited by Margo Swiss and David A. Kent, 135–57. Lewisburg, Pa.: Bucknell University Press, 1995.

Taylor, Edward W. *Donne's Idea of a Woman: Structure and Meaning in the Anniversaries.* New York: Columbia University Press, 1991.

Taylor, F. Sherwood. *The Alchemists: Founders of Modern Chemistry.* New York: Henry Schuman, 1949.

Thomas, Keith. *Religion and the Decline of Magic.* New York: Charles Scribner's Sons, 1971.

Thomson, Patricia. "Donne and the Poetry of Patronage." In *John Donne: Essays in Celebration,* edited by A. J. Smith, 308–23. London: Methuen, 1972.

Thorndike, Lynn. *A History of Magic and Experimental Science.* 8 vols. New York: Columbia University Press, 1923–58.
Tillyard, E. M. W. *The Elizabethan World Picture.* London: Chatto and Windus, 1943.
Tricomi, Albert H. *Reading Tudor-Stuart Texts Through Cultural Historicism.* Gainesville: University Press of Florida, 1996.
Tuve, Rosamund. *A Reading of George Herbert.* London: Faber & Faber, 1952.
Tyacke, Nicholas. *Anti-Calvinists: The Rise of English Arminianism, c. 1590–1640.* New York: Oxford University Press, 1987.
———. *Aspects of English Protestantism, c. 1530–1700.* New York: Manchester University Press, 2001.
———. *The Fortunes of English Puritanism, 1603–1640.* London: Dr. Williams's Trust, 1989.
———. "Puritan Politicians and King James VI and I, 1587–1604." In *Politics, Religion, and Popularity in Early Stuart Britain: Essays in Honour of Conrad Russell,* edited by Thomas Cogswell, Richard Cust, and Peter Lake, 21–44. New York: Cambridge University Press, 2002.
———. "The 'Rise of Puritanism' and the Legalizing of Dissent, 1571–1719." In *From Persecution to Toleration: The Glorious Revolution and Religion in England,* edited by Ole Peter Grell, Jonathan I. Israel, and Nicholas Tyacke, 17–49. New York: Oxford University Press, 1991.
———. "Science and Religion at Oxford before the Civil War." In *Puritans and Revolutionaries: Essays in Seventeenth-Century History presented to Christopher Hill,* edited by Donald Pennington and Keith Thomas, 73–93. Oxford: Clarendon, 1978.
Vassall-Phillips, O. R. C. Ss.R. "The Immaculate Conception in Theology." In *The Promised Woman: An Anthology of the Immaculate Conception,* edited by Stanley G. Mathews, 4–10. Meinrad, Ind.: Grail, 1954.
Vickers, Brian. "Donne's Eagle and Dove." *Notes and Queries* 32 (March 1985): 59–60.
———. "On the Function of Analogy in the Occult." In *Hermeticism and the Renaissance: Intellectual History and the Occult in Early Modern Europe,* edited by Ingrid Merkel and Allen G. Debus, 265–92. Washington, D.C.: Folger Shakespeare Library; ; London; Cranbury, New Jersey: Associated University Presses, 1988.
Viera, David J. "Exempla in the *Libre de Sancta Maria* [of Ramon Llull] and Traditional Medieval Marian Miracles." *Catalan Review* 4.1–2 (July–December 1990): 221–31.
Walker, Daniel P. *Spiritual and Demonic Magic from Ficino to Campanella.* London: Warburg Institute, 1958.
Walker, Julia M. "John Donne's 'The Extasie' as an Alchemical Process." *English Language Notes* 20 (September 1982): 1–8.
———. *Medusa's Mirrors: Spenser, Shakespeare, Milton, and the Metamorphosis of the Female Self.* Newark: University of Delaware Press; London: Associated University Presses, 1998.
Warlick, M. E. "The Domestic Alchemist: Women as Housewives in Alchemical Emblems." In *Emblems and Alchemy,* edited by Alison Adams and Stanton J. Linden, 25–47. Vol. 3, Glasgow Emblem Studies. Sherborne, Dorset: Remous Ltd., Milborne Port, 1998.
Watkins, John. "'Out of her Ashes May a Second Phoenix Rise': James I and the Legacy of Elizabethan Anti-Catholicism." In *Catholicism and Anti-Catholicism in Early Modern English Texts,* edited by Arthur F. Marotti, 116–36. New York: St. Martin's Press, 1999.

Weinhouse, Linda. "The Urim and Thummim in *Paradise Lost.*" *Milton Quarterly* 11 (March 1977): 9–12.

Werblowsky, R. J. Zwi. "Milton and the *Conjectura Cabbalistica.*" *Journal of the Warburg and Courtauld Institutes* 18.1–2 (January–June 1955): 90–102.

Whitaker, Virgil. *Shakespeare's Use of Learning.* San Marino: Huntington Library, 1953.

Wiggins, Peter D. "Preparing Towards Lucy: 'A Nocturnall' as Palinode." *Studies in Philology* 84 (1987): 483–93.

Wilcox, Helen. "Women, Reading, and Devotion in Seventeenth-Century England." In *Religion, Literature, and Politics in Post-Reformation England, 1540–1688,* edited by Donna B. Hamilton and Richard Strier, 187–207. New York: Cambridge University Press, 1996.

Willard, Thomas S. "Alchemy and the Bible." In *Centre and Labyrinth: Essays in Honour of Northrop Frye,* edited by Eleanor Cook, et al., 115–27. Toronto: University of Toronto Press, 1983.

Willey, Basil. *The Seventeenth Century Background.* London: Chatto and Windus, 1934.

Williamson, George C. *Lady Anne Clifford, Countess of Dorset, Pembroke, and Montgomery, 1590–1676.* London: Kendal (Titus Wilson and Son), 1922.

Yates, Frances. *The Art of Memory.* Chicago: University of Chicago Press, 1966.

———. "The Art of Ramon Lull: An Approach to it through Lull's Theory of the Elements." *Journal of the Warburg and Courtauld Institutes* 17 (1954): 115–73.

———. *Giordano Bruno and the Hermetic Tradition.* Chicago: University of Chicago Press, 1964.

———. *The Occult Philosophy in the Elizabethan Age.* London: Routledge and Kegan Paul, 1979.

———. "Ramon Lull and John Scotus Erigena." *Journal of the Warburg and Courtauld Institutes* 23 (1960): 1–44.

Young, R. V. *Doctrine and Devotion in Seventeenth-Century Poetry: Studies in Donne, Herbert, Crashaw, and Vaughan.* Rochester, N.Y.: D.S. Brewer, 2000.

Zambelli, Paola. *L'apprendista stregone: Astrologia, cabala e arte lulliana in Pico della Mirandola e seguaci.* Venezia: Marsilio Editori, 1995.

Zwicker, Steven N. "Introduction: Discovering the Renaissance Reader." In *Reading, Society and Politics in Early Modern England,* edited by Kevin Sharpe and Steven N. Zwicker, 1–37. New York: Cambridge University Press, 2003.

Index

Abelard, Peter (1079–1142), 26
Abraham, Lyndy, 11, 13,19, 42, 113, 183 n. 11, 188 n. 78, 191 n. 108, 191 n. 114, 197 n. 14, 199 n. 39, 209 n. 29
Adamic language. *See* International Language Project
Ad Herennium of pseudo-Cicero, 39, 40, 46–47, 141–42, 190 n. 102
Agrippa, Heinrich Cornelius von Nettesheim (1486?–1535), 41, 66–67, 81, 86, 199 n. 37
Albrecht, Roberta, 188 n. 76, 192 n. 126
alchemical emblems pertaining to the Virgin: androgyne, 73, 102, 145, 157; androgyne trampling the dragon, 67, 91, 108, 143; Aphrodite, 97–98, 208 n. 26; ark, 122, 136; breast suckling the Stone, 57, 75, 98, 107, 169, 209–10 n. 52; egg, 63, 67–73, 101, 112–13, 150–52, 199 nn. 39–40, 199 n. 42, 200 nn. 46–47, 208–9 n. 28, 209 n. 29, 219 nn. 63–64; grace, 115–18, 198 n. 22, 198 n. 24; hen, 65–72, 98, 112–13, 122, 140, 197 n. 18, 209 n. 29; hermaphroditic Adam, 38, 96, 146–47; *menstruum*, 116, 145; mercurial blood, 102, 115; Mercury, 49, 81, 91, 96–97, 101–2, 105, 108, 117–18, 145, 147, 208 n. 22, 210 n. 59; "middle nature," 64, 65, 108, 116–18, 122–23, 198 n. 22; *pneuma*, 49–50, 117, 211 n. 88; *prima materia* (or "Origin of all Reality"), 50, 95, 97, 219 n. 61; salt, 37–38, 80–81, 97, 117, 123, 136, 138, 202 n. 20; virtue, 110, 212 n. 95; womb, 61, 65–66, 94, 101, 112, 114–16, 118, 122, 130, 135–36, 141, 143–46, 155–56, 215 n.

4; worm, 64–65. *See also* Mary, Virgin: as Mint; coin
Alfonsi, Petrus (1062–1110?), 204 n. 60
Andreasen, N. J. C., 178
Anne of Denmark, wife of James I (1574–1619), 97, 110–12
Anselm, Saint (of Aosta [1093–1109]), 185 n. 39
Aquinas. *See* Thomas Aquinas, Saint (1226?–74)
Archangelus or Pozzo Archangelo da Borgo-Nuovo or Borgo Nuovensi Archangelus (fl. 1587), 66
Aristotle (384–322 B.C.): pertaining to, 26, 83, 89, 117, 120, 204 n. 60, 212 n. 93; *pneuma* in semen 211 n. 88
Arminianism, 12–13, 21, 31, 64–5, 92–93, 149, 183–84 n. 15, 184–85 n. 28, 187–88 n. 67, 194 n. 159
Arundel, 2nd Earl of, and Earl of Surrey (Thomas Howard [1585–1646]), 92
Ashmole, Elias (1617–92), 30, 102, 159, 162–63, 187 n. 63
Augustine, Saint (354–430), 26, 44–46, 201 n. 66; complication as concept in, 114, 139, 211 n. 77; function of intellect, memory, and will in, 100, 103, 170; memory buildings as conceptual metaphor in, 39, 46, 113–14, 121–22, 201 n. 66; rumination as conceptual metaphor in, 47, 51

Bacon, Francis (1561–1626), 23, 30, 42, 51, 102, 159, 162, 179, 184 n. 27, 187 n. 62, 187 n. 64
Bacon, Roger (ca. 1214–94?), 104, 113, 208 n. 22, 209 n. 34
Bald, R. C., 187 n. 55, 193 n. 150

251

INDEX

Baumlin, James S., 203 n. 40, 208 n. 10
Bedford, Countess of (Lucy Harington [1581–1627]), 77, 88, 97, 112, 145, 188–89 n. 79, 210 n. 66, 217 n. 43
Bernard, Saint (1090?–1153), 20, 25–26, 31, 121, 154, 157, 186 n. 46; Mary as aqueduct, 25, 117–18, 156; vision of Mary suckling him, 25, 183 n. 9
Besler, Michael Ruprecht (1607–61): compiler of alchemical emblems, 214 n. 120
birthing ceremonies, 31, 80, 82, 136–38, 188 n. 72, 202 n. 20, 215 nn. 9–10, 215 n. 12, 215 n. 14
Bolzoni, Lina, 49, 186 n. 48, 190 n. 97
Bonaventure, Saint, 219 n. 73
Bonner, Anthony, 186 n. 52
Bridgewater, Countess of (Frances Stanley Egerton [1585–1636]), 64
Bromley, Sir Henry (MP, fl. 1594–1604), 195 n. 166
Bruno, Giordano (1548–1600), 83, 85, 203 n. 45, 204 n. 55
Buckingham, 1st Duke of (George Villiers [1592–1628]), 92, 224 n. 98
Burland, C. A., 193 n. 149
Buxdorfius or Johann Buxdorf (1564–1629), 205 n. 79
Byrd, William (1543–1623), 158

cabala, 13, 19–20, 22–23, 26, 29, 30, 33, 39, 40–42, 66, 86–87, 102, 121, 159–61, 174–78, 186 n. 48, 190–91 n. 103, 191 n. 106, 192–93 n. 138, 201 n. 67, 204 n. 55, 204 n. 59, 220 n. 9, 223 n. 66
cabalists, 39, 82, 109, 159, 163, 187 n. 58, 205 n. 79
Calvin, John (1509–64), 13, 30, 161, 221 n. 29
Calvinism, moderate, 12, 91–92, 203 n. 37; radical, 12–13, 21, 31, 53–4, 92–3, 149, 160–61, 184–85 n. 28, 187–88 n. 67, 207 n. 105
Camillo, Giulio (ca. 1480–1544), 186 n. 48
Candlemas, 82, 184 n. 26, 203 n. 38
Carey, John, 79, 94, 112, 125, 163, 182 n. 2, 202 n. 11, 207 n. 3, 207–8 n. 10, 214 n. 118
Carlisle, 1st Earl of (James Hay [ca. 1580–1636]), 105, 180

Carruthers, Mary, 47, 124, 171, 191 n. 109, 192 n. 132, 201 n. 66, 214 n. 114
Chamberlain, John (1554–1628), 196 n. 6
Chamberlin, John, 40–41, 47, 86, 174, 181, 191 n. 105, 211 n. 77
Chanoff, David, 168
Charles I of England (1600–1649), 91–92, 194 n. 161, 220 n. 1
Chinese cryptograms, 30, 42, 45, 102, 159, 187 n. 62
Christian cabalists, 13, 19–20, 30, 41, 66, 81, 102, 160, 162, 167, 175, 187 n. 60, 187 n. 62, 189 n. 93, 190–91 n. 103
circle, as emblem, 33, 44, 95, 100–103, 105, 123, 132, 134, 138–40, 162. *See also* Copernican system and Ouroboros
Cistercians: alchemical motto, 25; breastfeeding priests, 26, 31; devotion to Mary, 25, 121, 186 n. 45
Clucas, Stephen, 189 n. 84, 192 n. 125
coin, 65, 116, 119, 122, 124–28, 130–31, 133, 143–44, 157, 202 n. 20, 207 n. 3, 210 n. 55, 213 n. 102, 214 n. 114, 214 n. 118, 214 n. 120
Comenius, Jan Amos (1592–1670), 42, 159, 187 n. 62
Comestor, Petrus (ca. 1100–ca. 1180), 26
Constable, Henry (1562–1613), 225 n. 119
Copernican system, 87
Copernicus, Nicholas (1473–1543), 89
Cotton, Sir Robert (1586–1631), 33, 88, 92, 159, 162, 188–89 n. 79, 220 n. 7
Crashaw, Richard (1612?–49), 13, 61, 220 n. 75
Crawshaw, Eluned, 63
Cressy, David, 21–22, 25, 30–31, 80, 136, 179, 183 n. 13, 184 n. 26, 184–85 n. 28, 188 n. 67, 188 n. 72, 188 n. 74, 189–90 n. 97, 202 n. 20, 202 n. 31, 203 n. 37, 206 n. 92, 215 nn. 9–10, 215 n. 14, 226 n. 126
Cromwell, Oliver (1599–1658): policies of, 30, 188 n. 69
Cromwell, Sir Oliver (fl. 1598–1617 [MP, Knight of the Bath]), 12–13, 195 n. 166

David (of the Bible), 54–55, 90
Davies, Julian, 21, 179, 183–84 n. 15, 184 n. 16, 192 n. 134, 202–3 n. 33
De auditu kabbalistico: pseudo-Lullian text, 12, 102
Debus, Allen G., 191 n. 118, 220 nn. 9–10
Dee, John (1527–1608), 32–33, 35, 44–45, 85, 88, 102, 188 n. 77–79, 189 n. 84, 192 n. 125, 205 nn. 75–76, 209 n. 40
Derby, 4th Earl of (Henry Stanley [1531–93]), 84
Derby, 6th Earl of (William Stanley [baptized 1561, d. 1642]), 84, 89, 206 nn. 82–83
Devereux, Robert (1567–1601). *See* Essex, Earl of
Diehl, Huston, 61–63
digestion (as reference in Herbert and Donne), 47–48, 50–53, 131. *See also* stomach
Dignities (or Divine Attributes) of God, 26–27, 29, 44, 86, 96, 123, 160–61, 164, 167, 170–71, 176, 186 n. 47, 204 n. 59, 205 n. 81. See also *hadras*
DiPasquale, Theresa, 14, 19, 120–21, 138, 143, 145, 182 n. 3, 212 n. 93, 215 n. 15, 217 n. 42
Dominicans, 27, 44, 185 n. 39, 186 n. 52, 192 n. 121
Donne, Elizabeth Heywood (d. 1631). *See* Heywood
Donne, Henry (1573–93) (brother of John), 83, 89
Donne, John (1572–1631), poetry: *The Anniversaries*, 89, 118–33, 140, 179, 213 n. 102, 213 n. 104; "The Annuntiation and Passion," 98–105, 138, 140, 159, 163; "The Autumnall," 223–24 n. 78; "The Canonization," 133; *La Corona*, 22, 63, 73, 89, 113, 134–50, 159, 171, 176, 215 n. 15, 216 n. 18, 216 n. 21, 218 n. 58; "To the Countesse of Bedford. Begun in France . . . ," 145, 196 n. 3; "Death be not proud," 146; "The Dissolution," 188 n. 76; "An Epithalamion, Or mariage Song on the Lady Elizabeth," 112; "The Extasie," 109; *The First Anniversarie*, 65–66, 72, 76, 140, 212 n. 97; "The Flea," 99; "Good Friday," 218 n. 58; "Lecture upon the Shadow," 109; "A Litanie," 19, 150–56, 176, 218 n. 58, 218–19 n. 59; "To Mr. Tilman after he had taken orders," 156–57, 219–20 n. 74, 220 n. 75; "A nocturnall upon S. Lucies day, Being the shortest day," 223 n. 61; "O my blacke Soule!" 65, 198 n. 25, 219 n. 60; "Resurrection, imperfect," 145–48, 217 n. 46; "Satyre III," 170; *The Second Anniversary*, 19, 162, 193–94 n. 158, 212 n. 97; "Show me deare Christ," 89, 159–74, 179, 222 n. 42, 222 n. 44, 222 n. 55, 223 n. 62, 223 n. 73, 223 n. 76; "To Sr. Edward Herbert. At Julyers," 51–53, 131; "A Valediction forbidding mourning," 109; "Valediction of the booke," 131–32; prose: *Biathanatos*, 79, 86, 191 n. 106; *Essays in Divinity*, 79, 86, 88, 163, 167, 169, 174–80, 186–87 n. 55, 191 n. 106; *Pseudo-Martyr*, 85, 89, 90; *Sermons*, "Death's Duel," 76–77, 180; 79, 80, 86, 113–14 191 n. 106; "To Sr. Henry Goodyere," 125, 210 n. 55. *See also* Heidelberg, Donne's sermon of 1619
Dort, Synod of (1618–19), 13
Dowland, John (1563–1626), 158
dragon. *See* alchemical emblems of the virgin
Drury, Elizabeth (1596–1610), 31, 65–66, 76, 106, 118, 129, 133, 140, 182 n. 3, 194 n. 162, 212 n. 93, 213 n. 102, 213 n. 104
Drury, Sir Robert (1575–1615), 112, 118, 124, 217 n. 43
Duncan, Edgar Hill, 19, 146
Duncan-Jones, E. E., 223–24 n. 78
Duodecim Principia Philosophiae: "spiritual logic" of Ramon Lull, 11, 84–85, 89, 119–20, 124, 161–62, 167, 178, 180, 204 n. 59, 221 n. 34
Duran, Manuel, 85, 204 n. 55, 204 n. 59, 204 n. 61, 221–22 n. 35

Edward VI of England (1537–53): Protestant reforms of, 25
Egerton, Frances Stanley (1585–1636). *See* Bridgewater, Countess of
Egerton, Thomas (1540?–1617). *See* Ellesmere, Baron

INDEX

Eisenstein, Sergei, 102–3, 209 n. 45
Elizabeth I of England (1533–1603), 31, 63, 90, 91, 108, 188 n. 77, 195 n. 166, 203 n. 41, 210 n. 57
Elizabeth, Queen of Bohemia and daughter of James I (1596–1662), 64, 109–18, 121, 210 n. 66
Ellesmere, Baron (Thomas Egerton [1540?–1617], also Lord Keeper of the Great Seal [1596] and Viscount Brackley [1616]), 83, 195 n. 166, 206 n. 101
Elohim: as concept in Donne, 175
Emerald Table, 104, 108, 110, 132
Emerson, Ralph Waldo (1803–82), 53, 106, 193–94 n. 158
Epicurus (341–270 B.C.), 21
Erigena, John Scotus (ca. 810–ca. 877), 186 n. 47, 204 n. 59, 205 n. 81
Erne, Lukas, 164, 168, 222 n. 55, 223 n. 73
Essex, 2nd Earl of (Robert Devereux [1567–1601]), 108, 195 n. 166

Feast of the Annunciation (Lady Day), 25, 91, 99, 103, 209 n. 31
Feast of the Passion, 99, 103, 209 n. 31
Fermi, Enrico, 178
Fernando, Diana, 183 n. 9, 195 n. 172, 218 n. 49
Ficino, Marsilio (1433–99), 19–20, 41, 76, 160, 178, 182 n. 7, 190–91 n. 103
Flamel, Nicholas (d.1418), 143
Fletcher, Harris Francis, 174, 177–78, 192 n. 138, 211 n. 72, 224 n. 85, 225 n. 103, 225 n. 121
Fludd, Robert (1574–1637), 172, 175
Flynn, Dennis, 84, 109, 182 n. 2, 206 n. 83, 207–8 n. 10
fragmentation: as concept in Donne, 41, 51, 122–23, 160, 166–67, 170–71, 179
Franciscans, 26, 27, 44, 186–87 n. 55
Frederick, the Winter King (1596–1632) [King of Bohemia (from 1619–20) and Elector Palatine (1610–20)], 64, 112–13, 163
free will: Arminian doctrine of, 53–54, 194 n. 159
Frontain, Raymond-Jean, 19, 213 n. 104, 215 n. 125
Frost, Kate Gartner, 139, 165, 217–18 n. 47

Galilei, Galileo (1564–1642), 89, 205 n. 79
Gardiner, Stephen (1483?–1555), 93
Gardner, Helen, 155, 164–65, 168, 207–8 n. 10, 216 n. 17, 216 n. 21, 222 n. 55, 223 n. 76
gematria: as cabalistic feature, 66, 159, 181, 191 n. 118, 220 n. 9
Gnosticism, 22, 35, 39, 49–50, 64, 82, 86, 121, 159, 200 n. 47, 205 n. 69
good works: Arminian concept of, 31, 54, 64–65
Goodyer, Sir Henry (baptized 1571, d. 1627), 125, 210 n. 55
Gosse, Edmund, 105, 209 n. 51, 224 n. 98
Green, Henry, 60
Gregory XV, pope (elected 1621, d. 1623), 219 n. 73
Grotius, Hugo (1583–1645), 194 n. 159
Guibbory, Achsah, 190 n. 99
Gunpowder Plot of 1605, 90–91

hadras, Islamic, 85, 160–61, 204 n. 59
Hall, Joseph, Bishop of Exeter and Norwich (1574–1656), 162
Hampton Court Conference of 1604, 54, 195 n. 166
Harington, Sir John (1st Baron of Exton [d. 1613], father of Lucy, Countess of Bedford), 110
Harington, Lucy, Countess of Bedford (1581–1627). *See* Bedford, Countess of
Harrington. *See* Harington
Harvey, William (1578–1657), 117, 131, 143, 211 nn. 85–86, 217 n. 38
Haskin, Dayton, 197 n. 9
Haskins, Susan, 182–83 n. 8
Hawkins, Henry, S.J. (1571?–1646), 60–61, 166, 178
Hay, James (ca. 1580–1636). *See* Carlisle, Earl of
Heidelberg, Donne's sermon of 1619, 113–18, 123, 153, 211 n. 87
Henry III of France (1551–89), 84
Henry VIII of England (1491–1547), 78–79, 109, 164
Heraclitus (or Heracleitus [ca. 535–ca. 475 B.C.]), 32–33, 38, 130, 188 n. 76, 196 n. 3

INDEX

Herbert, Edward, Lord of Cherbury (1582–1648), 51–53, 131, 138, 194 n. 159
Herbert, George (1593–1633), 13, 47, 50, 57, 138, 165, 185 n. 32, 189 n. 93, 201–2 n. 10, 220 n. 75
Herbert, Magdalen, Lady Danvers (d. 1627), 107, 138, 216 n. 18
Hester, M. Thomas, 170
Heywood, Elizabeth (d. 1631), 84, 109, 143
Heywood, Jasper, S.J., D.D. (1535–98), 83–84, 89, 93
Heywood, John (1497?–1580?), 78
Hickman, David, 79, 202 n. 32
Hippocrates (ca. 460–ca. 370 B.C.), 32, 188 n. 76
Hochmah, 13, 86, 182–83 n. 8, 198 n. 30. *See also* Wisdom
Howard, Thomas (1585–1646). *See* Arundel, 2nd Earl of
Hugh of St. Victor (1096?–1141), 124, 214 n. 114

Idel, Moshe, 186 n. 47
Immaculist doctrine of Mary, 25–29, 44, 94, 128, 141, 144–45, 176, 185 n. 40, 186 n. 46, 219 n. 73, 225 n. 119. *See also* Trinity.
Inns of Court (holy days observed by), 22–23
International Language Project of the seventeenth century, 29–30, 42, 49, 53, 82, 158–60, 162–63, 179–80, 220 n. 7
irresistible grace (Calvinist doctrine of), 54, 64, 161
Islam, 13, 29, 67, 85, 123, 160–62, 169–70, 221 n. 20

James I of England (James VI of Scotland [1566–1625]), 13, 53, 59, 64, 91, 110, 195 n. 166
Johnson, Jeffrey, 182 n. 2, 190 n. 99
Johnston, Mark, 88, 161, 170, 204 n. 59, 205 n. 81, 221 n. 34, 224 n. 98
John the Baptist, 25, 185 n. 39, 225 n. 119
Jonah, 51, 193 n. 151
Jonson, Ben (1572–1637), 119–20, 196 n. 3, 201 n. 62, 212 n. 94

Joseph, of the Old Testament (fed to the well), 51
Judaism, 13, 29, 30, 33, 66–67, 85, 123, 160–62, 169–70, 178, 186 n. 55, 187 n. 61, 188 n. 69, 221 n. 20
Jung, Carl Gustav, 95

Katz, David, 49, 82, 159–60, 179, 187 n. 58, 187 n. 60, 191 n. 103, 191 n. 104, 199 n. 37, 220 n. 7, 220 n. 9, 221 n. 17, 222 n. 43
Kelly, Edward (1555–97), 32, 65, 71, 75–76, 148, 188 n. 77, 195 n. 171, 196 n. 3, 198 n. 24, 199 n. 39
Kepler, Johannes (1571–1630), 89
Keynes, Geoffrey, 85, 204 n. 54, 204 n. 56
Klawitter, George, 19

Lactantius, (ca. 240–ca. 320), 135
Lady Day. *See* Feast of the Annunciation
Lake, Peter, 21, 83, 163, 179, 194 n. 164, 203 n. 43, 203 n. 46
Langer, Susanne, 90, 206 n. 85
Laud, William (1573–1645) (archbishop of Canterbury 1633–45), 87, 93, 179, 184 n. 16, 187–88 n. 67, 194 n. 163
Laudians, 53, 184 n. 18, 187–88 n. 67, 194 n. 165, 195 n. 167
Leo X, pope (elected 1513, d. 1521), 189 n. 82
Levi D'Ancona, Mirella, 209 n. 30, 212 n. 97
Levy-Navarro, Elena, 222 n. 42
Lewalski, Barbara Kiefer, 14, 60
Lewis, C. S., 79, 192–93 n. 138
limited atonement: Calvinist doctrine of, 54, 161
Linden, Stanton J., 11, 19, 23, 104, 183 n. 11, 184 n. 27, 185 n. 32, 192 n. 138, 195 n. 172, 204–5 n. 62, 218 n. 49
Lombard, Peter (ca. 1100–ca. 1160), 170, 221 n. 17
Loyola, Ignatius of (1491–1556), 44–45
Lucretius (ca. 99 B.C.–ca. 55 B.C.), 21
Lull, Ramon (or Llull [1235–1316?]), 11, 26–27, 29–30, 33, 44–46, 66–67, 77, 84–89, 93, 96, 100, 105, 108, 138,

Lull, Ramon (or Llull [1235–1316?])
(*continued*)
142, 152, 159, 164, 176, 186 n. 50,
203 n. 45, 204 n. 55, 204 n. 61, 204–
5 n. 62, 208 n. 17, 221 n. 23; *ars ascendendi*, 88; *ars combinatoria*, 11, 42–46,
86–88, 102–3, 160–61, 170, 178, 180,
201 n. 67, 205–6 n. 81; coessentiality
in the godhead, 96, 123, 142, 162,
169, 221 n. 34, 222 n. 38; system of
logic, 119–20, 124, 142, 149–50, 157,
161, 165, 167, 212 n. 93, 222 n. 38.
See also Dignities of God and
Duodecim Principia Philosophiae
Luther, Martin (1483–1546), 13, 60,
94, 161, 169

Maculist doctrine of Mary, 25–27, 94,
145, 186 n. 46, 216–17 n. 28
magic, 32, 41, 46, 55, 81–82, 93, 136–
38, 150, 160, 170, 203 n. 45; distinction between white and black, 39, 49,
189 nn. 92–93, 214 n. 120, 220 n. 10;
rejected by Calvin, 221 n. 17
Maier, Michael (ca. 1567–1622), 151–
52
Malpezzi, Frances M., 220 n. 75
Marotti, Arthur F., 14, 81, 182 n. 2
marriage, Donne's definition of, 171
Martz, Louis L., 14–15, 19, 119, 121,
140, 181 n. 1 ("Introduction"), 213 n.
102
Marvell, Andrew (1621–78), occult
codes in "Upon Appleton House,"
42
Mary, in alchemy. *See* alchemical emblems of the virgin
Mary Magdalen, 226 n. 126
Mary, Queen of Scots (1542–87), 112
Mary, Virgin: 140; as Adonai, 96; the
Annunciation, 101; as Glory, 86, 96,
100, 142, 161, 167, 171, 174, 182–
83 n. 8; as Grace, 59, 96, 114–16,
121, 139, 176, 225 n. 119; as Justice,
96, 143, 149–50, 167, 169, 171, 176,
218 n. 54, 224 n. 85; as Mercy, 13, 96,
143, 149–50, 167, 169, 171, 176,
218 n. 54, 224 n. 85; as Mint, 63, 65,
116, 124–28, 130, 133, 157; as Muse,
120, 139, 145; as Name, 13, 86, 121,
140, 176–77; as Patron Saint of
Sailors, 136, 142; as phoenix, 60–61,
65, 134–35, 147–49, 166, 171, 178;
as Power, 171; as Queen of Heaven,
102, 121, 139–40, 156, 216 n. 25; as
Rainbow, 122, 140; as Second Eve,
25, 67, 94, 121, 130, 154, 161, 199 n.
35; as Spouse of Christ, 25, 105, 135,
139, 144–45, 148–49, 166, 171, 178,
182–83 n. 8, 225 n. 119; as talisman,
41–42, 81–82, 136; as Truth, 96, 100,
142, 161; as Virtue, 96, 100, 142, 161;
the Coronation of, 29, 98, 144; in
the Apocalypse, 29; the Magnificat,
118; prayers to, 13, 66, 81–82, 136,
154, 210 n. 56, 215 n. 9; the rosary,
14, 106, 121, 140, 142, 216 n. 19,
216 n. 21; with the Holy Spirit, 66,
72, 86, 97, 133, 144, 153, 182–83 n.
8; with the Trinity, 25–26, 44, 95–98,
102, 154, 176–77, 187 n. 57. *See also*
Medieval iconography of the Virgin
and Wisdom
Masaccio, Tommaso di Ser Giovanni di
Mone (1401–28), 152
Massellink, Noralyn, 190 n. 99
Matar, N. I., 197 n. 20
Mazzeo, Joseph, 19, 196 n. 3, 197 n. 14
Meakin, Heather L., 53, 194 n. 162,
213 n. 102, 213 n. 104
Medieval iconography of the Virgin:
depicted with the egg or orb, 67, 72;
during the Creation, 144, 212 n. 97;
as Second Eve trampling the dragon,
67, 108; *Stabat Mater*, 152, 218–19 n.
59, 219 n. 65; in swaddling clothes,
25, 120, 144, 202 n. 20; with the Trinity, 26, 29, 95–98, 144, 176
Melville, Herman (1819–91), 106
metonymy, 72, 106, 108, 112, 131, 133,
167, 169, 198 n. 26
middle nature: in the blood, 65, 116–
17, 123, 198 n. 22
midwives: the role of, 31, 136, 138,
215 n. 10, 215 n. 14
millenarianism, 30, 187 n. 61
Milton, Anthony, 12, 21, 54, 78–79, 81,
83, 93, 149, 158, 179, 184 n. 18,
194 n. 165, 195 n. 167, 201 n. 2,
202 n. 29, 203 n. 44, 207 n. 105,
220 n. 1
Milton, John (1608–74), 49, 51, 112,
174, 178, 183 n. 11, 192–93 n. 138,
211 n. 72, 225 n. 103, 225 n. 121

INDEX

Minerva, 113. See also *Hochmah* and Wisdom
mint. *See* Mary, Virgin: as Mint
mise en scène (contrasted with montage), 46
montage (compared to Lullian mnemotechnics), 45–47, 171–72
Montaigne, Michel Eyquem, Seigneur de (1533–92), 172
More, Thomas (1478–1535) (Lord Chancellor [1529]), 35, 40, 78–79, 82, 85, 89, 93, 109, 160, 162, 164, 183 n. 13, 189–90 n. 97, 207 n. 111
Moses, 49, 167
Münster, Sebastian (1489–1552), 51, 186–87 n. 55, 193 n. 150

Native Americans, 222 n. 43
Nativity of the Virgin, 25–26, 185 n. 39, 186 n. 46
Neoplatonism, 29, 33, 109, 121, 178, 187 n. 58, 191 n. 105
New York Public Library, 163
Nicholas, Saint, 200 n. 59
notarikon, as cabalistic feature, 159, 220 n. 9
Novarr, David, 215 n. 17

O'Connell, Patrick F., 19, 154, 215–16 n. 17, 217 n. 40
Oppenheimer, J. Robert, 178
Ouroboros, 35–36, 79, 95, 99, 100, 102–3, 129, 132, 134, 138–42, 144, 150, 159, 162–63, 209 n. 35
Owen, John (?1563–1622), 63

Pantheo, Giovanni Agostino or Johannes Augustinus Pantheus (ca. 1517–35), 33, 42, 159–60, 174, 189 n. 82, 191 n. 118, 220 n. 9, 220–21 n. 14, 225 n. 102
Paracelsus (ca. 1493–1541), 37, 51, 96–97, 110, 120, 131, 136, 142–43, 146–47, 151, 155, 157, 205 n. 79, 208 n. 17, 211 n. 85, 211 n. 87, 212 n. 95, 214 n. 120, 215 n. 4, 219 n. 61, 220 n. 9
Paul V, pope (elected 1605, d. 1621), 219 n. 73
Paul's Cross. *See* St. Paul's Cross
pelican (as alchemical symbol), 75–76, 157, 169, 201 n. 62

Pereira, Michela, 221 n. 23
perseverance of the saints: Calvinist doctrine of, 55, 161
Philip II, of Spain (1527–98), 84, 204 n. 55
phoenix: as alchemical symbol, 32, 35, 60–64, 73, 134–35, 147–49–50, 163, 171, 178, 180, 197 n. 14, 197 n. 18, 213 n. 104; versions of, 60, 64, 75–76, 126, 148–50, 166, 223 n. 63
Pico della Mirandola (1463–94), 13, 20, 41, 66, 79, 81–82, 85–89, 102, 159–60, 174–75, 181, 187 n. 60, 189 n. 92, 190–91 n. 103, 191 n. 105, 204 n. 55, 205 n. 73, 205 n. 79, 205–6 n. 81
Piero della Francesca (ca. 1410/20–92), 67, 152
Pilarz, Scott R., S.J., 218–19 n. 59
Pistis Sophia: Gnostic myth of, 36
Pius V, pope (elected 1566, d. 1572), 219 n. 73
Pius IX, pope (elected 1846, d. 1878), 219 n. 73
Plato (427?–347 B.C.), 131, 212 n. 95
predestination: Calvinist doctrine of, 21, 194 n. 161. *See also* unconditional election
"puritan blueprint," 92, 195 n. 166, 206 n. 101. *See also* Hampton Court Conference of 1604
Puritanism. *See* Calvinism: radical

Questier, Michael, 83, 203 n. 43, 203 n. 46

Radzinowicz, Mary Ann, 207 n. 4
Raleigh, Sir Walter (1552?–1618), 195 n. 166
Read, John, 193 n. 148, 197 n. 14, 208 n. 26, 219 n. 67
Reuchlin, Johann (1455–1522), 41, 51, 81, 160, 181, 187 n. 60, 191 nn. 104–6, 205 n. 79
Reynolds, Sir Joshua (1723–1792), 40, 166, 190 n. 100
Ripley, George (ca. 1415–ca. 1490), 55–56, 105, 118, 184 n. 27, 204–5 n. 62, 210 n. 59, 218 n. 49
Roberts, Gareth, 11, 75, 198 n. 24, 209–10 n. 52
Roper, William (1496–1578), 109

Roth, Cecil, 188 n. 69
rumination: as conceptual metaphor, 53, 114. *See also* digestion; stomach
Russell, Anthony, 217 n. 41
Rutherford, Ernest, 225 n. 124

Sab'in, Ibn (1216 or 1217–70), 170
Sabine, Maureen, 213 n. 102, 213 n. 104, 216 n. 19, 216 n. 25
St. Paul's Cross (Simpson's identification for "Paul's Cross), 13, 57, 92, 93, 94, 129, 130, 177, 196 nn. 5–6
saliva: in alchemical theory, 51, 53
sanctum sanctorum (or the alchemical laboratory), 31, 33, 65, 110, 136, 150
Sapientia. See Wisdom
satire: as context for Donne, 23–24
Saurat, Denis, 168, 175, 177–78, 192–93 n. 138, 208 n. 23, 223 n. 66
Schekhina, 13, 20, 64, 77, 86, 167–68, 174–75, 177, 223 n. 66
Schoenfeldt, Michael, 51, 193 n. 153, 194 n. 160
Schubert, Franz Peter (1797–1828): the *Stabat Mater* in, 219 n. 65
Scotus, Duns (1266–1308), 26, 219 n. 73
Sebond, Raymond of, also Saibunde, Sabiende and Sabunde, (fl. 1432–36), 88, 172, 205 n. 79, 224 n. 98
Second Adam: Christ as, 67, 199 n. 35
Second Eve: Mary as, 25, 67, 129–30, 199 n. 35, 213 n. 102
Sefirot. *See* sephiroth
Sellin, Paul R., 207 n. 111
semen (*pneuma* in). *See* Aristotle
sephiroth, 26, 66–67, 186 n. 47, 198 n. 30, 199 n. 37, 204 n. 59
Shami, Jeanne, 149, 182 n. 2, 190 n. 99, 206 n. 96, 213 n. 104
Sharpe, Kevin, 11, 21, 23, 53, 88, 179, 183 n. 10, 183 n. 13, 184 n. 19, 188–89 n. 79, 205 nn. 75–76, 206 n. 97
Shawcross, John, 120, 150, 168, 182 n. 6, 212 n. 97, 216 n. 21, 218 n. 55, 218 n. 58, 219–20 n. 74, 222 n. 44; constants and variables defined by, 24, 48, 55, 63, 182 n. 6, 185 n. 35, 196 n. 2, 198 n. 26, 216 n. 17
Shell, Alison, 14, 158, 182 n. 2, 207–8 n. 10

Sheppard, H. J., 35, 72, 95, 100, 151, 208–9 n. 28, 216 n. 26, 219 nn. 63–64
Simpson, Evelyn M., 88, 190–91 n. 103, 191 n. 106, 205 n. 79, 209 n. 51, 224 n. 98
Sixtus IV, pope (elected 1471, d. 1484), 26, 44, 219 n. 73
Smith, Pamela H., 214 n. 119
Spanish motto, Donne's (according to Bishop Joseph Hall), 162, 221–22 n. 35
Spenser, Edmund (ca. 1552–99), 97, 174–75, 178, 207–8 n. 10, 208 n. 23, 220 n. 75
spiritual logic (of Ramon Lull). *See Duodecim Principia Philosophiae*
Spouse of Christ (in Donne). *See* Mary, Virgin: as Spouse of Christ
Spurr, Barry, 149, 216 n. 18, 218 n. 57
Stafford, Anthony (b. 1586/7, d. in or after 1645), 195 n. 167, 207 n. 105
Stanley, Henry (1531–93). *See* Derby, 4th Earl of
Stanley, William (baptized 1561, d.1642). *See* Derby, 6th Earl of
Stapleton, Laurence, 110, 212 n. 95
Star of David, 67
Stephen of Salley (thirteenth century), 121
Stoicism, 50, 194 n. 159
stomach: as alembic, 47, 51–53, 193 n. 148, 193 n. 155. *See also* Joseph and Jonah
Stone, Gregory B., 204 n. 60, 212 n. 93, 214 n. 111, 218 n. 53, 221 n. 21
Strier, Richard, 179
Sufi poetry. See *hadras*, Islamic
Summers, Joseph H., 226 n. 129
synecdoche, 106–7

Talbot, Edward (1555–97). *See* Edward Kelly
Tany, Thomas (fl. 1649–55): identification of Christ with Mary, 30
Taylor, F. Sherwood, 100, 209 n. 35
Taylor, Jeremy (1613?–67), 198 n. 33
Teller, Edward, 178
Tetragrammaton, 66, 71, 86, 174–75, 177, 198–99 n. 33, 225 n. 102

INDEX

Thomas Aquinas, Saint (1226?–74), 25, 185 n. 39, 190 n. 99, 216–17 n. 28, 219 n. 73, 222 n. 38
Thorndike, Lynn, 46, 183 n. 11, 189 n. 82, 211 n. 85, 220–21 n. 14, 225 n. 102
Tilenus, Daniel (1563–1633), 194 n. 159
Tillyard, E(ustace) M(andeville) W(etenhall), 172
Toleration Act of 1689, 179, 226 n. 127
total depravity: Calvinist doctrine of, 13, 54, 64, 161
Trent, Council of (1546), 219 n. 73
Tricomi, Albert H., 24, 65, 76, 169, 185 n. 36–37, 198 n. 26, 200 n. 56
Trinity, 13, 25–26, 29–30, 33, 38, 44, 66, 96–97, 99–100, 102, 144, 150–51, 153, 169–70, 176–77, 187 n. 60, 216 n. 19, 221 n. 17
Trismegistus, Hermes or Mercurius (fourth century A.D.), 33, 104, 109
Tuve, Rosemond, 20
Tyacke, Nicholas, 13, 21, 53, 87, 92–93, 164, 179, 183 n. 13, 184 n. 16, 187 n. 61, 194 n. 159, 194 n. 163, 203 n. 41, 210 n. 57

unconditional election (Calvinist doctrine of), 54, 161

Verstegan, Richard Rowlands (ca. 1550–1640), 220 n. 7
Viera, David J., 210 n. 56, 218 n. 54
Villiers, George (1592–1628). *See* Buckingham, 1st Duke of

Virgil or Publius Vergilius Maro (70 B.C.–19 B.C.), 223–24 n. 78

Warren, Austin, 207 n. 107
Watkins, John, 63
Webster, John (1580?– ca. 1630), 76, 207–8 n. 10
Werblowsky, R. J. Zwi, 187 n. 60
Whitney, Geffrey (1548?–1601?), 60, 75
Wilkins, John, Bishop of Chester (1614–72), 159, 187 n. 60, 199 n. 34
Wisdom, 13, 20, 29, 33, 36, 38, 66–67, 81, 86, 97, 108, 132, 161, 167, 172, 174–75, 178, 182 n. 8, 198 n. 30, 208 n. 23, 212 n. 97, 223 n. 66, 225 n. 121. See also *Hochmah*.
worm. *See* alchemical emblems pertaining to the Virgin: worm

Yates, Frances, 26, 29, 41–42, 44, 46, 66, 78–79, 81, 85–87, 102, 123, 160, 170, 180, 182 n. 7, 186 n. 50, 191 n. 105, 192 n. 121, 203 n. 45, 208 n. 17, 221 n. 20
Young, R. V., 14, 182 n. 2

Zambelli, Paola, 205 n. 73
zodiac, 12, 218 n. 49
Zohar, the, 13, 168, 175, 192–93 n. 138
Zorgi, F. or Francis George. Also Franciscus Georgius Venetus or Francesco Giorgi (1466–1540), 186 n. 55, 205 n. 79
Zwicker, Steven N., 11, 53, 183 n. 10, 184 n. 19